RICHAR[...] [...]ian and biographer. He won the [...] his first book, *Dudley Docker*. He has written biographies of W. H. Auden and Marcel Proust, and a highly acclaimed account of the Profumo scandal, *An English Affair*. He is an advisor to the Oxford Dictionary of National Biography, a Fellow of the Royal Historical Society and of the Royal Society of Literature. He reviews regularly for the *Guardian*, *Spectator* and *Literary Review* and he lives in London.

Praise for *Universal Man*:

'Treating Keynes's lives as interesting and valuable for their own sake, and not just as a means to his economics, gives them extra vividness … With a keen eye for telling detail and social connections, Davenport-Hines brilliantly conveys what one might call the peripheral atmospherics of Keynes's existence … Done with grace and insight'   ROBERT SKIDELSKY, *Observer*

'[A] first-class book, which I cannot praise highly enough … This admirable book does Keynes justice'   *Literary Review*

'An amusing, elegant and provocative writer … By focusing on Keynes as a private man and public figure rather than an academic economist, it is possible to see him as the last and greatest flowering of Edwardian Liberalism'

DOMINIC SANDBROOK, *Sunday Times*

'This thoughtful biography does justice both to Keynes's idiosyncrasies and to his influence … with wit and grace, as well as a good deal of scholarly digging … The book conveys its own vision of this wholly extraordinary and undeniably idiosyncratic figure with persuasive artistry and conviction'   *Financial Times*

'Worthy of its brilliant subject, *Universal Man* manages to expound Keynes's ideas while shining with his own optimistic spirit. The fact that this is a book about intellectuals and ideas, does not prevent it from shimmering with low gossip. Davenport-Hines is as deft at describing international political summit meetings as he is at evoking the ballet. Lively, funny, original and beautifully written'   A. N. WILSON, author of *Victoria: A Life*

'Davenport-Hines is incapable of writing a dull sentence. His prose sings, his curiosity is omnivorous and he has a piercingly sharp eye for detail'   *Mail on Sunday*

'As vivid as fresh paint. You can see the genius of many parts dashing to Number Ten Downing Street or dancing a jig with Lydia. It's wonderful'   SYLVIA NASAR, author of *A Beautiful Mind*

'Richard Davenport-Hines's fine series of sketches of Keynes makes a clear case that he was a great man ... *Universal Man* asserts that he was the chief intellectual influence on British public life in the 20th century and it is hard to argue with that ... a very readable single volume that succeeds in the manner of his previous book by providing a professional, temperate and clear account of a gripping subject'   *New Statesman*

'Utterly absorbing ... Davenport-Hines manages to pick out little-known stories, brilliant details and curiosities, relayed with affection ... [An] accomplished biography'   *The Economist*

'Daringly but sensibly, this renowned biographer, Richard Davenport-Hines, has studied Keynes from seven points of view – not one of them as an economist ... a rewarding and fascinating book'   *Daily Mail*

'Can a breezy 300-odd pages do justice to the man widely regarded as the greatest economist of the 20th century? Yes, they can … vividly. This is an entrancing book, always light but never weightless, and I am sure that Keynes would have enjoyed it' *The Oldie*

'Thoughtful and serious … For the reader already acquainted with the economics, or indeed not especially interested, there is a lot of fun to be had in this book' *The Times*

'A superb biography for the general reader … brilliant' *Standpoint*

'Richard Davenport-Hines heroically styles [Keynes] in this affectionate and occasionally delicious general biography … refreshingly unsanctimonious' *Times Literary Supplement*

'Elegantly, evocatively and movingly [chronicled] … an accomplished and impressive biography' *Country Life*

'The principal virtue of *Universal Man* is in reminding us of Keynes' life away from economics' *Prospect*

'John Maynard Keynes was indeed the central economist of the twentieth century, a thinker of unimaginable breadth and influence. Keynes lived at the white-hot center of British intellectual and social life in his times, and he seems never to have missed a moment to relish what lay at hand. In the superb hands of Richard Davenport-Hines, one of the most gifted of critics, historians, and biographers at work today, his large life quivers into being, fully fleshed and deeply imagined. This book should attract a wide, admiring audience'

JAY PARINI, author of *The Last Station: A Novel of Tolstoy's Final Year*

Also by Richard Davenport-Hines

Dudley Docker
Sex, Death and Punishment
The Macmillans
Glaxo
Vice
Auden
Gothic
The Pursuit of Oblivion
A Night at the Majestic
Ettie: The Intimate Life of Lady Desborough
Titanic Lives
An English Affair

Speculators and Patriots (edited)
British Business in Asia since 1860 (edited)
Hugh Trevor-Roper's Letters from Oxford (edited)
Hugh Trevor-Roper's Wartime Journals (edited)
One Hundred Letters from Hugh Trevor-Roper (edited)

UNIVERSAL MAN
The Seven Lives of
JOHN MAYNARD
KEYNES

RICHARD DAVENPORT-HINES

WILLIAM
COLLINS

William Collins
An imprint of HarperCollins Publishers
1 London Bridge Street
London SE1 9GF
www.WilliamCollinsBooks.com

First published in Great Britain by William Collins in 2015
This paperback edition first published in 2015

1

A catalogue record for this book is
available from the British Library

ISBN 978-0-00-751982-8

Printed and bound in Great Britain by
Clays Ltd, St Ives plc

MIX
Paper from
responsible sources
FSC **FSC® C007454**
www.fsc.org

FSC is a non-profit international organisation established to promote
the responsible management of the world's forests. Products carrying the
FSC label are independently certified to assure customers that they come
from forests that are managed to meet the social, economic and
ecological needs of present and future generations,
and other controlled sources.

Find out more about HarperCollins and the environment at
www.harpercollins.co.uk/green

For Selina Hastings and Jonno Keates
and again to the gentle memory of Cosmo Davenport-Hines

Contents

List of Illustrations

Page 1: Maynard Keynes as a figure of intellectual authority and cultural benevolence, surrounded by rare books in his Bloomsbury house. *(Tim Gidal/Picture Post/Getty Images)*

Page 19: Keynes, aged about fourteen, shortly before starting at Eton, where he won most school prizes and learnt the rudiments of statecraft. *(Archives Centre, King's College, Cambridge; by kind permission of Susannah Burn)*

Page 63: 'The peerless Maynard' was by his mid-thirties chief of the Treasury department responsible for the London government's external finances and inter-Allied finance. *(Archives Centre, King's College, Cambridge)*

Page 123: Keynes attended the Genoa Conference, which was charged with the conciliation of European capitalism with Russian communism, as special correspondent of the *Manchester Guardian. (Private Collection/© Leemage/ Bridgeman Images)*

Page 189: Duncan Grant with Keynes. In 1908 Keynes wrote to Grant: 'I want to see you again dreadfully and find that even in the midst of a crowd I am continually sinking into a trance and thinking about you.' *(Private Collection/Bridgeman Images)*

Page 249: Bertrand Russell, Keynes and Lytton Strachey in 1915: three Apostles, members of Cambridge's Immoral Front, conscientious objectors, skirmishers in Bloomsbury's cultural vanguard. *(© National Portrait Gallery, London)*

Page 305: Keynes addressing the Bretton Woods monetary and
    financial conference in 1944. He performed there, he said, the
    combined tasks of economist, financier, politician,
    propagandist, lawyer, prophet and soothsayer. *(akg-images)*
Page 361: Lydia Lopokova and Keynes on their balcony
    overlooking Gordon Square in 1940. Her protective love and
    gaiety kept him alive, and enabled his greatest
    accomplishments. *(© Hulton-Deutsch Collection/CORBIS)*

Good work is not done by 'humble' men. It is one of the first duties of a professor, for example, in any subject, to exaggerate a little both the importance of his subject and his own importance in it. A man who is always asking 'Is what I do worthwhile?' and 'Am I the right person to do it?' will always be ineffective himself and a discouragement to others. He must shut his eyes a little, and think a little more of his subject and himself than they deserve.

G. H. Hardy

It is, I think, of the essential nature of economic exposition that it gives, not a complete statement, which, even if it were possible, would be prolix and complicated to the point of obscurity but a sample statement, so to speak, out of all the things which could be said, intended to suggest to the reader the whole bundle of associated ideas, so that, if he catches the bundle, he will not in the least be confused by the technical incompleteness of the mere words which the author has written down ... This means, on the one hand, that an economic writer requires from his reader much goodwill and intelligence and a large measure of co-operation; and, on the other hand, that there are a thousand futile, yet verbally legitimate, objections which an objector can raise. In economics you cannot *convict* your opponent of error – you can only *convince* him of it.

Maynard Keynes

What do we do? What is the remedy? It would be most inappropriate for me to stand up here and tell you what Keynes would have thought. Goodness knows he would have thought of something much cleverer than I can think of.

Roy Harrod

CHAPTER ONE

ALTRUIST

Seven snapshots of a Universal Man:

An intellectual in his twenties in college rooms in Cambridge, hunched forward listening, lolling back in reflection, then standing on a hearth-rug speaking, eager, testing, provoking, always in passionate, lucid paragraphs, to the secretive discussion group called the Apostles, offering new intellectual or ethical systems, and later acting on his belief in the virtues of immorality, having energetic bouts of illegal, risky sex with men from all classes whom he picked up in museums, saunas, railway stations and streets.

A man of thirty-one perched in the side-car of a motorbike driven by his brother-in-law hurtling at top speed on the dusty hot roads from Cambridge to London on 3 August 1914. The young man is a Cambridge economist, and has been summoned to the Treasury to help with the crisis caused by the looming European war. This heretical outsider single-handedly dissuades the Chancellor of the Exchequer, Lloyd George, and the Treasury mandarins from taking a fatal step that the banks had convinced them was essential: the suspension of the Bank Charter Act. His advice is decisive in averting monetary panic and financial collapse in the first week of the war.

Less than four years later, during a critical phase of the world war, the Treasury official responsible for the government's external finances persuading the hard-bitten and visually insensitive Chancellor of the Exchequer, Bonar Law, whose home is notorious for its drabness, to allot £20,000 of government money to buy paintings for the National Gallery at the auction of the contents of Degas' studio; attending the auction in Paris, as the booms of advancing German artillery rattle the confidence of buyers; buying for himself works by Cézanne, Ingres, Delacroix and Degas; carrying the Cézanne back to England in his suitcase, and secreting it in the ditch of a Sussex farm-track, because it is too heavy for him to carry to the friends' house which he is visiting.

A man in his forties, a member of the Bloomsbury group, art collector, bibliophile, magazine proprietor, balletomane and husband of a dancer in Diaghilev's Ballets Russes named Lydia Lopokova, stumping round England on behalf of Liberal candidates during general elections, explaining taxation to Blackburn cotton operatives, slumps to Barrow shipyard workers, Russian loans to the shopkeepers of Cambridge, mobbed by railwaymen at Blackpool; becoming an international opinion-former as his articles in the *Manchester Guardian* are syndicated to newspapers in New York, Berlin, Paris, Milan, Vienna, Amsterdam and Stockholm.

As the Slump hits Britain, and the Great Depression looms over the United States, a Cambridge don leading an informal seminar, lasting several days, for members of a government committee on Finance and Industry, bewitching bankers, manufacturers, officials, trade unionists with piercing new insights (such as the difference between investment and saving) and radical proposals (public-works expenditure by the government to break the vicious cycle of underinvestment, cheap money through low interest rates, tariff barriers to protect home markets, and closing inefficient or surplus factories). 'You are a complete dramatist,' the committee chairman Lord Macmillan told him in admiration. His scrupulous, exact and judicious speeches captivate the committee into issuing the Macmillan Report of 1931 calling for a planned economy of a type that would later be known as Keynesian.[1]

A man in his fifties who knows the creativity of inconsistency, and defines someone of perfect consistency as 'the man who has his umbrella up whether it rains or not', revises his ideas, and publishes his *General Theory of Employment, Interest and Money* in 1936. This founding text (if not the absolutely original creator) of macroeconomics becomes the most important economics book of the twentieth century. It proves as important as Adam Smith's *Wealth of Nations* in inaugurating an economic era. 'We were pedestrian, perhaps a little complacent,' said A. C. Pigou, a senior Cambridge economist who often resisted his ideas. '*General Theory* broke resoundingly that dogmatic slumber. Whether in agreement or in disagreement with him discussion and controversy sprang up and spread over the world. Economics and economists came alive. The period of tranquillity was ended. A period of … creative thought was born.'[2]

A dauntless man in his sixties, a weary titan with heart disease, fighting daily, at interminable, closely argued and exhausting conferences, to save impoverished, war-wrecked Britain from being driven into bankruptcy by the Americans calling in their war loans; knowing that he is sacrificing his life in the effort; and then, in mid-Atlantic, on the liner *Queen Elizabeth*, while his exhausted colleagues are asleep, padding down the corridor to the radio-room to collect messages reporting how his Anglo-American financial settlement is being decried in England, and retreating to his state-room to prepare the speech of his lifetime, which will send his attackers scuttling into retreat.

Each snapshot shows the same man in similar postures: a disci-plined logician with a capacity for glee who persuaded people, seduced them, subverted old ideas, installed new ones; a man whose high brilliance did not give people vertigo, but clarified and lengthened their perspectives. The man was John Maynard Keynes (1883–1946).

Keynes was the chief intellectual influence on English public life in the twentieth century. He was England's paramount example of the scholar as man of action. He conceived economic theories in the solitude of his study, and in the cut and thrust of discussion. Then he persuaded the politicians and financiers of two continents to implement them. Isaiah Berlin, who worked with him in wartime Washington, thought him the cleverest man he knew – 'intellectually awe-inspiring'. Lord Beaverbrook, the newspaper magnate and master manipulator of opinion, called Keynes, in 1945, England's 'finest living propagandist'. Eric Hobsbawm put him in a list of political 'movers and shapers of the twentieth century' together with Lenin, Stalin, Roosevelt, Hitler, Churchill, Gandhi, Mao Tse-tung, Ho Chi Minh, de Gaulle, Mussolini and Franco. Before him, economic man lived by the fossil fragments of dinosaur systems. Phrases like 'Keynesian economics' and the 'Keynesian Revolution' testify to his influence on both economic theory and government policies. Indeed, 'Keynesian economics' was not as decisive to the world as the 'Keynesian era': that thirty-five-year period after the Second World War when versions of his economic ideas dominated the economic policies of Western governments, creating a boom that can now be seen as the most sustained period of rapid expansion in history. Keynesianism upheld regulated capitalism. It involved a commitment to full employment at any cost which, in England, dominated the economic policies of both Labour and Conservative governments from Attlee in 1945 to the onset of Thatcher in 1979.[3]

It is as an economist that Keynes is invoked, admired and deplored. His reputation rests on his writings and interventions in economic policy. Roy Harrod, who published the official biography of him in 1951, Robert Skidelsky, who wrote three masterly volumes at intervals from 1983, Donald Moggridge, who edited his papers in thirty volumes and then published his authoritative *Maynard Keynes: An Economist's Biography* in 1992, understandably all made economics paramount. Skidelsky's volumes amount to 1,758 pages: there are 990 pages in Moggridge. This approach is estimable; but it is not right for every reader. 'The worst of economics is that it really is a technical and complicated subject,' Keynes wrote in 1930. 'One can make approximate statements in a common-sense sort of way which may appear superficially satisfactory. But if someone begins to ask one intelligent and penetrating questions it is only possible to deal with them by means of something much more complicated.' This short book is notable for its technical omissions and for its selective emphasis in depicting Keynes.[4]

Leonard Woolf, who was a member of the same gifted esoteric clan in Cambridge and London, summarized Maynard Keynes: 'a don, a civil servant, a speculator, a businessman, a journalist, a writer, a farmer, a picture-dealer, a statesman, a theatrical manager, a book collector, and half a dozen other things'. Keynes was confident equally in Whitehall, Washington, Cambridge, Covent Garden, the Bank of England and the Arts Council. In each of these domains, and in the dining-clubs and private discussion groups of which he was an inveterate habitué, Keynes conjoined different networks of expertise, influence and ambitions. Woolf did not use the word 'economist' to characterize him: nor does the word occur in any chapter title in this book. Keynes was of a type that was more common in the sixteenth, seventeenth and eighteenth centuries than in the twentieth, whose ardent curiosity, knowledge, imagination and activity were directed at almost every aspect of humanity. He pursued multifarious interests, which fashioned the sort of economist that he became. The climate of his life – what Louis MacNeice in his poem 'Autumn Journal' called 'the frost that kills the germs of *laissez-faire*' – is the concern of this book.[5]

In the England of Keynes's generation, pleasures were seen as vices unless they had been deferred; instant gratification was immoral; joy-of-life was treated almost as a contraband luxury; and people tried to hide their emotions from indiscriminate gaze behind shutters which were fastened tight. Most accomplished and effective Englishmen of Keynes's class compartmentalized their lives. It was inherent in their cultural assumptions to categorize and segregate emotions and people according to their worth, to manage their conflicting motives and experiences by keeping them apart, and to be discerning in their evaluation of ideas and institutions. Compartmentalization was implanted by family circumstances, instilled by boyhood training, and found in manhood to be indispensable for forming priorities and making choices. If people were to enjoy clear, orderly, civilized, productive lives, without blurs, smudges, mess, waste and overlap, it was essential for them not to mix their friends, aims, urges and trepidation in an undifferentiated hotchpotch. Maynard Keynes exemplified the truth that compartmentalization is a mark of intelligence as well as requisite to successful intentions. Accordingly the structure of this book is not a chronological narrative. It treats him in turn as an exemplary figure, as a youthful prodigy, as a powerful government official, as an influential public man, as a private sensualist, as a devotee of the arts and as an international statesman. By showing the disconnections as well as the continuities, the distances as well as the intimacies, it tries to remind readers that Keynes believed that one's different traits and activities should be disposed with care like the freight separated and stowed in a ship's bulkheads to stop capsize.

Keynes was a great persuader. 'The misery of life was having to *persuade* people,' he told the Cambridge don Arthur Benson three months before the outbreak of the First World War (adding that the trouble was that few people halted to think before talking). 'Words ought to be a little wild,' he said in Dublin in 1933, 'for they are assaults of thoughts upon the unthinking.' Keynes spent his life trying to prompt, convince and stimulate people into right think-ing. He drew on his circumstances and surroundings as he resisted slogans, exposed lies, knocked aside people's crutch-words, insisted upon what was actual, built a bridgehead into reality. No account of his persuasive powers can omit a description of his voice. Austin Robinson, who worked with him in Cambridge seminars, official meetings and international diplomatic negotiations, stressed the sound of Keynes. 'That beautiful, musical, resonant voice, allied to an unparalleled power of lucid exposition and to a range of vocab-ulary and a joy in words comparable only to that of Winston Churchill in his generation, made him a pleasure to listen to, whether you agreed or disagreed, whether you knew all about what he was talking about, or nothing about it. He never bored. He never exhausted. He was never trite.'[6]

Keynes was a prolific contributor to daily newspapers, weekly magazines and learned journals. These articles were intended to have immediate influence on decisions, and to alter short-term opinion. There was immediacy, responsiveness and topicality in them: though his journalism was ephemeral, its persuasiveness was enduring. Keynes's books, by contrast, were meant to be re-read. They defined first principles, characterized problems, posed questions, established models and raised implications of enduring purpose. Their eloquence was meant to be persuasive beyond time. The most famous of them, *The Economic Consequences of the Peace*, which was published over ninety years ago, still reso-nates. In it Keynes addressed what he called the 'unusual, unstable, complicated, unreliable, temporary nature of [Europe's] economic organization'. Western economies, he emphasized, depended on 'the *inequality* of the distribution of wealth'. He identified the beginning of an aggressive, democratized new consumerism – 'the war has disclosed the possibility of consumption to all, and the vanity of abstinence to many' – and predicted that once 'the bluff is discovered, the labouring classes may no longer be willing to forgo so largely'. In consequence, the middle classes' conspicuous new consumption might provoke confiscatory tax regimes and political revenge.[7]

In the classical world – and classical training was instilled in Keynes by his education – the predominant question for thinking people was: 'How may I lead the Good Life?' After the religious wars of the seventeenth century had been fought to exhaustion, Europeans addressed the purpose of life with a different question: 'What must I do to be saved?' Keynes tried to answer these questions for Economic Man. In a review of *The Economic Consequences of the Peace* in 1920, Dennis Robertson, who knew Keynes well, wrote that he favoured 'hope against despair – of taking, where the future is at best uncertain, the risks of generosity rather than the risks of meanness. Perhaps – perhaps Mr Keynes himself is a bit of an old theologian, after all; and not a bad thing to be, either.'[8]

'It seems clearer every day', Keynes wrote in 1925,

that the moral problem of our age is concerned with the love of money, with the habitual appeal to the money motive in nine-tenths of the activities of life, with the universal striving after individual economic security as the prime object of endeavour, with the social approbation of money as the measure of constructive success, and with the social appeal to the hoarding instinct as the necessary provision for the family and for the future. The decaying religions around us, which have less and less interest for most people unless it be an agreeable form of magical ceremonial or of social observance, have lost their moral significance ... just because they do not touch in the least degree on these essential matters.

These attitudes to both money-making and religion set him at odds with many Americans in his lifetime and nowadays. Moreover, in both his private and official correspondence, he made sharp criticisms of American working methods and government organizations. However, he was not anti-American. There was no animosity in his remarks. His misgivings about the American way were expressed with the frankness with which he spoke of the misjudgements or inadequacies of the Bank of England, Eton College, the rump of Liberal party leaders after Asquith, the star columnists of the *New Statesman*, the Scottish members of the Arts Council of Great Britain. Hostility to the richest nation in the world would have seemed to him stupid, purblind, defeatist and regressive. The energy and optimism of the United States delighted him.[9]

Pessimism was an abomination to Keynes. He detested stupidity as a form of ugliness, and fought ignorance as the cause of pessimism, inhumanity, injustice and wastage. Humankind lived with some solid knowledge, an ungovernable welter of fragmentary information, a host of assumptions and many improvisational, day-to-day solutions. Keynes used both logic and instinct – adduced both neutral data and creative imagination – in order to make these cohere into clearer precepts for living. The motive force of his life was that, if only human stupidity could be overcome, and pessimism eradicated, most of the world's evils were remediable.

Keynes was a man of joyous vitality. At times he was too optimistic – so ardent was his faith in the power of reason and persuasion (especially his own). Always he was the centre of vigorous, disciplined activity. He believed that all problems were soluble in principle by rational thought – though obtuseness could prevent the solution being enacted. His method was first to identify the intellectual solution; then to devise an administrative technique to apply that solution; and finally to persuade others of the sense of his recommendations. He was a gregarious intellectual, who relied on the stimulus of fast, incisive discussion with his friends and protégés, although his constructive planning was detailed, methodical and sure. T. S. Eliot and other contemporaries extolled the concision, lucidity, word-perfect vocabulary and irony of his prose.

Not everyone liked Keynes. He was the model for a shifty stock-broker called Joseph Barralty in John Buchan's novel *The Island of Sheep* (1936): Buchan had ample chance to study Keynes, as they were fellow members of the Other Club, and dined together at the Savoy Hotel for a dozen years. 'Tallish, lean, big-nose, high cheek-bones,' an official from Scotland Yard says of Barralty. 'He has a moustache which has gone grey at the tips, and it gives him a queer look of innocence. That's one aspect – the English country gentle-man. In another light he is simply Don Quixote – the same unfin-ished face, the same mild sad eyes and the general air of being lost that one associates with the Don. That sounds rather attractive, doesn't it? – half adventurer, half squire? But there's a third light – for I have seen him look as ugly as sin. The pale eyes became mean and shallow and hard … and the brindled moustache with its white points looked like the tusks of an obscene boar.' Worst still, 'he's a first-class, six-cylindered, copper-bottomed highbrow. A gentle-manly Communist. An intellectual who doesn't forget to shave. The patron of every new fad in painting and sculpting and writing. Mighty condescending about all that ordinary chaps like you and me like, but liable to enthuse about monstrosities, provided that they're brand new and for preference foreign.' What made the Scotland Yard man long to finger Barralty's collar was his conde-scension: 'His line is not the fanatic, but the superior critic of human follies.'[10]

Intelligence cuts its way through conventions, beliefs, dogmas, traditions, sentiments, and social codes as an engineer hacks his way through forests and mountains, surmounts outcrops of nature, opening them up or slicing them away, forging ahead and imposing the shortest path. 'The mind of Maynard Keynes was an extraordinary instrument, powerful, subtle, swift and penetrating,' wrote Kingsley Martin, who worked with him for the last fifteen years of his life. 'It was silly to try to argue with it; you could only change his conclusion by offering a new premise. He could – and did – do most things better than anyone else.' Keynes reached rapid conclusions, and revised them just as swiftly. His reputed inconsistency 'was nothing of the sort; it was merely the mental gymnastics proper to a King's don', judged Martin (referring to the Cambridge college of which Keynes was a member for over forty years). 'He was willing to try any workable expedient.'[11]

Among those who only knew him socially, and had no working connection with him, Keynes was less intimidating. 'Maynard was the cleverest man I have ever known,' the art critic Clive Bell remembered. 'His cleverness was of a kind, gay and whimsical and civilized, which made his conversation a joy to every intelligent person who knew him. In addition he had been blest with a deeply affectionate nature.' Bell, in truth, was ambivalent about Keynes's worldliness, but acknowledged that 'he was magnificently generous: generous to his country, generous to his college … generous to his less fortunate friends.'[12]

Bell did not add that Keynes was the least envious of men. 'Envy' was a word that no one who knew Keynes associated with him. He was singular in lacking the faintest blotch of this trait. The thirty volumes of his collected works, the thousands of letters that he sent men and women, are devoid of envy, and of its attendant malice, discontent, grudges. Instead they show a man who was thankful to his core. Although Keynes's interest in money was intense, there was never a moment's covetousness: he wanted to share his gifts, and to spread abundance.

While writing this book my memory reverted to my first meeting with a Keynes. In June 1976, when I was working in the University of Cambridge on a doctoral dissertation on the history of English armaments companies between 1918 and 1936, I was taken up by a soppy old Swiss interior decorator named Konrad Kahl, who slunk about the purlieus of Cambridge colleges during May Week. He was missing either an eye or a leg (at this distance of time I forget which) and unable to drive. Offering me cooling drinks in compensation, he dragooned me into becoming his chauffeur, and hence his captive audience, for as we bowled along the byways of Cambridgeshire he pontificated in slow-moving monologues, full of periphrasis and coy hints and philosophical saws, about the sufferings of the artistic temperament, the nobility of Greek love of man for boy, the singularity of the Swiss soul, the harsh ingratitude of the world towards the elect who appreciate fine objects.

One afternoon Kahl took me to visit Sir Geoffrey Keynes, a spry, self-reliant and upright widower in his late eighties, who was the economist's younger brother and a renowned bibliographer. He lived at Lammas House near Newmarket. This was a solid, comfortable country house, with soothing shadows in the summer heat, which (as I learnt while writing this book) had been bought for him unseen, by his shrewd and decisive mother, in 1949. Konrad Kahl spoke with ersatz self-abasement to Geoffrey Keynes, whom he presented with a hideously printed and garishly designed volume, with something of the jazziness of the *Savoy Cocktail Book*, which contained dispiriting quotations from Swiss professors about the joys of literature. Keynes received this gift with grave courtesy, and assured his benefactor that he knew exactly where he was going to put this remarkable object. He adopted towards Kahl a manner of seasoned patience, civil but impersonal, which the interior decorator, on our return journey to Cambridge, fidgeting with delight, told me was so very English.

Towards me Sir Geoffrey Keynes was less unbending. He looked at me directly, with a scrutiny that was both friendly and appraising. He seemed pleased to have a young visitor. He was too honest to be flattering, but he asked interesting questions and seemed attentive to the answers. Our exchanges were not quite conspiratorial, but they had a clandestine touch to them, for they occurred in a complicit undertone, while Kahl orated about Rupert Brooke and Goethe with such satisfaction to himself that he remained oblivious to our minimal responses.

Three moments in my afternoon with Geoffrey Keynes I remember well. His wife Margaret (Charles Darwin's granddaughter) had died two years earlier. 'It was a good thing,' he said to me in a matter-of-fact way. 'She was quite off her head at the end.' This was my induction to the unusual and sometimes discomfiting truthfulness of the Keynes family.

The second moment came when we were ushered into a dining-room where a good old-fashioned tea was arrayed. Keynes took me aside, tugged from under the table an old deed-box and asked me what I thought of the contents. These were sheaves of pale-blue paper covered with firm handwriting in fading black ink, on which children's crayon drawings of animals and ships were superimposed. It was, he said, the manuscript of a book by Charles Darwin (either *On the Origin of Species* or *The Descent of Man*), which the frugal Victorian, receiving back from the printers, had handed to his small children as scrap-paper. While I handled these fragments, properly speechless, Konrad Kahl was reaching for some fruit-cake and dilating on the naturalness of men swimming naked together in Alpine lakes.

The third incident matters a trifle to this book of mine. Geoffrey Keynes – learning that I was training as a historian of the inter-war period – asked what I thought of Robert Skidelsky. Skidelsky had recently proposed to write an enlarged, modernized and comprehensive biography of Maynard Keynes, which was intended to replace the standard life written a quarter of a century earlier by Sir Roy Harrod. Geoffrey Keynes told me that a few interested parties (some at King's, but also, he implied, Harrod) had been deterring him from cooperating with Skidelsky. They had mentioned Skidelsky's previous interest in the economic schemes of Sir Oswald Mosley, and Geoffrey Keynes asked me if I thought that Skidelsky was a crypto-fascist, as he had been told. He asked, too, if Skidelsky resembled Michael Holroyd, which I did not understand until later was an enquiry whether Skidelsky would be as frank about Maynard Keynes's sex life, and in identifying his lovers, as Holroyd had been in his two recent volumes on Lytton Strachey. I extolled Skidelsky, whose *Politicians and the Slump* had taught me as a schoolboy the excitement of modern archives. Skidelsky was too enlightened in his ideas to be a crypto-fascist, I said: his imaginative gift was to interpret people who were far different from him. Geoffrey Keynes seemed to listen with surprising care to my blurting. It seems doubtful if he remembered what I said for long, but I am glad to have championed Skidelsky's cause against the mistrust and whispered impediments that confronted the early stages of his project.

This interlude at Lammas House left an abiding sense of the Keynes frame of mind. The punctilio, brisk competence, logic and discreet humour of Geoffrey Keynes were attractive. The way that he welcomed me with questions, without either reducing or emphasizing his own great authority, was signal. But his wish to hear well of Skidelsky, and his evident desire to find reasons for generous cooperation, were Keynesian. When I investigated Geoffrey Keynes in reference books afterwards, I found that he had worked in horrific conditions as a surgeon in casualty clearing stations on the Western Front in the first war and had held the rank of air vice-marshal as an RAF consulting surgeon in the second war. As a result of his experiences of trench warfare, he devised the Keynes flask for blood transfusion, founded the London Blood Transfusion Service and in 1922 published the first textbook on the subject. In the 1930s he pioneered the radium treatment of breast cancer and was a humane opponent of drastic surgical responses to that affliction. All the time he was assembling one of the best private book collections in England of his century, astounding other collectors by his generosity in sharing its treasures, and compiling magisterial scholarly bibliographies based on his holdings. He also wrote a ballet, with music by Ralph Vaughan Williams. This passionate, enriching diversity of interests, disciplines and powers was characteristic of the Keynes brothers.

In the University of Cambridge during the 1970s John Maynard Keynes was invoked as a man beyond emulation. Forty years later, my admiration for his self-control, authority and benevolence has intensified. He seems – more than ever – an inspiring example of an intellectual who was bold in his ideas and unselfish in the ways that he put them into action. If his life has one pre-eminent lesson, based not on wishy-washy hopes about human nature but on the probabilities for good outcomes, it is that if confronted by conflicting alternatives, when choosing the way forward in practical matters, the sound principle is to take the most generous course.

CHAPTER TWO
BOY PRODIGY

'The golden mediocrity of a successful English middle-class family' was John Maynard Keynes's phrase to describe the ancestry of his fellow economist Malthus. The calm, assuaging prosperity of his own family began with a teenage boy's stagecoach ride from Salisbury to Andover in the last years of the reign of King George III. His grandfather John Keynes (1805–78), who had been apprenticed at the age of eleven to his father's brush factory at Salisbury, admired a purple carnation (called Butt's Lord Rodney) in the buttonhole of a passenger sitting opposite him. He determined to cultivate carnations and pinks, and pawned his watch to buy his first plants. At the age of seventeen his pinks won his first prize in a garden-show: a pair of sugar-tongs. Within years his hobby was bringing him a respectable fortune. Thousands flocked to his dahlia exhibition at Stonehenge in 1841. Four years later he opened a nursery in Salisbury, where he produced dahlias, verbenas and carnations, and hybridized new roses. Copious hot-house beauty brought social opportunities that had been unimaginable to the apprentice in the brush factory. When the Prince Consort opened the Horticultural Society's new gardens at South Kensington in 1861, Keynes was a member of the committee that welcomed him.[1]

The success of John Keynes's nursery depended on the increased purchasing-power of middle-class Victorians and the confident assertion of their tastes. His customers rejected the aristocratic model of landscape gardening practised by William Kent, Capability Brown and Humphry Repton, whereby lawns swept up to the house and flowers were confined to the borders in the kitchen-garden. Instead of austere, distant and picturesque views, they wanted banks of colourful, floriferous, fragrant plants to abound in the beds around their houses. A description of the conservatory at a flower-show in Kensington in 1861, at which John Keynes took several prizes, encapsulates a Victorian world in which comfort, safety, abundance and colour were valued. The building was bestrewn with dahlia blooms, hollyhocks, gladioli, phloxes, petunias, roses, lilies, geraniums, verbenas, ferns. Mediterranean tree frogs, disporting themselves on mosses, lichens and ferns inside a glass case, fascinated onlookers, especially children. Military bands performed a selection of marches, overtures, fantasies, waltzes and operatic airs throughout the day.[2]

John Keynes, 'the principal grower of dahlias in the kingdom', was eminent in the cathedral city where he spent his life. He helped to build a school there, and was long-serving Sunday-school superintendent of Brown Street Baptist chapel. Education was seen as empowering, enriching, meritorious and fulfilling: it was not a chore, but a privilege. His household took *The Times*. For years before John Keynes's election as mayor in 1876 he served as a Liberal member of the municipal council. Such was the esteem in which his neighbours held him that most shops in Salisbury closed during his funeral in 1878. The old man left assets exceeding £40,000. Probably his profits from the nursery had been amplified by judicious investments in railways. A network of branch-lines and junction railways, some more profitable than others, were built to radiate from Salisbury during the 1850s. John Keynes probably joined in this local railway boom, and surely participated in the Salisbury Railway & Market House Company, which built a warehouse district on the edge of town and opened a profitable freight-line in 1859.[3]

The provincial prosperity of the old nurseryman seemed mellow to his descendants. 'Like everything English,' as Virginia Woolf wrote in 1937 of pre-war life, 'the past seemed near, domestic, friendly.' Maynard Keynes's sense of the brightness of English and European life before the lights were extinguished by continent-wide war was fundamental to what he thought and did. 'What an extraordinary episode in the economic progress of man that age was which came to an end in August 1914!' Keynes wrote in *The Economic Consequences of the Peace* – doubtless mindful of his family's burgeoning prosperity. Although most people were overworked, with few comforts, they were given hope by the pliancy of the class system. 'Escape was possible,' he felt convinced, 'for any man of capacity or character at all exceeding the average, into the middle and upper classes, for whom life offered, at a low cost and with the least trouble, conveniences, comforts and amenities beyond the compass of the richest and most powerful monarchs of other ages.'[4]

Neville Keynes (1852–1949) was the child of the floriculturist's second marriage to Anna Maynard Neville. She is often said to have been an Essex farmer's daughter; but her father, although descended from millers and yeomen, was in business in London: her childhood was mainly spent in the countrified suburb of Camberwell. The fact that the Keynes family were staunch Baptists predicated Neville's education. At the age of fifteen he was sent to a nonconformist boarding-school, where it was instilled in pupils that their hopes of salvation on Judgement Day lay in virtuous living and in passing the London University matriculation exam. Neville Keynes duly, in 1869, won a scholarship to University College, London, which, unlike the ancient universities of Oxford and Cambridge, accepted undergraduates from outside the Church of England. During his three years at University College, this young nonconformist, with his provincial background in trade, was shown longer horizons, which were to propel his children towards titles and academic honours, and to make their surname the basis for an adjective with world recognition, 'Keynesian'.

In 1871 Gladstone's Liberal government enacted the University Tests Act against Tory opposition. By this legislation, the Church of England lost its privilege to exclude religious dissenters and Roman Catholics from the universities of Oxford and Cambridge, and from their constituent colleges. This reform followed hard on Gladstone's order-in-council in 1870 that future permanent appointments to the civil service (excluding the Foreign Office) should be filled by open competitive examinations – for which university-trained candidates were most apt. Both the reform of civil service recruitment and the abolition of university tests dismantled England's traditional system of jobbery and sinecures; but although hailed as bold progressive measures they were also socially defensive. They occurred shortly after the Second Reform Act of 1867, which had broadened the electoral franchise: the dual reforms of 1870–1 were intended to bolster the established order by accommodating dissenters within both administrative govern-ment and the ancient universities, thus defusing the power of outsiders' dissident thinking and dispelling their grievances in a time of diffused democracy. Until the University Tests Act relaxed admissions policy to include religious nonconformists, most advanced, significant and enduring political, social, economic and scientific (although not theological) ideas had come from men working outside the ancient universities. After 1871, for nearly a century, until the two universities became less exclusive and less authoritative, the world of ideas was dominated by people who had trained at either Oxford or Cambridge.

These twin reforms of 1870–1 established a new governing order of trained, non-partisan expertise to regulate human affairs and national destinies. They were, incidentally, the making of Maynard Keynes. Nearly fifty years later, in scornful and unforgiving mood, he compiled one of the deadliest indictments and most rousing rallying-cries against the corrupt and botched old political order: *The Economic Consequences of the Peace* is one culmination of the trends began by open competitive examination and the University Tests Act. Moreover, university reform – as a tempered experiment designed to forestall social upheaval – proved a model for later Keynesian economics.

Social exclusions and cultural filters were retained in the ancient universities by the primacy of classical languages in the entrance requirements and by the narrow appeal of the curriculum. Dead languages were the antidote to the mercenary outlook that emphasized ownership, productivity, money-making, accumulation. The traditional educated classes feared that if the classics were ousted from their position as the chief instrument of education at Oxford and Cambridge, Greek would perish in the grammar schools and the ascent from elementary schools to those universities would become too easy. 'Ancient Colleges shd be fortresses of the humanities,' with newer universities in London, Manchester and Birmingham providing more utilitarian, modern systems, Maynard Keynes's teacher H. E. Luxmoore wrote in 1901, explaining why he opposed the abolition of Greek as a compulsory subject for university admission examinations. 'If a very smart Science or Math man knows no Greek I don't see *much* harm … but I had rather he went to Owens College or Liverpool. Is that pig-headed?'[5]

The University Tests Act enabled Neville Keynes to obtain promotion from London University to Cambridge a year after the legislation was ratified. In 1872 he won, at the age of twenty, the top entrance scholarship in classics and mathematics at Pembroke, one of the smaller Cambridge colleges. Dismayed by the drab, stilted teaching of mathematics by hacks who crammed their pupils for the examinations, he was drawn to moral sciences, where lively, innovative dons, notably Henry Sidgwick and Alfred Marshall, gave inspiring tuition in philosophy, political economy and logic. At the earliest possible moment, he transferred from mathematics to moral sciences, which he studied for two and a half years. He was elected as a Fellow of Pembroke in 1876 (the first nonconformist to be admitted into the fellowship), acquired the minor college office of domestic bursar, and for six years gave intercollegiate lectures on logic and political economy to male undergraduates and to students from the new women's colleges, Girton and Newnham.

Initially, as a provincial youth from a Baptist family in trade, Neville Keynes floundered in Cambridge college life. His isolation was mitigated by finding a congenial set of religious dissenters who met at a Congregationalist grocer's home a few minutes' walk from Pembroke: best of all, among them, a robust, clear-headed girl called Florence Brown (1861–1958). As the eldest child of John Brown, Minister of Bunyan's Meeting at Bedford, she had been reared in the manse in Dame Alice Street, Bedford. Her father was the biographer of Bunyan, wrote books on puritanism and on the Pilgrim Fathers, and received an honorary degree in divinity from Yale. Her brother Walter Langdon-Brown became Regius Professor of Physic at Cambridge in 1932, and was knighted three years later. At seventeen she went to Newnham, the Cambridge woman's college which had been founded in 1871 under the sponsorship of Henry Sidgwick. Although, from 1881, women students of Girton and Newnham were permitted to be examined and classed in tripos examinations, they were kept ineligible for titular degrees until 1923, and were not conceded membership of the university until 1947.

Neville Keynes married Florence Brown in 1882. His paternal inheritance of £17,000, which he invested on the Stock Exchange, ensured that they both had well-kept, orderly lives. After the outlay required to set up his household, and to run it harmoniously, he still had in 1887 investments with a net worth of about £17,300, which provided 60 per cent of his family's income. As a man who disliked uncertainty in all things, he was a fretful, pessimistic investor, who saw a steady increment in the net value of his investments: over £24,000 by 1900; £38,000 by 1908.

In November 1882 the newly-marrieds moved into a newly built semi-detached brick house at 6 Harvey Road, Cambridge. The kitchen and servants' room were in the basement; a study and dining-room lay on either side of the double-fronted, bay-windowed ground floor, with the larger drawing-room overlooking the small back garden; family bedrooms were on the first floor; with attic bedrooms for the cook, parlour-maid, and nursery-maid. The furnishings from Maple's furniture emporium in Tottenham Court Road were well polished, but not too shiny. The walls were covered with family photographs and etchings of reassuring conventionality. For Neville Keynes his home was a sanctum beneath its curtain pelmets.

The row of houses in Harvey Road, with their uniform bricks, angles and front steps, had been erected to accommodate married dons after the lifting of the celibacy restrictions on the tenure of fellowships. They were occupied, when Keynes was a child, by such Cambridge luminaries as the composer Sir Charles Villiers Stanford, the university's Professor of Music; Sir Donald Macalister, a Fellow of St John's for fifty-seven years and President of the General Medical Council for twenty-seven years; the physicist Sir Richard Glazebrook, senior bursar of Trinity; the mathematician William Besant, a Fellow of St John's; and Anchitel Boughey, vicar of Great St Mary's church, a lecturer in classics and theology, and a Fellow of Trinity. Harvey Road – a tree-lined residential street that was not a short-cut to anywhere except Fenner's cricket ground – stood about midway between Pembroke College and

Cambridge railway station (the latter within pleasant walking-distance). At the foot of the road a bulky Roman Catholic church was built in the early 1890s: it was said by E. M. Forster to have been funded by someone who made a fortune supplying movable eyes for dolls, but was in fact financed by a ballet-dancer who took to Christian repentance after marrying a banker.

Cambridge in the 1880s, and for another century, resembled a country town rather than a university city. It was nearer to John Keynes's native Salisbury than to Oxford. The atmosphere and values at 6 Harvey Road might have been those of a medical household in a provincial town if it had not been for the emphasis on educational striving, tripos results, the rating of young men as having 'first-class minds' or being 'unsound'. Maynard Keynes was always proud to identify himself as a member of the educated middle class: he saw education as enlarging and redemptive.

The Universities of Oxford and Cambridge Act of 1877 meanwhile facilitated reforms of college and university statutes, which came into force about the time of Neville Keynes's marriage in 1882. Life fellowships (unless held with a major college office) were abolished; a progressive levy on colleges redistributed income throughout the university; and the ban on the marriage of college fellows was lifted. As a practical idealist, keen to raise academic quality, Neville Keynes diverted his energies towards the administration of the reformed university, became assistant secretary of the Examinations Board at Cambridge and vacated his fellowship. Two years later, in 1884, he was included among the first Cambridge University lecturers ever appointed. He was thus a pioneer in Cambridge of a new type of university employee whose chief commitment was to teaching and administration for faculty boards rather than for colleges. As secretary of the Examination and Lectures Syndicate in 1892–1910, Neville Keynes was instrumental in starting the economics tripos in 1902–3. His link with Pembroke dwindled to dining-rights and combination-room privileges, until he was elected to an honorary fellowship at Pembroke after retiring as university lecturer in moral sciences in 1911.

Neville Keynes had a low estimate of himself. He needed calm and regular routines to fend off attacks of nerves. He preferred to stay in a level, straight rut than to take any path on which he might be surprised or jolted; was prone to migraines or hypochondria when faced with tricky personal decisions; took pride in never tampering with a fact; preferred steady, unimaginative, impartial but somehow restful desk-work to tasks that excited tension or doubts. Consequently, he did not seek the vacant chair in economics at University College, London for which Alfred Marshall recommended him. In 1887 he similarly declined requests from Marshall to become the first editor of the *Economic Journal* because he knew the responsibility would make him ill with worry. This timidity disappointed his wife, who sought substitute consolations in the later successes of her children. Maynard, significantly, became editor of the *Economic Journal* some twenty-one years after his father had shirked the task – and retained the editorship until February 1945.

Macmillan, the London publishers with Cambridge roots, published Neville Keynes's *Studies and Exercises in Formal Logic* in 1884, and *The Scope and Method of Political Economy* in 1891. Both books were painstaking but sterile; he revised each of them, but published little else. Instead, year after year, he churned out lucid, impersonal minutes and unfeeling, characterless memoranda for university committees. Repetitious, dutiful work made him feel better. He was described in 1904 by Arthur Benson of Magdalene as 'a nice little chippy, precise, solemn man – a good Secretary, I should think – not exciting'.[6]

Life for Neville Keynes was seated on well-cushioned comfort. It was protected by the broad, solid mass of unchallenged English prosperity. In one respect he was a model parent: he encouraged his children, wished them to succeed, and cherished their ambitions; he never wanted them to be smaller than him or dependent on him, never sought to overshadow them, or retard their progress. At work and at home he shrank from exaggeration or severity. Long after Queen Victoria had died at Windsor, Neville Keynes remained a mid-Victorian in his belief in preserving orderliness, exhibiting social deference, fulfilling personal obligations and public duties, and in Christian decency.

In 1882, after the celibacy restrictions on the tenure of fellowships had been lifted, there was a spurt of marriages among Fellows: it was said that all but one of the resident Fellows of Jesus married within a year. 'In that first age of married society in Cambridge, when the narrow circle of the spouses-regnant of the Heads of Colleges and of a few wives of Professors was first extended, several of the most notable dons, particularly in the School of Moral Science, married students of Newnham,' Maynard Keynes recalled in the 1920s of his parents and their circle. 'The double link between husbands and between wives bound together a small cultured society of great simplicity and distinction. This circle was at its full strength in my boyhood, and, when I was first old enough to be asked out to luncheon or to dinner, it was to these houses that I went.'[7]

In 1942 Maynard Keynes spoke at a family luncheon at King's to mark his father's ninetieth birthday and his parents' diamond wedding. He imagined his father sixty years earlier as an 'elegant, mid-Victorian high-brow, reading Swinburne, Meredith, Ibsen, buying William Morris wall-paper, whiskered, modest, and industrious, but rather rich, rather pleasure-loving, rather extravagant within carefully set limits, most generous; very sociable; loved entertaining, wine, games, novels, theatre, travel; but the shadow of work gradually growing, as migraine headaches set a readiness to look on the more gloomy or depressing side of any prospect.' Maynard Keynes praised his father, too, as a university administrator: 'He helped to create a framework within which learning and science and education could live and flourish without feeling ... a hampering hand.'[8]

Neville Keynes is easy to judge because he kept a moderately informative diary from 1864 until 1917. For his wife one must rely on public records and a memoir written in her old age. Florence Keynes bore three children (Maynard, Margaret and Geoffrey) between June 1883 and March 1887. She was an attentive, stimulating mother. When her eldest son Maynard was aged four and a half, she began teaching him the alphabet in hourly lessons each morning. 'Mother is such a clever person,' the child told his father, before adding, 'Mother is so kind. You are kind, too, but not so kind as Mother.'[9]

Once alphabets had been taught and her children launched into school life, Florence Keynes began to fulfil the ideals of service inculcated by her Baptist upbringing and Newnham training. She did not talk about the poor as if they were characters in a book; she had not a shred of the soft, subservient femininity of Victorian women; she was neither meddlesome nor domineering. Around 1895, deploring waste, confusion, insecurity and distress, she became founding secretary of the Cambridge branch of the Charity Organization Society, and began using her bracing virtuous intelligence to advance the education and health of girls and mothers. She entered local government in 1907 with her election to Cambridge's Board of Guardians (which oversaw the Poor Law workhouses), and served as chairman of the Board from 1922 until the modernization of social service provisions under the Local Government Act of 1929.

Although women had been entitled since 1894 to serve on urban and rural district councils, they were excluded from borough and county councils until the Liberal government enacted the Qualification of Women Act of 1907. Even then the qualification for candidates was to be a householder; and as in the eye of the law, only husbands could be householders, not married women, this meant that only spinsters and widows could stand for election. Florence Keynes brought this anomaly to the attention of a Liberal Cabinet minister, and the law was altered in the summer of 1914. In an uncontested election in October, Florence Keynes became the first woman member of Cambridge borough council – and probably the first married woman to serve on a town council. She was described in 1916 as the busiest woman in Cambridge. After the passage of the Sex Disqualification Removal Act of 1919, she was among the earliest women to become magistrates. She served as alderman of Cambridge from 1930 and as mayor in 1932.

It is notable that Maynard Keynes drew closer to his mother, consulted and respected her, as she became prominent in Cambridge civic life: his letters to her became informative, while his contacts with his father receded in importance. Public works lightened her domestic character. 'Florence is becoming quite frivolous – playing auction bridge, and solving crossword puzzles,' Neville Keynes noted in 1914. His devoted dependence on her increased with time. 'If possible I love my dear wife more than I ever did. I am always thinking about her.'[10]

As a Cambridge councillor Florence Keynes took up modernizing initiatives in both health and the law. During the Great War she was one of the doughty wives of Cambridge dons who helped Sir Pendrill Varrier-Jones to start the Papworth tuberculosis sanatorium outside the town. The Fulbourn mental asylum was another local cause that she adopted. She campaigned for the establishment of juvenile courts and for the appointment of women police; and urged women to serve as jurors. Sometimes by private lobbying, sometimes through voluntary organizations or in her official roles,

Florence Keynes helped to start an open-air school for sick children and the first English juvenile labour exchanges. The provision of free spectacles and dentistry for needy Cambridge schoolchildren, and the supply of gadgets or false limbs to help the disabled, were among her other good causes. She sat on a Whitehall committee on the recruitment and training of nurses. Many of her accomplishments were achieved through the National Council of Women, of which she became national president in 1930–2.

But all this came when her children were adults. A quarter-century of maternity had supervened. Florence Keynes became pregnant about a month into her marriage. The family doctor, who oversaw the pregnancy and delivery, was typical of the Harvey Road set. George Wherry, surgeon at Addenbrooke's hospital, Fellow of Downing College and University Lecturer on Surgery, was a lanky long-distance runner, who (like Neville Keynes) adored Switzerland and (unlike Neville Keynes) was a bold mountaineer. The author of *Alpine Notes and the Climbing Foot* (1896) and *Notes from a Knapsack* (1900), he savoured the inarticulate camaraderie of men who climbed steep mountains roped together. He had gone to Cambridge by an arbitrary route that was characteristic of its period. At the age of twenty-one, having qualified in medicine at a London teaching hospital, he was invited to a whist party by the house surgeon. There, when someone cited Tennyson's 'Northern Farmer', he capped the quotation with one from Virgil's *Aeneid*. Perhaps this seemed bumptious, for the surgeon retorted that Wherry was too immature to practise medicine, and sent him with a letter of recommendation for further studies at Cambridge. A young physician who quoted Virgil, climbed Alps, analysed old bones in the Fitzwilliam Museum and wrote a monograph on Charles Lamb was the only man present at the birth of Maynard Keynes.

Neville Keynes listened at the bedroom door (Tuesday 5 June 1883) as his mother-in-law Ada Brown and Dr Wherry handled the delivery. 'I saw her at intervals till about nine, but after that they wd not let me go into the room,' he recorded in his diary.

> At 9.30 I went to listen outside the door ... Florence was giving a slight groan every now & then (they say she was very brave) and at 9.45 I heard such a hullaballoo, & Mrs Brown just came to the door, & said it was a boy ... Everything went well, except for a little tear, wh Wherry sewed up. Just before eleven I was allowed in to see her, & I thought her looking bonny. They say that the boy is the image of me. It's ugly enough.

Next day Neville added in his diary: 'I am already getting very fond of him notwithstanding his ugliness ... I could sit & look at him for hours. I love the contortions of his little face and his little hands.' This harping on the baby's ugliness may have persisted: as a boy, Maynard Keynes was convinced of his ugliness, and in manhood he continued to feel that his appearance was repulsive.[11]

The forenames 'John Maynard' were chosen, but 'the little man' was never known to his family, friends and contemporaries by any forename except Maynard. The formulation 'John Maynard Keynes' is used on the title-page of his books, in library catalogues and by people who never knew him. He disliked this wording, and in letters to intimate friends always signed himself 'JMK': 'John' was used only by his mother at rare moments of stress.

The baby delighted his parents, who watched him with love and pride. 'With my own eyes I really did see him smile this morning,' Neville Keynes noted after a month. 'He is beginning to look about him a good deal, & he is particularly fond of colour. We think him the sweetest baby that ever was. Florence is getting so fond of him as almost to surprise herself.' And when the infant was approaching two months old: 'We don't think it possible that we could love any other baby as we do our little Maynard. He looks so sweet and so pathetic when he begins to cry. I would [that] I could photograph his looks upon my memory. I fear to forget them. His intelligence is increasing, & this enables him to be more patient when his Mother is getting ready to nurse him. He at least half understands what is going on.' A fortnight later, in mid-August 1883, the doting father noted (with a characteristic touch of unease behind his pleasure): 'the little man has again been making a distinct advance. He laughs a good deal and looks so pretty … He sometimes tries to sit up by himself, & he likes to feel his feet; but they say that is not good for him.'[12]

Neville Keynes loved the watchfulness, the receptivity, the thoughts and the growing articulacy of his children. He valued the childlike, and his children's pride of accomplishment. 'It is our dear little boy's third birthday,' Neville noted on 5 June 1886. 'He is quite a little man now; & we can send him to any part of the house by himself on errands. There is nothing he likes better than being entrusted with an errand … I wish he weighed more the little shrimp.' On summer holiday at Hunstanton in 1887, he grabbed his four-year-old for boisterous play: 'O Father,' Maynard remonstrated, 'you are so frisky!' When his aunt Fanny Purchase, who was married to a Weybridge grocer, remarked that she had a bad memory, Maynard chirped out, 'O, I have a very good one.' His aunt asked if he wouldn't give her a little bit of his memory. 'He thought for a moment and then he said, "But I don't know how to get it out of myself."' Just before Christmas of 1887 (aged four and a half) he impressed his father with his latest philosophic enquiry: 'How do things get their names?'[13]

When that same autumn Neville admitted 'that I shall be so sorry when he grows big so that I can no longer carry him about and hug him', Maynard promised to remain small and not grow up. Neville Keynes wanted his boy to remain a sprightly, skinny little darling full of bright quips and treasured confidences: half dreaded him turning into an independent, long-legged stripling striding away to an unpredictable future in which misfortunes could pounce on him.[14]

During the spring of 1888 Neville Keynes began reading aloud to his elder son for ten minutes every evening at bedtime, which increased their mutual trust, intimacy and pleasure. One night, when Neville was reading Grimm's tales, he spoke the sentence: 'A certain father had two sons, the elder of whom was sharp & sensible.' A little voice piped up, quite seriously, 'Why that is like me!' A few weeks later, Grimm was put aside, and *Alice in Wonderland* started. 'He is a delightful little man to read to. His attention never wanders for an instant, & he hardly misses a single point.' At the age of six he told his mother that he was interested in his own brain. 'Just now, it's wondering how it thinks. It ought to know.' Both parents read aloud to their children: on a holiday in 1894, for example, Florence read Anthony Hope's *Prisoner of Zenda*; Neville, Kipling's *Jungle Book*.[15]

For the nonconformist intelligentsia, for whom personal morals, religious faith and social duty were indivisible, it was inconceivable that godless people could remain good. Neville Keynes disliked the idea of his children being reared without religious influences. In January 1884, at six months of age, the baby was therefore baptized by his grandfather at the Bunyan Meeting in Bedford. Nevertheless, when Maynard was eleven, his father was 'appalled' by his 'ignorance of Bible History'. Maynard was a witty, self-confident boy who reacted against his father's pessimistic anxiety by developing an outlook of sunny optimism. He stuttered, especially if excited or tired by pressure, but was outspoken, as his father recorded in 1888 when the boy was five: 'Maynard generally likes to go to chapel with us in the morning, although he gets rather bored when he is there. To-day as we were returning home other members of the congregation surrounding us – he cried out in his loud clear voice "It is the prayers that I dislike the most!"'[16]

Maynard Keynes entered a kindergarten in 1889. Three years later he began at St Faith's preparatory school in Trumpington Road. The headmaster at St Faith's, Ralph Goodchild, proved to be a formative influence. Educated at the Clergy Orphan School at Canterbury and Sidney Sussex College, Cambridge, Goodchild had been appointed headmaster of St Faith's in 1883 at the age of twenty-three. He was trusted as a kindred spirit by Neville Keynes, who recruited him from St Faith's in 1909 to become assistant secretary of the Cambridge University Appointments Board. From the outset, Goodchild was impressed by Maynard's brightness and pluck. At the age of nine the boy had finished book 1 of Euclid, was studying quadratics in algebra, Ovid in Latin and *Samson Agonistes* in English. Algebra was his forte. 'Maynard', noted his father in 1894, 'is in high glee because he is to have two hours special mathematical teaching four days in the week.'[17]

Keynes absorbed much from his father. He did school work beside him in the study at Harvey Road, and dealt with his father's post when the latter was away. For a time the logician Willy Johnson, a Fellow of King's, lunched at Harvey Road almost once a week. The two men would sit endlessly over their meal discussing logic: 'I would be in a fidget to be allowed to get up and go,' Keynes recalled, and yet he learnt rudimentary ideas which contributed to his later work on probability. At his father's table he heard, said Jack Sheppard, his colleague at King's for forty years and occasional sexual partner, 'the courtesies of conversation and the thrust and parry of high argument', and thus enjoyed formative training. 'Maynard to me was', said Sheppard, 'always gracious and serene. Those who were privileged to visit Harvey Road with him, I think, know why.'[18]

While a pupil at St Faith's, Maynard shared his father's enthusiasm for stamp-collecting, golf, puns and word-play. Conning and appraising stamp catalogues as a boy was training for his adult skill in scrutinizing catalogues of rare books (butterfly-collecting and classification was the avocation which Neville shared with Margaret and Geoffrey). Maynard played golf with his father at Royston links, and compensated for his indifferent performance in competitive games by his cleverness at sporting statistics. Neville took him to circuses, firework displays and theatres. All the children enjoyed happy, revitalizing holidays at pretty, salubrious middle-class resorts, notably Hunstanton, Ventnor, Tintagel and the Lake District.

'Goodchild is still most enthusiastic about Maynard,' Neville Keynes noted in January 1897. 'I am already too proud of the dear boy. My pride in him and my love in him feed each other.' When Maynard went to his grandmother's house at Bedford for ten days that April (bicycling both ways), Neville was doleful and apprehensive. 'I have got Maynard & his school very much on my mind just now,' he wrote when the boy had been gone for twenty-four hours. His quandary was whether to enter the boy prodigy for Eton's scholarship examination. 'It worries me at night & in the early morning.' He brooded over the boy's imminent departure from day-school and home. The fact that the boy's voice began to break and that he grew three inches in the first half of 1897 only emphasized the looming changes, and the end of an idyll. In the week of Maynard's fourteenth birthday in June father and son began rising early so that they could have an hour's cramming before breakfast. He received intensive tuition in maths and classics from other coaches. His stammering increased under the pressure. 'It is a grief to me', wrote Neville that month, 'to think that the dear boy will not … do his work very much longer with me in his study. I like to see his books arranged opposite me; & I like all his little ways.'[19]

On 5 July both parents took their son to Eton, where they installed themselves in lodgings in the High Street. This intrusive parental involvement must have set Maynard apart. It is improbable that both parents of other scholarship candidates journeyed to the town in order to form a tight protective phalanx around their sons. Their fretting may not have helped. 'Frightfully noisy,' Neville fussed about their lodgings. 'Maynard went to bed a little after 8.30 and at 10.30 I found him still awake, and again at 11.15. We then went to bed ourselves but were worried at the idea that Maynard might still be staying awake.' The boy seemed calmer than his father. His parents fed him Valentine's Beef Extract to fortify him before the day's examinations. Sixty-two candidates sat seventeen papers over three and a half days: their examinations lasted from 7 a.m. until 5 p.m. The general paper required an essay of up to thirty lines on a choice of subjects which show the disposition of the Eton beaks: 'The uses of an aristocracy'; 'Your favourite poet with reasons for the choice'; 'Westward the tide of empire holds its course'; 'God made the country, but man made the town'; 'Free Trade and Protection'.[20]

Neville Keynes itched with disquiet until on 12 July a telegram confirmed that the boy was placed tenth among the scholars. Mathematics had proved Maynard's strongest subject. The family were acclaimed in Cambridge: congratulations tumbled through the letter-box; when Florence attended garden-parties, her reception 'seemed like a triumphal progress'. In addition to swimming-lessons as preparation for Eton, Maynard was taught by the Harvey Road cook how to fry, boil, scramble and poach eggs: 'Skill in this respect will be required of him by his fag master.'[21]

The squalls of puberty had blown up. 'The dear boy Maynard worries both Florence & me just now by a certain fractiousness & apparent want of consideration for others,' Neville noted in September. 'Every point must be argued, & to get him to do anything that he at all dislikes doing is an arduous task.' His parents hoped that school life would improve him, and 'correct our tendency to spoil him'. Certainly he was seldom punished as a child, but subjected to the discipline of reason.[22]

For five years, from September 1897, Maynard was a King's Scholar of Eton. He was demarcated from the ruck of Etonians by living in College – that is, at the centre of the school buildings rather than in one of the surrounding boarding-houses. The seventy Collegers were distinguished by wearing gowns, and hence had the epithet of 'Tugs' (alluding to togas) applied to them. Keynes as the star product of a Cambridge day-school was typical of Collegers in coming from a less smart preparatory school than most boarding-house boys. This disparity rooted the conviction in other pupils that Collegers were their social inferiors, and that 'brains were no part of a gentleman's make-up', according to Esmé Wingfield-Stratford, who went to Eton a year before Keynes and was elected a Fellow of King's in 1907. In Harvey Road Keynes had appreciated the studious habits, intellectual ambitions, restrained emotions and moderate behaviour of his parents: he found nothing there to resent or fight. At Eton, too, he found no causes for rebellion. His fag-master (son of the head of detectives at Scotland Yard) was considerate. There was much to stimulate, amuse and fulfil an inherently happy boy. The beauty of the buildings, their historic associations and time-worn fabric, enchanted and transmuted him: the imaginative pleasures of living in College amid such beauty made him a devoted Etonian for life. As a pupil there, he was flecked with the dust of apathy or boredom less than most. Living in College with other cerebral King's Scholars, there was little impingement from the unreflective games-players whom Rudyard Kipling in 1902 stigmatized as 'the flannelled fools at the wicket or the muddied oafs at the goals / Given to strong delusion, wholly believing a lie'.[23]

At Eton Keynes continued his family's process of social betterment by education. What sort of a school was it?

Eton was no longer the unruly schoolboy rough-house which had been notorious in the early Victorian period. It was more like a counterpart of the Indian Empire, with the head master as a remote, awe-inspiring viceroy, the house masters as state governors under him, and an administrative hierarchy which sometimes exerted rationality, but generally relied on violence. The Lower Master of the school, Edward Austen-Leigh, 'a shortish, potbellied, and apoplectic-visaged old boy, with a bull-terrier squeak and a sardonic manner', strong on wholesome piety, was known to boys as The Flea – acknowledgement of 'his skill, not to speak of delight, in drawing blood from the lower boys whom he was privileged … to birch'. Robert Vansittart, who overlapped for two years with Keynes and found Eton in the 1890s 'lovely', recalled that the birch, as swished by Austen-Leigh or other teachers, stung less than fag-masters' bamboo canes: 'we should all have been astonished to hear that corporal punishment ever harmed anybody'. As Maynard half boasted to his brother Geoffrey after a few weeks at the school, insubordinate boys were punished by older pupils whacking them with rubber tubes which were meant for siphoning water into baths.[24]

Percy Lubbock, the younger brother of Keynes's classics tutor and Keynes's near contemporary at Eton, said that their head master, the Reverend Edmond Warre, educated nobody. Neither 'his odd jumbled storehouse of a mind' nor 'his musing wandering speculating humour' caught the attention of boys. 'He brought forth his lore, he quoted the poets, he harangued us upon the grammar of the ancients; but he absolutely lacked the gift of the kindling spark, nothing that he touched ever sprang to fire in his teaching.' Warre was more voluble than intelligent – 'a portly dignified John Bullish sort of man', said Keynes's future sexual partner George Ives. Keynes was satirical about Warre's sermons on Sundays, with their mouldy ideas and asinine wordiness. 'In chapel he stirred nobody,' agreed Percy Lubbock, 'he was merely a headmaster doing his duty; he preached as the old head of an old school may be expected to preach, with all his dignity and sonority, with round faces that rolled away to the roof unnoticed till he came to an end.' Yet perhaps Warre's conventionality was apt for his audience, for Eton boys were shocked when a colonial bishop, preaching one Whitsunday, mentioned 'cigarettes'. Daily chapel attendance was obligatory. For Vansittart, the drowsy sermons might have been tolerable if he had not also been plagued by endless divinity papers.[25]

Although Keynes was loyal to Eton, his friend Bernard Swithinbank thought that the school's curriculum was narrow and class-room teaching was poor. He never learnt even the meaning of the words physics, biology and geology, as he recalled in 1948.

Somebody told us that Adam Smith had drawn attention to the division of labour, and of the harm done by restraints in trade, and that was all the Political Economy we knew. We heard of the Crusades vaguely, because some English princes took the cross, and we knew the names of two or three Popes who gave trouble to England, and that was all we knew of European history from 100 A.D. to 1453 A.D. Of the history of Asia and America, outside the British Empire, we learnt nothing. Of Architecture we learnt literally nothing: of how to look at pictures, or listen to music, only a few, who had a natural bent, learnt anything at all. Our classical reading may have been intensive, certainly it was not extensive (I remember taking three halves over one play of Sophocles) and it was almost wholly unillustrated from archaeological sources. There was a feeling that it was a good thing to read 'English Literature' in one's spare time.[26]

The view of what constituted literature was crabbed. When in 1902, Keynes had to prepare orations, he proposed to recite passages from Browning and Meredith; but as Warre forbade anything so modern, he was reduced to the stale patriotic resonances of Edmund Burke's panegyric on Charles James Fox.

Esmé Wingfield-Stratford thought Eton, under Warre's regime, was designed to churn out 'numskulls'. Pupils wasted their days construing sentences from printed sheets, copying words from lexicons, and in travesties of Latin verse composition which aped the way that Virgil might have written about cricket-pitches: 'what passed for education in the Eton of my day tended not so much to impart knowledge, as to plant an invincible distaste for every form of intellectual activity'. School work was a grind which conformist boys performed with 'the decent minimum of application necessary to avoid scandal'. Any boy who betrayed enthusiasm was 'branded as a prig and an outsider'. Wingfield-Stratford acknowledged that one quality distinguished Etonians of the 1890s, 'an ingrained self-possession and *savoir faire*', before concluding, 'the class from which Eton was recruited was in the lowest trough of intellectual depression'. It was a disheartening reflection on Victorian England that Warre's teaching methods 'gave those who paid for Eton precisely the sort of Eton they wanted'.[27]

As a King's Scholar in 1897–1902, Keynes had as his tutor (as opposed to his house master or form master) Samuel Gurney Lubbock, a newly appointed classics master known as 'Jimbo'. Lubbock was tall and trim, with gauntly sensitive features, and versatile as an oarsman, high-jumper, rifle-shot, carpenter and amateur of watercolours. He married a distinguished pianist after Keynes had left the school, and took over a boarding-house where the Duke of Brabant, afterwards King Leopold III of the Belgians, and Prince Henry, Duke of Gloucester, third son of King George V, were both inmates during the First World War. He enjoyed Maynard Keynes's mental nimbleness, felt sure in 1898 'that the boy can do well in almost anything' and ranked him 'much the best of his year in mathematics'. Yet at Eton, with Lubbock's support, Maynard refused to let himself be confined to mathematics.[28]

Another influence on Keynes was Henry Luxmoore, who like Lubbock spent his life as boy and man at Eton. Luxmoore was a revered figure, who fostered the artistic and intellectual leanings of favoured pupils, painted in watercolours and planted a beautiful garden. Fastidious and discriminating, 'an artist in life, and a scorner of materialism', he listed his recreations in *Who's Who* as 'ethics and economics'. Keynes, who was susceptible to the mood of rooms, will have appreciated the austere restraint about the rooms where Luxmoore entertained him: they 'excluded superfluity, cleared the way for a serious working life', wrote Percy Lubbock; 'no luxuriance, even of the best, was permitted in the good grave light of these rooms'. The King's Scholar from the donnish Cambridge household was soon a favourite with Luxmoore. 'I like Keynes much & think highly of his power – except in the direction of imagination,' he reported in 1900. 'He has a scholarly & rather mature mind, grasps & states a subject well, & can get the meaning of an author; he is very attentive, good, & interesting.'[29]

Neville Keynes enjoyed vicarious triumphs, and the fulfilment of his own forfeited academic hopes, through his prodigious son. 'I always feel a little depressed after parting from the dear Boy,' he wrote after a summer's day at Eton. He swelled to meet his son – 'a resplendent young Etonian with light blue favour, flower & umbrella tassel' – after the Eton & Harrow cricket match at Lord's, and to take him for dinner at a restaurant in Holborn before seeing Charles Hawtrey in the title role of *Lord and Lady Algy* at the Comedy Theatre. Watching the cricket, he relished sitting beside sprigs of the aristocracy. Florence, who accompanied him, was unlike most Eton mothers: a feathered, powdered, complacent, chattering flock. Back in Cambridge, a few days later, the Keyneses had dinner guests who 'seemed so much interested in hearing about Maynard & Eton that perhaps we talked about the school too much. I am afraid it is always what I like talking about most.'[30]

In January 1900, after notorious English defeats in the Boer War, Warre roused his pupils with a hortatory address on the Eton Volunteer Corps, as Maynard reported to his parents: 'For once his words have had effect and people are joining or being coerced into joining in throngs including all the Sixth Form and the greater part of the College. Am I to join? I am not keen and the drills will be a nuisance but I am perfectly willing to do so if I ought. It would be unpleasant to be almost the only non-shooter.' His parents, who loathed jingoism, replied that they preferred him not to enlist: 'but we pronounce no veto; he may join if his not joining would make him feel very much out of it'. In the event, less than half of the boys in Keynes's school year enlisted in the corps: he held out, thinking boy-soldiers no more useful than patriots flourishing Union Jacks.[31]

'Maynard's work seems to improve visibly every half,' Lubbock reported in 1901. 'It says a great deal for him that he has got on so thoroughly well with Luxmoore: certainly he has a remarkable mind, full of taste & perception, with all its precision and accuracy.' At English boarding-schools throughout the twentieth century it was the acme of splendour to be casual. Boys had to achieve their laurels by effortless talent: those who cultivated their nonchalance were preferred by masters as well as fellow pupils; swots who publicly strove in mental exertion were condemned as prigs. This sentiment underlay Lubbock's further approving comment on Maynard: 'there is never the slightest trace of the prig about him, a fact which I notice with continually increasing pleasure. No doubt he has a great deal of success before him.' There were imagined to be physiological arguments against priggery. 'On the whole,' Luxmoore wrote of Eton boys in 1905, 'they will resent any steady hard thorough study, whether cricket or farming or French or physics or Greek. Children have vast curiosity and eagerness, but after about 14 as the physique changes I believe intellectual application becomes tiresome generally except in a more or less desultory way.' It was because Luxmoore thought English literature so precious, and drilled subjects were so disliked by adolescent boys, that he opposed English becoming a standard subject in their teaching. 'History is less resented because it is easier ... & science sometimes because there is more to do with the hands.'[32]

Maynard Keynes won ten prizes during his first year at Eton, and eighteen in the next. By the time that he left Eton, he owned over 300 books: about half of them school prizes. In 1901 he achieved his greatest schoolboy triumph by his election to the most exclusive of the Eton societies, Pop. This was a self-selected group of leading boys, who monitored the other pupils as a preparation for running the country as adults. Usually members of Pop were sporting heroes in the school, and it was testimony to Keynes's power of leadership that he was elected without having athletic prowess. After his election, he sported white duck trousers with an ornate waistcoat and braid-edged tailcoat, and placed a daily order with a florist for a flower to sport in his buttonhole. 'This costume', as his mother proudly noted, 'was the outward mark of a position which entitled the wearer to certain privileges, such as the right to stand in the front row to watch matches, and to carry a small cane with which to castigate the ankles of unauthorised intruders, also to walk with other boys of similar standing arm in arm in the street.' Maynard was a good manager who, for example, organized the Collegers' Christmas supper in 1901: soup, fish, turkeys, partridges, plum puddings, mince-pies, pâté de foie gras and dessert were washed down by claret, moselle, champagne and coffee. He joined school committees, and was elected president of the Eton Literary Society in 1902. 'I am finding that', he told his father, 'when I am appointed to a committee I am invariably made to do all the work.'[33]

Harvey Road was a formative influence on Keynes, but neither the Salisbury nurseryman's son nor the Bedford minister's daughter gave him any expectation of governing. Eton did. It initiated him into notions of statecraft and techniques of rule. When later he became an economist, he did not give himself to analysis for its own sake, but directed his fertility of ideas towards problems of governance. He respected neutrality, and upheld practical justice, as an Olympian ruler should. Always, with his ruling assumptions, he devised economic solutions and recommended policies that promoted efficient administration.

Historically there was such a close connection between Eton and King's College, Cambridge that Isaac Newton had been rejected as Provost of the college because he was not an Etonian. Until the late Victorian period King's was perhaps the most intimate and cohesive of the Cambridge colleges because of the Eton schooling that united both Fellows and undergraduates. In the mid-1880s, with the increasing admission of non-Etonians, the undergraduates had split into two warring camps, Etonian and non-Etonian, bent on exasperating one another; and only the humorous tact of an outstanding Old Etonian undergraduate, John Withers, conciliated the factions. It was never doubted at Eton that Maynard would aim for King's. Armed with a scholarship in classics and mathematics, he began his undergraduate career there in the Michaelmas term of 1902.

The classical and mathematical tripos at Cambridge, like the Literae Humaniores course at Oxford, trained undergraduates in abstract thought, taught them to evaluate evidence, and to frame proofs and disproof. Studying the languages of ancient Greece and Rome was seen as a civilizing course: it clarified the English prose of able undergraduates, which helped to make them more honest in their thinking. By contrast, as Bertrand Russell noted with dismay in 1907, educated people were oblivious to the importance of mathematics to civilization. Numbers and calculations were treated as means to promote mechanization, faster transport and victory over foreigners in business or war. These ends seemed degrading to Russell, who found in mathematics 'a beauty cold and austere, like that of sculpture, without appeal to any part of our weaker nature, without the gorgeous trappings of painting or music, yet sublimely pure, and capable of a stern perfection such as only the greatest art can show'. Mathematics, for Russell, redeemed existence from being a useless chore. 'Real life is, to most men, a long second-best, a perpetual compromise between the ideal and the possible; but the world of pure reason knows no compromise, no practical limitations, no barrier to the creative activity embodying in splendid edifices the passionate aspiration after the perfect from which all great work springs.' Although Keynes appreciated the stern perfection and implacable rationality of mathematics, he felt unfulfilled by undergraduate work in the subject. He stuck with it until his final examinations in 1905, but never gave more than six hours a day to routine cramming. In college he found livelier interests.[34]

Although King's welcomed sturdy, open-air youngsters as well as studious, hunch-shouldered types, it discouraged lusty athletes who came to squander three years on the playing-fields, and condemned wasters slumped in tobacco-stained, drink-sodden lounging, with no more study of books than enabled them to scrape a pass degree. At most colleges, the dons were aloof and suspicious of the undergraduates, whom they punished for breaches of rules with fines, confinement within the college gates and expulsion. But, at King's, the Eton background shared by Fellows and undergraduates meant that the senior men aimed to treat their juniors with trust and informality as members of the same community.

William Herrick Macaulay, who as Senior Tutor of King's during 1902–13 was responsible for preserving order, was admired by

Keynes for respecting the privacy of young minds, and for extruding mindless, iron-clad discipline from the college. 'Rules, rules, what are rules for?' Macaulay would ask before answering himself: 'To be broken, to be broken.' This exemplary man, with his intuitive sense of justice, convinced Keynes that 'we most of us pay either too much or too little attention to rules'. The sentiment that creative minds were justified in breaking rules, when the results might be productive, was to underlie Keynes's rethinking of economic laws after 1924. Macaulay detested imprecision, insincerity and unfinished thoughts – all of which he challenged by feigning obtuseness. Deliberate miscomprehension 'was partly used by him as a form of criticism, not only of muddle and pretended knowledge, but of all kinds of nonsense and humbug, of conventional feeling, false sentiment and over-statement', Keynes wrote. He admired Macaulay's clear-cut feelings which 'made him live in a purer world than those who see round the corner of everything and know themselves and other people too much'.[35]

Luxmoore, who had polished Keynes's mind at Eton, liked to spend his Christmas holidays at King's. 'It is like a most splendidly appointed club in which each member has a suite of noble rooms to himself & is paid an income instead of subscribing,' he wrote in 1902 at the end of Keynes's first term. One night Montague Rhodes James, the first man to be successively Provost of King's and Provost of Eton, read a blood-curdling horror story, which he had written, to the other senior members of the college who had dined together in hall. Afterwards they played a card-game called 'animal grab' in which victorious players had to make the noises of animals and birds: 'Moo-Moo', they shouted for a cow, 'Hee-Haw' for a donkey, 'Hobble-gobble' for a turkey and so forth. 'The cleverness & gaiety of them all is wonderful & yet if it goes on like this in term time – & it does – where is the strenuous [intellectual] life, & search for truth & for knowledge that one looks for at College?' Luxmoore wondered. 'Chaff & extravagant fancy & mimicry & camaraderie & groups that gather & dissolve first in this room & then in that like the midges that dance their rings in the sunshine, ought to be only the fringe of life & I doubt if here it does not cover the whole, or nearly so.' Yet for all this frivolity, King's excelled most Cambridge colleges by standing out against the prevalent culture of insularity, obscurity, opacity and smugness. 'There are three things that no Cambridge man can endure,' one Fellow of King's, Oscar Browning, told another, Goldsworthy Lowes Dickinson. 'One is, that a man should know anything outside his own subject. The second is, that his name should be known outside the University. The third, that he should be able to express himself lucidly, either in speech or writing.' Rhodes James, Browning, Dickinson and other King's men did not bundle themselves inside the college, but pursued wide questing interests and national fame.[36]

Maynard Keynes was bought life membership of the Cambridge Union debating society by his father at the time of his matriculation in the university. There, in November 1902, he gave his maiden speech, four minutes long, in support of a motion deploring party government. This speech, which presaged a lifelong distaste for the waste of partisanship, drew the admiration of the Union's president, Edwin Montagu, who fostered him as a speaker at the Union, of which he was elected president in the Lent term of 1905. 'I owed – rather surprisingly – nearly all my steps up in life to him,' Keynes said of Montagu. He had his first experiences of electioneering in support of Montagu as (the successful) Liberal parliamentary candidate in 1905 for West Cambridgeshire ('the home of a peculiarly sturdy type of Nonconformity'). Later Montagu sponsored him as a Whitehall man of influence. As Under-Secretary of State for India, Montagu got Keynes on to the Royal Commission on Indian Currency in 1913. As Financial Secretary of the Treasury in

1915, he clinched his appointment as a Treasury official. Montagu introduced him to the world of political dinners, official secrets and confidential plans. 'He was so moody and temperamental and unhealthy and ugly to look at, that I daresay he wasn't very sorry to die,' Keynes reflected after Montagu wasted away at the age of forty-five. 'He was an Emperor, a tout and a child; also a wit, an actor and a gambler; he ate and drank too much and always had indigestion afterwards. Although he was extraordinarily hideous, I (unlike many) never found him physically repulsive.'[37]

At Cambridge Keynes was recruited to a body that – far more than the debating union – was crucial to the course of his life. In his second term at King's, Keynes was identified by two under-graduates from Trinity, Lytton Strachey and Leonard Woolf, as a potential member – in their private jargon, an embryo – of the Cambridge Conversazione Society, which had been founded in 1820 and was generally known as the Apostles. On 28 January 1903 he was initiated into the society as Apostle 243 in a ceremony which included the reading of a secret oath or curse. Election to the Apostles in his twentieth year forged much the strongest corporate bond of his life. For five or six years he thought, talked and confided about Apostle meetings, and plotted over Apostle elections, as much as about sex. The personal importance of indi-vidual Apostles, and of the Apostolic circle, to his thinking, choices and actions cannot be overstated. Their meetings accentuated his preoccupation with private intimacies and affinities; they promoted the priority he gave to aesthetics and philosophy; and they demoted his respect for political controversy.

The Apostles met every Saturday evening during term, behind a locked door, to eat anchovies on toast, drink tea or coffee and listen to a paper read by a member on a previously agreed subject. The members present drew lots to settle the order in which they questioned and discussed the paper. Like the speaker reading his paper, they stood in turn on the hearth-rug to deliver their remarks. Although they sometimes answered one another with vehemence, their remarks were hallmarked by precision and composure. As Keynes wrote, 'victory was with those who could speak with the greatest appearance of clear, undoubting conviction and could best use the accents of infallibility'.[38] The Apostles constituted a sort of intellectual freemasonry with their arcane ceremonials, exclusive jargon and oblique allusions that served as passwords. The anchovies on toast were known as Whales, for example, even after sardines had superseded anchovies. Philistines were called 'stumps'. The Apostles' stealthy exclusivity and air of clandestine privilege intensified the intellectual and emotional excitement of meetings.

At the time of Keynes's recruitment, the Apostles included two other King's undergraduates, the classicists Jack Sheppard and Leonard Greenwood, and three from Trinity, Saxon Sydney-Turner as well as Woolf and Strachey, who had recruited him. Older King's men, including the art critic Roger Fry and the novelist E. M. Forster, returned to the college for meetings. Goldsworthy Lowes Dickinson was resident in the college. The Trinity contingent was formidable: it included the philosophers Bertrand Russell, J. M. E. McTaggart, G. E. Moore and A. N. Whitehead, the mathematician G. H. Hardy, the historian G. M. Trevelyan, his poetaster brother R. C. Trevelyan, and the littérateur Desmond MacCarthy. McTaggart, Moore, Russell and Whitehead were preoccupied by moral philosophy, while Forster, MacCarthy, Strachey and others were drawn to aesthetics. Hardy had a maxim that it was never worth a first-class man's time to express a majority opinion: by definition, there were plenty of others to do that. The Apostles met to dispute and define minority views.

The Edwardian Apostles were ambitious men who wanted their work to endure in memory. They even had a code-word, 'footprints', for the guiding-marks which they hoped to leave for posterity. The best test of the value of work, they believed, is that it continues to please or impress future ages. Bertrand Russell once recounted to G. H. Hardy a distressing dream in which he stood among the book-stacks of Cambridge University Library two centuries in the future. A librarian was winnowing the shelves, taking down books in turn, glancing at them, restoring them to their places or dumping them into an enormous bucket. Finally he reached three volumes which Russell recognized as the last surviving copy of his *Principia Mathematica*. He took down one of the volumes, turned over a few pages, seemed puzzled by what he saw, shut the volume, balanced it in his hand and hesitated: Russell presumably awoke with a shuddering cry, for the devaluation of their work, or the absence of footprints, was the Apostles' nightmare.[39]

They liked in-jokes, teasing, cryptic allusions, irreverence, oblique personal meanings and passionate affection for friends. Imagination was as much valued by them as knowledge. They tended to mistrust showy brilliance, but prized integrity especially if it came in the wrappings of unworldliness. Henry Sidgwick, who had been elected to the Apostles in 1856, described their meetings as 'the pursuit of truth with absolute devotion and unreserved by a group of intimate friends, who were perfectly frank with each other and indulged in any amount of humorous sarcasm and playful banter, and yet each respects the other when he discourses, tries to learn from him and see what he sees. Absolute candour was the only duty that the tradition of the society enforced. No consistency was demanded with opinions previously held.'[40] The Apostles' state of mind can be summarized by the detail that Ellis McTaggart, the Hegelian philosopher and metaphysician from Trinity, always wore a string around one of his waistcoat buttons in case, as he explained, he should meet a playful kitten.

From their earliest meetings in the 1820s, Apostles discussed Christianity, doubts and heresies without reserve when they stood on the hearth-rug, although, until religious tests were abolished in 1871, doctrinal conformity was obligatory in Cambridge. The secrecy of the Apostles was therefore a precaution which allowed impartial analysis and fearless speculation during the half-century when the university authorities penalized religious dissent and repressed scepticism. The Cambridge outsiders who knew of the Apostles' existence tended to mock the society's self-mystification: in the late twentieth century, after the unmasking of the Apostle Sir Anthony Blunt as a communist spy, English journalists, with their hatred of locked doors, denounced the society as a nursery of espionage.

Although most Apostles in Keynes's time were vehement in their rejection of Christianity, and loathed the penitential temper, they had many residual Christian beliefs. Arthur Benson in 1905 noted that McTaggart 'tho' an Agnostic Philosopher is at heart a medieval prelate, a believer in privilege and tradition. "I believe in the Apostolic succession, but I don't believe in God" is one of McT's dicta.' Christianity stressed the importance of every moment: time was precious, and accounting for one's well-spent hours was the mark of a good Christian. There were few time-wasters among the Apostles: Keynes's fatal regime of overwork was instilled in him by ambitious, nonconformist parents, sermons heard in boyhood, but also by the example of his fellow Apostles. 'Most people can do nothing at all well,' wrote Hardy in true Apostolic spirit. 'Perhaps five or even ten per cent of men can do something rather well. It is a tiny minority who can do anything *really* well, and the number of men who can do two things well is negligible. If a man has any genuine talent, he should be ready to make almost any sacrifice in order to cultivate it to the full.'[41]

The Apostles could seem too isolated, rootless, impressionable and fervent. Virginia Woolf once watched Dickinson in intellectual contention: 'poor old Goldie wrinkled his forehead & flung himself lightly & ardently into one question after another in his usual way – the way of a bachelor who lives by plying his mind & moving by that means from person to person, having no settled abode'. Christians had been taught for nearly two millennia that they were never alone, because God was always with them; but the Apostles faced the metaphysical loneliness of a godless existence. They accentuated their isolation even as they sought to mitigate it by intellectual intensity. A pupil of McTaggart's described him: 'he did not smile or attempt to put you at your ease by any arts whatever; his manner of speaking was dry and terse; he appeared to care nothing for your feelings or your past history or tastes or anything like that; you knew at once that none of that was to the point – it had better not be spoken about; and yet you got an impression of utter benevolence'.[42]

The lovelorn earnestness of the Edwardian Apostles is indicated by Keynes's account of a conversation between McTaggart and a younger Apostle, Harry Norton, in 1908.

> McT has been in love five times and is still in love with all of them, one is now a farmer in New Zealand, two live together in London, one is his wife and the fifth I don't know about. Every week he writes to each of them and has these last twenty years, but some never reply. Very occasionally he meets them and is in a fever of excitement. At the end of the conversation he and Norton fell on one another's necks and shook one another warmly by the hand.

A year later, in 1909, Rupert Brooke described two Apostles, Jack Sheppard and Gerald Shove, walking round a country garden in pure-minded dispute about a candidate for the Apostles with whom Sheppard was in love.

They were both talking confusedly at once, expostulating 'Yes, but don't you see …', 'I cannot allow …', 'I don't think you quite understand …' They were always arm-in-arm, Gerald's left in Sheppard's right, and, very painfully, looking *outwards*, Gerald to his right, Sheppard to his left, and occasionally each on the ground, – but always each at his *own* toes, never at the other's. I think they never saw each other *at all*, much less met each other's eyes … Both faces were red (especially Gerald's) with nobility, and just perceptibly nervous.[43]

Collectively the Edwardian Apostles were intellectually aggressive, physically clumsy and timid, and prone to hypochondria and melancholy. With a few poetic exceptions, such as Rupert Brooke and Ferenc Békássy, they were charmless, gawky and unlovely. Keynes was convinced of his repulsiveness: he slouched. Lytton Strachey knew that he was ugly and maladroit, with a namby-pamby voice. Norton was a tall, round-faced, bespectacled invalid, disfigured by acne, who walked with comically small steps. Woolf had the face of an anxious, ill-used basset-hound and hands that shook uncontrollably. McTaggart was agoraphobic, and scuttled along streets with his backside to the wall like a crab scrabbling against the side of a bucket: he was too, said Lowes Dickinson, 'the poet of pedantry'. Virginia Woolf wondered at the anaemic ugliness of cloistered young Cambridge intellectuals: 'whether it was necessary that thought and scholarship should maltreat their bodies, and should thus elevate their minds to a very high tower from which the human race appeared to them like rats and mice squirming on the flat.' Their communal cleverness provided therapeutic compensation for their individual maladjustments: together they felt less embarrassing and exposed than as lone hobbledehoys. Their integrity, their moral courage, their ideals were cherished and magnified as a group. They claimed to be incorruptible. Many of them aspired to be numinous in a secularized vocabulary.[44]

Gossiping in 1904 about Etonian undergraduates at King's, Montague Rhodes James mused that 'Keynes seems to be an Apostle, full of argument & with no interest in humanity.' He was talking to Arthur Benson, who as an Eton beak had taught Keynes before migrating to Cambridge. Dialectical, robotic and therefore displeasing to his waggish elders Keynes seemed at twenty-one. This was midway through a three-year interval when (as described in chapter 5) he had no sexual partners: once he jettisoned celibacy in 1906, his racing mind and his angularities were somewhat slaked and softened. At an early age he was a noteworthy figure in the university. On a hot summer day in 1905, Benson met 'odd, shy, clever, influential Keynes' at Cambridge railway station, travelled to Royston with him and thought it worthwhile to jot his impressions of a youth of twenty-two. 'He had Jevons' *Economy* in his pocket; & was going to play golf. He talked: but his utterance is so low & rapid that the train, not I, had the benefit.'[45]

Some of the Edwardian intelligentsia outside Cambridge fretted about the Apostles – and especially at the conquest of their morals by the doctrines of G. E. Moore. 'There is a pernicious set presided over by Lowes Dickinson, which makes a sort of ideal of anarchic ways in sexual questions – we have, for a long time, been aware of its bad influence on our young Fabians,' Beatrice Webb wrote in 1911. 'The intellectual star is the metaphysical George Moore with his *Principia Ethica* – a book they all talk of as "The Truth"! I never can see anything in it, except a metaphysical justification for doing what you like and what other people disapprove of!'[46]

Just before the start of Keynes's second undergraduate year, in October 1903, he read Moore's recently published *Principia Ethica*. It came on him, and on his fellow Apostles, as a revelation that dominated their hearts and minds. A. J. Ayer's *Language, Truth and Logic* published in 1936 was a similar colossus for the next generation. Good was undefinable, Moore proposed, because it is an attribute which cannot be stated in terms of anything else. It must never be defined as that which promotes the greatest happiness of the greatest number, as Benthamites did. For Moore, states and emotions with intrinsic value – worth having for their own sakes, and capable of exact definition – were preferable to states or emotions that were judged best for society, and could only be described in woozy language.

'Its effect on *us*, and the talk which proceeded and followed it, dominated ... everything else,' Keynes recalled of *Principia Ethica* in his paper entitled 'My Early Beliefs', which he read in 1938 to the Memoir Club, where Apostles predominated. 'It was exciting, exhilarating, the beginning of a renaissance, the opening of a new heaven on a new earth, we were the forerunners of a new dispensation, we were not afraid of anything.' Moore's writings, he thought, freed him from conformity and accepted bounds. They made it permissible for him to choose his personal myth: the person he thought he was, the individual he wanted others to recognize, the man who took decisions and battled with circumstances and aimed at perfection as a way of putting a barrier around him. Or to put it differently, in words taken from Iris Murdoch, man is a creature who makes pictures of himself and then comes to resemble the picture: it is just a case of making the right picture; and Keynes's adult picture of himself was made by the Apostles.[47]

'We repudiated entirely a personal liability on us to obey general rules,' Keynes said of the Apostolic early readers of *Principia Ethica*. 'We claimed the right to judge every individual case on its merits, and the wisdom, experience and self-control to do so successfully. This was a very important part of our faith, violently and aggressively held, and for the outer world it was our most obvious and dangerous characteristic. We repudiated entirely customary morals, conventions and traditional wisdom. We were, in the strictest sense of the term, immoralists.' Moore's Apostolic followers, said Keynes, 'were among the last of the Utopians, or meliorists as they are sometimes called, who believe in continuing moral progress by virtue of which the human race already consists of reliable, rational, decent people, influenced by truth and objective standards, who can be safely released from the outward restraints of convention and traditional standards and inflexible rules of conduct, and left, from now onwards, to their own sensible devices, pure motives and reliable intuitions of the good'. Most Apostles believed in the rationality of human nature: 'we were not aware that civilisation was a thin and precarious crust erected by the personality and the will of a very few, and only maintained by rules and conventions skilfully put across and guilefully preserved. We had no respect for traditional wisdom or the restraints of custom. We lacked reverence ... for everything and everyone.'[48]

The objective world was discounted beneath the primacy of personal feelings by the Apostolic readers of *Principia Ethica*. 'Nothing mattered except states of mind, our own and other people's, of course, but chiefly our own,' as Keynes believed.

> These states of mind were not associated with action or achievement or with consequences. They consisted in timeless, passionate states of contemplation and communion ... The appropriate subjects of passionate contemplation and communion were a beloved person, beauty and truth, and one's prime objects in life were love, the creation and enjoyment of aesthetic experience and the pursuit of knowledge. Of these love came a long way first. But in the early days under Moore's influence the public treatment of this and its associated acts was, on the whole, austere and platonic.[49]

It is a measure of the daring of these ideas that Sir Roy Harrod in his official biography of Keynes published in 1951 omitted the phrase that 'love came a long way first' among his 'prime objects in life' – despite the remark being indispensable to understanding the trajectory of Keynes's career. Not everyone will be beguiled by *Principia Ethica*, as the Apostles were, into enthroning personal relationships and the contemplation of beauty as the principal ends of human life. But for Keynes these remained the purpose of civilized existence.

Keynes might have been a stony, sterile, mortifying intellectual, more an oblivious calculating-machine than a man, but for the loving attention and ease of his upbringing by two bright parents. His zest was all his own, from infancy onwards, but they nurtured his originality, his creativity and his love of imaginative play. Although Keynes read deeply from boyhood, the great influences on him were personal rather than bookish. He responded to some people with staunch loyalty, and incorporated the best of their ideas into his own. His upbringing and early manhood exemplify the suppleness of the English class system from the 1870s: Eton and King's set the ambit of his life; he learnt at school and college to discriminate between the shoddy, the stupid and the futile in ideas, amusements, objects and people and all that was well made, intelligent and purposive.

Clear thinking about other people's mazes of notions and impulses contributed less to Keynes's prodigious authority than the fact that all his conscious thoughts and deliberate acts were intended to serve what he believed to be true. No one, he thought, was entitled to accept a dogma unless he had thought or tested it himself. Few people had the disposition, the education, the strength of mind, the tenacity to think as he did: that is, to sift the weight of authority and tradition; to jettison much, but treasure a little. The urge to self-deception, which seemed to Keynes fundamental to untrained and thoughtless people, was what he most resisted. Public opinion he recognized as gullible, uninformed, wayward and super-abundant in misplaced confidence.

Improvisations, expedients and thoughtless half-truths led to blunders, as he was to demonstrate in *The Economic Consequences of the Peace*.

Keynes thought the Apostles stood apart from other Edwardians: 'We prefer to analyse and discuss ends; we have not very much to say about means and duties.' But they were akin to many of their contemporaries in feeling that traditional verities were flickering out. 'In all the fields of knowledge and action, boundaries are being broken down with a rapidity to which there is no kind of parallel whatever in the past history of the world,' he said in his paper on 'Modern Civilisation' delivered in 1905. 'I cannot believe that family relations, or business relations, or political relations will subsist much longer with any sincerity or useful purpose, unless we remember that all duties are with respect to time and place, and that sometimes old duties must go to be replaced by new.' Three years later, delivering his paper entitled 'Paradise', he reverted to this theme. 'Our old ideas are not so much overthrown as upset. The old is not destroyed; it is replaced. We simply learn to see new things in a different light.' His life as an economist, official, public man and benefactor of the arts held true to these beliefs. But he was an Edwardian, not a Victorian, so never caught unawares speaking in earnest. In submitting his credo in 1908, he chose to tease. His mother's enfranchisement, the destruction of bulwarks of boneheaded reaction, sexual liberty, affordable pleasures for poorer people, disseminated culture were all causes that he supported until his death – but without the solemnity that characterized so much twentieth-century progressive thinking in Cambridge. 'I believe', he affirmed on the Apostles' hearth-rug, 'in Woman's Suffrage and the New Mathematical Tripos, in the abolition of the House of Lords and the Sodomy Acts, in cheap weekend tickets, in Heaven and Hell and The Times Book Club.' And so he did.[50]

CHAPTER THREE
OFFICIAL

The universities of Oxford and Cambridge trained young men to serve the needs of an expansive imperial nation. They broadened admissions policy to include youths such as Neville Keynes – the provincial, non-Anglican son of a self-made businessman – whom they converted to their values by imposing Greek as a compulsory entrance requirement, and by providing a non-vocational curriculum based on classics. Both the entrance requirements and the curriculum were aimed at ensuring that neither university would be soiled by mercenary values. Thrusting businessmen would not pay for their sons to fritter away three years without promise of monetary profit. Still less would young men find that their undergraduate training disposed them towards life in business offices. Until the 1880s the academic cream of the undergraduates had become clergymen. Afterwards they entered government departments or the colonial service, enlisted as military officers, practised law or perhaps medicine. 'It is really most distressing the way the civil service swallows nearly all the best Cambridge men,' G. M. Trevelyan told Keynes around 1906.[1]

The Liberal legislation of 1870–1, which reformed entrance to both the civil service and the ancient universities, created a new governing order that was one of the glories of history. Compared with its forerunners, it was socially elastic. Its uppermost echelons were beguiling in their intelligence, and a tradition of adaptive self-renewal was instilled. The high officials in the ministries did not bend to populism; they stood beyond the swerves and crashes of public opinion; and they tempered the moody enthusiasms of voters and incoming ministers. There were neither political placelings in departments nor putsches of staff by politicians. Officials aspired to monastic clarity of thought. They honoured continuity, formality and objectivity. This system, it can be objected, discouraged initiative, venerated hierarchical authority and ossified departmental character; but until the late twentieth century it represented the acme of civilized organization.

Some commentators complain that this system produced administrators who were remote from the needs of industrial society, who disdained entrepreneurship, deprecated profit-chasing and, by valuing private avocations as well as productivity, brought amateurism to public life, and thus spread timidity, low productivity and economic failure. Such reproaches can be overdone. They ignore the extent that from 1915 onwards, in wartime and in peace, government departments recruited bankers, industrialists, merchants and tradesmen as privileged advisers and consultants. It undervalues the extent to which Whitehall – while trying to balance the counter-claims of trade unions and a globally dispersed empire – was receptive to the demands of the business community. Officials, if anything, had an inferiority complex where profit-making was concerned, and were at times too compliant with the imperatives that the business community brought them.

Lord Chalmers, Keynes's wartime chief at the Treasury, used to say that every man ought to drive two horses abreast, one his work and the other some scholarly enthusiasm which would give relief from his duties. Chalmers chose his hobby early: he took up the study of Pali, and translated sacred texts of Buddhism. As a further pastime he read and re-read Virgil, Homer's *Odyssey*, Dante's

Divina Commedia and Cervantes's *Don Quixote*. Basil Blackett, who first recruited Keynes to the Treasury, was an expert translator of Byzantine Greek. Otto Niemeyer, a classical scholar from Balliol who won first place in the civil service examinations of 1906, remained a keen classicist throughout his Treasury career. Sir George Barstow, Niemeyer's colleague, was a wit and versifier, and so polished an amateur of the arts as to be elected to the Society of Dilettanti. Frederick Leith-Ross for a time contributed a weekly article to *Vogue* as well as poems to the *Pall Mall Gazette*. One could feel pride in being governed by such men.

It was settled in the Keynes family that Maynard was to join this governing class. In the civil service entrance examinations of 1906, he came second out of 104 candidates, behind Niemeyer. The Foreign Office was unthinkable for Keynes, because it entailed overseas postings far from Saturdays with the Apostles, and from other precious King's affinities: he plumped for the India Office as the government department with the next highest prestige. It had a peaceable reputation – the Permanent Secretary of the Treasury had recently described the India Office as 'an office where everything goes right and there is little Parliamentary interference' – as well as the shortest working-hours of any of the great ministries: 11 a.m. to 5 p.m. on weekdays; 11 a.m. to 1 p.m. on Saturday; with an hour for lunch, two months' annual holiday, and remission from attendance on bank holidays and Derby Day. Keynes used these long hours of leisure to work at his *Treatise on Probability*, which was the first systematic English exploration of the logical foundations of probability since his father's mentor John Venn had published *Logic of Chance* in 1866.[2]

On 16 October 1906 Keynes began as a junior clerk in the Military Department of the India Office at a salary of £200 a year. His first task was to arrange the shipment of ten Ayrshire bulls to Bombay. From the outset he dreaded stagnation in lifeless routine, and feared that he might become a bore holding his friends in list-less conversation. Mary Berenson, wife and business manager of the art historian Bernard Berenson, with whom he had stayed at Villa I Tatti near Florence during the spring, visited the fledgling civil servant in the service flat, 125b St James's Court, which he leased for an annual rent of £90. 'I dined with Keynes last night, his first visitor in his bachelor quarters,' she reported to her husband on 27 October, 'a nice little flat, like College rooms, with a nice dinner, well served. He feels rather desperate at being labelled [as a government official] and is ready to do almost anything to escape from the impending monotony of doing the same thing every day at the same time for the next 40 years. I daresay he would get married – it is the psychological moment – if he weren't too wrapped up in his men Friendships.'[3]

Virginia Woolf pictured the clerks of Edwardian Whitehall as they transcribed documents, drafted memoranda, docketed new files, wrote minutes on circulating files and sent defunct ones to the registry. 'Papers accumulated, inscribed with the utterances of Kaisers, the statistics of rice-fields, the growling of hundreds of workpeople, plotting sedition in back streets, or gathering in the Calcutta bazaars, or mustering their forces in the uplands of Albania.' All went for the scrutiny of ministers, who inscribed comments in the margins or initialled their agreement at the bottom. At first Keynes liked his work, especially after being moved to the Revenue, Statistics and Commerce Department. 'There I sit in a charming room to myself, looking out over the park, writing a blue book on The Moral and Material Progress of India. A special feature of this year's edition is to be an illustrated appendix on Sodomy ... In the last census returns no less than 235,000 persons gave "catamite" as their trade, profession or occupation; I was surprised to see that quite a number were over 50 years of age.' He proved adept at mastering and synthesizing the circulating files on which the India Office's huge paper-bound bureaucracy depended. 'Foreign Office commercial negotiations with Germany, quarrels with Russia in the Persian Gulf, the regulation of opium in Central India, the Chinese opium proposals – I have great files to read on all of these.' He attended his first meeting of the Council of India, the official advisers to the Secretary of State: 'half of those present showed manifest signs of senile decay, and the rest didn't speak.'[4]

Keynes declined a resident clerkship, with higher pay, because he did not want to work longer hours, and valued his Saturday escapes to meet the Apostles during Cambridge term-time. 'I'm thoroughly sick of this place and would like to resign,' he wrote to Lytton Strachey after eleven months in the India Office. 'Now the novelty has worn off, I am bored nine tenths of the time and rather unreasonably irritated the other tenth whenever I can't have my own way. It's maddening to have thirty people who can reduce you to impotence when you're quite certain you are right.' He deplored the tendency of ministries never to admit mistakes or injustices. The shirking of individual initiative or responsibility by officials, and their evasion of any course for which they might be personally blamed, 'prevents any original or sporting proposal ever being made ... the risk to India of free speech in the India Office is nil. But you may be "snubbed".'[5]

In 1908 Keynes determined to resign from the India Office if he could get a fellowship at King's. 'He will be throwing up a certainty and taking risks,' his father noted. 'That fits in with his scheme of life but not with mine.' On his twenty-fourth birthday (5 June 1908), after being offered a lectureship in economics by the University of Cambridge, he resigned from the civil service. His last working day in Whitehall was 20 July. 'The peerless Maynard dined with me,' Mary Berenson reported. 'He is *too* happy at having shaken himself free of the India Office. He hopes to get a Fellowship at King's for £100, another £100 for lecturing in Economics, and his family will give him still another £100. But he will never rise to £1000 a year and a KCB.'[6]

The twenty months that Keynes spent in the India Office instilled in him the mental habit of seeking administrative solutions to economic problems, and of treating policy-making as a matter of management tactics rather than of dogma. As a result, he was not, until his late forties, a theoretical innovator as an economist. Well into middle age he trusted the classical economics taught by his father's Cambridge friend Alfred Marshall, who was his own sponsor in economics. He operated, until after Marshall's death in 1924, as a pragmatist who relied on his mastery of detail and adaptive intuitions.

Keynes was elected to a prize fellowship at King's on 16 March 1909. He returned to historic beauty, to old friends, to imposing dignity, to observances and amenities that he prized beyond measure. Soon he was allotted the rooms above the gatehouse leading from King's Lane to Webb's Court, where he stayed until his death. Arthur Benson began to meet him at college dinners in Cambridge: 'so much nicer & simpler & more humorous & charming than he used to be when younger'. Keynes went again to dine at Magdalene in 1913. 'A very intelligent creature', Benson wrote after a long talk 'about coercion – religious, parental, social. He took rather extravagant views of liberty, but no doubt believes that people are as reasonable as himself.'[7]

In 1913 Keynes was appointed a member of the Royal Commission investigating Indian Finance and Currency. He owed his nomination to his mentor Edwin Montagu, who was then Under-Secretary at the India Office. 'He was one of those who suffer violent fluctuations of mood, quickly passing from reckless courage and self-assertion to abject panic and dejection – always dramatizing life and his part in it,' Keynes wrote of Montagu. 'At one moment he would be Emperor of the East, riding upon an elephant, clothed in rhetoric and glory, but at the next a beggar in the dust of the road, crying for alms but murmuring under his breath cynical and outrageous wit.' The high-strung affinity between the two men was crucial to Keynes's precocious influence.[8]

No one outside Cambridge knew the name of Keynes at this time. The Royal Commission provided his first experience of being a professional economist exercising his influence on public affairs. It added an accretion of new contacts to those he had already made through Eton and Cambridge. His fellow Commissioners influenced and remembered him. He learnt the mannerisms, responsibilities and benefits of being a private man exerting public influence. The Commission's chairman was Austen Chamberlain, who had recently failed in his bid to become leader of the Conservative party and was to recur at intervals in Keynes's life for the next quarter-century. The secretary of the Commission was Basil Blackett of the Treasury. Sir Robert Chalmers, the then Permanent Secretary of the Treasury, was another colleague. Keynes impressed these men by his close questioning of witnesses, and by his meticulous approach. He mastered a welter of detail about the institutions and intricacies of India's financial and monetary system, the sub-continent's seasonal flows and crop variations, and the multitude of influences on transactions between England and India.

One of the Commissioners was a leading Calcutta merchant and industrialist called Sir Ernest Cable, who had recently acquired the Lindridge estate, near Bishopsteignton in Devon. Lord Cable, as he was to become, together with Keynes, prepared a scheme for the formation of a state central bank in India which was printed as an appendix to the main report and aroused wider interest. Keynes spent a week staying with Cable at Lindridge, during 1913, finalizing their bank proposal. Their discussions gave a far-reaching prompt to Keynes's thinking. Cable often complained that in India there was a huge discrepancy between savings and investment, and criticized the high rates of interest caused by people who did not lend their resources. He urged that the Indian public, instead of hoarding large amounts of sterile wealth, must be induced to fructify their stockpiles of gold and silver by investing in public works, railway-building and industrial enterprises. There can be small doubt that Keynes imbibed Lord Cable's opinion for future use.[9]

In November 1913 Archduke Franz Ferdinand (heir-presumptive to the Austrian and Hungarian thrones) was peppered with shot by a careless French marquis while shooting as the Duke of Portland's guest in Nottinghamshire. It would have been better for the world if he had been killed outright, on English soil, in an accident; for seven months later the assassin's shots that killed him at Sarajevo set Europe stumbling into war. Austria's belligerent ultimatum to Serbia on 23 July 1914 started a breakdown in London's financial markets – the foreign exchanges, the discount market and the stock market. Thus began the most severe financial crisis, worse than those of 1866 or 2007–8, ever to hit the City of London. In this emergency Keynes, at the age of thirty-one, made a decisive intervention.[10]

The problem was that foreigners could not meet their liabilities in London. After Austria's declaration of war on Serbia on Tuesday 28 July, the continental bourses shut; on Thursday 30 July a London stockbroking firm, which specialized in business with Germany, failed; and there was no doubt that other firms would be hammered because they could not get the sums due to them from Berlin or Paris for previous purchases. Therefore, on Friday 31 July, the London Stock Exchange closed in order to forestall further insolvencies: it did not reopen until 4 January 1915. Keynes regretted this closure, which he felt would have been avoidable if bankers had been less selfish and myopic in extending credit to stockbrokers. Newsreel photographers who went to capture pictures of gloom or panic outside the Stock Exchange and Bank of England were taunted by City workers brandishing their hats and sticks with defiant optimism, and were chased off. These images have been mistaken since as signs of jubilation in the City at the imminence of European war.

The devil take the hindmost was the spirit of the times. Apprehensive of insolvency, the joint-stock banks began cashing their notes for gold at the Bank of England, and on Friday 31 July began (in Keynes's words) 'the suicidal policy of making difficulties all over the country in paying out gold coin even to old customers who wanted £5 or £10 for petty cash, endeavouring to fob them off with Bank notes or silver'. This was folly, because the banks had gold, but insufficient £1 notes. 'Nothing could have been so well calculated to inspire the public with distrust or even panic, and to arouse in them the ancient instinct of hoarding.' Yet it was not the public running to the banks that caused the internal drain on gold, Keynes judged, but the joint-stock bankers' run on the Bank of England, which took three days to cut the Bank's gold reserve from £17.5 million to £11 million.[11]

The bankers devoted their weekend to cries of panic and despair. On Saturday 1 August a deputation of them called on Asquith and Lloyd George, the Prime Minister and Chancellor of the Exchequer, urging the suspension of the Bank Charter Act which obliged them to trade paper currency for gold ('specie payments'). Their heads were in such a muddle that they could not distinguish between suspending specie payments and the more momentous outright suspension of the Bank Charter Act. Lloyd George was disposed to concur with the bankers, but the Treasury and Bank of England demurred. As one interim holding measure, a month's moratorium on payments of bills of exchange was decreed.

This was the Saturday when war was declared between Russia and Germany. Money was owed in London from all over world.

Foreign remittances to London had broken down. Few capitalists could export goods, move holdings of gold or renew loans. In Keynes's words, 'just as the Stock Exchange was deranged by the failure of foreign debtors to remit what they were owing, so also the banks and discount houses, which had indirectly lent short money abroad, found their calculations utterly confounded by their inability to get this money back when they wanted it'. He deplored the precipitous way that the joint-stock banks recalled loans that they had made to London's bill brokers and discount houses for money owed by foreign buyers in London. The debts on these bills of exchange stood at £350 million. Once foreign debtors had defaulted, London's acceptance and discount markets juddered to a halt.[12]

At King's on Sunday 2 August Keynes received a letter from Basil Blackett of the Treasury. 'I wanted to pick your brains for your country's benefit and thought you might enjoy the process,' wrote Blackett. 'The Joint Stock Banks have made absolute fools of themselves and behaved very badly.' He hinted that a meeting on Monday might be too late. Rather than entrain for London, on a bank-holiday Sunday when services were disrupted, Keynes persuaded his brother-in-law Vivian Hill to hurtle him to London in the side-car of his motorcycle. Bertrand Russell met him hurrying across the Great Court of Trinity. Asking what the hurry was, Russell was told that Keynes needed Hill's motorcycle to reach London. 'Why don't you go by train?' Russell asked. 'Because there isn't time,' Keynes replied.[13]

Keynes was thus recruited to an advisory role in the first bailout by the British government of English bankers and London money-men. On Monday 3 August (with five European nations already at war on three frontiers, and the day on which English intervention became a certainty, but with London office-workers holidaying on day-trip excursions) he addressed a memorandum to Lloyd George which by its clarity and resolve changed the Chancellor's mind. Keynes opposed the suspension of specie payments during the war except as a last resort. Gold convertibility, he believed, was essential to Britain's ability to finance its allies. If specie payments were suspended at the outset of the crisis, trust in the credit of the City of London, and the word of its financiers, would be shaken for perpetuity. It was this international reliance on the City's probity that made it surpass Paris or Berlin as a financial capital: this confidence should not be endangered when the foreign drain on gold was unlikely to be large, and the internal drain could be obviated by the issue of notes. Keynes's advice that gold payments for foreign transactions should be protected, but that those for internal payments should be regulated, was adopted in essence. Gold payments for external debts survived, the joint-stock banks' gold reserves were centralized in the Bank of England, the Treasury issued emergency currency notes of £1 and ten shillings, and bank rate was reduced to 5 per cent on 8 August.[14]

In a further memorandum of 5 August, Keynes recommended that in order to restore the credit of the acceptance houses, revive discount business and restart foreign trade, the Bank of England should guarantee new pledges by the acceptance houses while a moratorium was declared on past acceptances – which would leave the banks and discount houses holding some bad debts but not on an intolerable scale. Instead, Lloyd George decided that the Bank of England should go the whole hog by guaranteeing all approved bills accepted before 4 August. Within four months the Bank had discounted bills worth £120 million. In effect, the government paid the City's bad debts, and rewarded those privileged citizens who happened to be engaged in financial business.[15]

'Financiers in a fright do not make an heroic picture,' Lloyd George wrote of this crisis. 'One must make allowances, however, for men who were millionaires with an assured credit which seemed as firm as the globe it girdled, and who suddenly found their fortunes scattered by a bomb hurled at random from a reckless hand.' Whereas Lloyd George was impressed by the most robust of the joint-stock bankers, Sir Edward Holden of the Midland, Keynes (in an essay written in August 1914 for his *Economic Journal*) characterized Holden as 'selfish', and Holden's chief abettor among the bank chairmen as 'cowardly'. The rest of the joint-stock banks he judged to be 'timid, voiceless and leaderless'. The trouble was that they were 'largely staffed, apart from the directors, on what in the Civil Service is called a second division basis'. Half of their directors were appointed because of their ancestral claims, and 'two-fifths, not on grounds of banking capacity, but because they are able, through their business connection, to bring to the bank a certain class of business'. By contrast, he admired the neutrality of servants of the Crown.

> The leaders of the City were many of them too much overwhelmed by the dangers, to which they saw their own fortunes and good name exposed, to have much wits left for the public interest and safety. At this point the Minister and the Civil Servant, with no affairs of their own to divert them from the affairs of the country, alone stood possessed of the qualities which were instantly required.

Keynes predicted that the government's intervention in City financial operations would prove a lasting precedent. As he explained, 'The world of borrowers and lenders, of bankers and discounters and stockbrokers, is to be galvanised by the wires of government into, at least, a marionette existence.'[16]

In January 1915 – again at the behest of Edwin Montagu – Keynes was recruited to the Treasury for the duration of hostilities. Six years later, when lecturing to the Society of Civil Servants, he depicted the department as an austere enemy of expenditure and waste, and regretted the destructive impact as Chancellor of Lloyd George, who 'never had the faintest idea of the meaning of money'. The Treasury had perfected a bureaucratic style which shielded its officials from attacks as they curbed the spending of other departments: 'precedent, formalism, aloofness, and even sometimes obstruction by the process of delay, and sometimes indefinite replies', as Keynes said. 'The aloofness of the Treasury was not a piece of old-fashioned absurdity, but a real part of the ritualism for the preservation of the prestige of the department.' The mandarins stayed in their offices while the politicians won power and lost it: they outlasted 'the whims of individual ministers and particular parties'; their longevity 'was aided by their impalpable and invisible character'. The Treasury's financial restraints shared some attributes with Church of England prelates, senior tutors in Oxbridge colleges and watch-committees in suppressing licence or immorality. 'There is a good deal of it rather tiresome and absurd once you begin to look into it, yet nevertheless it is an essential bulwark against overwhelming wickedness,' Keynes suggested. The Treasury cultivated wintry scepticism as the antidote to enthusiasm. Its group mentality was 'very clever, very dry and in a certain sense very cynical; intellectually self-confident and not subject to the whims of people who ... are not quite sure that they know their case'.[17]

Principia Ethica was a fine guide to success in the Treasury. Moore's method hoped 'to make essentially vague notions clear by using precise language about them and asking exact questions', as Keynes said. 'It was a method of discovery by the instrument of impeccable grammar and an unambiguous dictionary. "What *exactly* do you mean?" was the phrase most frequently on our lips.' This Cambridge frame of mind – 'a kind of combat in which strength of character was really much more valuable than subtlety of mind' – fitted Treasury needs.[18]

Keynes began work as a Treasury official on 18 January 1915 (living in rooms in Bloomsbury, but returning to Cambridge from Saturday to Monday when he could). He prepared an urgent briefing document for Lloyd George, 'Notes on French Finance', signalling the French central bank's conservatism ('compared with the Bank of France, the Bank of England is almost skittish'), indicting the commercial banking system as 'sordid, corrupt, disastrous and deeply intertwined with the basest features of French political life', and deploring the swindling of investors. While preparing it he went to dine with Leonard and Virginia Woolf. 'We gave him oysters,' she noted. 'He is like quicksilver on a sloping board – a little inhuman, but very kindly, as inhuman people are.' (It was often a problem for Keynes that his friends with subjective literary minds mistook the attempted impartiality of people with technical training for a deficiency in deep feelings.) 'We gossiped at full speed,' Woolf continued. 'Then we talked about the war. We aren't fighting now, he says, but only waiting for the spring. Meantime we lavish money, on a scale which makes the French, who are fearfully out at elbow, gape with admiration. We are bound to win – & in great style too, having at the last moment applied all our brains & all our wealth to the problem.'[19]

Keynes accompanied Lloyd George, Edwin Montagu and the Governor of the Bank of England, Lord Cunliffe, to a conference in Paris in February. Traditionally Britain had granted outright war subsidies to its allies. But the pride of the chief borrower, France, and considerations involving Dominion borrowers such as Canada, to say nothing of the scale of the European war, made the old practice insupportable. The Paris conference attended by Keynes settled an Anglo-French loan to Russia accompanied by Russian and French gold transfers to the Bank of England. This arrangement inaugurated the complex system of war credits between the Allies which created the post-war debt problem that bedevilled Europe. Over the next two years, Keynes helped to develop and manage a system of financial controls over the spending of Britain's allies, which entailed a centralized buying system, with orders being channelled through London, and payment coming from credits designated for Allied accounts at the Bank of England. 'His quick mind and inexhaustible capacity for work rapidly marked out a kingdom for him,' Niemeyer recalled. Keynes's powers increased after May 1915, with the formation of the wartime coalition government, in which Lloyd George became Minister of Munitions, and Reginald McKenna replaced him as Chancellor of the Exchequer. 'McK', wrote the Whitehall-watcher Sir Vincent Caillard a few months later, 'has an almost mysterious hold on the P.M.'s judgment and even affection.' Keynes soon acquired a similar lien on McKenna's views. He became the leading authority on questions of external, and particularly inter-Allied, debt.[20]

The government initially assumed that if it raised the money to pay for its wartime expenditure, there would be a corresponding fall in other expenditure. In expectation of a short war, it did not levy heavier taxes, but in November 1914 issued a war loan of £350 million to pay for its munitions. The banks subscribed for most of this loan, counted their Treasury bonds as part of their reserves and continued their lending as before. As a result, both public and private expenditure rose. Keynes helped McKenna to prepare his first budget, in September 1915, whereby income tax was raised to three shillings and sixpence in the pound, and an Excess Profits Duty of 50 per cent (raised to 80 per cent by 1917) was imposed together with the so-called McKenna Duties, which levied 33.3 per cent on luxury imports such as motor-vehicles and watches. These McKenna Duties were of signal importance: introduced by a free-trade Liberal, they were a victory for protectionists; intended as a wartime improvisation, they remained in force until the Labour government's free-trade budget of 1924; were reimposed in Winston Churchill's budget a year later; and continued until 1956 when they were abolished in Harold Macmillan's last budget before becoming Prime Minister. In effect, for forty years, the McKenna Duties served as a protective measure to defend British motor-car and lorry manufacturers from international competition.

Keynes toiled during September 1915 in negotiations that resulted in British financial credits to Russia, British control of Russian purchases and Russian loans of gold to Britain. 'I doubt if I've ever worked harder than during the last two weeks; but I'm wonderfully well all the same,' he told his parents on 18 September. 'The work has been as interesting as it could be. I've written three major memoranda, one of which has been circulated to the Cabinet, and about a dozen minor ones.' When the pressure of work relented, Keynes went for a Sussex weekend with Bloomsbury friends and showed no sign of strain: 'Maynard is equable and optimistic and very agreeable,' reported Clive Bell. Keynes's experiences at this time convinced him of the benefits of latitude and discretion. 'There is a case for controls which those in charge know to be imperfect and incomplete and deliberately leave so; especially in England. It is far more trouble than it is worth to be too logical about controls.' Only a day after establishing the principle that Russian credits should be confined to munitions, he had to initial a Bond Street bill for a Grand Duchess's underwear, and approved a shipment of beeswax to provide candles for Russian Orthodox churches. On another occasion, Spanish currency was urgently needed for Allied international transactions. With difficulty a smallish sum was raked up, as Keynes reported. Chalmers expressed relief that for a short time, at any rate, the Treasury had its reserve of pesetas. 'Oh no!' replied Keynes to his aghast chief, who like most civil servants had scant understanding of markets. 'I've sold them all again: I'm going to break the market.' By dumping the Treasury's holding, he jolted the value of Spanish pesetas downwards in international currency exchanges and was then able to buy back the necessary reserve of pesetas at lower prices than those for which he had sold them.[21]

From early in 1915 until the United States entered the war in 1917, there was a continuous exchange crisis of a gravity that became more acute as gold reserves were depleted. By the summer of 1916 Britain was paying for all of Italy's war expenditure, most of Russia's, two-thirds of France's, half of Belgium's and Serbia's. It did this by heavy borrowing from the United States (amounting to about 40 per cent of total war expenditure by September 1916). This sum was paid from dwindling gold reserves, the sale of American and Canadian securities under British ownership, the sale of Treasury bills, bond issues and collateral loans. Keynes estimated that British borrowing would soon have to rise to over $200 million a month in the USA. In a memorandum of 10 October 1916, he advised: 'the policy of this country towards the USA should be so directed as not only to avoid any form of reprisal or active irritation, but also to conciliate and please'. Robert Skidelsky has identified these words as fixing the moment when New York replaced London as the world's chief financial power.[22]

McKenna submitted on 24 October a Cabinet memorandum which Keynes had prepared for him on Britain's financial relations with the USA. In it McKenna warned of insolvency and concluded as a 'certainty that by next June or earlier the President of the American Republic will be in a position ... to dictate his own terms to us'. This infuriated Lloyd George, who rejected these views. On 27 November the US Federal Reserve Board instructed American banks to reduce their credit to foreign borrowers and warned private investors against advancing loans secured by Allied Treasury bills. The chief motive for this was to pressurize the Allies towards a negotiated peace, as Keynes had long wished the

Americans to do. In early December gold flowed out of Britain with startling speed.[23]

Chalmers and Sir John Bradbury, who were Joint Permanent Secretaries at the Treasury from 1916, were committed to the belief (as Keynes later wrote) 'that in a run one must pay out one's gold reserves to the last bean'. As a result, although they had prefigured this crisis to the War Cabinet, they kept the extent of the gold outflow from ministers. This was because they feared that politicians, in a funk, would jettison sterling's gold convertibility. 'I thought then, and I still think, that they were right', Keynes judged in 1939 of Chalmers and Bradbury. 'To have abandoned the [gold] peg would have destroyed our credit and brought chaos to business; and would have done no real good.' He recalled one occasion when the Treasury mandarins bamboozled the politicians. 'Well, Chalmers, what is the news?' Lloyd George, who became Prime Minister on 7 December 1916 after forcing Asquith's resignation, asked at the first meeting of his War Cabinet. Chalmers replied 'Splendid!' in his high, quavering voice. 'Two days ago we had to pay out $20 million,' he added, 'the next day it was $10 million; and yesterday only $5 million.' Chalmers did not add that a continuance at this rate for a week would finish Britain, and that the Treasury thought an average of $2 million too heavy. After outfoxing his political masters, Chalmers returned triumphant to his room at the Treasury, where Keynes was waiting apprehensively.[24]

In the government reconstruction of December 1916 the Canadian-born Andrew Bonar Law replaced McKenna as Chancellor of the Exchequer. Keynes found his dealings with Law easy: 'there was no one who could be briefed quicker than he and put *au courant* with the facts of the case in those hurried moments which a civil servant gets before his chief before a conference'. He found the Chancellor a grateful man: mistrustful of intellectual schemes, but with 'an inordinate respect for Success', and therefore 'capable of respecting even an intellectualist who turns out right'. As a Glasgow iron merchant, who had been reared in a wooden Presbyterian manse in New Brunswick, Law had (as Keynes wrote in 1923) 'no imaginative reverence for the traditions and symbols of the past, no special care for vested interests, no attachment whatever to the Upper Classes, the City, the Army, or the Church'. He regarded himself as 'a plain business man, who could have made a lot of money if he had chosen to, with a good judgment of markets rather than of long-term trends, right on the short swing, handling wars and empires and revolutions with the coolness and limited purpose of a first-class captain of industry'. It was to both men's credit that Keynes had a reciprocated liking for Law, an 'extreme partisan, a vehement mouthpiece for the Conservative party, who distrusted any emotional enthusiasm which grasped at an intangible object'.[25]

In an important memorandum of 17 January 1917, Keynes warned that if Britain suspended gold convertibility, the Germans would be alerted to Britain's dire position: "'If England has gone off the gold standard, she can't last six months more,' is what everybody would say, *whether it is true or not*.' Keynes was striving to ensure Britain's financial survival while not relinquishing his hope that President Wilson in Washington would force a negotiated peace by severing financial supplies and thus threatening Britain with ruin. On 22 January Wilson issued his manifesto for 'peace without victory' in the form of a message to the US Senate. He demanded freedom of the seas, limitation on military and naval armaments, self-determination of peoples, and a supranational world executive with overriding powers. 'In other words, an immediate utopia, machine-made and thoroughly American,' commented the German liberal Count Harry Kessler.[26]

In February 1917, at the age of thirty-three, Keynes was appointed to head a new Treasury department managing Britain's external finances and reporting directly to Chalmers and Law. His responsibilities covered banking, currency, foreign exchanges, inter-Allied finance. (As an Acting Principal Clerk at the Treasury, Keynes's toil never relented: contrary to Chalmers's peacetime hopes that his officials would make time for their hobbies, Keynes on the weekend of 18–19 August 1917 took home on Saturday some eighty-nine Treasury papers, which he had despatched by Sunday evening.) Keynes expected Britain's resources to be exhausted by the end of March. But the Germans – not realizing that the US Federal Reserve Board had already delivered a death-blow to the Allied effort – on 1 February launched unrestricted submarine attacks to stop American material supplies from reaching the British Isles, France and Italy. The German navy believed that they could defeat England in four months – and might have succeeded if the Admiralty had not introduced the convoy system whereby merchant ships put to sea in a tight group under escort from protective Royal Navy warships. German submarine attacks destroyed Wilson's notions of a negotiated peace, without victory. Publication of the Zimmermann telegram, in which the German Foreign Minister promised control of Texas, Arizona and New Mexico to Mexico as recompense for siding with Berlin in a war against the USA, outraged American opinion. On 6 April the US declared war on Germany.

After the American entry into the war, the US Treasury began limiting the release of dollars to Britain. In June US funds were withdrawn from London for investment in a $2 billion Liberty Loan. In a message drafted by Keynes, and sent on 20 July by Bonar Law, the US government was warned that the European Allies' finances would collapse within days unless the Americans undertook to pay all of the Allies' expenses in America, including exchange costs. Initiatives by Keynes were crucial in obtaining the release of funds by the US Treasury at the last moment. This emergency was for Keynes the worst period of strain since the beginning of the war. It confirmed that, by the summer of 1917, British financial dominance in the world had been ceded to the United States. After the resolution of the exchange crisis, Lord Cunliffe of the Bank of England demanded the dismissal of Chalmers and Keynes as punishment for their high-handed conduct. It was however Cunliffe whose retirement Bonar Law obtained.

Officials deal in public action: they operate in the public interest, they regulate civic affairs, they seek public stability; but Keynes was a man who cherished private intimacies, and cultivated the private domain. The tension between his official duties and personal loyalties was disturbing throughout the war.

Keynes wanted the war to be waged efficiently and to end swiftly. Its calamities convinced him that his early trust in the rationality of other people's feelings and conduct was specious. He said of the Apostles before August 1914, 'we completely misunderstood human nature, including our own'. He had no presentiment until the war that 'the springs of action lie deep in ignorance and madness'. He was not a pacifist who objected to fighting in principle, but a liberal who objected to compulsion in the form of conscription. 'He would not fight because Lloyd George, Horatio Bottomley and Lord Northcliffe told him to,' as Clive Bell recorded. 'He held that it was for the individual to decide whether the question at issue was worth killing and dying for; and surely he was ... a better judge than the newspapermen who at that time ruled the country.'[27]

In all this Keynes was a son of Harvey Road. Constance Garnett's translations of Tolstoy's major works had been read aloud by Florence Keynes to her family, who had heard (even if they did not fully accept) the Russian seer's message that violence is wicked, that all forms of state compulsion are criminal and that the aim of humankind should be to seek happiness by doing right. These ideals were out of kilter with wartime England. On 4 October 1915 Neville Keynes cancelled the household's order for *The Times*, which he had read since he was a boy in Salisbury, because he was disgusted by its bellicosity under Northcliffe's ownership. That day's issue included a jubilant account of the futile massacre of the Australian Light Horse Brigade when it had charged against a long line of Turkish machine-guns in the Dardanelles campaign; an endorsement of the Bishop of London's prudish campaign against night-clubs; and an editorial on the Battle of Loos which spoke of 'the utmost cheerfulness' prevailing among soldiers on the Western Front after 59,000 British soldiers had been killed. Perhaps most objectionable to Neville Keynes, who had not wanted Maynard to join the volunteer army corps at Eton, was the humbugging report of a London recruiting rally (which had singularly failed to excite many volunteers). There had been a booming oration on Shepherd's Bush Green by an MP with the apt name of Sir William Bull, but the leading jingo MP, Horatio Bottomley, failed to speak having sprained his ankle alighting from a taxicab. 'Everything was splendid,' *The Times* reported. 'There was plenty of popular music … The soldiers were in the pink of health and high spirits. Their bearing gave evidence of the contentment that comes when the call of duty has been responded to, and the virility and good humour imparted by military training.'[28]

In the opening phase of the war there had been a burst of genuinely voluntary enlistment by men seeking either to serve their country or to escape from their ruts into overseas adventures. This was followed by a period of voluntary enlistment under pressure of either public opinion or economic necessity. The army had more men than it could equip in 1915, but during that summer, as volunteers failed to meet the army's manpower targets, a bombastic newspaper agitation was launched against an estimated 650,000 slackers, who supposedly were shirking their country's call. The

Earl of Derby, Director-General of Recruiting, announced in October 1915 a scheme whereby men of military age 'attested' (or registered) their willingness to serve when called up. However, a man's decision to enlist in the army or navy still depended upon his sense of duty, his susceptibility to public opinion, and the attitude of his employer. The Derby scheme may have been intended to fail to meet its targets. Certainly, it incited agitators for compulsory military service rather than assuaging them.

In December 1915 the Cabinet was divided by a proposal to increase the army to seventy divisions by introducing conscription. Lloyd George, the newly appointed Minister of Munitions, was converted to conscription by his need to stop the unregulated, disruptive enlistment in the armed forces of skilled factory-workers, who were requisite for improving shell output. McKenna, who believed that seventy divisions were more than the country could afford, threatened to resign. Despite the resistance of McKenna, Walter Runciman and other Liberal ministers, the Military Service Act of January 1916 introduced conscription of all single men between the ages of eighteen and forty-one. Its achievements were mixed, for instead of catching the mooted 650,000 slackers, it produced 748,587 claims for exemption from miners, munitions workers, shipbuilders, farmworkers and others in protected jobs. Most of these claims were accepted as valid. A smaller category of men claiming conscientious objection to fighting were allowed to state their case before a local tribunal.

In total, during the war of 1914–18, there were 2.4 million volunteers in the United Kingdom and 2.5 million conscripts (although the nation contributed only 6 per cent of the total number of men mobilized on both sides). The issues of the war meant little to the majority of conscripts, who enlisted because they were scared to disobey the Military Service Act. That Act, combined with similar legislation in 1939–45 and the system of National Service whereby more than two million conscripts served in the armed forces between 1947 and 1963, meant that there had never been so many regimented citizens – ex-soldiers and ex-sailors – in English history as in the mid-twentieth century. The result was a divided manhood, with some of the population drilled, submissive to authority and intent on proving their virility by disciplined aggression, with others seething against deference, enforced uniformity and violence. Keynes and his friends anathematized this regimented, militarized culture in the making. They were not alone. Lord Sandhurst, son of an army commander-in-chief, himself formerly a Guards officer, Governor of Bombay and Under-Secretary of State for War, saw 'the agitation for conscription headed by *The Times* and *Daily Mail*' as an intrigue to topple Asquith as Prime Minister. If conscription comes, Sandhurst wrote in 1915, 'it will be the first time I shall feel low about the war ... the thing most to be dreaded, war or no war, is a military party'.[29]

'Here all is worry and confusion, everyone deeply depressed,' Keynes wrote from Whitehall to the literary hostess Lady Ottoline Morrell on 4 January 1916 – before quoting lines from Wordsworth's poem 'Andrew Jones' about a thieving bully: '"I wish the press-gang or the drum / With its tantara sound would come" and deal with all these bloody men who enrage and humiliate us.' He thought there was a chance that working-class protests might defeat the Military Service Act: 'I do not see the intellectuals can do anything – but ply a feeble pen occasionally and feel miserable.' He yearned 'for a general strike and a real uprising' against the political cowards who were submitting to newspaper bullying. In the meantime good people must '(a) intrigue to prevent a general election, which would bring the Jingos back absolute (b) keep all our spirits up (c) enflame the minds of everyone we meet'.[30]

'The Government have decided on compulsory service for single men,' Neville Keynes noted on 6 January. 'Maynard talks of resigning his post at the Treasury, and we are very much worried about him.' Maynard explained his position to his parents a week later: 'Things drift on, & I shall stay now, I expect, until they begin to torture one of my friends.' His friends demanded his resignation, and expected him to claim conscientious objection. However, he anticipated that Wilson would summon a peace conference and enforce a settlement, and felt loath to renounce the stimulation of his office life. 'He was sceptical about the value of almost all work, save for the pleasure it gives the worker,' reported Virginia Woolf. 'He works only because he likes it.' Moreover, his official position enabled him to help friends who had been summoned before conscientious-objection tribunals.[31]

In February 1916 Keynes received a certificate of exemption from military service on account of his Treasury duties. Nevertheless, five days later, he applied for exemption on grounds of conscientious objection, which suggests that he contemplated resignation in protest against militarist compulsion. When summoned to a tribunal scheduled for March he responded that he was too busy to attend. After his exemption had been renewed by the Treasury in August, he did not renew his application for exemption on grounds of conscientious objection – probably because his thoughts of resigning from the Treasury had been dispelled. Meanwhile, he had convinced his ex-boyfriends the painter Duncan Grant and the younger, more outdoorsy David 'Bunny' Garnett (later a novelist and literary editor) that their best hopes of exemption from military service lay in agricultural work. Grant rented a Suffolk landholding, where he and Garnett set up as fruit-farmers specializing in apples and blackberries. Keynes represented them both before the appeal tribunal at Ipswich. Appearing there with a locked bag bearing the royal cipher, he demanded that the cases be heard post-haste, as he had urgent matters of national importance pending at the Treasury.

'The Treasury depresses me just now,' Keynes told Grant in January 1917. 'I am badly overworked, need a holiday, and am filled with perpetual contempt and detestation of the new Govt. I should like to get away from it all.' Although McKenna assured him that peace must come soon, Keynes feared 'that L.G. will spin things out to let him taste a good draught of blood this spring. Did you read his last speech? "The war is a road paved with gold and cemented with blood." God curse him … I pray for the most absolute financial crash (and yet strive to prevent it – so that all I do is a contradiction with all I feel); but we always seem able to struggle on three months more.'[32]

Vanessa Bell's cherishing of Duncan Grant as both an artist and impish life force had developed into a sexual affair in 1915. This romance soon became one of the happiest partnerships between two painters in the history of art. Both lovers remained on the best terms with Vanessa Bell's husband Clive, who had long-term affairs of his own. At weekends Keynes often went to stay in the Sussex farmhouse occupied by Bell and Grant, Charleston, where the chickens were once painted red, white and blue in mockery of the surrounding patriotic fervour. He was there for a Friday-evening party, with Garnett and the painter Dora Carrington among the other visitors, in February 1917. 'Soups, Beef sausages and Leeks, Plum Pudding, Lemon Jellies, and Punches afterwards!!!' Carrington reported. Next day she and Keynes went slithering across the ice of a frozen pond, and walked on the Sussex downs above Charleston: 'I slid all the way down the Firle Beacon on Maynard's despatch case.' This was the black bag which made some villagers suspect him of being a spy engaged in nefarious deeds. Keynes was Charleston's most frequent London visitor. He would regale the household with his war news on the night of his arrival: his inside information was resolutely cheerful – 'he who knew what was happening always seemed to know the best'. He breakfasted in bed, where he spent the morning at work on a heap of official documents. The papers he tore up after dealing with them: he always took pride at weekends at filling his wastepaper basket to its brim before lunch. Keynes preserved his official air by wearing town clothes at Charleston, and looked incongruous among the shabby artists. Henry James, after meeting Vanessa Bell a few years earlier, said she looked as if she had been rolled in a duckpond. Following lunch, Keynes would go into the garden, kneel on a scrap of carpet that he carried, and spend an hour or two weeding the gravel path with his pocket-knife.[33]

Keynes went to Washington in September 1917 to help extract from the US Treasury an agreement to make monthly loans to schedule rather than in a sporadic dribble. This was the first of many momentous American visits. The Apostles, including him, tended to see the United States as a philistine and mechanized hellhole, where size, speed and money were fetishized. 'The two things rubbed into me in this country are (1) that the future of the world lies with America, (2) that radically and essentially America is a barbarous country,' Lowes Dickinson had written during an American tour. 'It is a country without leisure ... a country whose ideal is mere activity, without any reference to the quality of it; a country which holds competition and strife to be the only life worth living.'[34]

A sense of Europe's cultural primacy contributed to Keynes seeming 'rude, dogmatic and disobliging' on this visit, as Basil Blackett wrote from Washington. Keynes found the Washington administration to be serpentine, and was brusque with US Treasury officials whom he found verbose, dilatory and evasive. Washington seemed 'very oriental', he told Mary Berenson: 'Wilson like an invisible Sultan spending most of his time in the harem, and all the others talking endlessly and slowly and never getting to business.' He was displeased to find the US 'full of the utmost ferocity of war fever', he told Edwin Cannan of the London School of Economics. America seemed 'a country where minorities get precious little quarter; and to my astonishment I find myself looking back to England as a land of liberty!'[35]

By this time Keynes had reached the rank of Acting Principal Clerk: only Bradbury and Chalmers, the two Joint Permanent Secretaries, stood above him in the Treasury hierarchy. Yet he was discontent. 'My Christmas thoughts are that a further prolongation of the war, with the turn things have now taken, probably means the disappearance of the social order we have known hitherto,' he told his mother on Christmas Eve. 'I am on the whole not sorry. The abolition of the rich will be rather a comfort and serve them right anyhow. What frightens me more is the prospect of *general* impoverishment. In another year's time we shall have forfeited the claim we had staked out in the New World and in exchange this country will be mortgaged to America.' It seemed certain that the USA would supersede the British Empire in the world order. 'Well, the only course open to me is to be buoyantly bolshevik; and as I lie in bed in the morning I reflect with a good deal of satisfaction that, because our rulers are as incompetent as they are mad and wicked, one particular era of a particular kind of civilisation is very nearly over.' A few months later into 1918 he remained unwontedly gloomy about prospects. The Americans, he thought, were set on reducing Britain 'to a position of complete financial helplessness and dependence in which the call loan is a noose around our necks.'[36]

Alarms about German military advances in the spring of 1918 yielded to burgeoning Allied confidence in the approaching defeat of Germany. In a memorandum dated 31 October 1918 Keynes argued that in seeking war reparations from Germany, the Allies must assess Germany's capacity to pay, and must not destroy Germany's productive power. Germany needed to earn foreign currency by exports if it was to pay reparations, and could not export if its factories were unproductive. Keynes's paper was the basis for the Treasury memorandum of 26 November 1918 which offered the preliminary figure of £4,000 million as the Allies' claim for reparations, calculated that Germany could not afford to pay more than £3,000 million and, on the basis of Germany's expected post-war export surplus, judged that £2,000 million would represent a satisfactory achievement in the circumstances. It reiterated that if Germany was to make satisfactory reparations, it must not be impoverished. Yet there was a regiment of 'trade warriors' – Dudley Docker's Federation of British Industries (founded in 1916), the protectionists and the jingos – who wanted to disable the German manufacturing economy and leave the way unchallenged for English exporters. They resembled the hard-liners who supported the Morgenthau plan to dismantle German industry in 1944–5.

As a ploy to win votes in the general election called for 14 December 1918, Lloyd George appointed a committee to investigate the level of war reparations to be extracted from Germany. The committee was chaired by the Australian Prime Minister, Billy Hughes, who preened himself in the part of an audacious colonial teaching sense to starchy Europeans. It reported on 10 December that the war had cost the Allies £24,000 million (six times Keynes's provisional estimate), which Germany had the power to repay in annual instalments of £1,200 million. Hughes and Cunliffe, together with a judge, Lord Sumner, were selected to represent Britain on the Reparations Commission at the Paris Peace Conference: Keynes and the Treasury were excluded; and Cunliffe with Sumner confronted the Germans with exigent and swollen demands. Sumner was the most eloquent law lord of his day, famed for his cynical epigrams and acidulous sallies: Asquith had considered appointing him Lord Chancellor in a Liberal Cabinet as recently as 1915, for he had once been a radical, but by 1919 he was a last-ditch reactionary who kept to his brief and belaboured the German defendants. Keynes likened him to a vulture, and Cunliffe to a pig.[37]

At the general election of 1918 the most eminent Liberal leaders, namely Asquith, McKenna, Runciman, Sir John Simon and Sir Herbert Samuel, were defeated by a gaggle of unmemorable mediocrities. Lloyd George remained Prime Minister at the head of a coalition of Conservatives and his pick of Liberal candidates who held loyal to him. The rump of Asquith's supporters were derided as 'the old gang' in the gutter press, were reviled in the London clubs, cursed in the pubs, insulted in caricatures. Yet the electoral paroxysm that yelled for the Kaiser to be hanged, the obliteration of German prosperity and the humiliation of the Liberal leaders who had resisted conscription was already spent by April 1919, when the pro-Asquith Liberal candidate, Joseph Kenworthy, beat the coalition Conservative nominee, Lord Eustace Percy, in the Central Hull by-election.

Keynes was sitting in Chalmers's room in the Treasury drinking tea on the first day of the new Parliament while members were taking their seats. When Stanley Baldwin, the Financial Secretary to the Treasury, who had the next room to Chalmers, looked in from the doorway, Keynes asked of the new MPs, 'What do they look like?' Baldwin replied, with the phrase that Keynes made immortal by quoting it in his best-known book, *The Economic Consequences of the Peace*, 'A lot of hard-faced men who look as if they have done well out of the war.' Keynes annoyed R. B. McCallum, the Oxford election analyst and biographer of Asquith, by publicizing Baldwin's quip. McCallum, in his pioneering study *Public Opinion and the Last Peace* (1944), writing as a Scotsman, condemned *Economic Consequences* as 'characteristically English in that lack of emotional balance which made it so very fair to our enemies and so harsh to our allies'. This quotation of Baldwin by

Keynes insinuated that 'a new class of men had entered parliament, predatory capitalists, who made the peace with an eye to their own gain', McCallum thought, and it resounded through the century biasing 'generations of self-righteous young people'. In fact, as he showed, the MPs crying for vengeful punishing of Germany were Brigadier Henry Page-Croft, Colonel Walter Guinness, Colonel Claude Lowther, Colonel John Gretton, Colonel Burn (soon to transmogrify himself into Sir Charles Forbes-Leith of Fyvie), Major the Earl Winterton and the less martial Ronald McNeill.* It was not war profiteers who most wanted Germany to be powerless, dismembered and discounted from the European balance of power, but die-hard militarists.[38]

The armistice agreed with Germany on 11 November 1918 had been concluded by the Allies' naval and military representatives without consulting any civilian authorities. This made Marshal Foch the sole arbiter, untrammelled by military representatives of other Allies, of all negotiations with Germany involving the Blockade, the occupation of enemy territory and numerous financial questions. All negotiations involving ships and seas were, in Keynes's words, 'equally the uncriticised prerogative of the British Admiralty, represented by Admiral Browning, a most surly and ignorant sea-dog with a real and large hook instead of a hand, in the highest nautical tradition, with no idea in his head but the extirpation and further humiliation of a despised and defeated enemy'. The November armistice, which had been of only a month's duration, was renewed for a further month in December 1918 – with supplementary economic provisions imposed by French and Belgian financial representatives without American or English cognizance.[39]

---

* Burn's unsuccessful Liberal opponent in the 1918 general election at Torquay was Keynes's former lover and lifelong friend, Sidney Russell-Cooke.

Keynes was the principal Treasury representative at the Paris Peace Conference from January until June 1919. He installed himself with other British officials at the Hôtel Majestic on 10 January. 'No-one yet knew what the Conference was doing,' he recalled.

> But the peculiar atmosphere and routine of the Majestic were already compounded and established, the typists drank their tea in the lounge, the dining-room diners had distinguished themselves from the restaurant diners, the security officers from Scotland Yard burnt such of the waste paper as the French charwomen had no use of, much factitious work circulated in red boxes, and the feverish, persistent and boring gossip of that hellish place had already developed in full measure the peculiar flavour of smallness, cynicism, self-importance and bored excitement that it was never to lose.[40]

One of the Englishmen whom Keynes met at the Majestic was an elderly Apostle called Lord Moulton. Moulton was both a judge and Director-General of Explosives Supplies at the Ministry of Munitions. In addition to high explosives his department had charge of manufacturing poison gas, and controlled the country's gas-works, coke ovens and oil supplies. After the Armistice he became the first chairman of the British Dyestuffs Corporation, a newly formed combine of trade warriors, with government nominees among the directors, created to seize international trade from the dominant German chemical conglomerates, which before the war had been exporting 80 per cent of their output of synthetic dyestuffs. 'Moulton was visiting the Hôtel Majestic to promote a scheme by which German dyes might be secured and held off the market, to the advantage of the British Dye interests, but at the expense of the British Treasury,' as Keynes told the Apostles two years later, following the law lord's death. Knowing that Moulton

wished to meet him, as the Treasury representative, 'for the undignified purpose of using his eminence of position to influence me',
Keynes for some days avoided him; but Moulton's persistence
forced an interview. 'The old man, then in his 75th year, a Lord of
Appeal, with his great career behind him and substantial wealth at
his command, a little palsied and his slightly heavy features a little
quivering, but with his intellect undimmed, was not ashamed to
employ that intellect in an attempt to impose a sophistry on the
junior Treasury official in front of him.' (Keynes was Moulton's
junior in age, by thirty-nine years, but not his subordinate in official powers.) The interview – so eloquent of the grasping mood of
the time, and yet conducted with finesse – made Keynes both
ironical and inquisitive. He tried to discern, and even to sympathize with, the springs of motive that brought Moulton to the
Majestic. 'It was not a dull act,' he decided, 'but sprang out of a
vitality which still, in the evening of his life, was overflowing. The
old man was sensitive, capable of understanding and enjoyment,
apprehensive of the shifting movements of the visible world. I
fancy, therefore, that, rightly judged, his act was one of artistry, not
of avarice; and the impulse came, not at all from greed, but from
the necessity still to exercise a perfected talent.'[41]

Keynes's first active intervention in the peace negotiations
occurred in January 1919 when he and Norman Davis, a Tennessee-
born financier who had made a fortune in dealings with Cuba, and
was serving as Assistant Secretary of the US Treasury, boarded the
train carrying Marshal Foch and his entourage to Trèves (Trier),
where they were to meet Matthias Erzberger, the German Minister
of Finance, with his delegation to negotiate the second monthly
renewal of the Armistice agreement. Keynes, Davis, Sir John Beale,
Permanent Secretary of the Ministry of Food, and an American
functionary played bridge day and night throughout the journey,
and continued when they were not conferring with the Germans

in Trèves. The kings, queens and knaves falling on the bridge-table were like a dumb-show of what had been happening across Europe. 'It seemed to all of us an extraordinary adventure in January 1919 to step on German soil,' Keynes said. 'We wondered what the streets would look like, whether the children's ribs would be sticking through their clothes and what there would be in the shops.'[42]

Erzberger's negotiating team, which reached Trèves by a later train, was ushered into the saloon of the Allied officials' railway-carriage. 'We crushed together at one end of the carriage with a small bridge-table between us and the enemy,' Keynes wrote. 'They pressed into the carriage, bowing stiffly. We bowed stiffly also, for some of us had never bowed before. We nervously made a movement to shake hands and then didn't.' He studied the Germans across the bridge-table: 'a sad lot they were,' he thought, 'with drawn, dejected faces and tired staring eyes, like men who had been hammered on the Stock Exchange'. From among the hammered men, in Keynes's words, 'stepped forward into the middle place a very small man, very exquisitely clean, very well and neatly dressed, with a high stiff collar, which seemed cleaner and whiter than an ordinary collar, his round face covered with grizzled hair shaved so close as to be like in substance the pile of a close-made carpet, the line when the hair ended bounding his face and forehead in a very sharply defined and rather noble curve, his eyes gleaming straight at us, with an extraordinary sorrow in them, yet like an honest animal at bay'. This was Carl Melchior, a lawyer who was the first non-family partner in the Hamburg banking house of Warburg and the representative of the Ministry of Finance on Germany's delegation. Melchior was soon to emerge as German spokesman during negotiations and as a man of enduring significance in Keynes's life.[43]

No stipulation about Germany's mercantile marine had been included in the Armistice of November 1918. German submarine warfare had so depleted the mercantile shipping of Europe that the Allies determined to make the immediate surrender of all German merchant ships, and their transfer to other flags, a condition of the January renewal of the Armistice. The great shipowners of Hamburg hastened to Trèves on learning of the proposed confiscation of their assets. They were too numerous to fit inside the railway-carriage so the meeting was held in a public house near the railway station. As Keynes put it, 'We, the Allies, congregated in the parlour. They, the defeated, had no room given them, but collected uneasily in the bar, which continued, however, its usual business with the working men of Trèves drifting in and out.' The meeting was chaired by 'a vain and almost imbecile American who had made a fortune by purchasing for nothing from the inventor of it a small contrivance essential to the modern laundry machine'. He summoned the Germans into the parlour, where their leader made his opening address. The little French boy interpreter began, 'Thees mann sez', at which the German snapped in English, 'Thees mann! Say, if you pleese, thees gentlemann!' Keynes marvelled: 'Thus did these sea lords, about to die, salute their fate, and in the back parlour of the public house the German Mercantile Marine passed from her.'[44]

After this Trèves meeting, German negotiators demanded the liberty to use gold, which the victors had earmarked for reparation payments, to buy food before relinquishing their mercantile fleet. In March, at Spa, as negotiators with incompatible instructions skirmished over victualling Germany and receiving the surrendered ships, the prospect of German starvation loomed. Keynes retained every ounce of the Apostle creed that, although corruption and cruelty abounded in the world, truth, beauty and justice were attainable by imaginative sympathy. As a loyal Apostle, who sanctified the redemptive power of personal relations, he achieved moments of perceptive intimacy and collusive trust during the negotiations with unlikely men. One such moment happened at Spa with Carl Melchior, the Hamburg banker.

'As the time to adjourn drew near, I was in despair,' said Keynes. 'I looked across the table at Melchior. He seemed to feel as I did. Staring, heavy-lidded, helpless, looking, as I had seen him before, like an honourable animal in pain. Couldn't we break down the empty formalities of this Conference, the three-barred gate of triple interpretations, and talk about the truth and the reality like any sensible persons?' Keynes obtained consent from the Admiralty's chief negotiator to make a personal approach to Melchior. Despite the insolent obstruction of some mutinous German petty functionaries, the banker and the don found a small room in which they could be alone. 'I was quivering with excitement, terrified out of my wits at what I was doing, for the barriers of permitted intercourse had not then begun to crumble,' said Keynes. He urged on Melchior that if the German negotiators could reconcile themselves to transferring their merchant ships, the English would get food supplies moving to Germany without French obstruction. 'I begged him to believe that I, at least, at that moment was sincere and truthful. He was as much moved as I was, and I think he believed me. We both stood all through the interview. In a sort of way, I was in love with him.' At the end of this meeting, they pressed hands, and Keynes hastened away. Melchior failed to persuade his German colleagues to adjust their negotiating posture; but this moment when two men accepted their shared humanity and met in generous hope indicates the essence of the word 'Keynesian'.[45]

The literary counterpart of Melchior's meeting with Keynes is in *War and Peace*, when a ferocious French general, Davout, is about to condemn Pierre Bezukhov to death. For a few seconds Tolstoy makes them look at one another. Their exchanged stares take them beyond the annihilating impersonality of warfare: they become for an instant two men bonded in recognition of their common brother-hood. Feeling a flash of psychic unity, Davout withholds the death sentence. Keynes probably knew this passage from his mother's readings aloud of Tolstoy at Harvey Road: he took a translation of *Anna Karenina* with him to the French Riviera in 1912, and may well have read *War and Peace*. His account of the empathy between Melchior and him is certainly steeped in Tolstoyan sentiments.

Another affinity was struck by Keynes. On 12 March he went to Brussels with Admiral Sir Rosslyn Wemyss, the First Sea Lord and Chief of Naval Staff, soon to become Admiral of the Fleet Lord Wester Wemyss, but universally known as Rosie. 'The descendant of one of William IV's illegitimate children, with a comical, quiz-zical face and a single eye-glass, middle-aged, pleasure-loving, experienced and lazy, Rosie had still got a good many of the instincts of the flirtatious midshipman, and we had a very agree-able dinner in the restaurant car,' Keynes said. The Admiral had never sat beside a don at dinner, and was agreeably surprised that a professor, as he thought Keynes to be, should, before he had finished his soup, have used the word 'bloody'. Their larks contin-ued together.

There was one moment at the end of the Conference when the pre-siding German began to raise some financial point, of the answer to which Rosie hadn't the faintest conception. I was sitting three places down the table. So without any attempt at concealment from them sitting opposite, he hoisted a signal of distress and, turning my way with a comical, sea-sick-porpoise look, as good as said, 'For God's sake be quick and tell me what to say in answer to this silly ass's question.' I wrote the reply on the paper table-cloth and tearing it off passed it down to him; he, all the time I was writing, keeping up a look of mock despair.

The Germans were astonished by Wemyss abandoning any pretence of understanding what the conference was discussing. Keynes was attracted by the Admiral's 'self-possession and unassailable, as it were, social superiority, like a humorous and good-natured duchess presiding over the financial business of a local charity – which somehow made *them*, so serious and pompous, seem to be a little absurd'.[46]

'I'm absolutely absorbed in this extraordinary but miserable game,' Keynes wrote on 16 March to Vanessa Bell after his visit to Brussels with Wemyss. He was judging all that happened by the criterion of his friends in Bloomsbury and Charleston: measuring everything that befell him against their values, humour and curiosity. 'I wish I could tell you every evening the twists and turns of the day, for you'd be really amused by the amazing complications of psychology and intrigue which make such magnificent sport of the impending catastrophe of Europe.' The thought of his non-official existence sustained him under pressure. 'I am living for weeks together in a state of nervous excitement one would have thought only possible for hours,' he told Vanessa Bell. 'I hope you'll take me in at Charleston when I finally relapse into insanity.'[47]

The British Mission in Paris was not enthused by Lloyd George, as a government minister there, the Earl of Crawford, noted on 9 April: 'They slave away, produce admirable dates, statistics, résumés, argumentations – but they well know that he won't read them.' Crawford wished that Keynes, 'the Cambridge economist', had 'restrained the extravagance of ministerial promises'. Crawford judged him 'one of the most influential of men behind the scenes', but unsound in his advice, despite being 'clear-headed, self-confident, with an unerring memory'. The trouble seemed to Crawford that this admittedly 'wonderful fellow … has passed his life in a cloister'. Men like Crawford mistrusted Keynes because his views were unconfused. Throughout his life Keynes produced unimpeachable facts and figures, clear analyses, direct solutions and trenchant practical advice all based on the nitty-gritty of his subject, which were discounted by officials, politicians and bankers who dismissed him as academic, theoretical, quixotic, impractical. To them his clarity seemed too good to be true. It was even counter-productive to their aims, for politicians rely on diffusing apprehension, and use opacity and muddle to advance their interests. Keynes, however, held optimism to be one of the highest expressions of intelligence, and meant his proposals and doctrines to dispel fear.[48]

The change of mood in England, which was first indicated by the victory of the Asquith Liberal candidate in the Central Hull by-election, was confirmed in May 1919. Dorothy Buxton and her sister Eglantyne Jebb (the latter an associate of Keynes's mother in Cambridge social work, and pre-war girlfriend of Keynes's sister Margaret) founded the Save the Children Fund for the relief of starving and destitute Austrian and German children. They held a meeting at the Royal Albert Hall, and showed lantern-pictures 'so terrible that they ought to be seen by every mother and father in England', reported the *Manchester Guardian*. 'No famine pictures from India have been worse than these, of rickety bodies, horribly distended, shrunken limbs bent and twisted, wizened, old, questioning baby faces.' The Fund swiftly raised tens of thousands of pounds from magnanimous people whose outlook was not hobbled by the imbecilities of the *Daily Mail*.[49]

In contrast to the wizened, rickety Viennese children, Paris that May seemed resplendent with the richest English milords. The territorial magnate Lord Derby had recently been installed in the Embassy as Ambassador. When Marcel Proust caught a head-cold, he combined hypochondria with name-dropping by boasting for months that he had caught it from the great Derby. The head of Baring's bank, Lord Revelstoke, occupied an apartment in rue du

Faubourg Saint-Honoré. Lord Londonderry escorted peeresses to dressmakers. Lord Wimborne took a party of titled beauties to a ball at the Hôtel Majestic which shocked English officials by lasting until three in the morning. The Foreign Secretary, Arthur Balfour, viewed every historic decision at the conference with 'the detachment of a choir-boy at a funeral', according to one of his officials, Robert Vansittart, and regaled smart women with each day's diplomatic *va et vient, poste et riposte.*

'Paris was a nightmare, and every one there was morbid,' thought Keynes.

> A sense of impending catastrophe overhung the frivolous scene; the futility and smallness of man before the great events confronting him; the mingled significance and unreality of the decisions; levity, blindness, insolence, confused cries from without, – all the elements of ancient tragedy were there. Seated indeed amid the theatrical trappings of the French Saloons of State, one could wonder if the extraordinary visages of Wilson and Clemenceau, with their fixed hue and unchanging characterisation, were really faces at all and not the tragic-comic masks of some strange drama or puppet-show.[50]

Neither politicians nor civil servants at the conference had experience in managing economic affairs beyond their own borders. The pre-war international trade system had been developed by private capitalists. State intervention had been limited to adjusting trade barriers, protesting at breached contracts, giving diplomatic support to concession-hunters. There was no governmental expertise in international interventions when businesses or economies were failing. It is therefore not surprising that the victorious nations thought only in terms of seizing booty or of placating voters. 'The fundamental economic problem of a Europe starving and disintegrating before their eyes, was the one question in which it was impossible to arouse the interest of the Four,' Keynes lamented of the French Prime Minister Georges Clemenceau, his Italian counterpart Vittorio Orlando, Lloyd George and President Wilson, who comprised the conference's supreme Council of Four. 'Reparation was their main excursion into the economic field, and they settled it as a problem of theology, of politics, of electoral chicane, from every point of view except that of the economic future of the States whose destiny they were handling.'[51]

The Tory imperialist Leo Amery, who approached Keynes's Treasury department in 1917 about currency restrictions that he thought were hampering Canadian munitions production, recalled leaving a meeting with Keynes 'impressed with the brilliancy of his conversation, but still more with his unhelpful Little Englander outlook'. But Keynes was not a Little Englander: his outlook was European. He anticipated earlier than most that his country must begin to participate in continental Europe on a scale unprecedented in peacetime. No serious politician tried to dodge back into the Little Englander mentality after 1919. Germany was recognized as the fulcrum of Europe. Its prosperity, its frontiers, its temper and its leadership were the ruling factors in the continent, including the British Isles, then as now. A British army of occupation remained there until 1930.[52]

Duncan Grant was the Bloomsbury friend who was most sympathetic and magnanimous about Keynes's official life. To him Keynes wrote on 14 May 1919: 'I've been utterly worn out, partly by incessant work and partly by depression at the evil around me. I've been as miserable for the last two or three weeks as a fellow could be. The Peace is outrageous and impossible and can bring nothing but misfortune. To judge from the papers, no one in England yet has any conception of the iniquities in it.' If he was a German, he continued, 'I'd die rather than sign such a Peace.' He doubted if the

German delegates would accept the treaty, 'but if they do sign, that will really be the worst thing that could happen, as they can't possibly keep some of the terms, and general disorder and unrest will result everywhere. Meanwhile there is no food or employment anywhere, and the French and Italians are pouring munitions into Central Europe to arm everyone against everyone else. I sit in my room hour after hour receiving deputations from the new nations, who all ask not for food or raw materials, but primarily for instruments of murder against their neighbours.' This renewed arms-race made him despair. 'Anarchy and Revolution is the best thing that can happen, and the sooner the better,' he told Grant. 'I could cry all day for rage and vexation. The world can't be quite as bad as it looks from the Majestic.'[53]

'I am so sick at what goes on that I am near breaking point,' Keynes warned Bradbury on 27 May, 'and you must be prepared for my resignation by telegram at any moment.' Bradbury, tall, stooping, pale and ascetic, always, at this time, carried in his pocket a letter of resignation, for he was fighting against either a level of reparations that would destroy Germany's capacity to pay or terms that would seem too lenient. A few days later, Keynes took to his bed, exhausted by prolonged overwork, misery and rage. Once he dragged himself from bed to protest before the Reparations Commission against 'murdering Vienna', his favourite pre-war European capital, and achieved some alleviation. On 7 June he left Paris after resigning from the Treasury.[54]

The letters and diaries of other British Empire delegates in Paris expressed similar exasperation and misgivings to Keynes. Jan Christian Smuts, the South African leader who remembered negotiating the Anglo-Boer treaty of Vereeniging in 1902 and wanted a magnanimous peace to be made in Paris, urged Keynes to write an exposure of the political and economic dangers of the financial clauses of the treaty. More than that, Keynes determined to write a book that expounded the official mind, that upheld the neutral, non-partisan and expert cadre that had run government ministries during the previous half-century, that discredited the jockeying of parliamentary politics and berated the *Daily Mail* mentality that made its profits by bullying the weak and truckling to the strong. Implicitly he proposed technical experts, with economists foremost, as a new brand of world leader, beyond the clutches of traditional party politics, vote-buying and tribal loyalties. These were the new objective leaders who could best manage change now that old notions of statecraft were obsolete. Keynes pictured the patrician civilization that he valued as under threat from a mob that was massing and surging forward to breach the park gates. But economists offered a new statecraft that might prevent peoples, nations and continents from sliding into mutiny, decline, violence and waste.

Keynes wrote most of the book during two summer months staying at Bloomsbury's outpost beneath the Sussex Downs. 'I am absolutely glued to Charleston, writing a book against time and never daring to take a morning off,' he told Ottoline Morrell on 8 August. 'It is about the economic follies and wickedness of the Peace Treaty, and … if it is to be of any use, I have to write a preposterous and devastating number of words per diem.' Months later, after the final proofs had been checked, Keynes told Smuts that he had modified little of his frankness: 'attempts to humour or placate Americans or anyone else seem quite futile, and I personally despair of results from anything but violent and ruthless truth-telling.'[55]

The book was published by Macmillan, in London, on 12 December 1919. Commercially it sank *The Peace Conference*, by the veteran foreign correspondent E. J. Dillon, published by Hutchinson a few weeks earlier: 18,500 copies of *The Economic Consequences of the Peace* had been sold in England by April 1920, and almost 70,000 in the United States. There were translations into German, French, Italian, Spanish, Russian, Romanian, Danish, Dutch, Swedish, Chinese and Japanese. His book invites comparison with *The Last Days of Hitler* by Hugh Trevor-Roper as a bestseller that emerged in the aftermath of a world war, and had tremendous impact after publication as well as an enduring influence. It was the middle of a trio of books by Bloomsbury Apostles – Lytton Strachey's *Eminent Victorians* of 1918 and Leonard Woolf's *Empire and Commerce in Africa* of 1920 were the others – written in the ruins of Edwardian civilization. Strachey's iconoclasm in *Eminent Victorians*, and the critical acclaim and commercial success of the book, doubtless incited Keynes to irreverence about political leaders. Clive Bell's pamphlet of 1915, *Peace at Once*, also had a discernible influence on Keynes's ideas and expressions.

Robert Vansittart never forgave Keynes for resorting to calumny in order to score his points in *The Economic Consequences of the Peace*: 'no redeeming features were allowed to sophists, hypocrites, rogues, ninnies, who had fiddled and faddled with a treaty dishonourable, evil, odious, ridiculous, fraught with the decadence of European civilisation'. Vansittart had in mind the famous pen-portraits of Clemenceau, Wilson and Lloyd George, drenched in the teasing irony, startling candour and pictorial observation favoured by Keynes's friends, which were to be quoted round the world.[56]

Clemenceau was the most eminent of the peacemakers, with the best measure of other delegates, the most distinctive logic in his aims and the most decisive sense of himself. 'He alone both had an idea and had considered it in all its consequences,' wrote Keynes. 'His age, his character, his wit, and his appearance joined to give him objectivity and a defined outline in an environment of confusion.' He looked unmovable in his strength in conference sessions: 'he wore a square-tailed coat of very good, thick black broadcloth, and on his hands, which were never uncovered, grey suède gloves; his boots were of thick black leather, very good, but of a country style, and sometimes fastened in front, curiously, by a buckle instead of laces'. He needed no apparatus to impose his authority. 'He carried no papers and no portfolio, and was unattended by any personal secretary, though several French ministers and officials would be present round him … He spoke seldom, leaving the initial statement of the French case to his ministers or officials; he closed his eyes often and sat back in his chair with an impassive face of parchment, his grey gloved hands clasped in front of him. A short sentence, decisive or cynical, was generally sufficient.'[57]

President Woodrow Wilson's opponents in the United States exploited Keynes's depiction of his ineptness in diplomatic negotiations. 'When it came to practice his ideas were nebulous and incomplete,' Keynes judged. 'He had no plan, no scheme, no constructive ideas whatever for clothing with the flesh of life the commandments which he had thundered from the White House. He could have preached a sermon on any of them or addressed a stately prayer to the Almighty for their fulfilment; but he could not frame their concrete application to the state of Europe.' Wilson's air of sanctimonious and rigid Godliness irritated not only free thinkers like Keynes, but other Englishmen at the conference who professed a more discreet Christianity. The political culture of the United States seemed other-worldly if not theocratic to many European leaders in 1919: these divergences in national temperament did not diminish as the US moved, with evident chariness, into the position of a world power; and they became uncomfortably conspicuous when Keynes led negotiations in Washington during the 1940s. But in 1919 Keynes identified personal failings in the President rather than intrinsic faults in the nation that he led. He was not singular among officials in Paris in finding Wilson's diplomacy to be lumbering, stubborn and unadaptable. 'The

President's slowness amongst the Europeans was noteworthy. He could not, all in a minute, take in what the rest were saying, size up the situation with a glance, frame a reply, and meet the case by a slight change of ground.' Wilson seemed too mistrustful, too self-sufficient, too self-confident and jealous of his prerogatives as the only head of state among the negotiators. Consequently, he did not consult his entourage enough. In Keynes's words, 'the abnormal reserve of his nature did not allow him near any one who aspired to moral equality or the continuous exercise of influence. His fellow-plenipotentiaries were dummies.'[58]

Under advice, Keynes suppressed his most mordant references to Lloyd George, which he reserved to publish in his later *Essays in Biography*. But in 1919 he said enough. 'Lloyd George, after delivering a speech in English, would, during the period of its interpretation into French, cross the hearthrug to the President to reinforce his case by some *ad hominem* argument in private conversation, or to sound the possibilities for a compromise – and this would sometimes be the signal for a general upheaval,' Keynes recounted in his vivid way.

> The President's advisers would press round him, a moment later the British experts would dribble across to learn the result or to see that all was well, and next the French would be there, a little suspicious lest the others were arranging something behind them, until all the room were on their feet and conversation was general in both languages. My last and most vivid impression is of such a scene – the President and the Prime Minister at the centre of a surging mob and a babel of sound, a welter of eager, impromptu compromises and counter-compromises, all sound and fury signifying nothing, on what was an unreal question anyhow, the great issues of the morning's meeting forgotten and neglected; and Clemenceau, silent and aloof on the outskirts – for nothing which

touched the security of France was forward – throned, in his grey gloves, on the brocade chair, dry in soul and empty of hope, very old and tired, but surveying the scene with a cynical and almost impish air; and when at last silence was restored and the company had returned to their places, it was to discover that he had disappeared.[59]

Keynes had been transformed by his experiences in Paris from being an Englishman into a European in his cares and outlook. 'Europe is solid with herself,' he wrote in *Economic Consequences*. 'France, Germany, Italy, Austria, and Holland, Russia and Roumania and Poland, throb together, and their structure and civilisation are essentially one. They flourished together, they have rocked together in a war which we, in spite of our enormous contributions and sacrifices (like though in a less degree America), economically stood outside.' It was therefore a horrific realization for this newly converted European that Clemenceau 'took the view that European civil war is to be regarded as a normal, or at least a recurrent, state of affairs for the future, and that the sort of conflicts between organised great powers which have occupied the past hundred years will also engage the next. According to this vision of the future, European history is to be a perpetual prize-fight, of which France has won this round, but of which this round is certainly not the last.'[60]

The Economic Consequences of the Peace was written with pugnacious verve and brilliant insight to scourge the ignorance, caprices, hypocrisy and bad organization of the Paris delegates. It was recognized by reviewers as simultaneously a mordant political pamphlet and a masterly technical discussion of the economic provisions of the Versailles treaty. For many intelligent readers it was the first book of economics that they had found intelligible. Keynes argued that Europe could not prosper unless Germany was restored to economic vigour: he blamed the peacemakers for wrecking European prosperity by their punitive attitude to Germany. 'The policy of reducing Germany to servitude for a generation, of degrading the lives of millions of human beings, and of depriving a whole nation of happiness should be abhorrent and detestable – abhorrent and detestable, even if it were possible, even if it enriched ourselves, even if it did not sow the decay of the whole civilized life of Europe,' Keynes insisted. 'Some preach it in the name of justice. In the great events of man's history, in the unwinding of the complex fates of nations, justice is not so simple. And if it were, nations are not authorized, by religion or by natural morals, to visit on the children of their enemies, the misdoings of parents or of rulers.'[61]

He was aghast to see much of Europe, with its uplifting and enriching civilization, destitute and insurgent. The treaty did not promote the economic rehabilitation of Europe, but created new frontiers that were charged with economic as well as political significance. These entailed trade barriers, confiscations of private property, prohibitions and passport controls. The new states carved from the dismembered Habsburg and Romanov empires vied with each other for raw materials, foodstuffs, markets and capital. The treaty neither encouraged them to behave as good neighbours nor stabilized them. National rivalry, not continental cooperation, was let loose. The Versailles settlement cast Poland in the role that suited France, Keynes wrote: 'to be strong, Catholic, militarist, and faithful, the consort, or at least the favourite, of victorious France, prosperous and magnificent between the ashes of Russia and the ruin of Germany'. Russia was rejected, not reclaimed, by the treaty. Like Germany, it was excluded from the League of Nations, which was created partly in order to contain both countries through the territorial guarantees and disarmament clauses embedded in the treaty of Versailles. However, as Keynes warned, unless its neighbours Russia and Germany were prosperous and stable, 'Poland is an economic impossibility with no industry but Jew-baiting.'[62]

Keynes did not enthuse, as a good liberal might have done, that the peace treaty founded the League of Nations, or that its revision of frontiers brought liberty to Baltic and central European states that had previously been controlled by the Romanov and Habsburg empires. He saw the belligerence of the new states. The French armaments company Schneider, like its English rival Vickers, was offering to build arsenals and hunting for monopoly concessions in the new states of Poland and Estonia, in the enlarged kingdom of Romania and in the new kingdom of the Serbs, Croats and Slovenes. 'Crazy dreams and childish intrigue in Russia and Poland and thereabouts are the favourite indulgence at present of those Englishmen and Frenchmen who seek excitement in its least innocent form, and believe, or at least behave as if, foreign policy was of the same *genre* as a cheap melodrama,' Keynes wrote from firsthand experience. *Economic Consequences* assumed or asserted that prosperous, stable nations were less disposed to war than unstable, impoverished countries; but reviewers noted that Germany had been making the biggest profits from industrial success in 1914, yet still went eagerly to war – believing that conquests would enrich its economy.[63]

'You must get Keynes' book,' Austen Chamberlain urged his sister Ida on 21 December 1919. 'He ought not to have written it, for he held an official position and from an ex-official it is very indiscreet. But it is … brilliantly written & his … portraits of Clemenceau and Wilson are masterpieces. I read the description of Wilson with malicious pleasure. What irreparable harm that man has done by his ignorance, self-sufficiency, party spirit & obstinacy! And alas! we and all Europe pay the price whilst his countrymen disown him and all his works.' Chamberlain wished that he could differ from Keynes's estimate of Germany's inability to pay reparations or from his sense of the hopelessness of Austria under the treaty. 'There is only too much truth in Keynes' gloomy picture tho' his attack on politicians for fixing an impossible indemnity is unfair since ... the English ones followed the advice of an ex-Governor of the Bank, Lord Cunliffe, & one of the ablest of our Judges, Lord Sumner.' Similarly, Chamberlain's half-brother Neville recommended *Economic Consequences* to their sister Hilda. 'It is a brilliant piece of writing and the descriptions of the Big Three at the conference are masterly. All the same I guess this Keynes to be a crank.' The Cambridge man's recommendation of a capital levy to extinguish the debts of the belligerent European nations, as a device to restore sound finance, 'shows mental aberration of a dangerous kind'.[64]

'I find it distasteful that a man (apparently of military age) should enjoy a safe and cushy job, and then write a book criticising his official superiors and his government's policy,' wrote Lord Crawford on 22 December. The book was published while Wilson's Democrat administration was struggling without avail to secure the requisite two-thirds majority in the Republican-controlled Senate for the ratification of the Versailles treaty and of the League of Nations. Lord Reading, the former Ambassador Extraordinary in Washington who owed much to Lloyd George, deplored *Economic Consequences* to Crawford, who lamented that 'these clever men, and Keynes is among the cleverest I know, are often so tactless – say such unwise things'. Crawford's brother Sir Ronald Lindsay, who had charge of the Washington Embassy during Reading's frequent absences, reported in a despatch from there that the book's impact could not be exaggerated. 'Americans do not care for the political side of the Treaty. The disposition of frontiers and provinces in the complicated geography of Europe does not interest them ... But here is a book in eminently readable style and talking the international language of economics.' Lord Hardinge of Penshurst, the Permanent Under-Secretary at the Foreign Office, whose role at the Paris conference had been relegated by Lloyd George, deprecated 'the pernicious effects of Keynes's book on American public opinion'.[65]

Keynes's indictment of the fatally vindictive mood aroused by rabble-rousers at the time of the general election of 1918, which fashioned the reparations estimates of Cunliffe, Hughes and Sumner, was resented by such newspapers as the *Daily Mail*. The City banker Sir Charles Addis noted on 23 December 1919 that although Keynes's book was widely discussed, 'the Northcliffe Press boycott it'. The boycott was lifted on 5 January when *The Times* carried a long, hostile and well-informed article, written by its recently appointed editor Wickham Steed, a cosmopolitan linguist who had been a scouring critic of the pre-war Habsburg monarchy and was Northcliffe's dependable mouthpiece. Steed found *Economic Consequences* 'vitiated by a persistent pro-German bias'. How, he demanded, did Keynes 'come to hold the position of technical adviser to one of the most technical Departments of State? How, unless his bias had been throughout akin to that of the conscientious objector, could he place the Allies on the same moral level as Germany in regard to the war?' However, Steed, no more than other reviewers, did not pounce on a deficiency in *Economic Consequences*: Keynes elided the fact that the terms of the Versailles treaty were lenient compared with those imposed by Germany in the treaty of Brest-Litovsk in 1918, whereby Russia had been denuded of a third of its population, deprived of half its industrial capacity and nine-tenths of its coal-mines, and subjected to a massive indemnity. Similarly, the exactions which Germany had hoped to levy on the Allies in the event of winning the war were harsher than those of the Versailles treaty. But Keynes was too magnanimous to discuss Germany's actions and intentions in victory, and thus engendered a sentimental internationalism resting on a false realpolitik.[66]

As Keynes sat at Charleston writing in the summer of 1919, he surely had the subordinate aim of arming the dissident Asquith Liberals with weapons against the despised usurper, Lloyd George. Indeed, his ironical treatment of Clemenceau, Lloyd George and Wilson had perhaps been incited, in part, by a hint from Margot Asquith that the personalities and ambience of the peacemakers should be drawn for posterity. Certainly, the Asquith faction rejoiced in the skewering of their Welsh bugbear. Keynes was the literary lion at a post-Christmas house-party held by Henry and Margot Asquith at Sutton Courtenay. Asquith's elder daughter, Violet Bonham Carter, recorded guests clustering around him. 'He read it aloud to us,' she reported: 'brilliant – an unanswerable indictment.' Margot Asquith sent a telegram urging her friend Ettie Desborough to read *Economic Consequences*, while Violet praised its author as 'a most interesting & delightful creature with a mind like a blade'.[67]

The book impressed modernizing industrialists. Lord Perry, head of the Ford Motor Company operations in England, said he became 'a very humble pupil at the footstool of Lord Keynes' after reading *Economic Consequences* in the early 1920s. The younger Lord Melchett, vice-chairman of Imperial Chemical Industries, made similar tributes. Humbler office workers were also convinced. T. S. Eliot at this time headed the Intelligence Department of Lloyds Bank, where he compiled a daily sheet of commercial and financial extracts from foreign newspapers, and monitored the doings of businesses and officials in Germany, France, Italy, Spain, central Europe, the Balkans and the USA. Confined in a poky underground office, where his nerves were taxed by the hammering above his head of the heels of passers-by on the glass squares of pavement which roofed his room, his outlook embraced the continent, as Keynes's did. Compiling business synopses made him see Europe as a whole, and showed him the limits of national frontiers and of discredited notions of sovereignty. *Economic Consequences* he read and recommended soon after publication. Keynes's description of the 'blasted grandeur' of the Western Front, where 'for mile after mile nothing was left ... and no field fit for the plough', with devastated districts all 'a heap of rubble, a morass of shell-holes, and a tangle of wire', influenced Eliot's great poem of aridity, *The Waste Land*.[68]

It is often overlooked that the United States favoured the reduction of German reparation obligations while insisting that its former Allies repay all American loans. This would have saddled English taxpayers with most of the huge cost of the war. It is equally overlooked that Keynes advocated measures to promote French recovery as well as Austrian and German. In *Economic Consequences* he recommended that French war debts to the United Kingdom and the United States should be waived; that reparation claims by the London government should be deferred until those of the devastated areas of Belgium and France had been met; and that surplus coal production from England, Wales and Scotland should be allotted to the League of Nations for distribution to France and other European nations in need. These ideas were not conceived by someone who was antagonistic to the French. They were the work of a man who was not hobbled by narrow notions of national sovereignty, but saw Europe as a whole.

Keynes's book set the fashion for deploring the treaty of Versailles, as the Conservative politician Robert Boothby complained thirty years later.

What Lytton Strachey had already done for biography, he did for economics. They were dull no longer. On the contrary, they were deliciously exciting; and all mixed up with the most delectable debunking of world-famous political personalities. It was tremendous fun to find, in the middle of a table of reparations payments or coal deliveries, Mr Lloyd George described as a siren, and President Wilson as an old Presbyterian who could not be de-bamboozled. All the great men were pulled off their pedestals. Alas, nothing was put in their place. The passion in this book, its controversial sweep and imaginative power, the brilliance of the writing, combined to make it a bestseller which exercised a profound influence.

Boothby disliked the political results of *Economic Consequences*. 'It established, irrevocably, the legend of the *Diktat*, which, more than anything else, reduced the western democracies to paralysed political impotence, and enabled Hitler – only twenty years later – to trample the continent of Europe underfoot.'[69]

Robert Vansittart similarly complained that Keynes had treated Clemenceau's negotiating stance as akin to the German invasion of Belgium. Keynes's assertion that 'the perils of the future lie not in frontiers and sovereignties but in food, coal and transport' proved his distorted focus to a Foreign Office man. The real threat to European peace lurked in latent German militarism, Vansittart judged, 'not in the fact that France and Italy were broke, while Russia, Hungary, Austria and Poland were in worse case, nor in some undoubted rickets among German children who twenty years later were again sweeping lustily over Europe'. Germany was not economically crippled for long, Vansittart insisted. Ten years after the signature of the treaty of Versailles, German coal, iron and steel output beat all records, savings rose hugely, and national income was 60 per cent higher than before the war. There was a crisis of over-production in 1929; German exports exceeded British for the first time in 1930. It aggrieved Vansittart that 'Keynesian fallacies' fostered 'the myth that National Socialism was due to this much maligned treaty'. He noted that in 1924 French troops evacuated the Ruhr, as a rider of the Dawes Plan which provided Germany with a loan of $800 million to pay its greatly reduced obligations, and that nine months later Field Marshal von Hindenburg was elected President in an upsurge of nationalism. Similarly, in 1930, the Young Plan and loan eased German debts, and the last Allied troops left the Rhineland five years ahead of treaty-time: three months later the National Socialist Party won 107 seats in the Reichstag.[70]

Boothby, Vansittart, McCallum and like-minded critics seem to mean that Keynes created a guilt-complex among the victorious Allies which led to policies that fostered Nazism and incited Hitler's aggression. But Keynes's book had not yet been published when the US Congress first refused to ratify the treaty of Versailles and vetoed American participation in the League of Nations: it was America's entrenched isolationism, and Wilson's determination not to yield on amendments, that sundered hopes of the US participating fully in world affairs. Economic historians now tend to believe (on the basis of computations that the next generation will probably revise) that Germany could have afforded to pay the stipulated reparations, which were not as irrational as Keynes claimed. But less than half of the £6.6 billion demanded by the Allies under the Versailles treaty was reckoned by their experts to be recoverable. Consequently, throughout the 1920s, the Foreign Office's tactics – remotely influenced but by no means devised by Keynes – sought to pacify Europeans tensions by allowing reparations and then war debts to be winnowed, during thirteen years of wrangling, to about £1 billion. 'From the earliest years following the war,' explained a Foreign Office memorandum, 'it was our policy to eliminate those parts of the Peace Settlement which, as practical people, we knew to be untenable and indefensible.' The upshot of this policy was revisions, almost year by year, to the schedule of German repayments during the 1920s: ensuring, in the words of Lord Robert Cecil, the ex-Minister of Blockade who attended the early phase of the Paris conference, 'the maximum of financial disturbance with the minimum of result'. It was not Keynes's polemic that taught German voters that the Allies were yielding diplomatists. These reductions were not necessitated by Keynesian sophistry, but by the unenforceable provisions of which he had warned. The fact that there was no political will to collect punitive damages from Germany for the next thirty years was not of Keynes's making. If the adjustments of the financial clauses encouraged some Germans to expect comparable adjustments in the territorial clauses, as demanded by Hitler in the 1930s, this was the product of a faulty treaty, not of the book that pinpointed the faults. Revulsion at the futile slaughter of 1914–18 led all British political parties to endorse disarmament in the 1920s: any other course was unthinkable; but it was the unpreparedness in land, sea and air weaponry that made appeasement unavoidable after Hitler began a policy of European aggression.[71]

Nevertheless, the sense that Keynes had seized an unfair chance was prevalent. H. G. Wells described him to Siegfried Sassoon as 'a man who believes himself to have been brilliant, but was really only opportune'. His nomination for a fellowship of the Economic Section of the British Academy was rejected in 1920 by a cabal of literary critics and archaeologists led by the historian of English and French literature George Saintsbury. 'My earnest hope [is] that this ill-omened candidate will be either withdrawn or decisively rejected,' declared Saintsbury, who felt that Keynes's election would be construed as an affront to France, an encouragement to Germany and 'a definite expression of political partisanship' against the Lloyd George coalition. Keynes was indignant that the honour of election was thus 'tainted' by the demands of 'political, social and conventional orthodoxy', and warned that the British Academy risked becoming 'an undesirable, as well as an insincere, institution'. For some years he refused to allow his name to be renominated, but relented in 1929. He also seems to have been blackballed from the Royal Society for criticizing a government that he had recently served. The Cambridge physicist Sir J. J. Thomson, who was President of the Royal Society during 1916–20, was once asked if the good of *Economic Consequences* did not outweigh its irregularity. 'Not at all,' Thomson replied. 'What he said in that book was only what every sensible person knew already. He merely got easy publicity by mentioning things that he could have known only by being in the public service, such as Clemenceau's wearing mittens.'[72]

It was part of the genius of Keynes that, in writing of statecraft, he made the world remember mittens.

CHAPTER FOUR
PUBLIC MAN

'No-one ever became an economist through an uncontrollable impulse,' Robert Boothby declared at the London School of Economics in 1933. 'No-one, looking at an economist, ever said: "There but for the grace of God stand I."' Keynes began studying economics as a diversion from philosophy, with its thorny investigations of ethics, aesthetics and logic, but had only eight weeks' training in the subject. He was taught by his father's early mentor, Alfred Marshall, whom he had known from boyhood, and to whose wife Mary he felt lifelong devotion. Marshall urged that if booms and slumps were to be understood, monetary economics must be treated as a distinct speciality, and convinced him to specialize in money and banking. 'I find Economics increasingly satisfactory, and I think I am rather good at it,' Keynes told Lytton Strachey in 1905. 'I want to manage a railway or organise a Trust or at least swindle the investing public. It is so easy and fascinating to master the principles of these things.' He never sat an examination in economics: his knowledge came from pondering problems and discussing them as much as from book-learning. During his years at the India Office, his *Treatise on Probability* rather than economics provided his intellectual avocation. It was to escape from the Whitehall rut, and to recover the liveliness of the King's clerisy, that he became a lecturer in economics at Cambridge in 1910. The subject was subordinate to the location. The lectures themselves (covering credit, prices, the theory of money, the Stock Exchange, money markets, foreign exchanges and Indian finance) were popular because of their reliance on recent newspaper reports and their downplaying of abstractions.[1]

The technical intricacies and formidable explications in Keynes's major economic works – his *Tract on Monetary Reform* (1923), his *Treatise on Money* (1930) and his *General Theory of Employment, Interest and Money* (1936) – affright and beat the endurance of experts as well as of ordinary readers. Even Sir John Clapham, who held the chair of economic history at Cambridge from 1928, who was elected Vice-Provost of King's in 1933, who edited the *Cambridge Economic History of Europe* and who was President of the British Academy, never read *General Theory* because he concluded from talks with Keynes that he would never understand it. Keynes likened the attempt to explain monetary policy to intelligent non-specialists to that of describing the beauty of a painting to the colour-blind or of a sonata to the tone-deaf. This book is not an intellectual history of Keynes as an economist, and does not duplicate the compendious accounts of the development of his theories given by Peter Clarke, Donald Moggridge, Robert Skidelsky and other scholars. Instead, this chapter delineates Keynes's frame of mind as an economist: his disposition, his reactions to events, his partisan loyalties, his second thoughts and the inducements that he offered as he tried to educate opinion and alter policy. He trained as an economist under Alfred Marshall, broke free from classical economics after Marshall's death in 1924, proposed policies of 'Demand Management' whereby governments would substitute pragmatic short-term adjustments and policy wobbles for the rigid austerities of the classical cycle, and created a mentality which believed that states should intervene to reduce the instabilities, inefficiencies and waste of capitalism without stifling individual desires, interests, efforts and rewards. Keynes is often presented as having wrought a revolution in economic ideas or even as a revolutionary. It is true that he challenged taboos and prohibitions, and made people rethink what was permissible, but he was the antithesis of an insurgent, and his intentions were the reverse of seditious. He did not become an economist by uncontrollable impulse, in Boothby's phrase, but in response to the opportunities offered to him. Economics was paramount in making his reputation, but it was integrated in all his seven lives.

This chapter, too, explores Keynes's activities as a great persuader. He taught economics to undergraduates at Cambridge, and ran seminars with research fellows and more senior economists there. He edited the leading English journal in his discipline. He compiled European economic supplements for the *Manchester Guardian*. He was chairman of companies that published the foremost Liberal weekly magazine of the 1920s and the most influential progressive magazine of the 1930s. He was a profuse contributor to periodicals for most of the inter-war period. His Cambridge grounding made him impatient of the false fronts shown by many party politicians: 'As for Milner and Lyttelton,' he said in 1906 of two political hard-men, one Liberal and the other Conservative, 'they are merely effete, & I can hardly believe that any human being can be taken in by them.' Yet, despite his boredom with the ding-dong tussling of partisanship, Keynes was strenuous in both platform speeches and backroom work for the Liberal party until 1929. Prime Ministers and Chancellors of the Exchequer solicited his opinions, and took his advice – even when he was thought unsound in many quarters. He testified to government committees and Royal Commissions. He served on them, too. The fecundity of his second thoughts was such that an admirer joked in 1931, 'where six economists are joined together there are seven opinions, two of them Keynes's'. He was an inveterate diner-out, who developed extensive contacts at high altitudes of finance and government. In sum, he was a public man, who achieved influence and renown by his originality, by his eloquence and also by his social vitality.[2]

Virginia Woolf noted a talk with Keynes in 1919 after his resignation from the Treasury, but before his return to university life. He was disillusioned, and no longer trusted in the survival of his echelons. 'Eton is doomed; the governing classes, perhaps Cambridge too,' in Woolf's précis of his remarks. 'These conclusions were forced on him by the dismal degrading spectacle of the Peace Congress, where men played shamelessly, not for Europe, or even England, but for their own return to Parliament at the next election. They were not wholly vicious; they had spasms of well meaning; but a fate seemed to possess the business from the first, driving it all in the most fatal direction & soon no one had the strength to resist.' After his crisis in Paris, Keynes's economic thinking had these ends: to shore up the governing order, to preserve King's, Eton and all they represented, to repair the misfiring industrial economies, and thus to limit social instability. 'He detested the inefficiency of unregulated capitalism only less than he dreaded the waste and suffering of a proletarian revolution,' wrote Kingsley Martin, who edited the *New Statesman* when Keynes was chairman of its publishing company: 'he therefore made it his life's work to save capitalism by altering its nature.' King's and Eton were paramount in the explanatory narrative that he devised for his life. The images with which he imagined his past, ordered his present and planned his future came from them.[3]

It was impossible for Keynes, though he desired social justice, to be a socialist. 'The *class* war will find me on the side of the educated *bourgeoisie*,' he told the Liberal Summer School at Cambridge in 1925. In the Labour party, 'too much will always be decided by those who do not know *at all* what they are talking about' – and who were complacent about their ignorance. 'The Labour Party will always be flanked by the Party of Catastrophe – Jacobins, Communists, Bolshevists ... This is the party which hates or despises existing institutions and believes that great good will result merely from overthrowing them – or at least to overthrow them is the necessary preliminary to any great good.' *Three Guineas* (1938) was the book of Virginia Woolf's that Keynes liked least. He dismissed as silly its thesis that war could be averted by empowering women; and he was angered by its illustrations intended to depict the absurd pomposity of men. Apart from a jolly, bemedalled general in a plumed bearskin hat, Woolf chose photographs showing ceremonial processions: heralds in their tabards, Stanley Baldwin sumptuously garbed as Chancellor of Cambridge University, gaunt Archbishop Cosmo Lang in episcopal robes, chubby Lord Chief Justice Hewart processing out of a judges' service. Keynes had shed the Edwardian radicalism and Apostolic fervour that thirty years earlier had made him wish for the abolition of the House of Lords. In middle age he resented Woolf's derision of institutions that, regardless of individuals, merited respect because they represented centuries of English history and the acme of a certain culture.[4]

Keynes, who disliked egalitarian notions as much as he did envy, had no ethical dispute with capitalism. His objection was to capitalists who were too muddle-headed to distinguish new measures for safeguarding capitalism from Bolshevism. His criticisms of obsolete or wishful thinking made him unpopular. 'I am now told by a good many friends that I have become a sort of disreputable figure in some quarters because I do not agree with the maxims of City pundits,' he told a banker friend in 1924. 'I ought not to be so considered really! I seek to improve the machinery of Society, not to overturn it.' Truisms bored him, and conceptual imprecision annoyed him. Experiment and reason, tempered by intuition, were to him preferable to stolid plodding in the well-trodden paths of experience. 'The City editors, all bloody and blindfolded, still piteously bow down' before the false gods of the free market, he complained a year later. He never doubted that good ideas would ultimately prove stronger than vested interests; believed, too, that good ideas never start stampedes, and that the pace of a society's economic transformation should not be forced. Gaspard Farrer, a banking partner in Baring Brothers, felt 'dazzled by the brilliance and lucidity' of Keynes's writing, he said in 1925. 'The more I see of him, the more I am impressed by his ability and intellect, but as to his wisdom and judgment, well, that is another matter.' It did no good to hurry such men.[5]

Keynes had the greatness to say that economics is a matter of time and temper. A generation is usually reckoned as spanning a quarter of a century, but he saw that half that time turned a schoolchild into an adult with attitudes, choices and responses that could not be foretold. It took only a dozen years for new states of mind to arouse new quandaries, expectations and pressures of which political leaders must take account. He was an economist who thought more of generations than of immutable rules. 'What very odd, and sometimes terrible, things are strict principles!' he exclaimed. 'Why can an age only be great if it believes, or at least is bred up in believing, what is preposterous?' Keynes used the past to think ahead. His sense of history, of the crippling inhibitions laid by the previous generation's strict principles on free thinking about current needs and future prospects, is basic to his schemes of economic management. He was the first economist to stress how fast change came in the twentieth century. Hence the adaptive improvisation of his schemes, and the flexibility with which he used his historical sense to settle current and future tactics.[6]

Like many people Keynes cherished an imaginary past that was central to his ideas, reactions and behaviour. Recalling the pleasures of the past renewed them. 'The high comedy, the charm and security of the Edwardian age', as he remembered them, Eton and Cambridge before the deluge, framed his thoughts. He was the most nostalgic of modernizers. 'The Edwardian age is near enough for us quickly ... to be reminded of what it was like,' he said in 1936. 'We need only ... a few old photographs to bring back the taste of the biscuits we ate, and the inner feeling in the whole body of what it was like to be alive in the reign of King Edward and Queen Alexandra.'[7]

Generations diverged in their self-appraisals and reputations, in their exercise of power and in their expectations of prosperity, Keynes wrote in 1934. Victorian financiers and industrialists 'were tremendous boys at the height of their glory; and in due course they became tremendous old boys, with vision dimmed but tenacity and will-power untamed'. Successor generations seemed stunted saplings when compared with the old oaks. 'The capitalist has lost the source of his inner strength – his self-assurance, his self-confidence, his untameable will, his belief in his own beauty and unquestionable value to society.' Since the death of King Edward they had all gone to oblivion: 'the private bankers, the ship-owning families, the merchant princes, the world-embracing contractors, the self-made barons of Birmingham, Manchester, Liverpool, and Glasgow – where are they now?' They had vanished, and instead 'their office-boys (on salaries) rule in their mausoleums'. The rift between management and ownership made a great difference, Keynes understood. By the 1920s industrial combines were owned by numerous small shareholders, with holdings on average of £300 or £400, but run by salaried managers who risked little of their own money in their enterprises. 'These small investors who own these businesses have no power whatever of controlling them and no knowledge whatever of their real position. How remote that is from the old ... owners staking their fortunes on their judgements, and the most judicious surviving.'[8]

'The spirit of the age is not optimistic as it used to be,' Keynes said in a speech to the London Liberal Candidates Association in 1927. Disappointment was the Zeitgeist. 'We used to think that private ambition and compound interest would between them carry us to paradise. Our material conditions seemed to be steadily on the up-grade.' The Victorians and Edwardian gave thanks for a system promising a continuing crescendo of successes. But as the post-war system faltered and lurched, the neo-Georgians lost, said Keynes, 'sufficient confidence in the future to be satisfied with the present'.[9]

The state was mired in borrowings. The national debt rose from £650 million in 1914 to £7,832 in the financial year 1919–20. It cost £277 million to service the national debt in 1930 compared with £16 million in 1911. In 1914 Britain had been the world's largest trading economy, the world's third largest manufacturing economy, and the largest supplier of world investment and credit. After 1918, British trade did not regain its pre-war levels; British investors preferred opportunities within the British Empire, and skirted those elsewhere; increasingly money from Wall Street spurred the world's economic growth; domestic consumption mattered more to British economic growth, and exports counted for less. American, German and Japanese competition trounced some British producers. There was recession in 1920–1, stagnation in 1922–6 and boom in 1927–9. Cotton-mills, shipyards, iron foundries, steel-works and coal-mines went into decline, which sent unemployment soaring in northern regions. Products such as motor-cars and radiograms satisfied new consumer demands. Woollen and cotton clothes lost sales to those made from viscose or acetate.

With the onset of the Slump, trade in the United Kingdom was halved between 1929 and 1932, while output by heavy manufacturing fell by one-third. Registered unemployment peaked at 3.2

million in 1932, with millions more working short-time. The Slump drove the emergency coalition government to adopt in 1932 the Imperial Preference scheme, which guaranteed British markets to Empire producers of food and raw materials, and guaranteed export markets to Britain. Britain suffered less than other industrial economies at this time: the rise in living standards continued for those with jobs. After 1932, the economy revived slowly. House-building and rearmament generated prosperity, reduced regional unemployment, and raided the national debt. All this wastage, distress and instability provided the context for Keynes's activities as public man and innovating economist.

Group discussions were Keynes's preferred means of thinking and teaching: tutorial sessions with individual pupils dissipated his time. In 1909 he started a Cambridge economics discussion group called the Political Economy Club. It reflected the design of the Apostles and other college discussion societies: even the impecunious new college Selwyn had its Logarithms Society. Membership was by Keynes's invitation, and was limited to male economics undergraduates. The club met on Monday evenings in term-time in his rooms in King's. A paper was read; all those present would comment in an order determined by drawing lots; a masterly summary by Keynes would close the discussion. Some of the undergraduates who joined the Political Economy Club became future collaborators: Hubert Henderson (appointed a lecturer in economics at Cambridge in 1919), Dennis Robertson (elected to a fellowship at Trinity in 1914), Dominick Spring Rice (pre-war assistant City editor of the *Morning Post*, and a writer on finance and unemployment insurance), and Dudley Ward (pre-war assistant editor of the *Economist*, who went to the Treasury as a temporary official in 1914 and accompanied Keynes to Paris in 1919). Later recruits included the philosophers Richard Braithwaite and Frank Ramsey (who were both elected with Keynes's support as Fellows of King's in 1924), and the economist Austin Robinson. The Keynes Club, as it was called from the 1920s, continued until its founder's illness in 1937 kept him from King's for eighteen months.

The manuscripts submitted for publication in the *Economic Journal*, of which Keynes was a sedulous editor from 1911, set him thinking in diverse directions. His prompt responses to potential contributors, with his considered endorsements and criticisms, honed his mind. Editorial work on other people's sometimes diffuse efforts emphasized the importance of stripping arguments of non-essentials and irrelevancies, and leaving no loopholes for doubt. He learnt from his reactions as he worked: he sharpened his powers of persuasion, too, as he talked with other men of acumen.

Perhaps at the prompting of Edwin Montagu, Keynes joined the Eighty Club. This was an organization for Liberal supporters which, unlike the National Liberal Club, had associate women members and cultivated links with universities. Together with the Apostle and King's economist Gerald Shove, he enlisted in a fact-finding and speechifying tour made in Ireland by the Eighty Club in 1911, but defected from the group and explored Ireland alone for some days. 'A point came when I could support crowd life no longer and when I felt as if I should go mad if I heard another speech,' he explained to Duncan Grant. 'You haven't, I suppose, ever mixed with politicians at close quarters. They're *awful* ... dregs.' Among the Eighty, in Ireland, he discovered, 'what previously I didn't believe possible, that politicians behave in private life and say exactly the same things as they do in public. Their stupidity is inhuman.' Just as five years earlier Keynes had deplored the false fronts of Milner and Lyttelton, so again he found the emotional inauthenticity of political operators intolerable, because it suppressed all that made humanity original or interesting. A journalist from the *Morning Post* and 'a charming old peer called Lord Saye and Sele' were the most frank and unaffected of his fellow travellers. 'There were one or two others, whose characters were not particularly sympathetic to me, but were really all right. The rest of them had minds and opinions as deplorable as their characters.' Keynes excepted from his condemnation 'a young Jewish barrister, who seemed such a cad that I spent most of my time cutting him, [yet who] confided ... on the last evening that he thought buggery and bestiality ought to be permitted, due regard being had to the prevention of cruelty to children and animals'. Keynes also found an affinity with Mrs Max Muspratt, wife of Liverpool's leading alkali manufacturer, 'a middle aged lady with the character of a barmaid, whom I found very sympathetic and who thoroughly agreed with me over the rest of the company'.[10]

In 1912 Keynes was elected to the Political Economy Club, a London discussion-group cum dining-club for economists with a fine lineage dating back to 1821 (not to be confused with the Cambridge discussion group of the same name informally known as the Keynes Club). It was uncontaminated by partisanship or bores talking in public voices. For some years he journeyed to London for its Wednesday-evening dinners, and handled *Economic Journal* matters on Thursdays. Keynes learnt most when he was striving to prevail in argument by cool, relentless reason.

Most important of all to Keynes was the Tuesday Club, which he helped the stockbroker Oswald ('Foxy') Falk to start in 1917. The Tuesday was a dining-club of officials, City men and financial journalists which met to discuss monetary economics and business in a private room at the Café Royal once a month. Keynes became the most eloquent of the Tuesday Club men. He exerted his arts on fellow diners including Reginald McKenna of the Midland Bank, Sir Charles Addis of the Hongkong & Shanghai Bank, 'Bob' Brand of Lazards and the financier Sir Henry Strakosch. The Treasury knights included Sir George Barstow, Sir Basil Blackett, Sir Otto Niemeyer, Sir Richard Hopkins and Sir Frederick Leith-Ross. The

Inland Revenue was represented by its chairman, Sir John Anderson, later a Cabinet minister, and by the statistician Josiah Stamp, who collected industrial and railway directorships after 1919 and joined the Court of the Bank of England in 1928. Other Tuesday attenders included the Keynes Club regulars Dennis Robertson and Dudley Ward. The Tuesday Club's purpose was 'to educate the Civil Servants about the needs of practical finance and to give the City men some off-the-record tips about Government policy', said Leith-Ross, who found dinner discussions too taxing after a long day at the Treasury and ceased attendance.[11]

A second dining-club provided crucial linkages for his inter-war life as a Public Man. In 1927 Keynes was elected to the Other Club, which since 1911 had dined at the Savoy Hotel on alternate Thursdays when parliament was in session. Winston Churchill was the *genius loci* who dominated the Other. Smuts, the South African statesman whom Keynes had trusted during the Paris peace conference, was a member. So too were two devout Apostles, Eddie Marsh and Desmond MacCarthy; Robert Vansittart of the Foreign Office; Liberal politicians, including Lloyd George and Lord Reading; Churchill protégés, including Robert Boothby and Frederick Lindemann; Conservative frontbenchers, including Sir Arthur Steel-Maitland; the painters Sir John Lavery, Sir Alfred Munnings and Sir William Orpen; the architect Sir Edwin Lutyens; authors as varied as Arnold Bennett, P. G. Wodehouse and H. G. Wells; Rothschilds, newspaper tycoons and trade union leaders. Sir Oswald Mosley, the photogenic Labour minister charged with reducing unemployment, was proposed for membership by Churchill in 1930 (two years before his egotistical rowdiness veered into fascism). 'Very agreeable and rather brilliant', was Arnold Bennett's view of Keynes as a dinner companion at the Other Club, although the economist's murmured propaganda there failed to convert the novelist to tariff protection as a means of improving employment levels. It is notable that Steel-Maitland was the fore-most advocate in Baldwin's Cabinet in 1928–9 of road-building and public-works programmes to revive business confidence, to create jobs and thus to resist socialism: perhaps Keynes murmured to him at the Other Club more effectively.[12]

In the biographical essay that he wrote after Marshall's death, Keynes presented economics as 'a very easy subject compared with the higher branches of philosophy and pure science'. Why then, he asked, if it did not require specialist abilities of an exacting kind, did so few economists excel? The explanation, he suggested, was that:

the master-economist must possess a rare *combination* of gifts. He must reach a high standard in several different directions and must combine talents not often found together. He must be mathematician, historian, statesman, philosopher – in some degree. He must understand symbols and speak in words. He must contemplate the particular in terms of the general, and touch abstract and concrete in the same flight of thought. He must study the present in the light of the past for the purposes of the future. No part of man's nature or his institutions must lie entirely outside his regard. He must be purposeful and disinterested in a simultaneous mood; as aloof and incorruptible as an artist, yet sometimes as near the earth as a politician.

These were Keynes's own aspirations. There were introspective analogies, too, when later he wrote of Isaac Newton.[13]

In 1936 the family of Lord Portsmouth, descended from Isaac Newton's niece and coping with the heir's expensive divorce and remarriage, sent for auction the contents of Newton's wooden chest, which had been packed when he left Cambridge in 1696. Keynes attended the sale at Sotheby's, bought about forty lots, and added to his cache by purchases from other successful bidders. He also bought Newton's death-mask. During months of convalescence in 1937–8, he studied Newton's manuscripts. He found that while Newton was writing the *Principia* and laying the foundations of modern science, he was giving equal time and mental powers to medieval hocus-pocus, astrology, alchemy, chronological prophecy based on the measurements of Babylonian buildings, transmutation, the philosopher's stone and the elixir of life. His delving into Newton's papers led him to deliver a thrilling talk to the Royal Society in 1942 from which one extract can be quoted: 'He was the last of the magicians, the last of the Babylonians and Sumerians, the last great mind which looked out on the visible and intellectual world with the same eyes as those who began to build our intellectual inheritance rather less than 10,000 years ago. Isaac Newton, a posthumous child born with no father on Christmas Day, 1642, was the last wonder-child to whom the Magi could do sincere and appropriate homage.' This pioneer of the Enlightenment was sunk in occult and esoteric ideas, said Keynes, and thus simultaneously the first of the scientists and the last of the magicians.[14]

There is an element of self-description in this summary. Keynes, who became the first proponent of the managed economy and is sometimes hailed as a revolutionary influence, adhered to Marshall's classical economics until middle age. As a young lecturer, he upheld the quantity theory of money. This stated that the price level was determined by the quantity of money: that is, the greater the supply of money, the lower its value; as the quantity of money circulating in the economy rose, so would prices. A currency would thus be devalued if its supply was increased. This view precluded the possibility that increases or decreases in the quantity of money could stimulate or depress the demand for goods and services, and thus raise or lower production and employment. Keynes's *Tract on Monetary Reform*, published in

1923, was described by his coadjutor Richard Kahn as 'curiously conventional for a genius aged 40'. In it he shifted from classical orthodoxy by denying the short-term efficacy of the quantity theory of money, while accepting its truth '*in the long run* in which we are all dead. Economists set themselves too easy, too useless a task if in tempestuous seasons they can only tell us that when the storm is long past the ocean is flat again.'[15]

Marshall's death in 1924 loosened Keynes's loyalties to the old seer: he began to prepare for a Newtonian shift from his intellectual inheritance. 'Half the copybook wisdom of our statesmen is based on assumptions which were at one time true, or partly true, but are now less and less true by the day,' he told fellow Liberals in 1925. 'We have to invent new wisdom for a new age. And in the meantime we must, if we are to do any good, appear unorthodox, troublesome, dangerous, disobedient to them that begat us.' Although economic undergraduates knew that Thomas Carlyle called their subject 'the dismal science', few had the extra information that the Enlightenment economist Anne-Robert Turgot called political economy *la science du bonheur public*. The science of public happiness was how Keynes saw his work as an economist – which he undertook with the assumptions of an Apostle.[16]

Keynes indicted the utilitarian philosopher Jeremy Bentham as 'the origin of evil' for measuring human happiness by materialist criteria. He praised his Cambridge contemporaries who followed George Moore as 'amongst the first of our generation, perhaps alone amongst our generation, to escape from the Benthamite tradition'. He regarded that tradition 'as the worm which has been gnawing at the insides of modern civilisation and is responsible for its present moral decay. We used to regard the Christians as the enemy, because they appeared as the representatives of tradition, convention and hocus-pocus. In truth, it was the Benthamite calculus, based on an over-valuation of the economic criterion, which was destroying the quality of the popular Ideal.' The rejection of Bentham by his generation of Apostles protected them (as well as the Bloomsbury group) 'from the final *reductio ad absurdum* of Benthamism known as Marxism'.[17]

In pursuing the science of public happiness, Keynes scorned the nineteenth-century insistence on testing by its profitability the advisability of any course of action sponsored by private initiative or by collective action. 'The whole conduct of life was made into a sort of parody of an accountant's nightmare,' Keynes wrote in 1933. 'Instead of using their vastly increased material and technical resources to build a wonder-city, they built slums; and they thought it right and advisable to build slums because slums, on the test of private enterprise, "paid", whereas the wonder-city would, they thought, have been an act of foolish extravagance, which would, in the imbecile idiom of the financial fashion, have "mortgaged the future"; though how the construction to-day of great and glorious works can impoverish the future, no man can see until his mind is beset by false analogies from an irrelevant accountancy.' From about 1924 he urged, at first in vain, but with increasing success, that the nation would be enriched if unemployed men and machines were used in house-building and public-works programmes. He combated those 'bogus calculations' which led to the sanctimonious prudence of people who prefer hovels to palaces.[18]

Once, at the Apostles, when there was a joking discussion about the phrase 'have your cake and eat it', McTaggart said gravely, 'With a *proper* cake the more you eat the bigger it gets.' His pleasantry was adapted by Keynes to depict Victorian middle-class rentiers. In all their gradations 'the new rich of the nineteenth century', whether merchants, shopkeepers, factory-owners, office-workers, preferred the power which investment gave them to the pleasures of large expenditure. In his family, both his grandfather the nurseryman, and his father the university administrator, opted beyond a certain stage to save rather than spend. 'The Capitalist System', Keynes explained,

> depended for its growth on a double bluff or deception. On the one hand the labouring classes accepted from ignorance or power-lessness, or were compelled, persuaded or cajoled by custom, con-vention, authority and the well-established order of Society into accepting, a situation in which they could call their own very little of the cake, that they and Nature and the capitalists were co-oper-ating to produce. And on the other hand the capitalist classes were allowed to call the best part of the cake theirs and were theoretic-ally free to consume it, on the tacit underlying condition that they consumed very little of it in practice. The duty of 'saving' became nine-tenths of virtue and the growth of the cake the object of true religion.[19]

Keynes's observation about portions of cake dated from 1919. After the onset of the Slump ten years later, he became the most audible voice attributing national woes to the fact that people were withholding from consumption – not spending their money – a larger part of income than was being invested in constructive enterprises. This idea derived from the social theorist J. A. Hobson's collaboration in writing *The Physiology of Industry* (1889) with the Dover tanner Albert Mummery. Hobson and Mummery rejected the classical doctrine, known as Say's law, that money that is not spent on consumer goods is invested, for it would be irrational to hoard money – that is, to hold idle balances from which no income accrued. The flow of savings and the flow of investment – the supply of and the demand for loanable funds – are brought into balance by changes in interest rates. Mummery and Hobson however indicted the rich for 'over-saving', which produced 'under-consumption' of capital goods, production gluts, trade depression, and unemployment. The solution of these recurrent crises of capitalism lay either in encouraging the prosperous to consume more or in developing new forms of national expenditure.

Similar thinking had been instilled by the merchant and industrialist Lord Cable, with whom Keynes spent a week in Devon in 1913 talking economics. Cable was preoccupied by the gulf between savings and investment in India. In the Edwardian period he estimated that £11 million was hoarded yearly, which represented 'an enormous amount of wealth lying fallow'. There was a pressing need, said Cable, to induce 'the shy Indian capitalist to bring out his rupees', instead of secreting his gold and silver: 'our railways are being starved for want of capital, and industrial enterprise is being hampered'.[20]

In 1923–4 Keynes led a syndicate that bought control of the Liberal weekly magazine *Nation*. He became chairman of the publishing company, and installed as editor his former pupil Hubert Henderson, who had just published a monograph entitled *Supply and Demand* which challenged the influence of price on the total supply of factors of production. Virginia Woolf, meeting Henderson in 1923, found him 'a small, testy, unheroic man, vaguely on the look-out for offence, & suspecting I think our superior vitality, & longing for a compliment, which being honest for the moment, I could not give him. He ought to have stuck to Cambridge.' Perhaps it is not surprising that Henderson detested the Bloomsbury group. At Virginia Woolf's prompting, Keynes offered the literary editorship of the *Nation* to T. S. Eliot, fresh from writing *The Waste Land* and in the thrall of marital distress: Eliot havered before declining the offer in a neurotic letter. Instead, Leonard Woolf served as literary editor from 1923 until 1930.[21]

'Hubert is nervous of anything that might disturb him at all out of his fixed comfortable habits,' Keynes believed; but Henderson made bold editorial forays. Under Keynes's supervision and his editorship, the *Nation* supported the repeal of the McKenna duties on imported motor-cars in 1924, opposed the return to the gold standard in 1925, highlighted in 1926 the prosperity of the expanding industries of south-east England and the depressed northern manufacturing sectors, receded from laissez-faire Liberalism after 1927, and (reflecting the evolution of Keynes's views) in 1930 editorialized against the free traders' wish to rescind the reimposed McKenna duties.[22]

In two contributions to the *Nation* published in 1924, Keynes first advanced his notion of a programme of public works to reduce unemployment (which then stood at 770,000 men: women were discounted) and to avert wage reductions. Both articles were responses to a previous piece by Lloyd George about poor productivity. 'There is no place or time here for *laissez-faire*,' Keynes told his Liberal readers. 'We have stuck in a rut. We need an impulse, a jolt, an acceleration.' The country needed to give primacy 'to the principle that *prosperity is cumulative*'. Chancellors of the Exchequer should devote their sinking-fund and surplus resources to replacing unproductive debt by productive debt rather than to redeeming old debt and thus driving national savings to find a foreign outlet. Keynes enjoined the Treasury to promote expenditure up to £100,000,000 a year by capital works that enlisted 'the aid of private genius, temperament and skill'. He instanced the scheme of Lord Montagu of Beaulieu to build a motorway from London to Liverpool, passing near Birmingham, with the promoters providing one-third of costs, and the Ministry of Transport and local authorities the rest.[23]

Keynes in 1924 called for state intervention and abandoned laissez-faire, 'not from contempt of that good old doctrine, but because, whether we like it or not, the conditions for its success have disappeared'. The pre-war free-market system had entrusted prosperity 'to private enterprise *unchecked* and *unaided*'; but circumstances were irretrievably changed by the manufacturing mobilization and state controls that had entangled businesses with government in 1914–18. Private enterprise remained under regulation in many ways. 'There is no going back on this,' said Keynes in 1924, 'and if private enterprise is not unchecked, we cannot leave it unaided.' He challenged Labour and Conservatives leaders as well as Liberals: 'A drastic reduction of wages in certain industries, and a successful stand-up fight with the more powerful trade unions, might reduce unemployment in the long-run. If any party stands for this solution, let them say so.'[24]

What was Keynes's position in the 1920s as a renegade Treasury official dispensing provocative advice? 'The present age has no great faith in anything; but it still tries hard to believe in experts,' wrote F. L. ('Peter') Lucas, a literary critic and Fellow of King's, who revived the dormant Apostles after 1918, dedicated his superb scholarly edition of the plays of John Webster to Keynes, and based one of the characters in his novel *The River Flows* (1926) on his cherished friend. 'Not even the War, nor histories of the War, can quite cure it of that. And certainly the world grows in complexity so fast that we lie increasingly at their mercy.' The traditional governing classes – both political and official – had been convinced by their wartime experiences of their need of outsider technicians to help in managing public life. Business leaders, engineers, accountants, lawyers, financial experts, civil contractors, shipowners, educationalists were recruited to ministries, to advisory boards, to official inquiries, to supervisory committees. It was less than forty years since the Crown had interdicted anyone serving on a company board of directors from receiving a peerage; but by 1920 many pages of *Burke's Peerage*, the *Directory of Directors* and the *Stock Exchange Gazette* overlapped.[25]

Despite official displeasure, and Lloyd George's wrath, at publication of *Economic Consequences*, Keynes was at Edwin Montagu's behest appointed in 1921 to serve on the Royal Commission on Indian Tariffs. In fact, he resigned from the Commission after only six months, almost certainly in order to avoid a long absence in India early in his exciting love affair with his future wife Lydia Lopokova, although officially he pleaded that he must concentrate on editing a series of *Manchester Guardian* supplements on European finance and reconstruction. Keynes devilled hard at producing these supplements, forsaking Cambridge except at weekends, and recruiting a formidable range of contributors. The Germans, for example, included his friend Melchior, Hjalmar Schacht (President of the Reichsbank), Wilhelm Cuno (Chancellor of Germany in 1922–3), Rudolf Hilferding (then Minister of Finance, destined to die under Gestapo torture) and Walter Rathenau, the electrical manufacturing millionaire and Foreign Minister, who was assassinated before he could deliver his copy. English contributors included friends and ex-pupils (Falk, Lowes Dickinson, Dennis Robertson, Russell-Cooke, Dudley Ward); Blackett of the Treasury; and public men such as Asquith, Robert Cecil, Ramsay MacDonald, Philip Snowden and Sidney Webb.

In 1923 Bonar Law, recently installed as Conservative Prime Minister, consulted Keynes (who had worked for him in the wartime Treasury) about the Anglo-American debt settlement negotiated in Washington by his Chancellor of the Exchequer, Baldwin. 'I hope', replied Keynes, 'we refuse the American offer, in order to give them time to discover that they are at our mercy, as we are at France's, France at Germany's. It is the debtor who has the last word in these cases.' On 30 January, under Keynes's influence, Law told his Cabinet, which supported Baldwin's settlement almost uniformly, or thought it was too late to repudiate it, that he would rather resign as Prime Minister than agree. There was a day's

Cabinet crisis before Law conceded to imploring colleagues that he would withdraw his resignation; but he was so convinced by Keynes of the misjudgement of the American debt agreement that he pacified his conscience by writing an anonymous attack on his own government's policies for publication in *The Times*. Law's receptivity to outside thinking stood in contrast to his successor as Prime Minister, Baldwin, who, although responsive to the electorate's moods, was immune to ideas and averse to complexity. Lloyd George said: 'When a thing gets difficult, Baldwin's attention flags in three minutes.'[26]

Ingrained anti-intellectualism was an obstacle to Keynes. 'You seem to sneer at the Economist for trying to consider these questions strictly on their merits and with the scientific object of discovering which solution will most promote the prosperity of the world,' he protested to his fellow Tuesday Clubber Sir Charles Addis, who had disparaged professional economists in his presidential address to the Institute of Bankers in 1921. 'You prefer instead "the opposing interests, changing purposes, unruly affections and defective wills of ordinary men". That is to say, you set up as criterion, not the general advantage, but the conglomeration of self-interest, ignorance, passion and general stupidity, which will in fact prevent a scientific solution from being adopted. And not only so, but you suggest that you are being much more high-minded in doing so.'[27]

Legislation of 1919 kept the gold standard in suspension until 1 January 1926. Addis's recommendation in 1924 that Britain should commit forthwith to restore the gold standard by January 1926 drew another friendly rebuke. 'The proposals you outline do terrify me very considerably,' Keynes told him. Their subordination of the interests of industry to those of international finance was politically and socially fraught. Everything seemed set for better times if Britain kept off the gold standard. To risk misfortunes 'merely for the sake of linking up the London and New York money markets, and so facilitating the work of international financiers – for this in my judgment is all it comes to – is going to lay the City and the Bank of England open to popular attacks the violence of which might be very great'. He accepted that London's profits from international finance were valuable, but was 'not at all sure that we do not make more money out of the Americans and others in fluctuating conditions than in stable conditions, since they are generally wrong and we are generally right as to the prospective course of events'. It alarmed Keynes to see men 'in authority attacking the problems of the changed post-war world with ... unmodified pre-war views', he told Addis. 'To close the mind to the idea of revolutionary improvements in our control of money and credit is to sow the seeds of the downfall of individualistic capitalism.' He expected that 'enormous changes will come in the next twenty years, and they will be bad changes, unwisely and even disastrously carried out, if those of us who are aiming at the stability of society cannot agree in putting forward safe and sound reforms'.[28]

In April 1925 Keynes, McKenna and three Treasury officials of unrepentant pre-war outlook, Bradbury, Niemeyer and P. J. Grigg, were invited to a 'Brains Trust' dinner by Churchill, the Chancellor of the Exchequer, to discuss the restoration of the gold standard. Keynes and McKenna counselled that sterling would be overvalued by 10 per cent if the pre-war parity was restored. They reiterated that the restoration of the gold standard would subordinate the interests of export industries to those of bankers concerned to preserve London's position as a centre of international banking and exchange. They predicted rises in the prices at which British exports sold abroad, followed by increased unemployment and conflict with trade unions when employers cut wages in order to bolster profits. Bradbury's counter-arguments stressed that the gold standard was 'knave-proof', Grigg recalled. 'It could not be rigged for political or even more unworthy reasons. It would prevent our living in a fool's paradise of false prosperity, and would ensure our keeping on a competitive basis in our export business.' The symposium lasted until after midnight. Later that month Churchill made a sacrifice in homage to the Bradbury generation's shibboleths by announcing the gold standard's restoration for international dealings, although no gold currency was put into domestic circulation.[29]

As Keynes insisted in articles that *The Times* rejected but Lord Beaverbrook's *Evening Standard* published, the restored gold standard meant that bank rate would rise, industrial investment would become costlier, the country would grow less competitive in world markets (especially against the United States) and unemployment would therefore increase. In order to prevent workers in export industries (and in the docks) from bearing the brunt of this, Keynes suggested a 5 per cent levy on all wages together with a shilling increase in income tax. These articles were republished by Leonard and Virginia Woolf at their Hogarth Press as *The Economic Consequences of Mr Churchill*. When in a BBC radio dialogue Keynes again denounced the terms of Britain's return to the gold standard, Josiah Stamp (the Tuesday Clubber with whom he was broadcasting) retorted: 'Hush, Maynard; I cannot bear it. Remember I am a Director of the Bank of England.' There were many other men in authority who wanted to cry 'Hush, Maynard' when he voiced discomfiting truths.[30]

'At present,' Keynes said in 1926, 'everything is politics, and nothing policies.' What political affinities influenced his developing ideas in pursuit of the science of public happiness? He abominated the communist temper. He first visited Russia in 1925 (accompanied by his St Petersburg-born wife) as the University of Cambridge representative at the bicentenary celebrations of the Academy of Sciences in Leningrad. This was at the height of the

Politburo power struggle that followed Lenin's death. 'Red Russia holds too much which is detestable,' he reported. 'I am not ready for a creed which does not care how much it destroys the liberty and security of daily life, which uses deliberately the weapons of persecution, destruction and international strife. How can I admire a policy which finds a characteristic expression in spending millions to suborn spies in every family and group at home, and to stir up trouble abroad?' He was dismayed by the sovereign power of an ideology that seemed to him merely stupid. 'How can I accept a doctrine which sets up as its bible, above and beyond criticism, an obsolete economic textbook which I know to be not only scientifically erroneous but without interest or application in the modern world?' He loathed Soviet Russia's destruction of individual initiative, educational excellence and personal distinction. 'How can I adopt a creed which, preferring the mud to the fish, exalts the boorish proletariat above the bourgeois and the intelligentsia who, with whatever faults, are the quality in life and surely carry the seeds of all human advancement? Even if we need a religion, how can we find it in the turbid rubbish of the Red bookshops?' Everything in Soviet orthodoxy was a violent affront to the ideals that inspired Keynes.[31]

In 1928 the two Keyneses revisited Russia. 'We enjoyed the ballet and the opera ... but came back very depressed about the Bolshies,' Keynes reported to Ottoline Morrell. 'It is impossible to remember, until one gets in the country, how mad they are.' The vandalism of the communist economic system, in which doctrinal purity mattered more than making things work, left him aghast. 'Offered to us as a means of improving the economic situation, it is an insult to our intelligence,' he wrote in 1934. 'But offered as a means of making the economic situation *worse*, that is its subtle, its almost irresistible, attraction.' He saw communism not as a reaction against the nineteenth-century failure to organize optimal economic output, but as a reaction against agreeable prosperity. 'It is a protest against the emptiness of economic welfare, an appeal to the ascetic in us all ... When Cambridge undergraduates take their inevitable trip to Bolshiedom, are they disillusioned when they find it all dreadfully uncomfortable? Of course not. That is what they are looking for.' The free-thinking, free-speaking meetings of the Apostles had begun to be marred by young Communist party members parroting party doctrines.* Until then practical politics had been beneath discussion on the hearth-rug. The young communists' despoliation of a sacred Cambridge totem made Keynes condemn *Das Kapital* as he did the Koran. 'I know that many people, not all of whom are idiots, find it a sort of Rock of Ages,' he said to Bernard Shaw of Marx's monumental work. Yet its motivating ideas seemed redundant, otiose and barren in the twentieth century. 'How', he asked Shaw, 'could either of these books carry fire and sword round half the world? It beats me.'[32]

Socialism, too, seemed an irrational creed for any Apostle of Keynes's generation. There was no appeal for him in Sidney Webb's promised nirvana where the population would be bureaucratized and dutiful under governmental controls. 'You will have some small office no doubt,' Webb promised (or threatened) Virginia Woolf. 'My wife & I always say that a Railway Guard is the most enviable of men. He has authority, & is responsible to a government. That should be the state of each one of us.' Nothing was more alien to Keynes's outlook. Individual initiative was to him humane:

---

* The first communist was Alister Watson, a King's mathematician turned physicist. When Anthony Blunt was elected to the Apostles in 1928, Keynes co-hosted a celebratory supper party attended by Blunt, Dickinson, Rylands, Sheppard and George Thomson. Contrary to some tall tales, Blunt was neither solely responsible for the election to the Apostles in 1932 of the future Soviet spy Guy Burgess nor a pervasive communist influence: during 1933 he attended only two meetings of the society.

it enriched character, personal fulfilment, the arts, scholarship, benefactions as well as enterprise. Capitalist individualism was an outlet for masculine aggression and a safety-valve on the will to dominate. 'Dangerous human proclivities can be canalized into comparatively harmless channels by the existence of opportunity for money-making and private wealth, which, if they cannot be satisfied in this way, may find their outlet in cruelty, the reckless pursuit of personal power and authority, and other forms of self-aggrandizement,' Keynes judged in 1936. 'It is better that a man should tyrannize over his bank balance than over his fellow-citizens; and while the former is sometimes denounced as being but a means to the latter, sometimes at least it is an alternative.'[33]

The Labour party wanted a socialist system. Its supporters had little wish after 1918 to reconstruct the pre-war social and economic order for which Keynes hankered. They accordingly seldom participated in the planning or management of post-war reconstruction. The controlling heights of reform were left to Liberal intellectuals, with Keynes foremost. Labour's hope that unemployment could be eradicated by socialism in the form of state ownership (nationalization) and high taxation dismayed him by being both ardent and wishy-washy. Labour's assumption that there would be ample demand for goods, and therefore full employment, once capitalism was superseded by the supposed social justice of socialism seemed to him fuddled. He opposed those who planned to fleece investors of their dividends and to strip them of their comforts. English socialism was not as brutal as Russian communism, but nearly as drab in its attitude to money-making. Keynes's scorn made him unpopular with Labour doctrinaires. Harold Laski had not a vestige of doubt as to Keynes's brilliance, he told Oliver Wendell Holmes, 'but Keynes's personality seems to me not a national asset. He is sardonic where he might be perceptive and hard where kindness is needed.'[34]

By upbringing, temperament, conviction and his votes, Keynes was a Liberal. 'The Liberal Party is the centre of gravity of progressive forces,' he told its incoming leader, Sir Archibald Sinclair, in 1938. As a member of the House of Lords from 1942, working in the Treasury, he felt compelled to sit with the crossbencher peers; but he identified with the exiguous minority of coroneted Liberals. It might be hard to know what was best to do in either political economy or social policy, he thought; but the progressive and rational traditions of Liberalism provided the best frames of mind in which to manage changes and to persuade people to accept them. Yet Keynes was too questioning and too sharp in his definitions to be a good partisan. Always, as he wrote in 1913, he regretted good public initiatives being 'smothered in the magnificent and empty maxims of political wisdom'. Sir Eyre Crowe of the Foreign Office said of him in 1919, 'He has as little aptitude or taste for politics as you or I have for the refinements of economic speculation; but he is a very clever man, and has the talent of the good learner.'[35]

Traditional diplomacy, as practised by men like Crowe, was mistrusted by Keynes. 'There are two parties in Europe, two attitudes, two impulses; and it is time that they joined issue,' he told *Manchester Guardian* readers in 1922.

> The real struggle today, just as in the second quarter of the nineteenth century, is between that view of the world, termed liberalism or radicalism, for which the primary object of government and of foreign policy is peace, freedom of trade and intercourse, and economic wealth, and that other view, militarist or, rather, diplomatic, which thinks in terms of power, prestige, national or personal glory, the imposition of a culture, and hereditary or racial prejudice. To the good English radical the latter is so unreal, so crazy in its combination of futility and evil, that he is often in danger of forgetting, and disbelieving its actual existence.

He spoke here not only for the conscientious objectors of Bloomsbury and Charleston, and for Cambridge internationalists and combination-room idealists, but for professing Christians (Russell in his autobiography said that Keynes had the air of a bishop in a land of unbelievers), for Liberal leaders from the Marquess of Lincolnshire and the Marquess of Crewe down to constituency party volunteers, for the multitude who gave money to the Save the Children Fund to alleviate suffering in Austria, Germany and Soviet Russia – indeed for all the citizens to whose misgivings about the treaty of Versailles he had given voice in 1919. The old diplomacy believed that England had no permanent friends or enemies, only permanent interests, and should use the varying, adjustable balance of power to protect and extend national and imperial interests. The new diplomacy of the United States, against which Keynes struggled as a financial envoy in the 1940s, was to prove similar in its assumptions and tactics. 'Soldiers and diplomatists', Keynes reiterated, '– *they* are the permanent, the immortal foe.'[36]

One must take Keynes at his word. Politicians might be muddle-headed, keen to bamboozle voters and as socially uncongenial as Eighty Club members, but they were not his immortal foes. He worked and planned with them, sometimes at close quarters, for over thirty years. He was not indifferent to politics, but for a quarter of a century, from 1905 onwards, was a committed party worker who went on the stump at election times. Keynes used the Liberals to infiltrate his ideas into political discourse and to inject his reforms into policy-making. He was treated as a party man. In 1928, for example, he published an article in the *Evening Standard* urging Churchill to increase public spending: 'When we have unemployed men and unemployed plant and more savings than we are using at home, it is utterly imbecile to say that we cannot *afford* these things.' Inside the Treasury Frederick Leith-Ross,

Keynes's fellow Tuesday Clubber, retorted in a memorandum to Churchill: 'I am sorry to see that Keynes is renewing the Press propaganda which has done him little credit as a politician and considerable harm as an economist.' A year later, Sir Laming Worthington-Evans (a City solicitor and member of the Baldwin Cabinet whom Keynes had encountered ten years earlier when he was Minister of Blockade), striving to discredit Keynesian economics among *Evening Standard* readers, took a similar tack: 'It is difficult to reconcile Mr Keynes the politician with Professor Keynes the economist.'[37]*

Throughout the 1920s, when the Liberal party was contending with Labour to be the chief opposition to the Conservatives, Keynes performed as a Liberal platform speaker, and was besought to become a parliamentary candidate. In December 1923, for example, he toured north-west England during the general election called by Bonar Law's inexperienced successor as Prime Minister, Baldwin, to seek a mandate for the Conservatives to impose import tariffs intended to protect British manufacturing and thus to reduce unemployment. Keynes went first to speak at Blackburn for the Liberal candidate, John Duckworth, a cotton manufacturer. Blackburn was a two-member constituency, where the Liberal and Conservative associations each nominated a single candidate in order not to split the anti-socialist vote. Labour advanced two candidates who during the 1920s were always defeated. Keynes's Blackburn speech targeted Labour's fiscal plans for a confiscatory levy (which he had advocated four years earlier in *Economic Consequences*). 'The poor were already too heavily taxed,' he was reported as assuring the town's cotton operatives and

---

* 'Why is it', Keynes asked, 'that Sir Laming holds such very odd opinions? It is like asking me why he wears a top hat. He is a Conservative. The reasons are wrapped in the mists of history. But, roughly, I know them. He half understands an ancient theory, the premises of which he has forgotten.' (CW, XIX, p. 811)

middling classes, 'but there was a point beyond which they could not push the income-tax payer. The high income tax and the capital levy were both evil, but to make a levy for its own sake seemed to him to be absolute madness, and to put it forward as a cure for unemployment was not only madness but insincere.'[38]

From Blackburn Keynes went to Blackpool to speak on behalf of the Liberal candidate, Colonel Hugh Meyler, DSO, 'a Britisher who has fought for his country' in the words of his election literature (he was a solicitor who was to shoot himself in 1929 after sustaining losses on the Stock Exchange). Meyler stood a good chance, because the sitting Conservative MP for Blackpool, a Catholic with an Irish surname, had been ruthlessly deselected, and Admiral Sir Victor Stanley (brother of the Lancashire power-broker and Protestant leader Lord Derby) foisted on the constituency instead. Big crowds assembled in the Opera House of Blackpool Winter Gardens for the Liberal rally: Meyler and Keynes both 'delivered capital addresses', reported the *Blackpool Times* (although it elided details of the Cambridge man's rather technical speech). In the event Colonel Meyler beat Admiral Stanley – their prefixes indicate how the political parties and the nation had become psychologically militarized, as Keynes had feared during the battle over wartime conscription – by over 3,000 votes. Finally, Keynes went north to Barrow-in-Furness to speak for the Liberal candidate, Alderman William Wandless, a pharmacist, who opposed both 'revolutionary Socialism' and 'reactionary Protection', but believed in 'a middle policy' of social amelioration. Barrow was the site of the Vickers shipyards, where there was so little work that birds were nesting in the cranes and the men with jobs were met at the shipyard gates by barefoot children calling, 'Any bread left?' Keynes spoke with clarity about the surplus capacity for shipbuilding, but Wandless was trounced by a Conservative promising to drum up naval orders.[39]

'I did not like so well the atmosphere of last night's meeting at Blackpool, and I hated the sound of my own ugly voice more than ever,' Keynes wrote. 'It was much more enthusiastic than Blackburn but not so serious. The interest of the public is remarkable. I have never seen a theatre so packed (the whole of the stage behind me was full of people as well as the auditorium crammed to the roof, and they stood in queues to get in an hour before the doors were opened).' Railwaymen who had attended the rally recognized him next morning at Blackpool station. 'The station-master and the inspector came to the door of my carriage for a chat, and when the train started the porters jumped onto the steps to wish me good luck and to shout that "All our fellows are going to vote right."'[40]

Before the next general election, in 1924, Keynes was asked to stand as Liberal parliamentary candidate for the University of Cambridge constituency, and his mother for the town of Cambridge. Both felt that parliamentary duties in London would divert their energies and time from what they did best. Despite, like his mother, declining the flattering overture, Keynes spoke for the Liberals during the ensuing contest at a packed meeting of nearly 2,000 voters at Cambridge Corn Exchange. 'Keynes (pale as marble) began [with] an excellent dry speech,' which puzzled non-university members of the audience, Arthur Benson recorded. A barrister named Sydney Cope Morgan, who was the Liberal candidate adopted instead of Florence Keynes, followed with 'a loud fighting speech – really I almost expected to see tonsils & lungs blown from his mouth by his yells'. Cambridge's voters showed why Keynes shrank from parliamentary candidatures. 'The audience could not understand the simplest point & laughed only at the vulgarest jokes,' noted Benson. 'They were orderly & good humoured – but it was a low affair – the aspersions on fellow-candidates sickening. The room was hideous, & the constant singing of "For he's a jolly good fellow" was loathsome.' Keynes thought that as a political platform speaker he performed 'respectably but without éclat'. His Cambridge Corn Exchange tub-thumping prompted an outburst: 'I hate political meetings. They are always *exactly* the same – the same vamped-up atmosphere and the same underlying boredom. It makes one feel a fool and a liar. No, I'm not cut out for politics. I don't *enjoy* it enough.'[41]

It is understandable that Keynes felt disgusted with his speech and even self-demeaned. There was opportunism and hypocrisy in his denunciation of the first (minority) Labour government, led by Ramsay MacDonald, for its recent Anglo-Russian loan agreement. In addition to negotiating general and commercial treaties with Soviet Russia, MacDonald's government had proposed to guarantee the interest and sinking fund on a loan enabling the Bolsheviks to pay their international debts. Although similar financial devices had been used to help Germany, and despite the acknowledged need for an Anglo-Russian financial settlement, Lloyd George, who knew that he had little future if Labour governments succeeded, used the Russian loan proposals as a pretext to bludgeon socialism. Asquith, who also had hopes of returning to Downing Street, endorsed this approach. Accordingly Keynes (peddling the party line) decried the Russian loan to Cambridge voters as an unprecedented risk to taxpayers. It had been suggested that the loan would amount to £40 million. 'Would every single member of this audience be ready to hand over £1 to the Russian Government?' asked Keynes. 'How many of you feel inclined to do it?' He estimated that £40 million would build and equip five towns the size of Cambridge. Russia, added Keynes, had previously repudiated debts to Britain worth several hundred million pounds. He indulged in further red-baiting with his allusions to the Campbell case. Johnny Campbell was a Scottish communist, who had published 'An Open Letter to Fighting Forces' urging servicemen to refuse to shoot their fellow workers or to fight for profiteers. His prosecution under the Incitement to Mutiny Act was abandoned after representations by socialist MPs: the seeming leniency of the Labour government towards a Bolshevik subversive led to defeat in the House of Commons and triggered the general election of 1924. The Labour government was asking taxpayers, said Keynes, 'to make a loan to a country which, during the negotiations, had been inciting British subjects to work for the overthrow of present institutions by inciting a rising in the Army and the Navy. They were asked to loan this money to the most cruel, tyrannical and incompetent Government that existed.' To applause he continued, 'this Russian loan shows just how much we can trust the Labour Party to be sensible'.

As to the Conservatives, said Keynes, they still itched for tariff protection. Other reactionary measures could be expected from them. They yearned to enlarge the prerogatives of the House of Lords by repealing the Parliament Act passed by the Asquith government in 1911. 'In this age of transition there existed one danger. It was that the struggle should develop into a struggle between wealth and prosperity on the one hand, and poverty and revolution on the other.' Only the Liberals could save the nation from this. 'Every Government and every party makes mistakes sooner or later, and becomes unpopular,' said Keynes in his peroration. 'Let us suggest that Mr Baldwin and the Conservative Party were returned to power. In a year or two we shall be thoroughly sick of them – all of us – and the swing of the pendulum will come, and when that time arrives, do you want the Socialists to be the only alternative? Then use your votes and influence at this election to make the Liberal Party strong, self-confident and vigorous.'[42]

It is notable that, despite his mother's commitment to welfare work and medical charities, Keynes never referred in his campaign speeches, and seldom in his political writings, to the topics that a quarter of a century later would be covered by the terms 'welfare state' and 'National Health Service'. This was partly because state spending on welfare had a bigger leap under the predominantly Conservative governments of the early 1920s than under the Labour government of 1945–51. The opportunities for Liberal fault-finding were therefore limited. But, more than that, this was an area in which Keynes had neither close interest nor technical expertise.

In May 1926 Keynes and the *Nation* discarded their hopes of an Asquith revival and endorsed Lloyd George as leader of the Liberals following party ructions about the General Strike. 'I know what L.G. is like', he told Asquith's wife, but there was 'absolutely no choice. I find a unanimous – an astonishingly unanimous – feeling that this is so among every single leftist liberal whom I have spoken to in the last week. A party which has to look forward to consisting mainly of Simon and Runciman seems to me almost as gloomy and mouldering an affair as one can well conceive. I couldn't breathe in that mortuary.' His feelings for her husband were unchanged: he 'remains the one whom I should *like* to follow and whom I love and respect'. Thereafter, for three years, he worked hard for Lloyd George Liberalism.[43]

Political oratory, whether indoors or in the open air, went out of fashion in the 1920s, Keynes said. In an article for the *Radio Times* in 1926, he advocated the wireless broadcast of Churchill's budget speech, and the inauguration of party political broadcasts to interest and inform voters. However, as he lamented at a dinner of Lady Colefax's attended by among others H. G. Wells and Oswald Mosley, it was impossible to convey the complexities of an economic reform programme when voters only understood warcries or catchphrases. He was more effective at talking sense into people, and in improving their comprehension, by lecturing in honest language, shorn of slogans or attitudinizing, at Liberal summer schools to party workers.

Keynes was a strenuous member of the Liberal working-party that, often meeting at Lloyd George's house on a Surrey hilltop, produced the pioneering report entitled *Britain's Industrial Future* (also known as the *Liberal Yellow Book*). Sidney Russell-Cooke, his pre-war lover, now a partner in the stockbroking firm of Rowe & Pitman, was a colleague in this work. The drafting and revision was shared by all of the working-party, but Keynes took the labouring oar in writing the dry and formal chapters recommending various corporatist remedies for unemployment, including investment in modernized factories, a national investment board to regulate Stock Exchange issues made on behalf of foreign interests, public corporations intermediate between privately owned business and state-owned bodies, and reformed budgetary accounts. Editors however preferred to dramatize the obsequies for Field Marshal Earl Haig, whose state funeral clashed with publication of *Britain's Industrial Future*, rather than to dissect technical expositions and mince economic niceties. 'The Liberal Enquiry has had rather a bad press,' Keynes noted, 'but I daresay it deserves it. Long-winded, speaking when it has nothing to say, as well as when it has … it would have been so much better at half the length splashing only what is new and interesting.' Beatrice Webb, who had a high tolerance of prolixity, said the Report 'read as if it were a Fabian document tempered by a desire *not* to appear socialistic'.[44]

After Keynes again declined the Liberal candidature for the University of Cambridge seat, his protégé Hubert Henderson was adopted in his place to fight the 1929 general election. The two men in the meantime prepared a pamphlet advancing the Liberal programme entitled *Can Lloyd George Do It?* They indicted the Treasury for upholding the notion that 'the less the government borrows, the better … are the chances of converting the national debt into loans carrying a lower rate of interest'. To facilitate debt conversion, the Treasury had striven to curb 'all public borrowing, all capital expenditure by the State, no matter how productive or desirable in itself'. The futility of this, given that the capital market was international, was protested by Henderson and Keynes. 'All sorts of influences which are outside our control go to determine the gilt-edged rate of interest; and the effect which the British government can exert on it by curtailing or expanding its capital programme is limited. Suppose, which is putting the case extremely high, that the effect might be as much as a ¼ per cent.' This percentage, when applied to the £2,000 million of War Loan, which was ripe for conversion, represented a difference in the annual debt charge of £5 million, which was nugatory compared with over £50 million spent in the previous year on the Unemployment Fund.[45]

Henderson and Keynes, as Liberal election propagandists, stressed that nations are enriched by the positive act of people using their savings to augment the country's capital equipment – not by the negative act of individuals restraining their consumption. 'It is not the miser who gets rich; but he who lays out his money in fruitful investments.' They inveighed against the Baldwin government with its campaign slogan 'Safety first'. 'Negation, restriction, inactivity – these are the government's watchwords. Under their leadership we have been forced to button up our waistcoats and compress our lungs. Fears and doubts and hypochondriac precautions are keeping us muffled up indoors. But we are not tottering to our graves. We are healthy children. We need the breath of life. There is nothing to be afraid of.' Britain should feel 'free to be bold, to be open, to experiment, to take action, to try the possibilities of things. And over against us, standing in the path, there is nothing but a few old gentlemen tightly buttoned-up in their frock coats, who need only to be treated with a little friendly disrespect and bowled over like ninepins.'[46]

The Lloyd George Liberals fought the general election of June 1929 on an economic programme (which few of its candidates understood) that repudiated laissez-faire and budgets founded in classical economics. Lloyd George advocated a programme of road-building, house-building, electricity and railway development to reduce the suffering caused by unemployment. He published an election pamphlet entitled *We Can Conquer Unemployment* with the sub-title 'We Mobilised for War – Let us Mobilise for Prosperity'. It pledged to reduce unemployment to the pre-1914 level of 570,000, and claimed that its schemes would provide work for 586,000 men in the first year. Keynes and Henderson suspected that the schemes would need longer to take effect, and might reduce unemployment by as little as 400,000. Later calculations by economic historians put the likely figure at 300,000.

Encouraged by a run of Liberal by-election victories, Keynes expected that the Liberals would win between 100 and 150 seats in the new House of Commons. In fact the Liberals secured only fifty-nine MPs: Hubert Henderson, at Cambridge, was not one of them. It was evident that the electoral advantage had passed from liberalism to socialism since 1923, when for the last time a third party attained over 100 seats in a general election. Ramsay MacDonald, as Prime Minister of the Labour government which took office in 1929, began to consult Keynes in an encouraging manner. It took two years for it to become clear how little was achieved by MacDonald's overtures.

Eighteen months after the general election a minor – but significant – episode taxed Keynes's loyalty to Liberalism. In December 1930 a young woman called Millie Orpen, who was Jewish, not Christian, brought an action against a cinema chain in the High Court under the Sunday Observances Act of 1780. The judge ruled that cinemas were illegal on Sundays, and cast doubt on the legality of Sunday concerts, the Sunday opening of the Royal Zoological Gardens and the holding of educational lectures for which tickets were sold. Moreover, under the 1780 Act, a common informer could obtain a reward of up to £200 for every Sunday performance that he or she denounced: Orpen claimed £25,000, and the judge reluctantly awarded her £5,000. Within a week of winning her case, she issued further writs claiming a total of £195,000 from other cinema companies, and also sued Sunday newspapers. In April 1931 the Labour government brought to the House of Commons the so-called Sunday Cinema Bill, which permitted film-shows on the Sabbath and mitigated the law of 1780. The Home Secretary (a trade unionist named Clynes, who had begun work in a Lancashire cotton mill at the age of ten) gave an apologetic, tepid recommendation of the Bill, which was treated as a free vote of conscience. It was left to the Conservative frontbenchers Neville Chamberlain and Lord Eustace Percy to prove the Bill's necessity in robust speeches.

Ian Macpherson, the Gaelic-speaking Liberal MP for faraway Ross & Cromarty and President of the Free Trade Union, who had earlier caused controversy by enforcing his right, as a Presbyterian MP, to have his son baptized in the crypt of the House of Commons chapel, led the speeches against Sunday cinema opening. Liberals with Cornish, Welsh and Scots constituencies spoke and voted against Sunday cinemas, including Megan Lloyd George, Sir Donald Maclean, Goronwy Owen and Walter Runciman. So did Sir Herbert Samuel, who a few months later replaced Lloyd George as Leader of the Liberal party. Large crowds gathered outside the Commons awaiting the vote: cries of 'Give Us Liberty!' and 'Down with the Continental Sunday!' were heard from opposing sides. The Bill was carried, to cheers, by just 258 to 210 votes. Keynes, who upheld people's freedom to choose to enjoy secular Sundays and mistrusted anti-European slogans, was so riled by the Liberal nonconformists that he told Clive Bell and the parliamentarian and former diplomat Harold Nicolson that the Sunday Cinema vote, coupled with the free-trade propensities of the puritans, was enough to make him think of forsaking the Liberals and vote for Oswald Mosley's New Party, which was campaigning for tariffs to protect manufacturers from imports, public-works programmes to provide employment, and state ownership of key industries.[47]

A financial journalist once praised Keynes's *Essays in Persuasion* (the selection of his livelier, less technical writings of the 1920s that he described on their publication in 1931 as the croakings of a Cassandra who had never influenced the course of events in time) for its tendency 'to relegate economics to the back seat where it belongs leaving us free to discuss the things that really matter, such as human relationships and religion'. In his evidence of 1932 to the Royal Commission on Lotteries and Betting, Keynes indulged human psychology, derogated religious proprieties and presented the private vice of 'occasional flutters' as conducive to the public good. 'Gambling should be cheap, fair, frivolous and on a small scale, if its evil economic results are to be reduced to a minimum, and the fun and mild excitement to be maximised,' he urged. He mistrusted the pretence of skill in gambling, preferring the chance wins of lotteries or sweepstakes to horse-racing and Stock Exchange speculation, because the latter category wasted people's time in trying to perfect a spurious system. In a passage based on a witty paragraph in Clive Bell's tract *On British Freedom* (1923), Keynes proposed a weekly state lottery, raising about £10 million a year for the Treasury in taxation, with the operating expenses paid by the Sunday newspapers in return for a monopoly of publishing each Sunday the numbers of the winning tickets. He twitted the solemn godliness surrounding the Christian day of rest, as exemplified by the killjoys who defended the Sunday Observance Act, and irritated the chapel-goers among the Royal Commissioners, by suggesting that 'it would add to the cheerfulness of life if practically everyone in the country was to wake up each Sunday morning stretching out for the Sunday paper with just a possibility that they had won a small fortune'.[48]

Lloyd George, despite his debt to Keynes in preparing *Britain's Industrial Future* and for writing *Can Lloyd George Do It?*, was so irritated by the references to him in Keynes's *Essays in Biography* that he retaliated in his *War Memoirs* of 1933. 'He is an entertaining economist whose bright but shallow dissertations on finance and political economy, when not taken seriously, always provide a source of innocent merriment,' Lloyd George wrote in his sly way. The don had perched himself in 'the rocking-chair of a pundit' during McKenna's tenure as Chancellor of the Exchequer, Lloyd George continued: 'it seems rather absurd now, when not even his friends – least of all his friends – have any longer the slightest faith in his judgments on finance'. With these petulant and ungrateful words Lloyd George proved himself yesterday's man. Even as they were published Keynes's influence was reaching a new ascendancy. This was achieved by him as a public man, talking and acting in London, rather than by academic thinking in his university.[49]

The French economist Jacques Rueff, speaking at Cambridge, extolled the English as a logical people – 'unique in a government that thinks economic reasons are worth applying to daily life or have anything to do with politics, and which asks Royal Commissions for reasons for changes that it contemplates'. To which Keynes, who was present, retorted that the English pride themselves on reaching the right solution in the wrong way. In November 1929, hard on the Wall Street crash and the rise in bank rate to 6 per cent, he was appointed to an official inquiry instigated by the newly elected Labour government. The Committee on Finance and Industry had a remit to investigate the banking system's impact on manufacturers. Labour's Chancellor of the Exchequer, Philip Snowden, a fervent free trader, stipulated that the abandonment of the gold standard was beyond the committee's remit. Its chairmanship was first offered to Keynes's admirer Lord D'Abernon, an international financier who had recently retired as Ambassador in Berlin and was the very model of what Keynes meant by the 'Ins'. After D'Abernon's refusal (he had leased a Venetian palazzo where he was intent on enjoying leisure), it was taken by a barrister called Hugh Macmillan, who was soon afterwards promoted to the judicial bench as a lord of appeal.[50]

Keynes dominated the deliberations of Lord Macmillan's committee. He took a leading part in questioning fifty-seven witnesses over forty-nine days; he attended 100 meetings. He explained his views to the committee during five lengthy sessions in February and March 1930 and on a further three occasions in November. This extended seminar on the monetary system's workings was commanding and incontrovertible: he taught his fellow committee-members the difference between investment and saving; argued that the world's wealth had been accumulated by enterprise rather than thrift; insisted that savings achieved nothing unless they were put to work. He explained the operation of bank rate, and stressed the difficulties for an economy dependent on foreign trade when wages were high (as Britain's were). He told fellow committee-members that if bank rate was raised to protect the balance of payments, investment would fall, business would report losses and prices would follow downwards. If losses continued without a drop in costs, unemployment would ensue. He recommended home investment by the government to remedy underinvestment and to increase domestic demand. Hopefulness that export expansion would reduce unemployment was insufficient. Keynes recommended cheap money (low interest rates), tariff barriers to protect home markets (forsaking his traditional free-trade loyalties) and the rationalization of industry (the closure of inefficient or surplus factories, the amalgamation of businesses that were competing in contracting markets, and the shedding of duplicated managerial, technical and sales staff).

Keynes criticized the Bank of England's secretiveness about its concealed reserves, which he estimated at between £50 million and £100 million, and the obscurity of the Bank's published figures about its earnings (he suspected that its earning assets were put too low). The trouble arose, he said, from the Bank still pretending to be a private institution (it was not nationalized until 1946), and therefore fearful of disclosing its profits. The neurotic aberrations of its cryptic, self-mystifying Governor, Montagu Norman, and the Bank directors' belief that banking mystique was helpful rather than befuddling, were further obstacles. 'I attach enormous importance ... to getting rid of unnecessary secrecy and mystery of all kinds,' Keynes told the Macmillan committee. 'If everything is secret and everything has to be discussed in confidence the circle within which opinions can be freely exchanged is unduly narrowed.' Open discussion about the Bank's intentions was not to be mistrusted: it would help the market to adapt to the Bank's intentions – not fight or bet against them. Publicity about the Bank's operations would 'educate the public ... and bring much nearer the day', Keynes urged with touching optimism, 'when the principles of central banking will be utterly removed from popular controversy and will be regarded as a kind of beneficent technique of scientific control such as electricity or other branches of science are'. The Bank of England's abstruseness made it vulnerable 'to popular pressure and to dangerous charges'.[51]

Secrecy camouflaged financiers' intractability, Keynes told a closed session of the Macmillan deliberations, in which he reverted to the Bank's reluctance to state its objectives or discuss its tactics. 'Industry has no orthodoxy; industry is changing all the time, industry is not governed by wise sayings and traditions; it is all the time experimenting; it is opportunist,' said Keynes, 'but the extraordinary character of finance is the extent to which it is governed by orthodoxy, it is kept back by maxims, and things handed down, and things that were established as sound a long time ago.'[52]

For Keynes, furtiveness was a protection for illusions and delusions. As an Apostle and as a Bloomsbury grouper, he believed in frank truths. The passion for detailed precision that he had shown before 1914 when investigating Indian finance led him always to press for improved statistics and their free discussion. He did more than anyone after 1919 to integrate statistical analysis into administrative practice. He was active in the Royal Statistical Society, and took a lead in 1922 in starting the pioneering London and Cambridge Economic Service, which compiled and disseminated statistics. After his return to the Treasury in 1940, he encouraged the decision to collect national income statistics and other financial data that came to be indispensable in budget-making.

Witnesses from the Treasury, the Bank of England, the joint-stock banks, the Trades Union Council and business gave evidence to the Committee on Finance and Industry, and were cross-examined. Along with Lord Macmillan, Keynes was the most vocal member of the committee. His Tuesday Club banker friends Reginald McKenna and Robert Brand, together with Theodor Gregory (Professor of Banking at London University) and the trade unionist Ernest Bevin, also intervened effectively. Lord Bradbury, Keynes's former chief at the Treasury, indicated his demurral from Keynesian ideas by his frosty, stilted taciturnity. Keynes's disquisitions on the arcana of monetary policy baffled some of his committee colleagues, including Macmillan, who was impressed when Keynes was putting his case, but forgot it swiftly. Geoffrey Crowther, who was awarded a double first in economics at Cambridge in 1928 and afterwards became editor of the *Economist*, said that Keynes's lectures were so brilliant and clarifying that he never needed to write notes; but that whenever it came to writing an essay, he could never recall the lecture's substance.[53]

Economic fluctuations had become more violent since the war, as Keynes stressed. The existence of the 'dole' for the unemployed meant that wages did not fall even at times of falling prices, a falling cost of living and higher unemployment. After the onset of the Slump, real wages increased faster than ever before: the dole had altered the nature of all traditional market adjustments. Within a dozen years – which in economics amounted to a generation for Keynes – there had been an about-face in economic factors and expectations. He found a set determination in most quarters not to reduce wages except as a last resort. The employers who testified before Macmillan, and whom he questioned on this point, were all averse to wage reductions.

The drafting of the committee's report was undertaken by Brand, Gregory, Keynes, Macmillan and a long-serving Bank of England director Cecil Lubbock (the brother of Keynes's Eton tutor, Lubbock had been a social worker in Whitechapel before joining the Home Office, and then entered business as managing director of Whitbread's brewery). A hostile Treasury official, P. J. Grigg, characterized the finished document as a long, 'wishy-washy report which tended slightly in the Keynes direction. At the same time there were a number of addenda with variations on or divergences from the central theme, the most important of these being signed by Keynes, McKenna, Ernest Bevin and others, advocating the whole paraphernalia of public works plus tariffs or devaluation, according to the varying tastes of the signatories.' Bradbury submitted a solo dissentient report 'saying that the rest of the committee were talking something like nonsense.'[54]

Grigg's Treasury colleague Leith-Ross however thought the Macmillan Report remained 'a classic review' of the banking system and its relations with industry for three decades. It called for a managed economy – with a currency that would be managed in the interests of price stability – that would later be known as Keynesian. Bankers were recommended to adopt policies that, at home and abroad, would help enterprise by providing better and cheaper facilities for credit. An international fund to guarantee loans was proposed. So, too, were reforms at the Bank of England. Improved cooperation between the City and manufacturers – a subject that had been repeatedly but inconclusively discussed in Whitehall since 1916 – was again recommended. Austerity measures were opposed. Keynes, McKenna and Bevin submitted a powerful addendum to the main report recommending a tariff on imports and a bounty on exports, urging productive capital expenditure through a National Investment Board, and deprecating wage reductions.[55]

Keynes ensured that the Macmillan Report corrected an entrenched delusion about the balance of payments. The British thought of themselves as a trading nation which exported manufactured goods to pay for the food and raw materials that were imported: in fact this trading account had not shown a credit balance since 1822. Banking, shipping and interest on foreign investment – so-called invisible earnings – had adjusted this balance in every year except 1847, 1918 and 1926. After the publication of the Macmillan Report in 1931, politicians and the public could no longer duck the reality.

The Macmillan Report was not released until mid-July 1931. At almost 200 pages long, it seemed too technical and prolix to read on hot summer days in town. MPs therefore deferred their scrutiny until the parliamentary recess. But disastrously, on 1 August, just as the House of Commons was rising, Snowden published a four-page report on the national economy, tendered by a small committee, working to narrow terms of reference, headed by Lord May, an actuary lately retired as company secretary of Prudential

Assurance. One of May's committee-members was Sir Mark Webster Jenkinson, an accountant associated with the English Steel Corporation and the Vickers-Armstrong group, who in his testimony to the Macmillan committee had advocated forming a financial trust charged with providing capital for industry, industrial banks to promote the rationalization of different industrial sectors, and an expanded contracts-guarantee scheme to enable manufacturers to take foreign contracts on deferred payment terms. Jenkinson was evidently receptive to institutional change; but he and his fellow accountant Lord Plender, together with May, treated the national economy as if it was a shaky business needing rescue from crushing debts. They made alarmist predictions of budget deficits, and proposed inordinate cuts in government spending. International confidence in British economic viability was damaged. Keynes told Ramsay MacDonald that his views of the May Report were unprintable.

Publication of May's recommendations precipitated a run on sterling. Moves towards a balanced budget were suddenly considered essential to restore confidence in sterling. MacDonald's Labour government disintegrated, a coalition government was formed on 24 August, on 15 September sailors of the Royal Navy mutinied in protest at pay cuts, and on 21 September Montagu Norman, returning from Canada by ocean-liner, received the cryptic telegram 'Old Lady goes off on Monday', which signalled that Britain was abandoning the gold standard (but which he interpreted as meaning that his ancient mother was leaving for an unexpected holiday). 'Our departure from the Gold Standard', P. J. Grigg judged in 1948, 'heralded the beginning of our repellent modern world.'[56]

In the autumn of 1928 T. S. Eliot, as a commissioning editor at Faber, had proposed to Keynes that he should write a book about free trade and protection, 'giving a Liberal view of the situation', to be published before the general election due in 1929. 'As for the length of the book,' wrote Eliot, 'it might be hardly more than a pamphlet, or it might be two volumes: that would be for you to decide.' Keynes declined, stating 'I am struggling to finish a big Treatise on Money, which has been turbulently gestating for four years now, and has the claim on all my time.' He did not add that he could not be a sound guide to best Liberal opinion on free trade, as he was rescinding, in his own mind, his opposition to tariffs.[57]

Keynes's public switch to protection began to emerge after February 1930, when he attended the first of the monthly meetings of the businessmen, trade union leaders and technical experts of the newly convened Economic Advisory Council, chaired by the Prime Minister, MacDonald. These Council meetings proved to be a diffuse and frustrating talking-shop, which spawned numerable sub-committees of indifferent value. After six months of hubbub, Keynes convinced MacDonald to appoint a sub-committee of economists to provide an agreed diagnosis of contemporary problems and recommendations of remedies. He promised the Prime Minister, in effect, that, if the economists were left alone, they would reach unanimous recommendations. Under his chairmanship the sub-committee comprised Henderson, the Cambridge classical economist A. C. Pigou, Lionel Robbins (newly appointed to the chair of economics at the London School of Economics) and Stamp (with Keynes's King's protégé Richard Kahn as joint secretary).

During intense day-long meetings, amid a blizzard of papers, Keynes was an inspiring and dominant leader. 'To witness those bird-like swoops of intuition with which he opened up a subject, to listen to that unique voice expatiating with wit, understanding and compassion upon problems of life and politics, and to enjoy his genial company ... were indeed privileges,' recalled Robbins. He was entranced, almost against his will, by Keynes's 'idealism and moral fervour; above all, the life-enhancing quality of his presence'. And yet there were blazing rows. Robbins was an austere free trader and upholder of laissez-faire, who saw the Slump as the healthy antidote to the insalubrious years of over-expanded credit. The nation had consumed its capital during the war, but had not accordingly reduced its standard of living, which the downturn was now enforcing as a matter of hygiene. Robbins insisted upon appending a separate document in which he explained his support of free trade and opposition to increased public expenditure. 'Keynes, who, then as always, was capable of fits of almost ungovernable anger, was furious,' said Robbins. 'In his wrath he treated me very roughly.' Robbins later recanted his views on public investment, and came to regret this dispute as the biggest mistake of his academic life. As a result, the diagnosis and remedies proposed by the economists' sub-committee were neither unanimous nor cogent, as Keynes had all but pledged to MacDonald.[58]

One of the issues considered by Keynes at the Economic Advisory Council was tariff protection. 'The arguments against tariffs on the grounds of political morality, national and international, and of the invariable tendency of tariffs, once started, to be overdone and irrecoverable, are just as strong as ever they were,' he averred in a memorandum circulated to the Council in 1930. Nevertheless, he was no longer a free trader, and doubted that anyone else was in the old sense of the term. The traditional doctrine of abandoning industries that could not compete, or closing operations that no longer held their own, was inoperative when wages were immobile. The nation would always need motor-cars, steel and agriculture, and it would be foolish to let them go out of business in order to preserve doctrinal purity. 'Ever since 1918 we, alone amongst the nations of the world, have been the slaves of "sound" general principles regardless of particular circumstances … Nearly all our difficulties have been traceable to an unfaltering service to the principles of "sound finance" which all our neigh-bours have neglected.'[59]

On this subject, as on others, Keynes thought that one-third of the way through the twentieth century, the English, and indeed other industrial nations, were still trying to escape from the nine-teenth. 'I was brought up, like most Englishmen, to respect free trade not only as an economic doctrine, which a rational and instructed person could not doubt, but almost as a part of the moral law,' he said in a lecture on 'National Self-Sufficiency' deliv-ered in Dublin in 1933. Departures from it, he thought when young, were 'an imbecility and an outrage'. Speeches by Edwardian tariff reformers had seemed to him as authoritarian, life-diminish-ing, backward and crabbed as pulpit sermons. But although free trade remained to him a banner of decency in the world, circum-stances changed. He attributed his altered outlook 'to my hopes and fears and preoccupations, along with those of many or most … of this generation throughout the world, being different from what they were'. He came to want an internationalized outlook for humanity, but national self-sufficiency in business. 'Ideas, know-ledge, science, hospitality, travel – these are the things that should of their nature be international. But let goods be homespun when-ever it is reasonably and conveniently possible, and, above all, let finance be primarily national.' The economic internationalism of the developed world before 1914 had not proved peaceable: perhaps economic isolation would do better. 'The decadent international but individualistic capitalism, in the hands of which we found ourselves after the war, is not a success. It is not intelligent, it is not beautiful, it is not just, it is not virtuous – and it doesn't deliver the goods. In short, we dislike it, and we are beginning to despise it.' It had been possible to idealize the pre-war system whereby British savings were invested in railways installed by British engineers to carry British emigrants to new areas of development, but Keynes felt that it was hard to feel pride in the virtues of international investments in the 1930s, when Chicago speculators had stakes in Germany's Allgemeine Elektricitäts-Gesellschaft or English spinsters put their savings into a loan for the municipal improvement of Rio de Janeiro.[60]

The shrivelling of Liberal certitudes about free trade and unregulated markets was reflected in the decision to absorb the Liberal *Nation and Athenæum* into the Labour-inclined *New Statesman*. Keynes had first proposed this merger in the aftermath of the depressing result for Liberals of the general election of 1929. His overture was rejected by the board of the *New Statesman*, which was then chaired by Arnold Bennett. Keynes renewed his advance a year later for reasons of personnel: Henderson had left the editorship of the *Nation* to become joint secretary of the Economic Advisory Council; his counterpart at the *New Statesman* was an inebriate; and Kingsley Martin, a former London School of Economics lecturer who had become an intemperate editorial writer on the *Manchester Guardian*, was ready to assume the combined posts. The merger was implemented on terms that favoured the financially stronger *New Statesman*, and the first issue of the *New Statesman and Nation* appeared on 28 February 1931. Keynes rather than Bennett became chairman of the combined company.

The *New Statesman and Nation* did not become the rational, constructive influence that Keynes wished for. Kingsley Martin was a restless, melodramatic man who postured as the torchbearer of a righteous, harassed minority. He established the 'Staggers' as the leading exponent of democratic socialism, and as a recruiting-sergeant for anti-colonialism and other progressive causes; but editorially he proved hot-headed, unsteady and devious. From the mid-1930s he lived with Dorothy Woodman, secretary of the Union of Democratic Control, who juggled the ideologies of pacifism, anti-fascism and anti-capitalism, and wrote unscrupulous conspiracy-theorist bestsellers belabouring armaments companies, *The Secret International* (1932) and *Patriotism Ltd* (1933). She and Martin converged in their politics, and his judgement became more suspect under her influence. One of the *New Statesman*'s star columnists was Noel Brailsford, whom Keynes anathematized to Martin in revealing terms: 'He seems to me to have almost every defect – almost incredibly misinformed and ill-informed, carrying credulity to the point when it is almost certifiable, extraordinarily tendentious in a frightfully boring way, with bees in bonnets that entirely distort the right balance.' Brailsford's pathology contaminated the magazine: 'all the weeklies are mere homes for inferiority complexes', Keynes told Virginia Woolf in 1935. He was wary of zealots who embraced good causes only to turn other people against them.[61]

Keynes used the second issue of the *New Statesman and Nation*, published on 7 March 1931, to announce his conversion to support for a revenue tariff and export subsidy scheme to make industry more profitable at the 1925 gold-standard exchange rate. His arguments followed from his privately circulated memorandum to the Economic Advisory Council. In these public proposals, he advocated a 15 per cent tariff on all manufactured and semi-manufactured goods, and 5 per cent on foodstuffs and some raw materials. As he wrote in a gloss for the *Daily Mail* on 13 March, 'Unqualified free trade is part of an austere philosophy which depends, and indeed insists, on things being allowed to find their own level without interference. But if economic changes are very violent and very rapid, human nature makes it impossible for some things to find their proper levels quick enough.' Uproar followed, with vehement counter-blasts from free-trade economists. Keynes regretted that his critics ignored his analysis of the crisis in order to inveigh against the tariff proposals. 'Is it that economics is a queer subject, or is in a queer state?' he asked. 'New paths of thought have no appeal to the fundamentalists of free trade. They have been forcing me to chew over a lot of stale mutton, dragging me along a route I have known all about as long as I have known anything, which cannot ... lead one to a solution of our present difficulties – a peregrination of the catacombs with a guttering candle.'[62]

The failure on 11 May 1931 of the Austrian bank Credit-Anstalt was the Lehmann Brothers moment of the 1930s. Keynes visited the USA in June and July of that year (his first trip since 1917). Back in England, he wrote a report on US economic conditions, which was circulated by direction of Ramsay MacDonald to the Economic Advisory Council, with further copies going to Cecil Lubbock, Walter Layton of the *Economist* and other experts. Keynes found 'an absolute mania for liquidity' among small-town banks which feared runs by depositors. 'Moreover I fancy that the great New York institutions have more skeletons in their cupboards than anyone yet knows for certain, and that their concealed anxieties cramp their action more than is admitted.' By mid-August Keynes was despondent. 'A general breakdown is inevitable,' he told the connoisseur of arts and letters Raymond Mortimer. 'America will revert to a Texas type of civilisation. France and Germany will go to war. Russia will starve. And we, though impoverished, may just survive ... Food will be cheap, and thus riots not too serious.'[63]

After the coalition National Government had been elected in October 1931, Keynes's public interventions were shorn of party affiliation. As the onset of the Depression hit banks across Europe and America, nervous investors shifted their money between countries, always seeking a safer haven for their funds, and leaving bank runs and currency crises in their wake. Nations devalued their currencies as a ploy to attract funds; they imposed exchange regulations, and erected protectionist barriers. 'Well, we're about as bad as we can be,' Keynes told Mrs George Bernard Shaw during luncheon in June 1932. 'Never been so bad. We may go over the edge – but as it's never been like this, nobody knows.' He spoke, said Virginia Woolf, who overhead him, 'in the low tone of a doctor saying a man was dying in the next room; but didn't want to disturb the company'. This was a new mood for Keynes, who was no longer flicking taunts at the stupidity of politicians and bankers. The time was past for making a show of unorthodoxy, rebellion and disobedience to the established order. Now he found a new tone to conciliate and convince.[64]

This change of tack was clear in the four articles that Keynes wrote in February 1933 for *The Times*. These were intended to influence both the budget which Neville Chamberlain and his Treasury officials were preparing for April and the deliberations of the World Economic Conference, which was to convene in London in June (which the USA had agreed to attend on condition that inter-Allied debts were not discussed). Accordingly a stately sobriety pervades the four articles. Publication had to be deferred to allow the publicity storm aroused by the arson attack on the Reichstag to subside, and they finally appeared on 13–16 March. With the World Economic Conference in mind, Keynes addressed global problems: he did not so much prescribe remedies for his own country as advance an international recovery plan, and outlined the means to induce world reflation. He renewed his call for public works financed by loans. He urged that taxation should be remitted without reducing public expenditure, thus adding purchasing power to the economy to help depressed business. It is significant that, when the articles were expanded into a pamphlet (entitled *The Means to Prosperity*), Keynes chose Macmillan as the publisher rather than the Woolfs' Hogarth Press: their tone was grave not teasing; he wrote as an assured public man rather than as a Bloomsbury gadfly.

In *The Means to Prosperity* articles Keynes publicized the 'multiplier effect', which had been recently identified by his young co-adjutor Richard Kahn. In his famous article 'The Relation of Home Investment to Unemployment', published in 1931 in the *Economic Journal*, under Keynes's editorship, Kahn put a precise order of magnitude on the total increase in employment that would ensue from a primary increase of employment created by public works. He showed by mathematical proof, under specified conditions, the ripple-effect of investment expenditure on levels of total economic activity: the initial expenditure multiplies income in the national economy. A proportion of the income generated by the purchase of extra capital goods will be spent on consumer goods. Part of that income from consumer goods will be spent too, and thus generate more income than the initial outlay. Rising national income will induce business people to invest.

The Means to Prosperity articles had momentous impact – not only because the pleasure felt in understanding subtle arguments predisposes people towards accepting their conclusions. The articles sparked international discussions which inaugurated the oncoming Keynesian Revolution. They established Keynes as a constant factor in world opinion on economic policy. Reviewing *The Means to Prosperity* in the *Manchester Guardian*, Sir Arthur Salter (a fellow member of the Economic Advisory Council) wrote: 'He has expressed the strong, and now almost overwhelming, mass of opinion, lay and expert alike, that the time has come for expanding public investment and for more effectively assisting an upward movement of prices by monetary action.' Salter endorsed the Keynesian view that increased public expenditure on capital work would radiate economic activity over the economy, stimulate a trade revival, reduce the costs of unemployment and increase taxable income for the Exchequer. Salter was tantalized by the possibilities of the Keynesian global programme. An international authority would issue certificates, to be treated as the equivalent of gold, worth up to $5 billion to be distributed among participating nations. The certificates would increase each country's current resources and relieve budget deficits or taxation. They would strengthen the reserves of countries striving to maintain the gold standard by means of exchange restrictions, and enable those restrictions to be lifted. They would stimulate public expenditure and increase the general level of prices.[65]

Keynes had to contend, however, with the English mistrust of a smartiboots. Austen Chamberlain spoke for many of his compatriots who mistook conformist notions of common sense for actual good sense when he wrote on 26 March: 'Keynes is extraordinarily clever & marvellously lucid; he has it to his credit that he was the one man who at the moment of the peace negotiations made a true estimate of Germany's capacity to pay; but he is not, I am convinced, a safe guide in business or politics. He excels in theory, but his theories are too fine-spun to stand the wear-and-tear of workaday practice.'[66]

'With mingled hopes and doubts,' Keynes told BBC radio listeners in June 1933 on the eve of the opening of the World Economic Conference, 'sixty-six nations are assembling: statesmen and financiers arrive by every train. The world's needs are desperate: we have, all of us, mismanaged our affairs, we live miserably in a world of the greatest potential wealth.' But most people expected a fiasco. 'Every previous conference ... has ended in empty platitudes and ambiguous phrases so boring and vapid that they have expired in a universal yawn. Isn't the present shocking state of the world partly due to the lack of imagination which they have shown?' He banked his hopes on Britain and the USA agreeing a programme.[67]

France and its allies insisted at the World Economic Conference that monetary stabilization must precede tariff reductions. The British and American delegations conciliated the French by indicating willingness to negotiate; but then President Roosevelt in Washington disclaimed the attitude taken by his own negotiators, and sent a man from the US Treasury hurrying across the Atlantic to undermine the American delegation. 'This undignified incident was the death-blow of the conference,' wrote E. H. Carr, then a Foreign Office expert on eastern Europe. 'The World Economic Conference failed because the delegates, whatever their opinions as to the next step, were all seeking ultimately to bring back an irrevocable past – the regime of low tariffs and fixed currencies.' After this diplomatic failure, economic nationalism and state regulation of trade became fixed features of the balance of power. This outcome was a victory for Keynes's immortal foes who framed policies while contemplating national glory, cultural hegemony and racial superiority.[68]

This was the frustrating context for Keynes's turn in his late forties to his great work of theoretical revision. Early in the 1920s, at one of the meetings of the Keynes Club in his room at King's, he told the assembled younger economists that the implicit working assumptions of classical economists offered a fruitful area of investigation. The biographical essays on Marshall and others that he wrote over the next ten years were part of his investigatory programme. This was not far under way when in 1923 he published his *Tract on Monetary Reform*, which proposed a new institutional framework to improve economic performance, but made no theoretical advances. In 1924 he started a sequel, which did not proceed to schedule, missed self-imposed deadlines and took six years to complete. During those years, Keynes wrested himself, in Richard Kahn's words, 'from the stranglehold of the Quantity Theory of Money in its crude form'. In doing so, he jettisoned by the age of forty-seven what he had upheld at the age of forty: Keynesian economics developed from its progenitor's rejection of the quantity theory of money. He once told Austin Robinson that he reached his best ideas 'from messing about with figures and seeing what they must mean'. They were not derived from painstaking mathematical model-making. Keynes liked to recount the story of Newton explaining his discoveries of planetary motion to Edmond Halley, who asked, 'but how do you know that? Have you proved it?' Newton was startled. 'Why I have known it for years,' he replied. 'If you give me a few days, I'll certainly find a proof for it.' Robinson thought Newton's remark a perfect description of Keynesian methods in the 1930s, 'when there was no doubt about the truth, but a good deal of trouble about the proof'.[69]

The two volumes of Keynes's *Treatise on Money* were published in October 1930. The book's primary purpose was to advance towards a managed world currency. He argued that monetary policy should adapt to social tendencies and the level of earnings: that nations should not rely on market forces. The Bank of England policy of directing monetary policy with the priority of protecting gold reserves – necessitated by the return to the gold standard – was injurious to profit-making and levels of employment. Expectations of profit stimulated enterprise, which built and improved the world's possessions. 'Not only may thrift exist without enterprise, but as soon as thrift gets ahead of enterprise, it positively discourages the recovery of enterprise and sets up a vicious circle by its adverse effect on profits.' The banking and monetary system, even more than peace, warfare, inventions, laws or educational levels, governed both expectations of profit and levels of enterprise.[70]

Richard Kahn was the key figure in the Cambridge 'Circus' which started to meet in the autumn of 1930 to discuss the newly published *Treatise*. Joan Robinson, Piero Sraffa, Austin Robinson and James Meade were its other luminaries. Keynes did not attend the weekly Circus meetings, the results of which were retailed to him by Kahn. When the Circus levelled criticisms at his assumptions regarding employment and output levels, he never used his authority to quash the youngsters. Nor did he justify every position that he had taken. Instead, he welcomed goading to revise his ideas. 'Keynes never even appeared to hesitate,' Austin Robinson recalled. 'He was off with the rest of us in pursuit of truth with as enthusiastic a zest as if he were demolishing the work of his worst enemy.' Yet, as Joan Robinson said, 'there were moments when we had some trouble in getting Maynard to see what the point of his revolution really was'.[71]

Having explored the implicit assumptions of classical economists, Keynes turned to the implicit assumptions of his own mindset. It was assumed, often wrongly, he realized, that achieving more of one thing required the acceptance of less of another. 'It was', said Austin Robinson in 1947,

a great step forward in economic thought when Keynes insisted that we should have a *general* theory – a theory which was valid not only with full (or near-full) employment, but also with unemployment – and that we should know clearly which of the propositions of economics were universally valid, and which were valid only in conditions in which it might be true that an increase of one activity was possible *only* at the expense of another activity. In the Cambridge thought of my time I believe that no single forward step has been so important. It has gone right to the heart of the method of estimation of the opportunity costs of doing anything.[72]

Keynes determined to write a book that would free savings and investment from their neo-classical straitjacket: explicitly addressed to fellow economists, his *General Theory of Employment, Interest and Money* was published in 1936. It is one of the most influential works of economic thought, and arguably the most intellectually audacious, ever published. Kahn called it 'a world-shattering book'. The central argument, which seemed revolutionary to classical economists, was that the economy had no natural tendency towards full employment. High unemployment could persist indefinitely if governments did not intervene forcefully. Although Keynes denied the classical nineteenth-century liberal faith in the self-regulation of the free market, there was minimal promotion in his *General Theory* of the policies that were later called Keynesian. 'Our final task', he wrote, 'might be to select those variables which can be deliberately controlled or managed by central authority in the kind of system in which we actually live.' The variables which were apt for management by central authorities were interest rates and taxation, which he proposed that governments should adjust in order to stimulate investment and to seek full employment. However, he said little of emergency public works, and nothing about fiscal methods of demand management. He did not recommend increasing the government's current expenditure by running a budget deficit to meet a deficiency of demand. He gave no encouragement to profligate finance ministers. He urged that additional government expenditure should be on capital account and financed from a separate capital budget while so far as possible the regular budget should be kept in balance. He suggested that full employment might be maintained by redistribution of income. If wealth was more equitably dispersed in the population, effective demand would be stimulated and would thus help capital growth. As the scarcity of capital diminished, investors would be rewarded less. He never believed that state planning would eliminate economic instability. He saw national economies as inherently wobbling: they were susceptible to rational management, but with irrational elements.[73]

'If economists could manage to get themselves thought of as humble, competent people, on a level with dentists, that would be splendid', Keynes wrote. He wished his colleagues to recognize the limitations of economic theory, to accept that they were not omniscient and thus to make themselves useful in formulating policy without banging the kettledrum of absolutist authority. Yet Keynes's braininess was too obvious for him to be mistaken for a white-coated drone who extracted wisdom teeth week after week. Similarly *General Theory* aroused hostility, because it was a technical work, which proclaimed abstraction in its title and used terminology directed at his technical peers. 'Enveloped in a vast cobweb of abstract definition, eked out by algebraic formulas, it contains a few commonplaces, obvious to all except the "classical" economists, to the effect that full employment depends upon a due adjustment between consumption and productive investment, that over-investment in productive equipment, coupled with frenzied Stock Exchange gambling, can produce a disastrous slump, that lowering wages all round reduces the consuming power on which employment depends,' the Conservative politician Leo Amery concluded after his second reading. And yet to many economists *General Theory* has seemed light on data, and certainly less filled with quantitative facts than the *Tract on Monetary Reform*.[74]

Keynes is the economist who plumbed ulterior motives: who appraised instincts, shibboleths, memories, national customs and liberties, opportunities taken and missed – and incorporated his sense of them into his economic schemes. He was a public figure, who happened to be an economist: a quondam official, still consulted by government ministers, departmental heads, City directors and Royal Commissions, an inveterate diner-out who listened, argued and spread his influence at the tables, the chairman of a weekly magazine which formed opinion on the Liberal left, the editor of an eminent academic journal who saw all the submissions, a newspaper commentator, platform speaker and broadcaster. His great book of 1936 arose from all this: derived, too, from his earlier work and thought on behalf of the Liberal party.

Keynes had no illusions about Liberalism. Writing of *Britain's Industrial Future* to the editor of the *Observer* in 1928, he said that the report received more publicity by appearing as a party manifesto than it would have done as a pamphlet co-authored by neutral economists. Its ideas, he predicted, would be purloined over the years by rival parties. 'If one regards the activities and existence of a Liberal Party as a route to power, I agree that one is probably wasting one's time'; but as a source of influence and as an accelerator of reforms, it was useful. 'As things stand at present, the Liberal Party, split and divided as it is and with uncertain aims, provides an almost perfect tabernacle for independent thought which shall at the same time be … in touch with the realities of politics.' In this Keynes proved right: the dangerous Liberal prescriptions of 1928–9 seemed safe enough by the general election year of 1935, when Treasury officials advised their Chancellor of the Exchequer, Neville Chamberlain, that expanded public borrowing would help to maintain the impetus of economic recovery. Chamberlain, among other acts, authorized a road-building programme costing £100 million.[75]

For a time Keynes gave vitality and even militancy to the Liberals: he saw himself as a lancer riding into the thick of the fight against impractical stupidity. Asked in 1926 to define the three groups of non-revolutionary reformers, Keynes had his answer pat. 'A whig is a perfectly sensible Conservative. A radical is a perfectly sensible Labourite. A Liberal is anyone who is perfectly sensible.'[76]

CHAPTER FIVE
LOVER

Keynes thought himself ugly in appearance and voice. 'Yes, I have a clever head, a weak character, an affectionate disposition, and a repulsive appearance,' he told Arthur Hobhouse, whom he found sexually desirable but was hesitant to seduce. Repulsive was a repeated word with him. 'My dear,' he told Lytton Strachey in the year that they became lovers, 'I have always suffered and I suppose always will from a most unalterable obsession that I am so physically repulsive that I've no business to hurl my body on anyone else's. The idea is so fixed and constant that I don't think anything … could ever shake it.' Other people agreed that he had horrid looks for which he atoned by his talents. 'He is an ugly devil, but said to be a financial genius,' Lady Cynthia Asquith, the ex-Prime Minister's beautiful and clever daughter-in-law, noted after walking with him in 1918. Two years later Virginia Woolf likened him to 'a gorged seal, double chin, ledge of red lip, little eyes, sensual, brutal, unimaginative'. After his fortieth birthday she revised her opinion: she still found him 'very gross', with 'a queer swollen eel look, not very pleasant', but his eyes she conceded were 'remarkable'. Keynes compensated for feeling unattractive by flirting. Men and women who interested him were likely to have his toying charm exerted on them. Flirtation was part of his equipment – along with his intelligence, intuition, lucidity and improvisation – as the great persuader.[1]

Ottoline Morrell described Keynes's flirtatious technique as projecting 'the atmosphere of his personality'. He gave 'a detached, meditating and yet half-caressing interest in those he is speaking to, head on one side, a kindly, tolerant smile and very charming eyes, wandering, speculating, then probably a frank, intimate and perhaps laughing home-thrust'. Harold Nicolson, who had been Raymond Mortimer's lover and knew other cadet Bloomsbury groupers, recalled Keynes gazing with 'probing, gentle eyes' at 'the humble or the young' as if they were 'about to say something supremely important'. His approach must have been similar when, in 1909, after dinner at Simpson's in the Strand, he walked to Liverpool Street station for a late-night Cambridge train. 'I got into a carriage with three sailors and an exquisite young cavalry man. The Jacks fell deeply in love with the Tommy, who really was *lovely*. The conversation was general; we all drank a great deal of neat whisky out of a bottle, and everything became very friendly. They were going onto Norwich and must have been in one another's arms before 2.20 a.m.' Keynes was open to the possibilities in many people and situations when young. His enduring humanity rested on these early perceptions. Moreover, he created fresh prospects for others. 'You … manage to create an atmosphere in which all is possible,' Vanessa Bell told him in 1914. 'One can talk of fucking and Sodomy and sucking and bushes and all without turning a hair.'[2]

Flirtation launched Keynes's career as a public man. His appointment to the Royal Commission on Indian Finance, his discovery by politicians such as Austen Chamberlain and businessmen such as Lord Cable, the impression he made on *hautes fonctionnaires* such as Blackett and Chalmers, his recruitment to the Treasury in 1915 and his introductions to the Asquiths and to smart Liberal society – all these he owed to Edwin Montagu, who had first spotted him when he was an undergraduate at Cambridge. During the general election of 1910 he and Montagu addressed a political meeting attended by Chivers jam-makers at Histon: 'the audience', he said, 'was entirely male and very much excited in our behaviour'. Montagu treated Keynes with nervy, chattering coquetry in which he approached close and then started back. 'He was an inveterate gossip in the servants' hall of secretaries and officials,' Keynes wrote. 'It was his delight to debate, at the Cabinet, affairs of State, and then to come and deliver, to a little group, a brilliant and exposing parody, aided by mimicry, of what each of the great ones, himself included, had said.' What Montagu loved most, Keynes continued, was 'when he could push gossip over into intimacy. He never went for long without an intense desire to unbosom himself, even to exhibit himself, and to squeeze out of his confidant a drop of – perhaps reluctant – affection. And then again he would be silent and reserved beyond bearing, staring stonily with his great hand across his mouth and a staring monocle.' Montagu said that the two people who meant most to him in life were Asquith's paramour Venetia Stanley, with whom he had an undersexed if not unconsummated marriage, and the youngest member of Asquith's Cabinet, Bron Lucas, a one-legged misogynist. Montagu and Lucas were self-torturing men; and there were knotty, non-avowable complications in the former's mentorship of Keynes.[3]

There are many grades to flirtation. During 1921 Keynes gave a series of evening lectures at the London School of Economics. The banker Sir Charles Addis was one of the eminent men in the audience. Afterwards, despite the damp, dark nights, the two men, who belonged to a hardy generation, walked and talked together, from Aldwych to King's Cross station, where Keynes entrained for Cambridge. 'I like him much,' Addis noted, 'such a luminous intelligence!' It was Keynes's radiance, his attentive intensity and desire to impress his personality on listeners that made him such a seductive talker. He dallied with people as different as Lloyd George and

Albert Einstein. 'I had a terrible flirtation with Ll.G. yesterday,' he confessed to his wife Lydia Lopokova, 'and have been feeling ashamed of myself ever since!' As to the theoretician of relativity, whom he first met in Berlin in 1926, 'A naughty Jew-boy, covered with ink, pulling a long nose as the world kicks his bottom; a sweet imp, pure and giggling' was his description. Keynes discussed politics and life with Einstein: 'I had indeed a little flirt with him.'[4]

Keynes was a demonstrative man who liked physical contact. After a dinner of the Tuesday Club in 1930, at which he had led a discussion about free trade, he walked away from the Café Royal arm in arm with Reginald McKenna. Still linked, they strolled down Regent Street, across Piccadilly, to McKenna's flat in Pall Mall, discussing a gold speculation. Ten years later Virginia Woolf met Keynes: 'A blank wall of disapproval; till I kissed him, on wh. he talked of Lydia, having a book about the ballet, in his eager stammering way.'[5]

Many of Keynes's dealings had an amorous undertow in which sexual desire had no part. He cherished his lively, diminutive aunt, Fanny Purchase: 'the one I always flirt with', he called her in 1923. Another redoubtable old lady, Mary Marshall, was delighted by his flirting, and insisted that his tender solicitude saved her life during a grievous illness of the 1930s. Only coarse spirits would take all his expressions of love as lustful. It would be absurd to find eroticism in Keynes's remark, while a guest at Sutton Courtenay in 1917, less than a month after Asquith's ejection from Downing Street, that he found himself 'falling in love' with the deposed Prime Minister, 'sweet and gentle but bruised in spirit'. Yet the meanings of Keynes's affections have been degraded. As recounted in chapter 3, he closed his account of his meeting at Spa with the banker Melchior, in which two men on opposing sides recognized their brotherhood and strove to avert German starvation, with words reminiscent of Tolstoy's faith in the boundless power of loving humanity: 'In a way, I was in love with him.' The historian Niall Ferguson, who has shown a reiterative need to make illiberal references to Keynes's carnality, reinterpreted these words. Keynes, he wrote in 2010, 'felt an almost sexual attraction to Melchior'.[6]

Keynes thought that his sexual history mattered. He wished his experiences to be understood. Accordingly he preserved, with care, his incriminating correspondence written during his early manhood with Lytton Strachey, Duncan Grant and others. The letters were exchanged at a time when it was unlawful for men to have sex with one another. They were secreted by him from prying eyes. Although they chronicle, with more vivid authenticity than is possible for most historical figures, the initiations, experiments, risks, sprees, settled confidence and ultimate stability of his sexual history, from pre-pubescent schoolboy to late-middle-aged invalid with waning libido, his first biographer, Roy Harrod, writing long before the partial decriminalization of male homosexuality in 1967, quoted them gingerly. Yet euphemisms, suppressions and guesses were contemptible to Keynes. Although he felt ashamed of his looks, and unlovable because of them, he was unapologetic about his sexual preferences.

The English disease is that 'one's private life is so damned private that there is too great a gulf between it and the public appearance', he told the vicar's son Bernard Swithinbank in 1906. Few people had true communion with one another: 'their privies are so private that they don't even know themselves that they have got them'. Yet there were prurient nosey-parkers in many households, including parents, butlers, housekeepers and landladies, spying, eavesdropping, reading intimate letters and sending denunciations, as Hobhouse, Grant, Keynes and others found. Mummification best describes the mentality that Keynes withstood. This chapter unravels the mummy to find what lay beneath the stifling, tight-bound linen cloth.[7]

Keynes's sex life was one of the seven activities that made the universal man. His affections and desires permeated, although they never dominated, his development at Eton, his influence at King's, his epiphany as an Apostle, his ambivalence about his responsibilities as a government official, his flinching from the false fronts of politicians, his irresistible persuasiveness, his developing interest in the arts and his commitment to the public patronage of private creativity. As with classical economic orthodoxy, so with homosexuality: around the age of forty he had second thoughts, and changed the direction of his ideas. More than that, his flirtatious powers – his mixture of intensity, frivolity and flattering attention – were akin to his persuasive powers. He studied people, impressed his personality on them, charmed and subjugated their resistance, in similar ways. Intelligence was a major component in his sexuality. So, too, was the compartmentalization that he practised in common with most intelligent Englishmen of his class. He measured distances and evaluated reciprocities between people. Although he felt unashamed of his intimacies and longings, Keynes kept them in a discreet compartment of their own. Some trusted colleagues and contemporaries had easy admittance, but Tuesday Club members, Liberal party associates, Treasury officials and many others were excluded.

The ghost of Oscar Wilde haunted the sex education of middle-class Edwardians. His degradation and imprisonment defined how young men of comparable tastes thought of themselves after 1895. 'I'm an unspeakable of the Oscar Wilde sort,' says the hero of Morgan Forster's novel *Maurice*. In 1914 Forster lent Keynes the manuscript, which was only published posthumously, because he feared that the police might open a criminal investigation into his friends or start a prosecution for obscenity. Forster instructed Keynes in the sexual samizdat of their generation: 'Give back M.S. to Dickinson when you've done with it – don't show or mention it to anyone.' Wilde's trials taught several generations of Englishmen that certain sexual acts, if detected or avowed, brought criminal prosecution or social ruin. The reverberations of his case suggested that practitioners of those acts were a freakish minority of intermediates, distinct and estranged from the rest of manhood, or an unruly tribe, with weird rites, launching raiding-parties on the normal majority of the human race, and with a tendency for their lives to plunge into calamitous disorder.[8]

Oscar Wilde's name recurred at defining moments among the Keynes children. In 1906 the two brothers travelled together in Germany. Geoffrey had recently left Rugby School, where he had been swaddled, it seemed, in sexual ignorance. 'My dear, here he is at nineteen and all agog to hear what any self-respecting lower boy would die of boredom to hear repeated,' Maynard told Strachey. 'It all came out at once and quite suddenly. He has found Germany all ears for O.W. and has read a brochure hinting.' Geoffrey asked what Wilde had been accused of. 'Sodomy,' said his brother. 'What's that?'

> I fell pale and shivering on the ground: and it then transpired that although he vaguely knew that people were sometimes 'bunked' for it, he had never known a case and had never even heard the question raised on a single occasion during his whole time at school.
> 'Do they do it at Eton?' said he.
> 'Yes,' said I – giggling. And he looked a little interested, but nervous.[9]

Geoffrey Keynes had an inquisitive sexuality. Rupert Brooke was not the only male beauty to whom he was susceptible when young. However, as a physician in a London teaching hospital, he was cowed by the threat of scandal into personifying discretion. As Brooke's literary executor, he went to lengths that now seem pitiful to suppress evidence of his hero's slight relations with men. His frets, too, inhibited Roy Harrod, whose cryptic treatment of homosexuality, in his official Keynes biography, was however chiefly necessitated by the criminal sanctions in force when it was published in 1951. It is impossible to know what loneliness, fear, frustration and regret he may have endured in the sixty years after the revelation to him in Germany of Oscar Wilde's abasement, gaoling, ostracism and ruin. In old age Geoffrey Keynes's inhibitions relaxed. Someone close to him said with a grin that you only had to walk down the street with him and see him swivel his head after certain passers-by, to see the appeal to him of young men. During the 1970s he was charmingly attentive to a series of handsome Cambridge undergraduates. As a widower, he seemed to be in love with an artistic blond at King's, who did not mind being caressed as he knew the old man was too ancient to follow through. He enjoyed a pleasant swansong of affections.[10]

Two years after the Wilde explanation in Germany, at Christmas of 1908, the three Keynes children were invited to a fancy-dress dance. Margaret startled Maynard by saying, 'I think *you* had better go as Oscar Wilde,' but he found with relief that she was addressing Geoffrey; and their mother immediately quashed the idea, exclaiming 'Oh! that would be a horrid thing to do.' That afternoon the Keynes family went for tea with the Darwins. There Maynard heard Margaret Darwin (aged eighteen), who married Geoffrey Keynes nine years later, ask Margaret Keynes (aged twenty-four), 'Was Oscar Wilde imprisoned for stealing?' His sister replied, slightly flustered, 'Oh I don't know: for that and other things.' This made him suspect that she knew what she had implied in the morning.[11]

Margaret Keynes's artless candour more than once disturbed the equanimity of her elder brother. It seems as if she sometimes set him teasing tests. In 1908 Keynes discussed with her and their mother a short-lived university scandal caused by the bursar of Trinity Hall marrying the daughter of a lodging-house keeper. 'Most unwise,' said Mrs Keynes, 'he'll find her dreadfully dull in the end.' The dialogue continued:

> Me – Not much duller, I expect, than most women dons marry.
> Margaret to me – I expect you know lots of men you wouldn't mind marrying, don't you?
> I (hedging) – Well, they wouldn't be so dull anyhow.
> My mother – You mean to live with.
> Margaret – Anyhow, I know several females *I'd* be quite willing to marry. We'd better arrange it that way.
> My mother laughs at our absurdity and the conversation veers off to the question whether it wouldn't be a good thing to clear out the *Atlantic Monthlys* and make more room on the shelves opposite.

In 1910, at one of his weekly lunches at Harvey Road, Keynes was cornered by his sister into what would a century later be called a coming-out. 'I had a dreadful conversation on Sunday with my mother and Margaret about marriage,' he reported to Grant, 'and had practically to admit to them what I was! How much they grasped I don't know.'[12]

Margaret Keynes, before her marriage in 1913 to Vivian Hill (a physiologist who was a Fellow of King's 1916–20, elected Fellow of the Royal Society in 1918 and co-winner of a Nobel prize in 1922), had 'a Sapphistic affair', in her elder brother's phrase, with Eglantyne Jebb, who had been taught economics at Cambridge by Mary Marshall, worked with Florence Keynes in Cambridge charities and wrote a path-breaking treatise on social policy in Edwardian Cambridge. Jebb later compiled the authoritative, neutral-spirited 'Notes from the Foreign Press' in the wartime *Cambridge Review*, which led to the magazine's offices being ransacked by rowdy patriots. In 1919 she co-founded the Save the Children Fund. 'She's much too sensible to make a fuss,' Margaret said of Jebb after her engagement to Hill was announced. The Hills – conversationally at least – became an eccentric couple. At family meals they would take turns to speak at inordinate, unbreakable length for minutes on end without any reference to what the other had said.[13]

The three Keynes children were boxed together in the high-minded, liberal, open-hearted, smothering household in Harvey Road. Their undisclosed sexual imagination and clandestine initiatives provided a way to evade the fine mesh of their family cage. Willa Cather in an essay once praised Katherine Mansfield (Keynes's sometime tenant in Bloomsbury) for portraying in her stories 'happy families' living unremarkable lives, without crises, shocks or bewildering complications, 'yet every individual in that household (even the children) is clinging passionately to his individual soul, is in terror of losing it in the general family flavour'. Within Mansfield's precincts, said Cather, 'the mere struggle to have anything of one's own, to be oneself at all', creates tension 'even in harmonious families'. The result is a double life: the outward respectability of households, and their underworld, 'secret and passionate and intense – which is the real life that stamps the faces and gives character to the voices of our friends. Always in his mind each member of these social units is escaping, running away, trying to break the net which circumstances and his own affections have woven about him.' Aside from their inborn predilections, Maynard and Margaret Keynes, if not their anxious younger brother, enjoyed the surreptitious excitement, private dialects and specialized nuances of their illicit desires. Bisexuality provided one way of saving their souls from being quenched in the family's collective identity. It offered miscreant vividness beyond the inexpressive and perpendicular rectitude of Harvey Road.[14]

One physical fact about Maynard Keynes's childhood raises both probabilities and hypotheses. He and his brother were subjected to late circumcisions: probably in 1891, when Maynard was eight and Geoffrey four. The motive was to discourage masturbation, which the Victorians feared as enervating of virility and deprecated because it was the one sexual act that they could not sentimentalize. Neville Keynes was sufficiently anxious about his sons feeling themselves to make a cryptic diary entry when Maynard was eleven: 'the poor boy was very sad this morning because the pockets of his overcoat were sewn up'.[15]

Circumcision was coming into vogue at this time. It was believed that the retractable foreskin drew boys' attention to their genitals at an age when sexuality was supposed to be latent. John Harvey Kellogg, in *Plain Facts for Old and Young* (1888), recommended that circumcision should be performed on pre-pubescent boys without anaesthetic, 'as the brief pain attending the operation will have a salutary effect upon the mind, especially if it be connected with the idea of punishment'. Discouragement of masturbation was Kellogg's aim: 'the soreness which continues for several weeks interrupts the practice, and if it had not previously become too firmly fixed, it may be forgotten'. The foreskin 'conduces to masturbation and adds to the difficulties of sexual continence', a physician urged in the *British Medical Journal* in 1890. Another physician reading 'A Few Notes on Foreskins' to a medical conference at Sheffield in 1891 'attributed the frequency of hip-joint disease, of affections of the spinal cord, of hernia, of epilepsy in young subjects, to the neglect of the condition of the prepuce'. A medical practitioner in Hertfordshire reported in 1899 that 'of late years most parents' asked him to circumcise their newborn sons. Nevertheless another surgical discussion concluded: 'circumcision is a relic of barbarism ... practised by many of the least civilised peoples on the face of the globe'. It counselled that 'the prepuce is not the valueless or mischievous appendage that some represent it to be, nor is its removal so entirely harmless as some would have us believe.[16]

The politician Lord Hailsham, who was born in 1907, recalled after seventy years his experience of being circumcised at a similar age to Maynard Keynes just before being sent to boarding-school. The first page of his memoirs opens with the shock of the event. 'I was not told that it was going to be done; no anaesthetic was administered; I was just laid across the doctor's knees,' Hailsham recalled in 1990. 'I can still remember the pain, the blood, and my sense of total betrayal by the adult world.'[17]

Hailsham's coeval, the poet W. H. Auden, also underwent circumcision, at the age of seven, in 1914. These late circumcisions made some boys feel impaired, injured or incomplete, and influenced the direction of their adult sexual activity. Auden, in his Berlin journal of 1929, noted as a driving impulse of men's sexual interest in other men the 'comparison of circumcised with uncircumcised and vice versa'. Neither the physicians who performed nor the parents who paid for these mutilations (especially those inflicted in mid-childhood) foresaw the effect on some young Englishmen, already desirous of their own sex, whose quests for other men were spurred by their delighted curiosity about foreskins, their identification of them with real men, and their connotation of circumcision with reduced manliness. For such youngsters lust was intensified by the inquisitive belief that there is as much interesting variety in the shape, size and character of men's penises as there is in their faces. There are signs that Keynes's sex life when young was influenced by his late circumcision. He liked to discover whether other men were cut or uncut. 'He is charming and he is affectionate,' he wrote of his first Eton boyfriend Dillwyn Knox in 1906, 'and he is uncircumcised.' Of his first great love, Arthur Hobhouse, he added, 'you will hardly believe it, but I don't know whether Hobby is circumcised or not – you can't conceive his precautions.[18]

At Eton, when new boys arrived, they were addressed by the head master, Warre. 'There he stood, waiting, this great square man, with a broad, silk band round his middle, gazing at a high window, and chewing the inside of his cheek,' recalled Sir Lawrence Jones, who overlapped at Eton with Keynes. 'Then he spoke to us, paternally, dropping his final G's, moving his strong lips as one does to a lip-reader, now in a vibrant bass, now in a sudden tenor. He spoke of our responsibility as Etonians … He told us to beware of "filth", to avoid even talking "filth".' Jones at thirteen was baffled: 'Could he be telling us to look where we trod, because of the occasional dog-mess on the pavements? And who ever wanted to talk about these horrors?' In old age it saddened Jones that it had been axiomatic at Eton in the 1890s, 'uncontested by masters or boys, and a particular obsession of visiting preachers, that sex, although given to us by God, was a dirty little secret. The strongest of human impulses, the most delectable of human enjoyments, was equated, in our hierarchy of values, with ordure.'[19]

There were scandals of the usual sort often enough. In 1899 Richard Powell, one of Keynes's election at Eton, was (as Neville Keynes noted in his diary) 'made to withdraw from College for reasons more or less veiled in mystery. Maynard understands that he has been received at Haileybury.' In adulthood, Powell became sports editor of *The Times*, married Lord Courthope's sister and was killed in action in 1915. When Cecilia Fisher expressed shock after learning of a schoolboy misdemeanour similar to Powell's, she was rebuked by her mother Blanche Warre-Cornish, the wife of a house master. 'Don't be a prig!' Mrs Cornish said. 'It's the traditional, ancient, aristocratic vice of Eton. What do they know of it in those modern, sanitary, linoleum schools?'[20]

Sublimation predominated at Eton, among masters as well as boys. Percy Lubbock wrote of Keynes's mentor Henry Luxmoore that his passion for beauty was too purified. 'It was bigoted, it was repressed and encroached upon by many a prejudice,' Lubbock observed: 'it suffered much from an obstinate fear of the devil and his works ... he hid it, screened it, and denied its air. He worshipped beauty, but he couldn't trust it.' Whatever may have happened in boarding-houses, in College, among King's Scholars such as Keynes, so his Eton contemporary Bernard Swithinbank recalled in 1948, 'emotion and desire were directed almost exclusively towards the male sex – I knew hardly anyone who ever thought of women. This does not mean that there was a great deal of "vice"; indeed, it was looked on with disapproval, not untinged with envy, by the many who repressed their desires through shyness or virtue.'[21]

Keynes first had sex with another boy in 1901 when he was seventeen or so. We know this from a list of sexual partners, identified by their initials and years, which he compiled in 1915 or 1916, and which was released into the Keynes archive at King's years after the bulk of his papers were accessioned. The boy was Dillwyn Knox, known as 'Dilly'. In a cool, inquisitive and systematic way, the two youths set themselves sexual and mental tests to resolve the question of what choices, feelings and acts were requisite to live well. Pleasure, they decided, was more essential than morality or duty. Knox had vowed to be impregnable in his feelings after being bereft by his mother's early death: as grandson and son of bishops, he had much to reject. Keynes's classical education ensured that his limited susceptibility to guilt was nearer to Plato's than to a Christian's. Together they defied the preachers' admonitions against 'filth' and explored possibilities. Sexual incidents between them recurred throughout 1901–2. Knox went in 1903 as a scholar to King's College, Cambridge, where he became a Fellow in classics in 1909. He had a passion for solving puzzles, discovered a genius for cryptography while working in naval intelligence during 1914–18 and after the war forsook Cambridge for the Government Code and Cypher School, where he became a leading man.[22]

Keynes's second Eton boyfriend was Daniel Macmillan, son of the publisher and elder brother of the future Prime Minister. Their affair during 1902 ended when they left school, but the attraction did not peter out. When in 1906 Keynes visited Oxford, where Macmillan was an undergraduate, it reignited. 'I succeeded yesterday in catching Dan alone – for about an hour,' he told Strachey. 'We sat on a sofa together and things ended in only a semi-embrace, but I could have done anything – if only I had the nerve. He goes on about the most silly Eton Oppidans [those who were not King's Scholars] and likes to talk theoretically about women.' The difficulty in renewing 'l'affaire Dan' was Keynes's inhibition in going too far. 'You see, I am so terrified of losing the right to fondle him and hold his hand. I feel that if I once attempted rape, he would never [again] sit close to me on a sofa and rub his knee against mine.' Keynes was sympathetic when Macmillan caught venereal disease in 1909. A year later he invited his friend to stay in a house which he rented for August in a pretty little market town in the Cotswold hills. 'Dan I find in a rather distressed condition – verging on melancholia. Very nervous, very depressed, not able to sleep, worrying over every detail of life, and – chiefly – thinking himself an utterly worthless creature, foolishly repining over all his supposed misdeeds. Isn't it dreadful? I believe it's due to the nature of his family life.'[23]

Keith Murray and Alwyn Scholfield, two Cambridge undergraduates recently arrived from Eton, went to tea with the former Eton master Arthur Benson in 1904. 'Both strong against "the aesthetes" like Keynes – but I couldn't find out what they meant, except that K talked of things they didn't understand,' recorded

Benson, who well knew what the code-word 'aesthete' denoted after the Wilde trials. 'Altogether,' Benson continued, 'I felt the tinge of complacency about Murray which I did not quite like – the public-school Pharisaism.'[24]

There were Pharisees enough in Cambridge. A scholar of Trinity who went for tea in Lytton Strachey's rooms said through blanched lips afterwards: 'The conversation was too horrible! And the pictures and atmosphere!' Leonard Woolf warned Strachey, whose talk was lascivious as compensation for being sunk in the isolation of timid chastity: 'they think you are a witch and given up to the most abandoned and horrible practices'. Puritanism stifled the university. It vexed Keynes when, in 1909, the theologian Arthur Mason, who was Vice-Chancellor, prohibited the award of Swinburne's poems as a university prize, because he judged them 'immoral'.[25]

The Pharisees were muted at King's, where to Keynes's benefit the domineering figure of Oscar Browning sponsored a different sexual tone. The Keyneses' Harvey Road neighbour Sir Charles Villiers Stanford complained in 1904 that Browning was depleting the membership of the Athenæum club in London by signing his name for everyone he found without a seconder in the candidates' book: 'O.B. has an unfortunate way of running candidates of the Oscar Wilde type – & so there are members who blackball everyone he seconds.' Among King's undergraduates, though, the sayings and doings of the second most famous Oscar were magnified and reverberated. In his rooms, on Sunday evenings, he would entertain scholars, creative types, fit lads and noblemen. No one was fazed by a Tommy in scarlet uniform playing the clarinet there or, when 'O.B.' finished his boisterous rendition of a Mozart aria on the piano, by the clarinet-player spanking him. His erotic friendships were never soulful, but merry, hospitable bouts with young soldiers, artisans and stable-lads. He joked that he preferred to sleep at night with a muscular companion lest he was seized by sudden illness.[26]

The classicist Sir Maurice Bowra famously described his allies in Oxford university during 1920–39 as variously the Immoral Front, the Homintern and the 69th International. A generation earlier Browning cultivated a similar Immoral Front at King's, which upheld and affirmed young men like Keynes. As an undergraduate Keynes was not a favourite with Browning – perhaps he was too ugly or acerbic. But after O.B.'s reluctant retirement in 1908, he sympathized with the old man's boredom and poverty, and helped him with financial advice. In affectionate gratitude O.B. in 1918 urged Keynes, as 'the most distinguished of the young Kingsmen', to stand for the provostship and make King's 'the most intellectual college in the university'. Goldsworthy Lowes Dickinson's phrase, in his *Dictionary of National Biography* article on Browning, that O.B. during his last years in Rome 'assisted young Italians, as he had young Englishmen, towards the openings they desired', conveys the arch hints of the happy world in which Keynes dwelt at King's.[27]

Dickinson's character and ideas mattered to the young Keynes: 'I had a lot of letters from Goldie at different times, but was apt to throw them away out of dislike for the paper and the typing,' he told Dickinson's biographer E. M. Forster. Although 'Goldie' found no sexual appeal in Keynes, his influence helped to turn the Apostles into an adjunct of Cambridge's Immoral Front and thus to disinhibit its younger members such as Keynes. He was a masochist who yearned to be trampled by the boots of strapping young men of normal tastes but extra-normal kindness. The earliest of these obliging friends was Roger Fry, an Apostle of unfaltering heterosexuality. 'Sex of course is one long muddle, and I suppose always will and must be,' Dickinson later wrote to Fry. He was then preparing his memoir of another Apostle, McTaggart, who, said

Dickinson, 'had a *nonsexual ideal passion for men*, but sexually only for women'.[28]

The Apostles' notion that the love of man for man, when it precluded sexual acts, surpassed the love of man for woman was known as 'Higher Sodomy'. They considered that sexual activity was abasing, which is why they coined the phrase 'Lower Sodomy' to indicate sexual acts between men. Many of the Edwardian Apostles were sexually abstinent, which exacted as heavy a tax on their nerves and happiness as Luxmoore's idealization of beauty at Eton. At Trinity, for example, G. H. Hardy seems to have been a practitioner of the higher sodomy with Russell Gaye, who held a temporary classics fellowship there. In 1909, aged thirty-one, Gaye was found by his bed-maker in his college rooms, having shot himself in the mouth. Lytton Strachey attributed the suicide to Gaye's mortification at failing to convert his fellowship into a permanent post, and to stress in his relationship with Hardy. James Strachey described Hardy's Trinity rooms as they looked in 1911: 'There's an appalling life size head of the Dear Departed over the mantelpiece with an eye that one's forever catching. The whole suite has the air of a mortuary chapel and I felt sure that the drawers contained endless love letters and relics. I only ventured to open one – and found a pair of poor Gaye's fives-gloves, and a cricket ball.' Remnants and keepsakes seemed safer to some Edwardians than flesh on flesh.[29]

Keynes began at King's as a higher sodomite. He recorded no sexual contacts in 1903–5. With his friends discussing sex incessantly, this felt frustrating and futile. As the young Apostle and Trinity mathematician Harry Norton lamented to him, after a reading-party with the economist Ralph Hawtrey and Arthur Hobhouse, 'we all talk of sodomy & fornication & none of us have any practical knowledge of either carnal act'. In his paper entitled 'Modern Civilisation', delivered to the Apostles in 1905, Keynes criticized the brotherhood for insular theorizing and for unadventurous libidos. 'We cannot', he urged, 'ignore the outside world, [nor] real life – London and New York and Paris and Vienna, where fortunes are made and tragedies enacted, where men really bugger and go to prison for it, where some are hungry and others are cruel and rapacious, not because they are wicked, but because they are in the grip of the machine.' Just as at Eton he and Knox had determined to expand their experiences and test their reactions together, so he was preparing for further exploratory advances.[30]

Keynes's timid paces began in 1905 when he helped to secure Hobhouse's election as an Apostle, and then spent three weeks with him at Truro cramming for examinations: they indulged intense emotions together, but remained chaste. Strachey, who was infatuated by the boy, felt supplanted by Keynes, against whom for months he evinced virulent, demented loathing. Despite these tantrums, when a few months later Strachey's closest friend at Trinity, Leonard Woolf, went to Ceylon, Keynes was promoted to the role of Strachey's chief confidant. Around the same time Hobhouse became the boyfriend of Strachey's cousin Duncan Grant, with whom he spent rapturous summer weeks in Scotland. Hobhouse, however, had to hide his affections from his suspicious, controlling mother, and halted their activities after Grant's ardent pleadings were overheard by a butler. The cousins Strachey and Grant had previously enjoyed sexual exchanges together: for Grant their tussles were simple fun; but for Strachey, 'I kissed Duncan for the first time – oh! it was hardly a kiss – and plunged into a sea of passion.'[31]

These Strachey–Grant–Hobhouse manoeuvres preceded Keynes's overdue relinquishment of the higher sodomy. During 1906 he had three sexual partners: Lytton Strachey, the latter's younger brother James, and Hobhouse. They made a safe quartet, all of them Apostles, who kept one another's secrets. They were, in this phase, experimenters, who knew that if experiments are to have value, they must be repeated and refined. Neither Keynes nor Hobhouse considered themselves to be effeminate. Only Hobhouse was handsome.

Lytton Strachey was tall, skinny, ungainly, bespectacled, with a beaky nose, shrill voice, unkempt reddish beard, lank hair and an air of debility. He yearned to prove his genius, but feared that he was a fool or, worse still, ordinary. Perhaps to expunge any taint of ordinariness, he was self-dramatizing. He had an affinity with other Cambridge puritans who felt it was impermissible to enjoy pleasure without agonized soul-searching. His temperament was dogmatic yet irresolute. Although he demanded sincerity in others, he had a forte for self-deception. Neither Strachey nor Keynes could forget their physical inferiority; but Keynes did not submit, as Strachey did, to self-victimization. Strachey was astounded if a younger man responded to anyone as unappetizing, if not absurd, as him. He reacted with precarious neediness, with disabling insecurity, with self-mortifying, theatrical misery. His bodily discomfort held him captive. By contrast, from the age of twenty-four or so, Keynes set out to enjoy his body, even if it looked repugnant, rather than accept a life sentence of solitary confinement within it.

The fact that Lytton Strachey was a vivid, inveterate letter-writer has pushed him unduly to prominence in the Keynesian narrative. It is true that his allegiances, jokes, gossip, jealousy, histrionics and spite marked Keynes's life before 1920. Yet there were other men, admittedly less articulate, who mattered to Keynes, and who were more generous in their influence. Strachey was the good friend who did Keynes most harm. He tried to spoil Keynes's happiness during the most important male love affair of his life. In talk with their mutual friends he scratched at Keynes with feline claws and left wounds that festered: he depicted him as selfish, greedy, coarse and sexually mechanical. Strachey's jibes at Keynes's collusion with the wartime government smarted too. He envied, though he affected to despise, the Whitehall officials with whom Keynes mixed: 'those infinitely cultivated and embittered eunuchs', he called them against the background din of japanned pots insulting black kettles.[32]

James Strachey (the thirteenth child in his family, born when his father was seventy and his mother forty-four) was pallid, flimsy and epicene. Keynes regarded him as a winning proselytizer for homosexuality among Edwardian undergraduates. As one example of his reach, he was in 1909 invited by Keynes for Sunday parental lunch in Harvey Road. Another guest was George Mallory, who fifteen years later became an English hero second only to Scott of the Antarctic when he perished near the summit of Everest. Mallory did not match the Harvey Road measurement of a first-class mind – he thought Ibsen was an English dramatist – but James Strachey and Mallory fell for one another. They spent six months communing, exploring their emotions and stroking one another's faces in public before consummating their affair in July.

James Strachey met Rupert Brooke at the age of ten: they were best friends at preparatory school; were separated when they went to different schools aged thirteen; but were reunited at Cambridge in 1906. When Geoffrey Keynes, as Brooke's literary executor, edited and published Brooke's correspondence in 1968, he excluded the poet's remarkable exchanges with Strachey, which were not published for another thirty years. Their voluminous letters chronicle an ardent but sexually unconsummated relationship at Cambridge and afterwards: Strachey, normally objective about life, is fervent, possessive and vulnerable towards Brooke; Brooke's responses are alternately demure, obscene, patronizing and unkindly teasing. Brooke, who felt embarrassed by his virginity at the age of twenty-two, went to bed one night in 1909, not with his adoring suitor, but with an amenable young man called Denham

Russell-Smith – having calculated that it would be easier to have sex with a young man than with a young woman. 'I wanted to have some fun, &, still more, to see what it was *like*, and to do away with the shame … of being a virgin,' he told Strachey. 'I thought, I shall know something of all that James & Norton & Maynard & Lytton know & hold over me.' The experiment, and James Strachey's frequent talk of his experiences, doubtless shaped the lines in Brooke's poem 'The Great Lover': 'the cool kindliness of sheets, that soon / Smooth away trouble; and the rough male kiss / Of blankets.'[33]

James Strachey was sacked from his job as assistant editor of the *Spectator* when he refused to register his availability for military service under Lord Derby's wartime recruitment scheme of 1915. He began to cohabit with a manly, deep-voiced woman in 1919: the couple underwent psychoanalysis by Sigmund Freud in 1920–2, and subsequently translated and edited twenty-four volumes of Freud's psychoanalytical works. When Keynes described Strachey to the Apostles in 1921 as 'being disintegrated at the hands of Professor Freud, rendered immortal by Professor Steinach, and being fitted out with a more than ordinarily complete sex apparatus at the expense of the poorer classes of Vienna', he was making a Keynesian topical joke. Eugen Steinach was a physician who promoted vasectomies as a means of rejuvenation: a satisfied patient, who had paid £700 for a Steinach vasectomy, had a month before booked the Royal Albert Hall to give a lecture entitled 'How I Was Made Twenty Years Younger', but dropped dead just before going to the podium.[34]

Keynes continued to have sexual encounters with James and Lytton Strachey throughout 1906–8, and indeed sexual activity with the former continued into 1909. This was more than many Cambridge contemporaries achieved, although their earnest prattle about sex continued day and night. One evening in 1908 Keynes attended a talk given to the university's Fabian Society by a King's classics scholar who was later known as Arthur Waley. 'A dreadful, silly, maundering paper, followed by a blithering speech from Daddy Dalton,' he reported to Grant (his disdain for Hugh Dalton as a bumptious undergraduate tinged his later estimate of Dalton both as an economist and as a Labour minister). 'In spite of the serried ranks of females, the paper was chiefly about sodomy which is called "the passionate love of comrades".' Each generation was prone to think that homosexuality was more prevalent than in the preceding age: Keynes, recently returned to King's after his stint at the India Office, felt 'the thing has grown in leaps and bounds in my two years of absence and practically everybody in Cambridge … is an open and avowed sodomite.'[35]

In his first week as an undergraduate Keynes had befriended a fellow King's freshman called Charles Fay. He liked Fay – a sturdy youth who played rugby for Lancashire – for his 'hearty, broad-bottomed wit', for talking with 'superb inconsequence' and for his eager, random curiosity about people and places. Fay, who left Cambridge in 1906 to become a research student at the London School of Economics, seems to have been the friend who nudged Keynes towards questing for men in London. 'I am off to dine at a low sodomitical haunt in Soho which Fay has discovered, where guardsmen offer their services at half a crown a bottom,' Keynes trilled to Lytton Strachey in 1906. 'This seems to me a sordid oriental vice without warrant in Hellenic literature; I haven't found any philosopher who thought it the part of a sage.' This was some ten years after the Wilde trials, but he assured Strachey, 'so long as no one has anything to do with the lower classes or people off the streets, there is not a scrap of risk – or hardly a scrap.'[36]

The sexual statistics for the period before 1916, which Keynes compiled and preserved, record four encounters between 13 May and 12 August 1906, and roughly the same hit-rate during 1907. His partners were presumably the Stracheys and Hobhouse rather than guardsmen in Soho. From May 1908 to February 1909 he had sixty-one encounters: mainly with Grant, but some still with Stracheys. After renting his own London bedroom in Fitzroy Square, he became emboldened, trawled the haunts to which Fay had alerted him and picked up young men off the streets. He loved the onrush of the pavements, and making eye-contact with the one person in a hundred who was not hastening by with scared eyes downcast towards their feet. From February 1909 until February 1910 he had sixty-five encounters: some months later the young King's economist and Apostle Gerald Shove warned that, unless he kept his taste for picking-up working-class Londoners within bounds, he would end up in the dock. There were twenty-six encounters in the same period 1910–11; thirty-nine in 1911–12. 'Nothing,' he told Ottoline Morrell, 'absolutely nothing, pays in love like perseverance.'[37]

How did he meet his partners? Offering or lighting cigarettes, asking the time of day, standing side by side gazing into shop windows (the duller the contents, the better the sexual prospects), spotting a young man with his fingers crossed or with both hands crossed behind his back, friendly glances at passers-by – these were discreet openings to sexual overtures. There were numerous pick-up points in London: the bronze statue of Achilles, showing naked muscles and an adamant look, near Lover's Walk at Hyde Park Corner, was popular (not least for its proximity to the Horse Guards' barracks). There were twenty-five public baths, ranging downwards in cost from the Savoy Turkish Baths in Jermyn Street and the basement amenities of the Imperial Hotel in Russell Square to those in Whitechapel and Bermondsey. Frank sexual approaches and uninhibited responses, without fear of complaints or arrest, were possible in most sauna-baths: it was enough to watch the movements of other men's eyes, and to see whom their looks were following, to discover whom it was safe to accost. The Jermyn Street baths were also conveniently located for those who preferred to scrutinize younger men, with towels girding their loins, before offering to take them for tea at Lyons Corner House or home for bed.

These forays were fun for Keynes. But he retained an ironical curiosity about himself and his partners; liked to quantify and analyse his experiences; and brought his love of classification, first learnt in stamp-collecting with his father, later exemplified in his cataloguing as a bibliophile, to his sex life. Accordingly, he kept lists of his pick-ups, sometimes specifying nationality as with foreign stamps, and recording other descriptive features, as if to note Elzevir editions, Baskerville typeface, blue morocco binding, duodecimo pages, mottled paper:

Stable Boy of Park Lane
The Swede of the National Gallery
The American of Victoria Street
The Sculptor of Florence
The Baron of Mentone
The Soldier of the Baths
The Bootmaker of Bordeaux
The Art dealer on the Quays
The French Conscript
The Shoemaker of the Hague
The young American near the British Museum
The young man in the Park
The Medical Student
The beautiful young man in the P. shed
The clergyman
The chemist's boy of Paris

The Irish nobleman of the Whitechapel Baths
The Blackmailer
The Actor of Whitechapel
Sixteen year old under Etna
Lift boy of Vauxhall
Jewboy
Grand Duke Cyril of the Paris Baths.[38]

Grand Duke Cyril is presumably Keynes's soubriquet for a man who was either haughty or *très bien monté*. It is more than improbable that Keynes had an encounter with the authentic Grand Duke, who became the senior Romanov claimant to Russia's imperial throne after the massacres of 1917. The cosmopolitanism of this preceding list – Americans, Frenchmen, Italians, a Dutchman and a Swede if not a genuine Russian – shows that national distinctions meant less in this sexual market than in other contemporary spheres. Each generation had its own test questions for sounding the availability of foreign men whom they met: the German baron in Christopher Isherwood's *Mr Norris Changes Trains* asks the young Englishman, do you know Naples, how are the Horse Guards, have you read *Winnie the Pooh*?

Naturally Keynes paid on some occasions. One September night in 1911 he went strolling in London and brought a youth to his Bloomsbury room. His pick-up told him that boys were sparser than usual because policemen had been detaining them on the streets. The police had been goaded to action by the previous Sunday's assembly at Speaker's Corner, by the Marble Arch, where soap-box orators had decried 'hundreds of painted boys fighting the women for a living'. This conjured up to Keynes 'a sublime scene', he told Grant. 'What a superb place London now is. But I'm afraid it must have reached or almost reached the zenith of its accomplishment.'[39]

Some London partners were given surnames in Keynes's lists: Ives, Erskine and Bonnyman, for example; and they are worth attention.

Ives was George Ives, the Primrose Hill penal reformer and campaigner against sexual taboos, who was sixteen years older than Keynes. He had been an undergraduate at Cambridge, which he often revisited at weekends. Oscar Browning professed devotion to him, and he was a friend of many men known to Keynes – Arthur Benson, Lowes Dickinson, Magnus Hirschfeld, Robert Ross, Jack Sheppard, Esmé Wingfield-Stratford, John Withers and an Austrian-Dutch undergraduate at Trinity named Ernst Goldschmidt who had once worked as an expensive Vienna rent-boy. Ives was an ardent cricketer, who played in teams organized by Arthur Conan Doyle and J. M. Barrie, and was supposedly a model for Willie Hornung's fictional gentleman-thief Raffles. He had a broad, endearing smile, which got him likened to the Cheshire cat. His fervent belief that sexual liberation would improve human nature and accelerate social progress made him seem in 1906 either 'an optimist lost in the glamour of the Future' or 'a Pagan missionary, looking towards dead cities [Sodom and Gomorrah] for a cult'. He liked prowling in dark recesses of public parks, and hankered for London to be provided with a 'spoonitor-ium' – a bushy Arcadia where young people and lovers could disport without fear of arrest for public indecency. He venerated the memory of Oscar Wilde, whom he had known, and advocated repeal of the law which had sent Wilde to prison when Keynes was twelve.

In short doses Ives was a winning character, but his voluminous diaries reveal him as self-obsessed, histrionic, platitudinous, a lovelorn and mawkish lecher, timid and yet longing for destiny to call him to greatness. He could be absurd, travelling in crowded railway-carriages with a silk handkerchief over his face to preserve his aloofness, and finicky ('I utterly refuse to mix with the common herd, and always have. Nice people occur in every social scale'). He disapproved of frivolity (unlike Keynes, he hated dancing and dancers), and believed that women, liking to be tyrannized by male brutes, were happiest in harems. Ives was avid in devouring newspapers, and compiled forty-five volumes of newspaper cuttings, many of them concerned with sexual policing, judicial prejudice, parapsychology and human absurdity. Keynes, who read all the criminal reports and smutty stories in *Reynold's News*, would have been delighted if shown the black and gold albums that Ives kept.[40]

David Erskine was the laird of Linlathen, outside Dundee, and scion of a family that had graced Scotland's Enlightenment. He was seven years older than Keynes, served as Liberal MP for West Perthshire in 1906–10, and was chairman of the trustees of the National Gallery of Scotland from 1908 until his death in 1922. 'His stalwart figure might have been that of a typical Norse hero, and his sunny, cheerful presence was ever welcome,' said an obituarist. 'Soon after leaving Harrow, he spent some time in France and Germany, thus early encouraging his love of art and travel, which were perhaps hereditary tastes and certainly two of his main interests.' Like many of Keynes's sexual partners he was the reverse of self-seeking or immodest. Indeed, his character sounds like that of a dilettante version of Grant: 'tolerant judgment … delicate consideration, and … unselfish nature' were his governing traits. Erskine was the sort of partner who might have been encountered in the Jermyn Street baths.[41]

So, too, was Charles Bonnyman, a captain in the Duke of Cornwall's Light Infantry. In May 1911, at the age of twenty-nine, within a year or so of meeting Keynes, Bonnyman took a fatal dose of potassium cyanide in Hyde Park. His suicide occurred a fortnight after the *London Gazette* had published a notice stating that he had relinquished his commission in the army. The coroner's inquest was told that Bonnyman had been dismissed from his regiment on account of a kidney stone, was appealing against his dismissal and was distressed that people might think that he had been cashiered on other grounds. Perhaps his sexual inclination had been betrayed to his commanding officer and talk of the kidney stone was intended to save his family from disgrace. Reports of the inquest suggest a concerted attempt to minimize discussion. Twentieth-century physicians often reported that sodomites had an inherent tendency to suicide without reflecting that the vulnerability of men like Bonnyman, facing criminal sanctions or wrecked careers, herded them into isolated despair from which only death brought release.[42]

All these preceding men were bits of fun – although Bonnyman's death agonies in Hyde Park were not a happy sequel. Much more than fun – indeed the supreme male love of Keynes's life – was Duncan Grant. Eighteen months younger than Keynes, he had lived with the Strachey family while he was a day-boy at St Paul's School, and then used a legacy of £100 to study art in Paris in 1906–7. The affair between Grant and Keynes began in June 1908. They continued to have friendly sex until at least 1915, although the intensity of their meetings dwindled in 1909 chiefly because Grant became jaded by monogamy, secondarily because Keynes cherished Cambridge while Grant thrived in London, and perhaps also because Keynes's disheartening shows of intellectual superiority sometimes made Grant pettish. 'The Idiot', Virginia Woolf called Grant – meaning a holy fool or divine simpleton of the Russian sort. He was ill-educated, scatter-brained, disorganized, with limited numeracy, but shrewd and intelligent. Although moody, he was never unmannerly without intention. He loved music and dance as much as pictorial art. He was a delicious tease.

'Duncan was the most entertaining companion I have ever known,' recorded his lover Bunny Garnett – who later married Grant's daughter.

> He was intensely observant and amused and interested in everything he saw: and the things he saw were especially those to which the majority of people are blind. One only had to walk down the street with him to find this out. Duncan's eyes were always roving; he would notice a woman brushing her hair in front of a second-floor window, or a cat stealing fish on a basement table while the cook's back was turned: all the little dramas which were going on were instantly perceived, and they delighted him.

Grant's vision was watchful, percipient and with an arresting slant: it enlivened Keynes's scrutiny of the universe, as passages in his writings demonstrate over and again.[43]

Like many painters and sculptors Grant was a good listener. His judgements were magnanimous and sincere. He became the most important man in Keynes's life, as Lydia Lopokova was the most important woman. The painter and the dancer had similar sensibilities: they were responsive, instinctual, imaginative, sympathetic, astute and unstudied. Keynes saw rare integrity in each of them, and liked to be protective of them. One of Grant's greatest gifts to Keynes is seldom noticed. The two men were bound together in their sexual imaginations as men who have had sex together for seven years always must be. If it had not been for the example of Grant's fulfilling affair with Vanessa Bell, which produced the child whom Garnett married, it is doubtful that Keynes would have been inspired to pursue, set up home with and marry Lopokova. Without her, he would have been less happy in his forties; without her, his great academic work might not have been accomplished in his fifties;

and without her vigilant love, he must have died years before he did.

Lytton Strachey screamed like a herring gull when he discovered that his ex-boyfriend Duncan Grant had become Keynes's lover. 'Oh heaven! heaven! the thought recoils, and I find myself shrieking and raving,' he wrote to his brother James on 15 July 1908 after a confrontation with Keynes, who, he claimed, had 'come to me reeking with that semen' spent on Grant. Imagining Keynes coupling with Grant pitched him into 'wretched agony'. He flinched at the memory of 'that spectre grinning with amusement, and retailing to me how well it had been done, and the narrow escapes, and all the statistical details – ugh!' Keynes and Strachey met again a week later with similarly stagey effects. 'It went off on the whole as well as might have been expected,' the latter reported. 'He wept, and I had an erection, and that was all.' Through all these storms James tried to commiserate with his brother, 'whom the Universe tortures quite incredibly', as he told Brooke.[44]

These scenes did not succeed in wrecking Keynes's happiness. 'Dear, dear Duncan I love you very much,' Keynes wrote on 28 July: 'if I could kiss you and hold your hand I should be perfectly happy.' Grant was staying with his cousin Thomas Middlemore, a hardy mountaineer with sporty, hard-drinking house-guests, who had sold his Birmingham leather-goods business and Coventry bicycle-saddle factory and spent the proceeds on buying the 40,000-acre Melsetter estate in the Orkneys. 'You are the only person I feel I can speak to,' Grant replied on 2 August. 'You cannot imagine how much I want to scream sometimes here for want of being able to say something that I mean. It's not only that one's a sodomite that one has to hide but one's whole philosophy of life; one's feeling even for inanimate things I feel would shock some people.' Keynes wrote daily to Melsetter during five days that he and his sister spent with Mary Berenson at Iffley near Oxford: 'We bathe and lie naked in the sun and eat too much and hear conversations on the principles of ART and punt out on the Thames at night with the beautiful body of the punter black against the moon,' he told Grant. 'I want to see you again dreadfully and find that even in the midst of a crowd I am continually sinking into a trance and thinking about you.'[45]

Keynes was reunited with Grant on 18 August. They spent a fortnight together in a hotel at Stromness; rented a ground-floor bedroom at Orgill Farm on the isle of Hoy for several weeks; moved to Melsetter on 18 September for ten days; returned to Orgill; and did not leave Hoy until 22 October. These two months, with Grant painting and Keynes writing his *Treatise on Probability*, were blissful to both men, as Grant's tender portrait of Keynes at work attests.

During 1909 the Strachey brothers pursued a sly, deadly denigration of Keynes as a heartless lecher, greedy eater and crude-minded technician. Their target felt temporarily shunned by some Cambridge friends, and suffered more lasting damage. The denigration even reached to Ceylon, where Leonard Woolf was then working: his lifelong ambivalence towards Keynes, despite their cooperation in inter-war work, dates from this time. It was unforgivable to Lytton Strachey to be bested in love by Keynes; but hurtful, too, that Keynes prospered and fulfilled his ambitions in Cambridge while he drudged in Belsize Park as a magazine reviewer. Lytton coined the nickname Pozzo de Bongo, which alluded to a sewer and was not used affectionately. Grant, by contrast, helped to conciliate Bloomsbury friends to Keynes.

One sequel to Keynes's love affair with Grant was his cheerful romance with St George Nelson. Keynes first met this lissom, sprightly, happy seventeen-year-old when the boy was posing as a model for Grant in 1909. They became sexual partners swiftly. Francis Arthur St George Nelson had been born on St George's day in 1892, at Brockley on the south-east edge of London. His father was a commercial clerk and insurance agent, his grandfathers were respectively a cheesemonger and a farm bailiff, and his younger brother became an electrician. He grew up in meanly proportioned Deptford streets. Unusually for people of their class, his parents divorced when he was a child.

The boy, who in addition to occasional work as an artist's model joined a succession of financially precarious theatrical touring companies, deserves commemoration. He and Keynes continued to meet and live together intermittently in every year between 1909 and the outbreak of war in 1914. Keynes spent the December holidays of 1910 not at Harvey Road but with Nelson. 'What do you think I'm doing at the Victoria Commercial Hotel, Ramsgate?' he asked Grant on Christmas Eve. 'A letter came from St George yesterday asking me to come down here and stay with him, so I came, and spend my evenings in the basement of a lodging house chatting with low comedians – whose chief characteristic seems to be their extraordinary kindness.' The rest of Keynes's letter shows his humanity, his openness and his sympathies – qualities that he would never have developed so well without the sexual expertise that he had developed since sampling the haunts recommended by Charles Fay. 'Poor St George I found in rather a bad way. He has had the clap from which he's only just recovered; and weakened by that he's been suffering a great deal from toothache and a bad throat. In addition his mother has gone bankrupt and been sold up.' Nelson, he said, had been overworked and depressed.

After touring Wales, where he was always cold and wet and stopt at a different place every night, he had to hurry here where he rehearses the pantomime from 9 to 6 without meals … However he's in very good looks, with rather long hair and handsomely dressed (in complete taste); and has a great deal to recount. He's really quite unchanged after a year's adventures. His companions seem very fond of him, and call him Bubbles (or Bubs). It seems this has always been his pet name, because of his former devotion to the blowing of soap bubbles. Don't you think Bubbles a very good name for him?

While Nelson was in rehearsals, Keynes worked all morning before walking to Broadstairs in the afternoon. 'This is a most remarkable place. Lodging houses and hotels tower one above another to an incredible height against a lurid sky, and below long empty esplanades ... and a muddy sea. The streets are full of sailors home for Christmas. Everything is second or third class.'[46]

A month or so after the Ramsgate holiday James Strachey regaled Rupert Brooke with an incriminating story in which he bestowed protective aliases on Keynes (whom he called 'Leigh'), Grant ('Applegate') and Nelson ('Herbert') in case the letter was snitched. 'Herbert, though a member of the lower classes, was just seventeen, at the amiable age when one's on the turn – hoping, a little shyly, for a pair of breasts to put one's hands between, but oh! ready in one's randiness for narrower hips and shorter hair. Well, as it rained so, Leigh said one morning: "Let's go up to London for the night, Herbert, and I'll give you a woman."' The pair met Grant in the brilliantly lighted saloons of the Hôtel & Grand Café de l'Europe in Leicester Square. Nelson was attracted by a woman sipping whisky and soda, who chatted to them. She proved to be Mrs Anderson, whose husband was a physician in Brighton. She murmured to Keynes that she'd like to go to bed with Nelson: 'as for *you*, my dear, it's easy enough to see which way your tastes lie, you and your other friend' – nodding at Grant.

On the following Saturday, Mrs Anderson, Keynes and Nelson dined in a Soho restaurant before going to a nearby hotel. She wanted to watch 'you two boys having a bit of fun together'. Keynes refused from nervousness, left the hotel and strolled to the Lyons Corner House in Coventry Street: a notable congregation point for clerks, shop assistants, civil servants and workmen who could afford its low prices and wanted to meet other men (on the first floor was a Sunday tea-time venue nicknamed the Lily Pond, which was a recognized pick-up point). Outside the Corner House Keynes met a young man from Ealing wearing a bowler hat, who typified the Edwardians who 'went up West' to stroll the teeming streets at the heart of the capital, or to loiter at busy spots, hoping to pass unnoticed by the mass, but exchanging covert recognition signals with like-minded men out on the pick. Keynes and the Ealing man returned to Mrs Anderson's room, where they found the lady in a pair of stays and Nelson naked in bed except for her boa and muff. Keynes was shy at this sight, and retreated to an upstairs bedroom with his Ealing companion: 'After long embraces, they undressed and lay on the bed and embraced again for a long, long time, and copulated, and remained at last in a quiet naked ecstasy.' Then Nelson appeared in their room wrapped in a blanket, and took them downstairs, where the three men joined Mrs Anderson in bed. Although the young men were excited by her, Keynes 'was horrified; all his elevation of spirits left him' as she kissed and licked his genitalia. He lay frigid until she slung Nelson and the Ealing youngster on him: then 'he was happy again, and grew warmer, and stirred his legs, and panted a little, and was passionate at last. The six arms wreathed together, the six legs were interlaced, the kisses rained.'[47]

In 1913, when Keynes attended a conference of the British Association for the Advancement of Science in Birmingham, the lovers were reunited. They shared a bedroom in a superior public house called Bullivant's Hotel. 'I found St George last night (cured, thank God, of his disease) and he's living with me at this quasi-hotel, – though, in effect, only at night, as I desert him all day for my scientific friends,' Keynes reported to Grant. The lovers went to the theatre together, and on Saturday afternoon watched a football match between Aston Villa and Blackburn Rovers attended by 40,000 spectators. 'The scene was very much as I imagine the Coliseum,' he told Grant. 'The ground is built on the same model, – an immense oval rising all round tier above tier in about 50 rows … The crowd maintain a dull roar nearly all the time, rising into a frenzy of excitement and rage when the slightest thing happened. The match was between the two principal "league" teams of England. The local people were beaten by a team from Lancashire, who had, so I was told, "the best right wing in England, and the most expensive".' Each evening the two young men returned to Bullivant's for bed. 'Last night, when I got back, it was seething with "young laads" and their lasses slightly tipsy, – there was scarcely a customer over 25. They drink, the host told me, mainly beer and "French wines" – namely Benedictine and Cream de Ment [sic]; and the combination naturally makes them very sick, which I suppose is healthy.'[48]

This is the last documented meeting with Nelson, although Keynes certainly continued their liaison into 1914. It is likely that neither Grant nor Keynes knew Nelson's fate: gentle, frolicsome 'Bubbles' was caught in the war, sent to the Western Front (where it is hateful to imagine him) and killed on 11 September 1916 on the Somme. His name is inscribed on the war memorial at Cromer, where his mother retreated after her bankruptcy.

In his sexual adventures, as in other aspects of his public and private lives, Keynes held fast to his principle of intelligent compartmentalization. In London he met boys on the streets and strangers in sauna-baths. So far as one can tell, they were not camp, although they doubtless had discreet inflexions that indicated their interests. In his Cambridge compartment he limited affairs to younger men of his own class, whom he met in college rooms. He did not waste time, make himself conspicuous or risk adverse reactions by pursuing ambivalent, strapping, demanding types such as George Mallory. He never jeopardized his position by looking at youths from the town. Some of his Cambridge boyfriends – Francis Birrell and Nigel Farnell, for example – were effeminate. Others, such as Sidney Russell-Cooke, were simply gentle and affectionate. It is unlikely that they were as exciting as the Londoners, but softer intimacies can be pleasurable enough.

Keynes first had sex with Francis Birrell in 1910. Birrell was an undergraduate reading history at King's, six years younger than Keynes, an Old Etonian, and son of an ineffectual Liberal politician. Keynes and Birrell revived their bouts in 1913, when Birrell was working in the textile department of the Victoria & Albert Museum, and again in 1915 before Birrell, as a conscientious objector, joined the Quakers' War Victims' Relief Mission rebuilding devastated villages on the French battlefields. Birrell convinced another of Keynes's boyfriends at this time, Bunny Garnett, to join the Quaker Relief Mission: after the war, in 1920, they became partners operating as antiquarian booksellers. Birrell had a will-to-failure without being enervate. He treated the shop not as a profit-earning enterprise, but as a *salon* where he could amuse customers with his picturesque exaggerations, playful malice and provocative sallies. He had a pert face, with flitting expressions, as if interior facial strings were being pulled on a marionette. Keynes got him work as theatre critic of the *Nation*, for which he also reviewed books. He translated Diderot, and became expert on the works of Proust and Pirandello. He broadcast film reviews on BBC radio, and wrote a short, lively biography of Gladstone; but his mind raced too fast for the task of literary composition. He lacked ambition, mistrusted successful people and rejected the obvious.[49]

When Garnett brought Birrell to visit D. H. Lawrence in 1915, there was a panicky outburst of repudiation from Lawrence. 'Never bring Birrell to see me any more,' he ordered Garnett. 'There is something nasty about him, like black-beetles. He is horrible and unclean.' Lawrence knew or intuited that Garnett, then aged twenty-three, had had sexual exchanges with Keynes. 'I never myself considered Plato very wrong, or Oscar Wilde,' he explained to Garnett. 'Why is there this horrible sense of frowstiness, so repulsive, as if it came from deep inward dirt – a sort of sewer – deep in men like K?' After seeing Keynes in his King's rooms, in pyjamas and blinking with sleep, he felt repulsion. 'David, in the name of everything that is called love, leave this sect and stop this blasphemy ... Truly I didn't know it was wrong, till I saw K. that morning in Cambridge. It was one of the crises of my life. It sent me mad with misery and hostility and rage. Go away, David, and try to love a woman.'[50]

Nigel Farnell, son of an Eastbourne surgeon, and nephew of the head of an Oxford college, was three years younger than Keynes. He attended St Paul's School in Kensington at the same time as Grant and James Strachey (he was midway between the two in age). In 1906 he was sent down from Corpus Christi College, Oxford without taking a degree. He was admitted at Jesus College, Cambridge in 1907, and remained on the college books until 1910, but again failed to take a degree. James Strachey found him rather a compromising acquaintance, 'whom one really can't have about', in the Cambridge of 1908, because he wore cosmetics at a Fabian tea-party. He taught at a preparatory school in Winchester before starting as assistant master at the City of London School in January 1914. He soon left to serve as a private in the Great War, but after demobilization returned to teach English, history and French at the school until 1938. He proved a vivifying aesthete with a flair for instilling a love of literature in his pupils. The compelling effervescence of his readings and recitations, whether in prose or verse, captivated even dull youths (Shakespeare, Dickens, Hardy and

George Eliot were his favourites). Pupils relished his quirky benevolence: he studied their latent gifts, and developed an instinct for what was best in them. He was acclaimed for his zest in directing school plays, and for casting unlikely boys in parts in which they triumphed. He married in his late forties, and bequeathed his library on the arts, archaeology, the classics and music to City of London School.[51]

Farnell receded from Keynes's life, but Sidney Russell-Cooke, with whom he had intermittent sexual bouts in 1913–15, remained a lifelong friend and colleague: they lunched together on the day of Russell-Cooke's death. 'Cookie', who had been an undergraduate at King's, lived with his twice-widowed mother in a spacious villa called Bellecroft at Newport on the Isle of Wight. First married to a Liberal MP (brother of Sir Charles Dilke, whose political career was ruined by being cited in a divorce), she then married Russell-Cooke's father, who had been legal adviser to the Liberal party. There was gentle but solid affection between the two men: Keynes tried to get Russell-Cooke to accompany him on a gambling spree at Monte Carlo in 1913; Russell-Cooke sought his advice in Stock Exchange flutters. Russell-Cooke had a reputation as a yachtsman and all-round sportsman, and passed as a hale fellow in the stockbroking firm in which he became a partner.

The statistics of his sexual conquests that Keynes compiled between 1906 and 1915 were shown to selected friends, some of whom gasped. 'Maynard, the iron copulating machine', James Strachey described him to Brooke in 1909 after seeing the figures. The statistics, or a version of them, were possibly displayed in 1910, when Keynes, Lowes Dickinson and Hugh Dalton were invited to dine by Edward Dent, a Fellow of King's and a musicologist, to meet Magnus Hirschfeld, the Berlin campaigner for the decriminalization of homosexuality, who was investigating the scene in London ('particularly baths in the East End, Dent says'). 'Now his investigations have reached Cambridge. So Dickinson and I have been selected as leading cases for him to begin on!' Keynes thus became one of the 10,000 case-studies in Hirschfeld's treatise *Die Homosexualität* (1913). He may have completed one of Hirschfeld's questionnaires aimed at defining the physical and psychological traits of his sample: 'Can you easily separate your big toe from the other toes by its own force? ... Are you a good whistler, and do you like to whistle? ... During intercourse, do you imagine performing the act with another person? ... Are you talkative? Are you logical?'[52]

In 1906 Alys Russell, first wife of Bertrand Russell and sister of Mary Berenson, mustered a reading-party of young Englishmen as companions for her nieces, Karin and Ray Costelloe, at the Berenson villa, I Tatti, near Florence. The Englishmen were Geoffrey Scott, a nephew of the editor of the *Manchester Guardian*, and Maynard Keynes. Arthur Hobhouse was forbidden to join the party by his mother, who overheard her sister Beatrice Webb discussing Mary Berenson's adultery. Keynes was collected at the Uffizi Gallery, taken for tea, quizzed by Bernard Berenson about mathematics, and invited to install himself with Scott at I Tatti. Three weeks later, on Easter Monday, Mrs Berenson pictured her guest: 'Keynes was too funny, he lay curled up in a rug, all huddled together and looking indescribably wicked. He is quite a clown in his way, and now that he feels at home, he does the most ridiculous things.'[53]

The excursions and luxuries that Hobhouse had been forbidden from sharing were reported to him by Keynes. 'We have seen an incredible number of places, the laughter has been continuous and La Belle B. has treated us sumptuous.' The house-party had toured the countryside and historic towns in sybaritic motor-cars. 'The boys are good looking – but only in some villages; and the whole country is lunatic with excitement over a visit of Buffalo Bill's Wild

West. Even the Franciscan friars at Assisi would speak of little else.' A child whom they stopped to ask the way said that his school had closed for the day because all the schoolmasters had gone to Perugia to see Buffalo Bill. 'So we whisked him into our car and swept him along fourteen miles across the plain to Perugia and landed him at the gates of the Wild West with 5 francs in his hand.' (This was in the happy heyday of the Latin Monetary Union, when the silver and gold coins of Mediterranean countries, including the French franc and the Italian lira, were readily exchangeable.)[54]

That summer of 1906 Mary Berenson visited England, where she saw both Keynes and Scott. The latter confided in her about a love affair. 'I had to be very careful', she reported to her husband,

> not to encourage him in what will probably lead to disaster. So I took the line that such affections might well be beautiful and inspiring in youth but become dotty and disgusting if men persisted in them into middle age. He knew this, and cited several Dons and said he knew he must get out of it in time – but then, he said, it was so wonderful to adore a handsome, talented, beautiful youth, he wasn't sure that it might not be worth everything in life.

A flirtation had begun in Italy between Mary Berenson's daughter Ray Costelloe and Keynes. They were together in the house-party at Iffley which Keynes joined before going to the Orkneys. He was elated by irrepressible thoughts of Grant, for the young woman 'gathered from his talk, which is sometimes rather wild and mystical, the whole doctrine of the peculiar *culte* to which he and Scott belong.'[55]

In the spring of 1907 Mary Berenson summoned Scott after receiving an anonymous letter, in disguised handwriting, with an Oxford postmark. It warned against letting her 'innocent' daughters associate with Scott, 'known in Oxford as a disciple of the deplorable practices of Oscar Wilde', and added that 'under the pretence of "Greek fiendships" [sic]' some of Scott's friends 'cloak the most unnatural & shocking form of vice'. In alarm at the risk of criminal prosecution, but with studied flippancy, Scott informed Keynes: 'Funny thing – what? You & I will pick oakum yet.* Or if you get off I look to you to raise the fuss in the Press & to petition the Home Secretary.'[56]

Keynes tried to persuade himself that Mary Berenson's mischievous brother Logan Pearsall Smith was responsible. In fact, her housekeeper at the rented Iffley house had sent the denunciation. 'One of the recurrent scares which terrify you more than me has occurred,' Keynes told Lytton Strachey on India Office notepaper. 'It just shows how damned careful one has to be … and in this respect one is so hopelessly in the hands of others.' Two days later he wrote again to Strachey from his Whitehall desk. 'Worse and worse – at least so it seems to me. I have never felt more nervous.' It had become obvious from Mary Berenson's letters to Scott that she 'knows about me. This is news: I have always been a model of discretion – neither word nor hint.' Moreover, 'La B has told Ray and goodness knows who else besides.' In saying this, he underestimated both mother and daughter, to whom his interests had become obvious respectively at I Tatti and Iffley. 'I have no doubt now, that, although they are too polite to mention it, everybody in England is perfectly well aware of everything. Well, I suppose it is a fair penalty for going about with such people. But – in the present state of public opinion – damn and damn and damn.'[57]

The only solid upshot of this affair was that Alys Russell, hearing that Scott, and probably Keynes, was 'a sod', struck them off her visiting list. Not everyone was as silly. Vanessa Bell, after spending

---

* Picking oakum was a monotonous and humiliating chore imposed on inmates of Victorian prisons.

a country weekend with him at Easter of 1914, imagined him enjoying 'all the ecstatic preliminaries of Sucking Sodomy' before 'buggering one or more of the young men whom we left for you'. Similarly, his sexual rapacity was obvious to Ottoline Morrell. 'That satyr Keynes, greedy of work, fame, influence, domination, admiration; *soigné* and attractive, and desirous of being attractive, very sympathetic to the ambitions of young men', she called him in 1915.[58]

Scott exemplified the hazard – one of which Keynes was at small risk – of a man wasting his energies chasing after other men and therefore, in the Apostles' parlance, leaving no footprints with his work. Virginia Woolf first met Scott at Florence in 1909, and then did not see him for sixteen years. In the interval, he acquired 'the distinguished face of a failure', she noted, and came to resemble all the 'other "brilliant" young men, who remain "brilliant" & young well into their 40ties [sic] & never do anything to prove it'. Scott, like Farnell, Birrell and other Keynesian friends such as Swithinbank, was intelligent, cultured, insightful, but too pliable and self-conscious to impress the world. Oscar Wilde's short story, 'The Remarkable Rocket', is a parable of their pathos. Hard work saved Keynes from this.[59]

Wars provide opportunities for casual sexual encounters between men; but there were mounting suspicions, dangers and antipathies for Keynes. In September 1914 he took a set of rooms at 10 Great Ormond Street in Bloomsbury. There he went to bed with Birrell and Garnett, and took some casual pick-ups. His landlord or landlady became aware of his habits, and made blackmailing hints: as a result, in February 1915, he moved to a nearby house of his own at 3 Gower Street. There was another disturbing incident in 1917 when Keynes was staying in Paris as part of a delegation led by Balfour, Reading and Northcliffe. He was intercepted at the Hôtel de Crillon by a young man sporting a French aviator's uniform, and resisted an invitation to the bedroom of the tempting pilot, whom he suspected of being a German agent set on compromising him. Some months later, amid lurid publicity, a disreputable MP named Pemberton-Billing set himself up as a vigilante rampaging against homosexuality and espionage. Clarence Barron, publisher of the *Wall Street Journal*, who visited London in 1918, had an interview with 'Professor Keynes of the British Treasury' on the subject of the exorbitant levels of tax levied on the Duchess of Marlborough, Lord Astor and other American millionaires resident in England. Keynes was 'a kind of Socialist', the San Francisco-born London hostess Lady Cunard had forewarned Barron, who commented after meeting the so-called professor, 'My judgment is that he is a Socialist of the type that does not believe in the family.' ('Lady Cunard is rather a sport, with her frankly lower-class bounce,' wrote Lytton Strachey. 'She takes to me, she says, for the sake of that dear nice Bernard Keynes, who's such an intimate friend of hers.') The queer-hating Robert Vansittart, who saw much of Keynes during 1919, recalled: 'I liked him, but not much; he smelled of Bloomsbury.'[60]

The perils of bachelor life in Bloomsbury were discovered by Sydney Cope Morgan, the barrister who was the Liberal parliamentary candidate instead of Florence Keynes at Cambridge in 1924. He lived in Woburn Place, and one night, wearing evening-dress after dinner, he visited the dark urinals in Percy Mews. There a half-undressed young man, whom he mistook for a 'tough', but who was an off-duty police constable and (the newspapers insisted) 'an old public-schoolboy', accused him of indecent assault and dragged him all the way to Oxford Street struggling and protesting. At one point another man, who had followed the wrestling pair from the urinal, where he had been loitering, broke Cope Morgan free from the constable's clutches. After two court appearances and a masterly defence, the barrister was acquitted: 'if he has friends who alter their relationships to him following the misfortune of this charge', declared the magistrate, 'he is as well without them, for they are fools'. Despite coming close to ruin, Cope Morgan later became leader of the Parliamentary Bar.[61]

Various wartime circumstances shifted the direction of Keynes's affections. As previously signalled, the sexual excitements between Vanessa Bell and Duncan Grant, which had begun in 1915 when Keynes was still going to bed with Grant, were doubtless crucial in arousing his imagination with bisexual curiosity. During the war years, there were no undergraduates to interest him in Cambridge: previous boyfriends, and congenial male beauties, were away in the armed forces, or dispersed in rural districts where they laboured on farms. Grant's former lover Adrian Stephen (Virginia Woolf's brother) married Mary Berenson's daughter Karin Costelloe in 1914. Gerald Shove, who had been in love with Rupert Brooke, and a lover of Birrell and Ferenc Békássy, married Virginia Woolf's niece, Fredegond Maitland, in 1915. Lytton Strachey was drawn to Dora Carrington, with whom in 1916 he went to live in a mill-house (Keynes contributed £20 a year towards the rent). In 1917 Geoffrey Keynes married Margaret Darwin (then working in an Admiralty department which deciphered German codes). Geoffrey Scott had an unsettled affair with Mary Berenson followed by an unsuccessful marriage with one of her Tuscan neighbours in 1918. Grant fathered Vanessa Bell's daughter Angelica, who was born on Christmas day of 1918. After the androgynous couple of James Strachey and Alix Sargant-Florence had married in 1920, Fredegond and Gerald Shove assured them that it was 'such a comfort to be married', so 'convenient', without making 'any difference' to basic feelings. Bunny Garnett, the former lover of both Keynes and Grant, married in 1921. 'Logic, like lyrical poetry, is no employment for the middle-aged,' Keynes wrote in 1930: so, too, it seemed to be thought, is sodomy.[62]

Keynes first had sex with a woman – presumably paying money for the experience – at Alexandria in 1913. Although he liked Ray Costelloe and other young women from the intelligentsia, they were too similar in their patterns and colour, and too familiar in their histories, to fascinate him. Then, two months before the end of the war, he first saw the Russian ballerina Lydia Lopokova. She was fathoms deep in exoticism and furlongs distant from any blue-stocking. Her unprecedented originality – her difference from all he knew – intrigued him.

Born in 1891, Lopokova was the daughter of a handsome, almost illiterate peasant, who served as a soldier, learnt German and became a well-tipped usher at the best theatre in St Petersburg. In relative prosperity, he became drunken, foul-mouthed and loutish: his death in 1912 was hastened by alcoholism. It was, however, his pushing that got Lopokova enrolled in the Imperial Theatre School in 1901. She first danced with Nijinsky in 1905, joined Diaghilev's Ballets Russes in 1910 and became a favourite of the impresario during a European tour. After conquering Paris in the lead role in Stravinsky's *The Firebird* choreographed by Fokine, she was lured by lavish fees to dance in the United States, where she worked for five years. The theatre critic Heywood Broun wanted to marry her and became her lover; but on a rash impulse, in 1916, at Minneapolis, she underwent a secret marriage ceremony with Diaghilev's sleek business manager, Randolfo Barocchi, whose divorce from his previous wife had not yet been finalized. The marriage soon failed: during the Spanish tour by the Ballets Russes in 1916–17, Lopokova probably slept with Stravinsky. She definitively separated from Barocchi, possibly after he stole her wages. Vague tales hint that she became pregnant by a Russian officer.[63]

Lopokova reached England for the first time in August 1918. She delighted London balletomanes when the Ballets Russes season opened a month later with *Cléopâtre* and *Les Femmes de bonne humeur*: 'the personification of gaiety and spontaneity', as Osbert Sitwell recalled, 'her wit entered into every gesture'. Keynes first went to see the Ballets Russes in September, kept returning to the spectacle, and began visiting 'Loppy' in her back-stage dressing-room after performances. But his flirtation with the Russian dancer made no advance for three years. Then, in November 1921, Diaghilev staged, at the Alhambra in London, Petipa's *The Sleeping Beauty* (retitled *The Sleeping Princess*) to the music of Tchaikovsky. Lopokova danced two secondary parts, the Lilac Fairy and Princess Florine, and undertook limited performances as Aurora. London audiences wanted modernism from the Ballets Russes, not a nine-teenth-century treasure of the imperial Russian repertoire, so the production was a financial failure: it ended months early in February 1922. Keynes, however, took his brother to meet Lopokova in her dressing-room after the opening night, and returned over and over again. In December he told Vanessa Bell that he was 'very much in love' with the dancer: 'she seems to be perfect in every way'. This was information, too, for Duncan Grant, with whom Vanessa Bell was wintering in St Tropez. His letter to them presaged a love affair every bit as improbable as theirs.[64]

There was perhaps another influence at work. In mid-December 1921 his ex-lover and continuing friend Sidney Russell-Cooke announced his engagement to marry Helen Smith, the only child of the captain of the *Titanic*. The couple were quickly married, in January 1922, at a smart Mayfair church. Russell-Cooke's choice of best man was significant: Sir Campbell Stuart, 'a pansy' in the words of Hugh Gaitskell, 'a very odd fish indeed' in the words of C. P. Snow. Inviting Keynes to meet his fiancée, Russell-Cooke wrote: 'She's certainly lovely, reasonably intelligent, some money (more in prospect), damn randy & good tempered. In addition she is ambitious & adventurous.' The couple had two children. In July 1930, while his wife was in a nursing-home, Russell-Cooke lunched with Keynes in London. 'He seemed in absolutely good spirits,' Keynes told Jack Sheppard after hearing that a few hours later their friend had been killed by a gun-shot wound to the abdomen in his chambers in King's Bench Walk. He was 'much upset by poor Cookie's death. It's difficult in such a case to believe in an accident, but I really think it is the more probable explanation.' The suggestion by Skidelsky that Russell-Cooke shot himself after sustaining Stock Exchange losses must be wrong: he left an estate exceeding £120,000. The fact that Russell-Cooke had been shell-shocked was mentioned at the inquest; but his happy lunch, hours before his death, with an ex-lover who continued to matter to him, raises the possibility that he shot himself in a lonely paroxysm of miserable regrets at his married life.[65]

Keynes was in 1921 deep in his last romance with a man: in this case, a bright, handsome youngster, fourteen years his junior, who was known as Sebastian Sprott. Sprott had reacted against a harsh boarding-school by becoming a dashing, quick-witted aesthete when he started as a Cambridge undergraduate in the first post-war intake of 1919. He was elected to the Apostles in 1920, graduated with a double first in moral sciences in 1922, and then obtained work in the university's Psychological Laboratory. He was a protégé of both Strachey brothers, and was appointed by Forster as his literary executor. For Keynes their affair was a fling: 'shallow waters are the attraction – up to the middle, not head over ears, at my age'. For Sprott, who hoped to anchor himself in Cambridge and dreaded a provincial future, the affair was more fraught. 'A gentle, clever, courteous creature, in considerable depression as to prospects &c, but really conversable,' Arthur Benson described him after lunching together in 1924. The following year Sprott left Cambridge with sorrow to become a lecturer in psychology at University College, Nottingham, which was being expanded by the benefactions of Jesse Boot the retail chemist. In Nottingham he became a pioneering sociologist, a befriender of ex-prisoners and a sponsor of criminology as an academic subject. He resembled many of Keynes's boyfriends in being hard-working but unsoiled by ruthless ambition. Like others, he tended in adversity towards passivity.[66]

Keynes spent Christmas of 1921 staying with Lytton Strachey, Carrington and Sprott. Shortly afterwards, on a foggy Sunday, he and Lopokova went to bed together at the Waldorf Hotel, where she was living. Early in 1922 he arranged for her to move to rooms in Gordon Square a few doors from the house where he lived. His subsequent resignation from the Royal Commission on Indian Tariffs was surely prompted by his wish to stay in Bloomsbury with her rather than be separated for months while he journeyed with his fellow Commissioners to the sub-continent.

Lopokova's biographer, Judith Mackrell, concludes that the affair succeeded by its gratifying play of fingers and mouths. In their letters there are merry references to fellatio: Keynes, for example, wrote from Genoa, where he was working as special correspondent of the *Manchester Guardian*, 'I want to be foxed and gobbled abundantly. It is only half a life here, says the fountain pen to the metronome.' Lopokova makes grateful references to her lover's 'subtle fingers'. Mackrell also suggests that Keynes, as a don who valued background research, bought a copy of Marie Stopes's sex manual *Married Love*, which explained female orgasm and how a man might 'charm and stimulate' the clitoris to achieve it. As a corollary, Roy Harrod once asked Frances Partridge if it was true that Keynes inclined to premature ejaculation in penetrative sex. 'I hadn't ever been in a position to know,' she recorded, 'but had always heard so.'[67]

Throughout this time Keynes was still involved with Sprott, as Lopokova knew. The plan that the two men would spend the Easter holidays of 1923 together in north Africa roused her to protests which routed Sprott from Keynes's sex life. Soon Loppy (acting under her lover's guidance) began legal proceedings to break her ties to Barocchi. The divorce was complicated, rather than eased, by the fact that the Minneapolis marriage of 1916 was bigamous; but eventually, after wearisome and costly legal proceedings, she received the decree absolute of her divorce, and a few days later, in August 1925, at St Pancras Registry Office, she married Keynes. Grant was the only male friend invited: he took the part of Sir Campbell Stuart at the Russell-Cooke wedding and acted as best man. The couple honeymooned in a rented house in Sussex, where Wittgenstein came to stay for six days and made the bride's life miserable with his ferocious questions and rasping contempt for her. But Keynes gave his bride the best of wedding presents: a visit to her surviving family in Russia.

Generally the Bloomsbury group mixed hedonism with steady work. Lydia Keynes irritated them because she disrupted their schedules at their easels and desks. Vanessa Bell, in particular, was annoyed by her chatter, inane jokes and time-wasting, and became a cruel critic of the Russian interloper. Lytton Strachey and others were grudging too; but Virginia Woolf liked the dancer's non-cerebral influence. 'How does her mind work? Like a lark soaring; a sort of glorified instinct inspires her.' Woolf recognized, too, the reliability under the skittishness. 'Lydia is composed, & controlled. She says very sensible things.' Even so, Loppy inspired aspects of a character in Woolf's novel *Mrs Dalloway* (1925): Lucrezia Warren-Smith, the lonely Italian floundering in an uncomprehending marriage to a shell-shocked, hallucinating Englishman, who defenestrates himself from their Bloomsbury boarding-house and is impaled on spiky railings below.[68]

Lydia Keynes had a tight grasp of facts, but a pleasing way with fancies. She had none of the prevalent vinegary Bloomsbury flavour. Her puckishness relied on intentional malapropisms to jolt people out of their settled lines. Before taking her to meet Geoffrey Keynes's wife Margaret Darwin, Keynes primed her, perhaps excessively, about *On the Origin of Species*. 'So you are the granddaughter of the man who wrote *Genesis*,' she said on being introduced.[69]

In middling successful marriages involving a gay man and a straight woman one cause of discontent, or depression, is the woman's realization that what matters primarily to her sense of herself, her femininity, is valued less by her husband than her secondary characteristics. Loppy, for example, knew that Keynes liked her to dress in boyish clothes resembling a frivolous parody of a midshipman. But she was also confident that he loved and needed her above all else. Her assurance made their marriage a mutual delight. The revolution in Keynes's sexual order perhaps freed him to disarrange and then remodel other aspects of his life. He made a revealing aside when A. C. Pigou's book *Industrial Fluctuations* was published in 1927. 'Rather miserable', Keynes thought Pigou's ideas. He was busy revising his own economic principles, and moving in as different a direction as when he gave Sprott his marching-orders and committed himself to Lopokova. She was said to be the only woman ever to have kissed Pigou, whose sex life was supposedly limited to inviting young male alpinists to stay at his cottage overlooking Lake Buttermere, encouraging them to swim naked and watching through binoculars. So there is significance in Keynes's criticism to his wife of Pigou as a hidebound bachelor who had not renewed or enlivened himself by trying new lines: 'perhaps ... he should have married, his mind is dead, he just arranges in a logical order all the things we knew before'.[70]

Despite the known difficulties for ballet-dancers in bringing pregnancies to term, the Keyneses tried to conceive a child during 1926. He was a sympathetic monitor of her menstrual cycle – what she called 'a certain lunar complaint which even the best behaved women have sometimes'. In the spring of 1927 they were briefly in hopes that she was pregnant. Even Keynes's optimism was quelled by repeated disappointments: the couple had stopped discussing conception in their letters by 1928.[71]

It was characteristic of Keynes's brisk liberal humanitarianism that having got the knack of heterosexuality, he took up the cause of contraception for men and women who did not want children. Earlier, in 1907, he had been scornful to discover from a Customs manual that condoms were treated as contraband: 'presumably in order that the God-sent syphilis may prosper'. (Until the 1980s English Customs officers were instructed to treat any traveller carrying condoms in their luggage as a suspect person, and to search for drugs or other unlawful items.) Keynes advocated the easy availability of contraceptives as well as instruction in their use. Accordingly, in 1923, perhaps through the influence of his former pupil Dominick Spring Rice, who helped to run a birth-control centre in north Kensington, Keynes agreed to serve as a vice-president of the Society for Constructive Birth Control and Racial Progress, which had been founded by Marie Stopes to provide contraceptive advice to married people. Other vice-presidents included such progressive physicians as Sir Archdall Reid and Sir Arbuthnot Lane, together with Julian Huxley and Sir Anthony Hope Hawkins (author of *The Prisoner of Zenda*). However, the unstable enthusiasms of Stopes annoyed Keynes, who effaced himself from her organization. He was irritated to discover in 1939 that he was still on its letter-head as a vice-president.[72]

In Moscow in 1925 Keynes gave a lecture on 'birth control for Russia' which aroused hilarity in his communist-ridden audience. This lecture doubtless resembled his address to the Liberal Summer School at Cambridge in that same year. He urged that Liberals should break bounds by *public* discussion of 'sex questions', which were so widely discussed in *private*. As 'there are no subjects about which the general public is more interested … I cannot doubt that sex questions are about to enter the political arena', he assured fellow Liberals, who did not titter like the Muscovites. Readers of Clive Bell's polemic *On British Freedom* will have recognized phrases as well as sentiments in Keynes's speech. 'Birth control and the use of contraceptives, marriage laws, the treatment of sexual offences and abnormalities, the economic position of women, the economic position of the family – in all these matters the existing state of the law and of orthodoxy is still medieval – altogether out of touch with civilised opinion and civilised practices and with what individuals, educated and uneducated alike, say to one another in private.' These were not the minority concerns of a sophisticated elite, but urgent issues that offered 'new liberty, emancipation from the most intolerable of tyrannies' to all women. 'A party which would discuss these things openly and wisely at its meetings would discover a new and living interest in the electorate – because politics would be dealing once more with matters about which everyone wants to know and which deeply affect everyone's own life.' Contraception was an issue of women's freedom for Keynes, who also recommended in 1925 that women's pay must be regulated to ensure fairness. It took over forty years for Keynes's pioneering views to be met by legislation: male homosexuality was partially decriminalized and contraception made available to all women under the Sexual Offences and Family Planning Acts of 1967; the injustice of women's low earnings was first addressed in the Equal Pay Act of 1970.[73]

In 1929 Keynes was enlisted in support of the literary critic William Empson, who was deprived of his fellowship at Magdalene after condoms had been found in his rooms by college porters. Empson was the secretary of the Heretics, a Cambridge society which excluded Christians from membership, met to discuss religion, philosophy and art, and had elected Keynes to honorary membership. Arthur Benson had been succeeded four years earlier as Master of Magdalene by another virginal bachelor, Allen Beville Ramsay, who had been an Eton master when Keynes was a pupil. Ramsay, who had founded Eton's boy scouts troop and delighted youngsters by reciting his version of 'Little Jack Horner' in Latin, told Empson with sorrowful emphasis 'that anybody who had ever touched a French letter, no matter when or why, could never again be allowed with safety in the company of young men, because he was sure … to pollute their innocence; and this in spite of the fact that his own intellectual powers would have been destroyed'.[74]

Openness in sexual discourse rather than witless repression was what Keynes wanted. He was unrepentant when, in 1938, the *New Statesman*, of which he was chairman, was criticized by rival magazines for carrying personal advertisements that enabled men to make contacts with one another: man 'not interested in the fair sex' seeking holiday companion; 'young man of aesthetic, philosophic interests, unaffected, wants another to share *gemütlich* [homely] villa, lovely situation, above Ancona'; 'cultured young man wishes another to share modern flat … Music-lover'; 'young woman, married, travelled, adventurous but not adventuress, with happy background, no complexes; with only a restricted circle of mediocre friends, would like to meet another woman for companionship'. The *New Statesman* had become 'a recognised clearing-house for this type of "personal"', Keynes noted with satisfaction. 'I wonder how many replies are received!'[75]

In one respect, though, marriage did not improve Keynes. Back in 1907 he had gone with Charles Fay on a holiday centred on Biarritz. One excursion took him to the Val d'Aran, the only part of Catalonia on the northern side of the Pyrenees. 'As I sat in it, gazing on the irises and lilies, its waterfalls and fountains, its forest and glades, and high red battlemented cliffs with the snow mountains beyond, I heard a laugh from the top of the rock under which I lay,' he told Lytton Strachey.

> As I looked up, there was the most beautiful shepherd boy in the world, smiling and holding up my aluminium flask which I had lost and he had found. I offered him half a franc. Nanni, nanni [sic] he cried, waving it from him with a laugh and a gesture. Then we fell into conversation; and when every minute or so he discovered that I couldn't understand a word of Spanish or speak one, another roar of laughter and a glance and a smile. So he prattled on and I helped him drive his two cows with their calves about 8 miles down the valley. When we reached his father's house which was almost next door to where I was staying, he tried most desperately to explain something to me; but it was no good. Only with Fay's assistance afterwards did I discover that he was offering me a bed in his father's house at a franc a night for ever ... there was no kiss, only a hand lightly on the shoulder.

This Arcadian scene reaches to the heart of the young Keynes. Such flirtations ensured that 'he suffered fools and foolish thoughts, not gladly, but patiently and kindly', as Fay remembered him at this time.[76]

This was decreasingly true after his marriage. He had never spared his intellectual peers. 'Keynes' intellect was the sharpest and clearest that I have ever known,' said Bertrand Russell. 'Annihilating argument darted out of him with the swiftness of an adder's tongue. When I argued with him, I felt that I took my life in my hands, and I seldom emerged without feeling something of a fool.' But when Keynes halted in his intellectual onslaught for carefree interludes with a Catalonian shepherd, with sailors on the late train to Norwich, with a youth from Ealing loitering outside Lyons Corner House, with Aston Villa supporters saturating themselves with

Benedictine, he had patience with slower minds, tolerance for cloudy thought, avidity for larks. After 1925, the old captivating dalliance receded, though it never quite expired. His illness of 1937–8, and the certainty that his time was foreshortened, exacerbated the tendency of his married life: impatience with dullards and sluggards. Sir Kenneth Clark, who worked closely with Keynes in the 1940s, thought he displayed his brilliance 'too unsparingly'. He saw him, despite his kindness, 'humiliate people in a cruel way'. Keynes had the happiest of marriages, and the best of wives for him, but marital contentment narrowed his outlook and temper.[77]

This does not mean that the glee ended. Let one cameo represent over twenty years of jinx. In July 1944 Lord and Lady Keynes arrived by air at Ottawa. They were met on the tarmac by Malcolm MacDonald, the High Commissioner of Canada, together with several officials, bedecked in morning suits. Lydia Keynes alighted from the aircraft in a voluminous fur coat, and embraced MacDonald, whom she had never met before. 'O, my dear High Commissar, how are you?' she cried. 'Last night I dreamed zat I was lying in bed, and zat you were lying in my arms.' Some hours later, the High Commissar and his apparatchiks arrived in the Keyneses' hotel suite hoping to open discussions. They found the two Keyneses rummaging for the key to open his official red box where confidential papers were held securely. The search had been abandoned, and the official talks were under way, when Lady Keynes reappeared. She was clad in a short, flimsy white chemise (MacDonald hoped for underwear beneath).

In that state of near nudity she stood in apologetic manner casting a half-guilty, half-mischievous look at Keynes as she said: 'O Maynard darling, I am so sorry. You did give me ze key; and I forgot zat I hid it for safety between my little bosoms.' At that she clutched in her hands a ribbon hanging round her neck, and as she lifted it over her head raised from between her breasts – which so far as we could detect were not quite so small as she suggested – the lost article.

With Keynes chuckling, 'she blew him a kiss, turned in a ballerina's pirouette on her toes, glided through the door, and closed it behind her'.[78]

So might St George Nelson have pranced before going on stage in the Christmas pantomime at Ramsgate. Loppy was the right wife for Keynes.

CHAPTER SIX
CONNOISSEUR

One of the seven lives of Maynard Keynes was that of a connoisseur. The paramount trait of connoisseurship is discrimination. Connoisseurs need not be aristocratic, but must adopt or reject people and tastes according to a patrician sensibility that ignores the worlds of productivity and profit. Money is esteemed as a means to acquire what they value, but despised as a provider of power, showiness, luxury, over-eating or barbarous hobbies. Connoisseurs are fastidious, privileged and more ornamental than useful. Their opinions are trenchant, not insipid; but never hectoring. Spontaneity is not much prized. Connoisseurs play with their senses, memories, perceptions and instincts. They share affinities and antipathies. They adopt foreign fashions; they have their own decorum.

As an Apostle Keynes had disputed, elaborated and sharpened his answers to the ethical question: how best should humankind live? An abiding concern for him was how civilized people could use their time and abilities well, and fulfil themselves in virtuous, responsible, productive lives. All his intuitions, expertise, priorities and advice revolved around these quandaries. His lives as an economist, as an official, as a pundit, as a lover, as a patron of creativity, as a Londoner and latterly as a country gentleman might seem to be sealed in distant compartments; but they were indivisible in their ethical underpinning.

Keynes's life as a connoisseur began in 1909, when he rented a back bedroom in a ground-floor flat which Duncan Grant had leased at 21 Fitzroy Square, in the north-western corner of Bloomsbury (the front room was used by Grant as a studio). In 1911, together with Grant, Keynes became an inmate at 38 Brunswick Square – the home of Virginia Stephen and her brother Adrian. George Duckworth, the elder half-brother who had earlier molested her, was sufficiently shameless to remonstrate in prudish tones about a household containing unmarried people of opposite sexes. 'Oh, it's quite alright, George,' she replied, 'it's so near the Foundling Hospital.' This communal household was joined by Leonard Woolf, whom Virginia Stephen soon married. Keynes was allotted the ground-floor dining-room, on the walls of which Grant painted a London street scene dominated by a fallen cab-horse, the cab tilting forward on to the pavement, with the driver of the hansom perched precariously aloft.[1]

During the early war years Keynes rented Bloomsbury footholds in Great Ormond Street and Gower Street. At the latter house Keynes aimed to achieve a form of 'salon civilization', so Clive Bell reported in 1915, as an antidote to war barbarities and gloom. Bell however hoped that 'when the Barbarians come they will find something prettier than a gramophone party in corduroy trousers'. In 1916 Keynes and Jack Sheppard, a King's man who was a temporary official at the War Office and had recently been his sexual partner, moved a couple of streets eastwards in Bloomsbury to Bell's house at 46 Gordon Square. Keynes let his Gower Street house to Katherine Mansfield and Middleton Murry, who occupied the ground floor, while the painters Dorothy Brett and Dora Carrington took upper storeys. Subsequently Keynes took over the lease of 46 Gordon Square, which remained his London home until his death. The Duke of Bedford was his ground landlord: the Duke's other houses in the square had black or navy-blue front doors; number

46 signalled its distinctiveness by having vermilion paint on its front door. Later Keynes leased 47 Gordon Square, next door to his house, demolished the wall separating the adjacent first-floor drawing-rooms, and thus created a spacious new room. In this he emulated his father, who had bought the next-door house in Harvey Road and demolished a wall to create an enlarged study.[2]

These scene-shifts installed Keynes at the centre of what was called in his lifetime the Bloomsbury Set. Its thirteen core members in 1912–14 were Vanessa Bell, Virginia Woolf and Adrian Stephen – painter, novelist and future Freudian psychoanalyst respectively; the novelists Morgan Forster and Molly MacCarthy; the novelist turned political commentator and literary editor Leonard Woolf; the bellettrist Lytton Strachey; the painters Duncan Grant and Roger Fry; the critics Clive Bell and Desmond MacCarthy; Keynes; and Saxon Sydney-Turner, now a cultivated Treasury official with the manner of an automaton. Most of them gelled together by sharing households or living in proximity in Bloomsbury: the MacCarthys lived in Chelsea; otherwise even Forster, who was based in Surrey, kept rooms in Brunswick Square. Seven of the ten men had been Apostles: Forster, Fry, Keynes, MacCarthy, Strachey, Sydney-Turner and Woolf. However, Quentin Bell (the observant son of Clive and Vanessa Bell) said that Keynes, his mother, his uncle Adrian Stephen, Fry and Grant were the only Bloomsbury groupers who reckoned themselves to be adherents of Moore. Forster denied that he had ever read *Principia Ethica*.

This gifted little clan liked to startle with their daring, to scorn sentimentality, to trust instinct, and yet to cultivate mental order. They tended to frugality and even discomfort, in a high-minded way, rather than to profusion; but they found drabness intolerable. This was what parted them from many of Keynes's Cambridge colleagues: his fellow economist Dennis Robertson was an extreme case of a wider tendency in making his splendid rooms overlooking

Trinity Great Court so unsightly, mortifying and comfortless as to convince Lionel Robbins that he was a domestic masochist. It was perhaps inevitable that Robertson broke over economic principles with Keynes, who visualized rooms when he was trying to recall a mood or evoke an incident, and to whose imagination the shape of houses mattered. Bloomsbury groupers strove to be observant, and had painterly ways of regarding people, rooms and street-scenes. They took pride in spotting outlandish possibilities in the mundane: Keynes savoured incongruities.

The clan felt compelled to confide, gossip, analyse, dispute, convince, explain. Their stock phrases – 'exquisitely civilized', 'How *simply too* extraordinary!' – stressed their amused wonder, incredulity, tolerance. These virtuosi maintained that whatever has been believed by everyone, always and everywhere, is likely to be untrue. They were not prattlers whose highest aim was irresponsible brilliance in their talk. They did not indulge in the battledore and shuttlecock style of chatter, which sends mindless blurts winging back and forth to prevent uncomfortable silences. They recognized anecdotes as inimical to good conversation: Bloomsbury groupers never hoarded yarns to let loose on captive listeners; never began their remarks with those depressing phrases, 'That reminds me …' or 'Did I ever tell you …'; they felt anecdotists to be egotistical, disruptive and indecent among intelligent companions. Instead, they met Percy Lubbock's excellent definition of friends as 'the people who put a fine edge on one's mind'. Some of their best thinking was done in analogies. They refused to be captives of Victorian or Edwardian taboos, conventions or fears. It had been instilled in most women to promote men's self-important talk without listening to it. But Bloomsbury men and women talked and listened on equal terms, and valued one another's wit. The Edwardians' crushing insensitivity to other people's ideas and florid philistinism repelled them. Twittering fin-de-siècle aesthetes, with their exalted talk of the sublime and the infinite, bored them. They believed, and acted on the belief, that human affairs, public and personal, should be guided by reason. They upheld all that they judged truthful, but decried all that seemed shoddy and meretricious.[3]

Clive Bell's tract *On British Freedom* (1923) is a key Bloomsbury text, which Keynes often paraphrased. It denounced, with a welter of convincing detail, 'the Goody-Goody gang', the 'busybodies and spoil-sports', who had 'converted what once was merry England into a place of proverbial gloom'. The Goody-Goodies were, said Bell, in a quintessential Bloomsbury dismissal, 'mainly recruited from the class which has a passionate love of self-expression and nothing of value to express: also, since by joining it, mediocrity stands a chance of cutting a figure, vanity without talent rallies to the black flag'. It was Bell's spry wit and his countryman's earthiness that saved the Bloomsbury group from being frigid, other-worldly zealots in their aestheticism and pursuit of abstract truth. The other wits who redeemed the sect from priggery were Lytton Strachey, Virginia Woolf, Desmond MacCarthy, Keynes and an outlying Cambridge-based Bloomsbury grouper, Harry Norton. Keynes was the toughest and supplest among this brittle crew. In the early years his popularity with them was undermined by Strachey, who felt unforgiving of his sexual success with Grant. During 1915–18 his collusion with a government that imposed conscription and waged war *à l'outrance* renewed the group's distaste for him. He reclaimed his standing by publishing *Economic Consequences* in 1919, but found in the 1920s that once people reach their forties, conversational brilliance replaces sexual success as a cause of jealousy.[4]

'No subject of conversation has been taboo, no tradition accepted without examination, and no conclusion evaded,' a young man down from Cambridge, Raymond Mortimer, reported in 1928 of his incursions into the Bloomsbury Group.

In a hypocritical society, they have been indecent; in a conservative society, curious; in a gentlemanly society, ruthless; and in a fighting society, pacifist. They have been passionate in their devotion to what they thought good, brutal in their rejection of what they thought second rate; resolute in their refusal to compromise. 'Narrow in their tastes, loose in their view of morals, irreverent, unpatriotic, remote, and superior,' their enemies say. And, I think, truly. For will not relentless reasoning and delicate discrimination make a man all of these things?

Notoriously, though, Bloomsbury conversations nauseated D. H. Lawrence. 'To hear these young people talking really fills me with black fury: they talk endlessly, but endlessly – and never, never a good or real thing said,' he raged to Ottoline Morrell in 1915 after meetings with Keynes, Grant and Birrell. The dandyish witticisms and unassailable self-assurance of the Cambridge youngsters riled Lawrence, who was socially insecure and cankered by class resentment. The prolix gaiety of these young men who had been each other's lovers, their abrupt shifts and interruptions, the ways they made life into a collage of jokes, vehemence and passive-toned subversion, above all their gamesmanship in immorality, repelled Lawrence's earnest puritanism: 'Their attitude is so irreverent and so blatant. They are cased, each in a hard little shell of his own, and out of this they talk words.'[5]

The Bloomsbury group was 'rooted in the previous age', said a younger outlying Cambridge-based member, George 'Dadie' Rylands. Proletarian taste, new-money ostentation, patriotic swagger and provincialism revolted them. Egalitarianism dismayed them. A world without social barriers 'would be a rice-pudding world, a white counterpane world', said Virginia Woolf. 'Democracy and civilization are incompatible,' preached Clive Bell. Triumphant masses marching in step to authoritarian music aroused fear and contempt in them. Bloomsbury agreed with Sir Osbert Sitwell who averred in his *Who's Who* entry that he favoured the suppression of Public Opinion in the interests of Free Speech.[6]

Bloomsbury groupers thought political talk was boring because it made people speak in catchphrases. 'Liberty, Justice, Equality, Fraternity, Sanctities, Rights, Duties, Honour, all these expensive vocables may mean anything or nothing,' said Clive Bell. 'There are few things for which a good-natured, liberty-loving man or woman cares less than political activity.' To his set of friends, living through the parliamentary clichés, blunders and chicanery of the 1920s, it seemed undeniable that party passions led to muddled or dishonest thinking, made people unreasonable or stereotypical, and lacked long-term perspective. 'Politics have always bewildered me and always will,' Grant said, 'because I do not keep time with events.' When driving-tests became compulsory shortly before the general election of 1935, he was astonished that so many Liberals with motor-cars were proclaiming their party allegiance with L-plates tied to their bumpers. The influence of Bloomsbury dwindled in the culturally politicized 1930s. The deaths of Lytton Strachey in 1932 and of Roger Fry in 1934 eroded the group's cohesive identity; but the chief damage was inflicted by Bloomsbury values seeming obsolete to young Marxists and to the Auden generation resisting cultural fascism in the 1930s.[7]

If Bloomsbury's ideas were progressive, they did not rest on brotherly love. Lord Chalmers at the Treasury, Cecil Lubbock at the Bank of England, all manner of men whom Bloomsbury would have deprecated as sterile, cautious, conservative and Christian, had gone to live in the slums of Whitechapel after university with the hope of regenerating the East End's suffering poor. Bloomsbury did nothing of the sort: they saw themselves as raffish nobility with a taste for innovation. 'They did things better before the French Revolution came and made such a mess,' Lytton Strachey complained in 1912. 'In the 18th century the aristocracy *was* the intelligent class. In the Victorian age, it was the upper middle class. And now – ! – What's the intelligent class now? A few queer people scattered over London, and occasionally to be found in the Upper Circle during the Russian Ballet!' Fourteen years later, in 1926, Keynes lectured on Britain's industrial future to a working-class socialist summer school held at the Essex country home of an extinct aristocratic family for whom some of his paternal ancestors had been tenants or employees, and from whom his forename was derived: the Maynards. Beatrice Webb, who heard and watched him among the factory-workers in the Maynard house and grounds, afterwards wrote a pithy assessment of his temperament. 'He is contemptuous of common men, especially when gathered together in herds. He dislikes the human herd and has no desire to enlist the herd instinct on his side. Hence his antipathy to trade unions, to proletarian culture, to nationalism and patriotism as distinguished from public spirit. The common interests and vulgar prejudices of aristocracies and plutocracies are equally displeasing to him – in fact he dislikes all the common-or-garden thoughts and emotions that bind men together in bundles.'[8]

Keynes was patrician in outlook. He suspected that liberty was incompatible with equality, and had a sharp preference for liberty over the chimera of equality. His copious historical imagination had been enriched by the opulent beauty of Eton and King's: he trusted educational or creative elites. With his nonconformist ancestry and lifelong exposure to the puritanism of Cambridge University, sloth and waste were unforgivable to him. Accordingly, he tended to dismiss the aristocracy as idlers, spendthrifts, sots, philanderers, or as strenuous out-doors bores; but his intolerance receded when he met noblemen who were informative, pictur-esque, amusing or public-spirited. Shortly before his death he described a House of Lords debate in which Lord Cranborne, with his 'pure Cecilian utterance', delivered a 'masterly' snub to the millionaire arch-spiv Lord Beaverbrook. What attracted Keynes to Cranborne was 'the combination of his diffidence and unimpressive appearance with some inherent quality of dignity and authority'. Cranborne's father, 'old Lord Salisbury, as beautiful and pure a picture as ever, was there to hear him', Keynes told Lord Halifax. 'I have never in my life been able to resist a Cecil.' Thirty-five years earlier Keynes had been happy to spend his nights chatting in the basement of a Ramsgate lodging-house with ill-paid Christmas pantomime comedians, whose merriness he found seductive. At the end of his life he was still attracted to opposites, was still curious about other people's experiences and expectations, and still savoured whatever seemed romantic, vivid or theatrical. But the international statesman, uxorial husband and twentieth-century philosopher-prince was susceptible to different performers, sporting different costumes and playing different parts, from the edgy young don chasing other men.[9]

The Cecils represented historic stability, caste manners, hereditary authority and a tradition of public service perpetuated since Elizabethan England. These factors pleased Keynes, who was (like most Bloomsbury groupers) saddened by the transience of human memories, and shocked by the way that emotions of once solid intensity were vaporized by the unforgiving passage of time. In this respect the archetypal Bloomsbury novel is Virginia Woolf's threnody on historical change, *The Years*. The past, one of her characters thinks, 'so interesting; so safe; so unreal … and, to her, so beautiful in its unreality'. Keynes said that it was her best book. One scene, he thought, surpassed even Chekhov's *Cherry Orchard* for its poignancy. On a snowy day in 1913, after the death of old Colonel Pargiter, his spinster daughter in her fifties, Eleanor, and an old maidservant, Crosby, leave for ever the vacant white-stuccoed town-house, emptied of furniture, bare of carpets and pictures, damp-stains showing on the walls, where they have lived for forty years. Inwardly Eleanor rejoices at her liberation, sees all the old impediments crumbling away, plans journeys to Italy and India; 'but for Crosby it was the end of everything'. The old servant weeps: 'She had known every cupboard, flagstone, chair and table in that large rambling house, not from five or six feet of distance as they had known it; but from her knees, as she scrubbed and polished; she had known every groove, stain, fork, knife, napkin and cupboard. They and their doings had made her entire world. And now she was going off, alone, to a single room at Richmond.'[10]

Keynes's mourning for defunct times, his wish to resuscitate the best of pre-1914 England, his sensual memories of the scrub and polish of Edwardian flagstones, were central to his outlook after his return from the Paris conference. 'To resist living in one's own time, to attempt to live in an imaginary past,' the American scholar Edward Mendelson has written, 'is human in the same way that being neurotic is human.' Bloomsbury groupers – the novelists among them particularly, but also Keynes – had a propensity to resist the contemporary drift, and to devise imaginary pasts that were more hospitable. Keynes's imagination, his nerves and his sensibility all leant this way. This was not hackneyed nostalgia for pre-war scenes or sensations: cricket played on a village green, raspberries and cream, wicker chairs in sunny gardens, the smell of lily-of-the-valley, shire horses standing high on the horizon. Instead, Keynes honoured, as he said in 1938, 'the undisturbed individualism which was the extraordinary achievement of the early Edwardian days, not for our little lot only, but for everyone else, too'. After the shocks, calamities and European *dégringolade* of 1914–18, the past came to represent the old calm sanity in ways that would have been unimaginable to him as a restive young Apostle.[11]

His friends in Cambridge thought this way. As early as 1920, after reading *The Economic Consequences of the Peace*, Lowes

Dickinson expected 'bolshevism and anarchy from Vladivostok to the Rhine'. The men who concocted the treaty of Versailles had 'destroyed Europe and the whole heritage of its civilisation'. Younger Apostles agreed that they lived in degenerate times. 'More and more … the old ideals of liberty [tend] to be replaced by the organization, discipline and efficiency of the Termite State,' F. L. Lucas grumbled in 1929. 'There are, indeed, countries where bodies and souls are nationalized and rationalized already. The process is said to be excellent for the train services; but for the human beings?'[12]

Leonard Woolf was a grave, wintry man with an ardent sense of justice who saw much of Keynes for forty years, but never warmed to him. He, too, harked back to Edwardian England and pre-war Europe as forfeited civilizations. 'In those days there *was* an ordered way of life, a law, a temple and a city … there *were* certain standards of public right and wrong, of justice, law and humanity.' Violence was endemic, but systematized atrocities were unknown before the First World War. 'If you opened your *Times* on a morning in say 1907, you did not expect to find its columns filled with horror piled upon horror, fear treading upon the tail of hatred, and hatred upon the tail of fear,' Woolf wrote in his jeremiad *Barbarians at the Gate* published in 1939. In Europe before 1914, innocent men were imprisoned, judicial killings were perpetrated, Russian Jews and Armenian Christians were hunted and killed, but there was no political culture requiring 'the wholesale torture, persecution, expropriation, imprisonment or liquidation of hundreds of thousands of persons'. Woolf conceded that the ruling culture was based on class privilege and colonial exploitation, but felt that undeniably it was 'a progressing and expanding civilization'. The ease of travel across Europe without a passport showed how pre-war European nations had seemed bound together in assumptions that made national frontiers seem nugatory.[13]

Unguarded European borders remained a mark of civilization to Keynes's friends. So, too, did the existence of the Latin Monetary Union, which came into force in the 1860s with Belgium, France, Greece, Italy, Spain and Switzerland as early members. The Union, which was emulated by the Scandinavian Monetary Union of 1873, was joined in 1889 by Bulgaria, Romania and Serbia, but juddered apart under the strains of continent-wide war after 1914. Keynes, in his pre-war travels, found Belgian, French and Swiss francs, Italian lire, Spanish pesetas, Greek drachmae, Bulgarian lev, Romanian lei and Serbian dinars all pegged and exchangeable in gold and silver coins across most of non-German-speaking Europe. The system worked well, except when Vatican cardinals or Greek finance ministers tried to cheat, and seemed a generous-spirited antidote to aggressive nationalism and frontier disputes. 'To our trusting youth it seemed a pleasant and a vivid world,' Lucas recalled of going to Trinity with a classical scholarship in 1913. 'Travel was free – we had never even seen a passport – should as soon have thought of taking a stage-coach. The same silver coinage circulated freely from Brussels to Athens.' Thanks to the Latin Monetary Union, he remembered the thrill of receiving as change in the Roman Forum a Greek five-drachma silver coin as if Pericles was still alive.[14]

Although Keynes mourned the past as much as anyone in Bloomsbury, and was susceptible to the despondent alarms of Dickinson, Lucas and Woolf, he had a dissident optimism. In boyhood he had been a sunny creature who never submitted to his father's overloaded apprehensions. He was resolved, too, to resist Bloomsbury's woefulness as best he could. He would not see the world as doomed, broken, inane. Keynes felt sure that he could help by not thinking like that.

The morbid mood of his friends must have been affected by the district where they lived. Bloomsbury should have been a graceful, sacrosanct purlieu; but its houses, built for the Georgian mercantile gentry, seeming too big for single families in a democratic age, were sub-divided into boarding-houses for poor foreigners and University of London students. Houses were grimy from the smoke and fogs of the city; they looked lacklustre in daylight with their chipped or faded paint; seemed unwelcoming at night with their shuttered windows. Keynes, when young, expressed 'that intense sense of infinite multitudes and endless whirl of traffic that alike oppresses and excites me in London'. The hooting motor-traffic puffed exhaust-fumes, which mixed with other urban pollution to give Bloomsbury the colour of a dirty dishcloth: houses and pavements looked as if they had been smeared with a film of grease.[15]

The district may have influenced Keynes when he wrote in 1940, 'Civilization is a tradition from the past, a miraculous construction made by our fathers of which they knew the vulnerability better than we do, hard to come by and easily lost.' Bloomsbury stretched northwards from Covent Garden towards the great railway termini of Euston, St Pancras and King's Cross – the last with its trains, on which Keynes travelled thousands of times, to Cambridge. Bloomsbury was owned partly by Herbrand Russell, eleventh Duke of Bedford and partly by the Foundling Hospital. Ill-advisedly, in 1913, the Duke gave an option to buy nineteen acres of his Covent Garden estate, which had been owned by his family since 1552, to a property dealer and cut-price tailor called Sir Harry Mallaby-Deeley, who swiftly sold his option to Sir Joseph Beecham, the patent medicines millionaire. The Duke invested his £2 million from the Covent Garden sale in Russia, lost the lot in 1917 and felt obliged to sell yet more Bloomsbury property. In 1924 the Foundling Hospital sold its adjoining fifty-six acres to the Dunlop Pneumatic Tyre Company, which sold on to Mallaby-Deeley in 1933. These transactions – the careless Duke dispersing the miraculous construction of his patrimony, glossy but unsavoury Mallaby-Deeley seizing his chances – signalled the loss of a precious form of urban order.[16]

The ducal estate was honeycombed with spacious squares between the straight lines of tall houses. These squares were private gardens, with gates that could be opened only by key-holders, and with gravel paths raked by gardeners. 'On summer evenings there is tennis on the lawns, and the Vicar's daughters can be seen playing with the bigwigs,' Raymond Mortimer wrote in 1928. 'Around are figures reading and talking, and as night falls, the mourning veils in which London soot has dressed the Georgian façades become unnoticeable, and in these gardens you may fancy yourself in the precincts of a college.' By contrast Coram's Fields, part of the Foundling Hospital property, which local outcry had prevented Mallaby-Deeley from building over, was opened in 1936 as a public park, with asphalt paths and boisterous playgrounds.[17]

Pre-war Vienna was Keynes's ideal city. He stayed there in 1912 while returning from a holiday in Hungary with the endearing bisexual Apostle Ferenc Békássy. 'I've never found a town so completely to my taste – it's *by far* the pleasantest European capital to visit,' he told Duncan Grant. 'You can imagine nothing more civilised or magnificent or comfortable. One's never bored and never tired. The part of the town that matters is very compactly placed and is nearly all of the most splendid baroque.' There was abundant and confident modern architecture 'of which I am told Viennese taste complains but which I think very fine and which fits in quite well with the old baroque'. He admired the yellow-painted palace of Schönbrunn, 'in the style of Versailles but more austere, with endless allées of enormous clipt trees', and its zoological gardens displaying outlandish animals with unscientific frivolity. 'And the Prater – Vienna's Hyde Park – but wild and most beautiful, in the dark recesses of which one buggers wild Bosnian soldiers. And excellent food and cafés to give one a club at every street corner. And excellent theatres, splendid pictures and streets packed with gay people as charming and polite as the Berliners are not.' He spent his mornings in picture galleries, where he was excited by the work of Breughel and Rubens, and his evenings at theatres, including the Opera House, where he was impressed by Bruno Walter conducting *Figaro*.[18]

When, as a half-the-week Londoner, Keynes became interested in the redevelopment of the capital, his imagination recalled Habsburg Vienna. 'Why not pull down the whole of South London from Westminster to Greenwich, and make a good job of it?' he asked in a radio broadcast in 1931 on unemployment. It would be possible to house there, 'near to their work, a much greater population than at present, in far better buildings with all the conveniences of modern life, yet at the same time providing hundreds of acres of squares and avenues, parks and public spaces, having, when it was finished, something magnificent to the eye, yet useful and convenient to human life as a monument to our age. Would that employ men? Of course it would!' Five years later he was posing more rhetorical questions for BBC listeners. 'Why should not all London be the equal of St James's Park and its surroundings? The river might become one of the sights of the world with a range of terraces and buildings rising from the river. The schools of South London should have the dignity of Universities with courts, colonnades, fountains, libraries, galleries, dining-halls, cinemas and theatres for their own use.'[19]

Keynes had scant interest in painting until he met Grant. He stopped work on his *Treatise on Probability* to sit for Grant's portrait of him, because it was important to Grant. His love for Grant made him want to see with Grant's vision. The Post-Impressionist exhibition of 1910, in which the Bloomsbury grouper Roger Fry introduced Cézanne, Gauguin, Matisse, Picasso and Van Gogh to England, stimulated his imagination. So, too, did the Omega workshop (supplying furniture, textiles, mosaics and stained glass, with designs influenced by Post-Impressionism, Cubism and Fauvism), which Fry, abetted by Grant and Vanessa Bell, opened at 33 Fitzroy Square in 1913, and which survived until 1919.

But the decisive episode came in 1918 a year after the death of Degas. Hearing that the contents of Degas' studio were to be sold, Grant obtained a catalogue, and convinced Keynes that this was an unprecedented chance for the National Gallery to buy major Impressionist paintings. Keynes first squared a crucially placed Treasury official; then visited Sir Charles Holmes, Director of the National Gallery; drafted a letter which Holmes agreed to send him; arranged for Holmes to nobble Lord Curzon of Kedleston, a Cabinet minister and Gallery trustee; and (armed with Holmes's letter and Curzon's endorsement) won the support of Bonar Law, the Chancellor of the Exchequer. Law, who was amused by his zeal in the cause, allotted £20,000 (550,000 francs) to buy works for the National Gallery. Keynes accompanied Holmes to Paris in March 1918 in a party led by Austen Chamberlain. Holmes shaved his moustache and wore spectacles to disguise himself from Paris dealers.

The auction occurred in the week that German troops broke through the Allied line at the Somme, and advanced forty miles. The French Commander-in-Chief predicted that capitulation by English soldiers would lead to the vanquishing of his own armies. Preliminaries for evacuating the French government from Paris were initiated. Keynes's rail journey took him within seventeen miles of the fighting, as he told Ottoline Morrell, through 'stations full once again of peasant refugees with bundles, parrots and babies'. This crisis, emphasized by shell-bursts from Big Bertha which punctuated the bidding, worked to the advantage of buyers. Prices were low. Keynes secured for under £500 a small Cézanne painting of seven apples, a drawing *Femme nue* by Ingres, several large charcoal drawings by Degas and a small picture *Cheval au pâturage* by Delacroix, together with a drawing by Delacroix which he gave to Grant. The Franco-American art-dealing firm of

Knoedler bid on behalf of Holmes, who refused to buy any Cézannes, missed the chance of an El Greco and returned with £5,000 unspent – but who did bag works by Delacroix, Ingres, Corot, Manet and Gauguin. Keynes returned from Paris, via Folkestone, with Austen Chamberlain, whose motor-car dropped him at the end of the lane leading to Charleston. 'I've got a Cézanne in my suitcase,' he announced after trudging to the farmhouse. 'It was too heavy for me to carry, so I've left it in the ditch, behind the gate.' Grant and Bunny Garnett loped away to retrieve the bag, and bore it back in triumph between them.[20]

Keynes amassed the collection that Grant would have made if he had been richer. With advice from friends, he attended sales and exhibitions, and scrutinized catalogues. He had particular bursts of buying in 1924 (Cézanne, Derain) and 1937 (Braque, Cézanne, Delacroix, Picasso). His taste was 'rather Cambridge in its austerity', but more eclectic than scholarly. Ultimately he bequeathed 150 works to King's, including the works of friends alongside modern masters. Many of these works are now at the Fitzwilliam Museum.[21]*

After starting to collect paintings, Keynes considered how best he might help painters. In 1925, at the prompting of Roger Fry and with support from Samuel Courtauld, the millionaire collector of Impressionists, he started the London Artists' Association, which opened a gallery in Old Bond Street to hold exhibitions of modern

* The pick of his collection were: Delacroix, *Cheval au pâturage* (1819?), *La Fiancée d'Abydos* (1842) and *Lion à la couleuvre* (1847); Paul Cézanne, *Oncle Dominique* (c. 1866), *L'Enlèvement* (1867), *Pommes* (c. 1877) and *Sous-bois* (c. 1880); Auguste Renoir, *Paysages avec Oliviers, Cagnes* (1912); Walter Sickert, *Théâtre de Montmartre* (c. 1900) and *The Bar-parlour* (1922); Georges Braque, *Nature morte* (1911) and *Femme nue* (1925); Henri Matisse, *Déshabillé* (1917?); Pablo Picasso, *Nature morte* (1923) and *Nature morte avec fruites* (1924); Georges Seurat, study for *Un dimanche après-midi à l'île de la Grand Jatte* (1884?); André Derain, *Nature morte* (pre-1920) and *Dormeuse aux mains croisées* (pre-1924). Grant, William Roberts, Ivon Hitchens and Henry Moore's 'Shelter' drawings were included in his collection.

works and thus to improve the prosperity of individual artists. William Coldstream and Victor Pasmore both held their first solo exhibitions under the Association's auspices. Ivon Hitchens, Henry Moore, William Roberts and Paul Nash sold works there. Keynes was disappointed when Vanessa Bell and Grant defected to a more lucrative dealer, and the Association succumbed in 1933. Clive Bell thought Keynes had a poor eye for a picture: where John Buchan found Keynes offensively cosmopolitan, Bell thought him insular. 'France, Italy, America even, he saw them all from the White Cliffs of Dover, or, to be more exact, from Whitehall or King's combination room.'[22]

Keynes used to speak of 'the Ins': the politicians, officials, administrators and educated readers of the weekly journals who ran or participated in public life. He knew the importance of being recognized among the 'Ins' – what came to be called, ten years after Keynes's death, the Establishment – and was careful to attend such clan gatherings of the 'Ins' as the imposing memorial service for Lord Bryce, the Liberal statesman, at Westminster Abbey in 1922. He was the only Bloomsbury grouper to enjoy an entrenched position in this smart, veneered set: his more unworldly confrères thought that '"Society" is the affectation of everything – of wit, good manners, art, literature, and, above all, love.' Perhaps, too, some felt that his aspirations beyond Bloomsbury were social adultery.[23]

Edwin Montagu sponsored Keynes among the 'Ins' by introducing him to the Asquiths. In 1915 Keynes stayed for his debut weekend with the Prime Minister at Sutton Courtenay, where he and Margot Asquith won £9 at bridge from Montagu and Lady de Trafford. A year later, when Keynes was again visiting Sutton Courtenay, his hostess reproached him for not playing tennis: 'You're an ass not to play. Think of your bridge – if you didn't play, you wouldn't know a cat.' Keynes admired the working-habits of a man whom others found too casual or tipsy in wartime Downing Street. 'He worked, as a Prime Minister must if he is to survive, with great economy of effort,' he wrote in 1928 after the death of the Earl of Oxford and Asquith (as Asquith became in retirement). 'He could deal with printed and written matter with the rapidity of a scholar. He never succumbed to the modern curse of shorthand and the verbosity it brings. Lord Oxford belonged to the lineage of great men, which will, I pray, never die out, who can take up a pen and do what is necessary in short notes written in their own hand.' (Unlike Keynes, Asquith detested using telephones, and on one occasion, when he was forced to take a call from an importunate and annoying man, was surprised in the act of pouring a bottle of black ink into the telephone's mouthpiece in the belief that the ink would leak out at the other end into the ear of his antagonist.) It was a signal mistake of Asquith's, though, to forget about a piece of business once he had signed it off, thought Keynes, 'not to carry it about with him in his mind and on his tongue when the official day's work was done'.[24]

After Keynes had been stricken by appendicitis in 1915, he spent part of his recuperation among the droves of Lady Ottoline Morrell's guests at Garsington, near Oxford. She was tall and haggard with the sovereign warmth of a character-actress forcing emotional intensity on her audience. Her husband was also stagey in his vigorous geniality: he strode about in leather boots, riding-breeches, double-breasted waistcoat and rat-catcher coat; unsure of himself, a little bogus. Together they made wartime Garsington into a privileged place. Oak-panelled rooms were painted peacock blue-green or dark sealing-wax red. There were silk curtains, Persian carpets, bowls of pot-pourri, orris-root and desiccated oranges studded with cloves; knick-knacks abounded; gregarious pugs trotted underfoot snuffling. Keynes was pictured by his hostess, lying convalescent on the lawn, which sloped towards an oblong stretch of ornamental water screened by yew hedges fronted by statuary: 'His influence and advice are always in favour of hard work, and point towards the high road of life, not to flights and dilettantisms. His intellect is of a fine steel-like quality, and his mind works more rapidly than any I have ever known.'[25]

At this stage of his life Keynes liked to change compartments at short intervals. Accordingly, he left plush Garsington to go to stay at Bellecroft, the seaside villa on the Isle of Wight which his boyfriend Sidney Russell-Cooke had inherited from his mother in 1914. Russell-Cooke had enlisted in the Post Office Rifles after the outbreak of European war, but had recently been invalided home with shell-shock, and spent the duration of the fighting in the Intelligence Department of the War Office. The two invalids found sexual consolations together during their convalescence.

The leading Liberal households, the Asquiths, McKennas and Runcimans, became Keynes's familiars. They introduced him to people as varied as King Edward VII's 'Court Jew' Sir Ernest Cassel and Mrs Winston Churchill. After the war, the Asquiths retrenched by moving to Bedford Square in Bloomsbury. There, during a typical occasion in 1923, Keynes was placed between Lady Desborough and the equally aristocratic and glamorous Lady Hartington: Siegfried Sassoon was among the other guests. In 1925 Sir Abe Bailey, the South African financier, gave a dinner to honour the role of Lord D'Abernon, the British Ambassador in Berlin, in the seeming triumph for peace represented by the treaty of Locarno. 'A Belshazzar feast, of a refined order, with a wonderful collection of guests,' noted D'Abernon. 'Two ex-Prime Ministers, Balfour and Asquith, the Chancellor of the Exchequer, Winston Churchill, Geoffrey Dawson, the Editor of *The Times*, Keynes, Philip Kerr, and several newspaper magnates.' A few years later, when Lady Desborough's daughter married Keynes's Sussex landlord, George Gage, the names of Mr and Mrs Keynes appeared on the guest-list along with those of the G. K. Chestertons, the Walter de la Mares, the Kiplings, Osbert Sitwell. There were also couples with historically resonant territorial names: Devonshire, Lansdowne,

Linlithgow, Londonderry, Northampton, Plymouth, Portland, Rutland, Westminster, Westmorland.[26]

From 1916 onwards Lytton Strachey, Clive Bell, Norton, Sheppard and others regretted that Keynes was betraying his principles to serve his ambitions, and prostituting his gifts to what Bell called 'the dirty work of governing'. Grant was the only Bloomsbury friend to sympathize with Keynes's testiness when – working long hours under strain, and bearing heavy responsibilities – he heard his friends offer glib, ill-informed opinions which he could not counter without betraying official secrets.[27]

One evening in 1918, Keynes returned from late work at the Treasury to find the Gordon Square household discussing the London government's rejection of the Vienna peace initiative of Emperor Karl. He showed brusque contempt for their views before denying that anyone could be a genuine conscientious objector. When Vanessa Bell and Norton contested this, he said crossly, several times, 'Go to bed, go to bed,' at which Sheppard, who was the angriest after the Emperor Karl dispute, grew pompous: 'Maynard, you will find it a mistake to despise your old friends.' Sheppard condemned Keynes for self-importance and snobbery: he had been incensed by hearing Keynes say to Jessie, their cook, as he left for Lady Cunard's, 'I'm going to dine with the Duke of Connaught. Isn't that grand?' Yet the antagonism of Bloomsbury groupers to Keynes's worldliness advanced his career. Their fault-finding led him to scour his motives and to subject government policies to searing scrutiny. 'His friends', said Garnett, 'kept him aware of the danger that he might, for the sake of a brilliant official career, be a party to bringing about terrible evils.' Bloomsbury's scolding put him in the mood to resign from the Treasury and to write his protest against the terms of the peace treaty. His dissent, in turn, brought international fame.[28]

One instance of his celebrity occurred in 1920. He was travelling in Italy with Vanessa Bell and Grant, whom he chivvied into accompanying him on a visit to Mary and Bernard Berenson at I Tatti. The Berensons had assembled a house-party including her brother Logan Pearsall Smith, Keynes's fellow Apostle Robert Trevelyan, and Bella Greene, Pierpont Morgan's librarian in New York. 'Everybody in Florence wanted to crowd up and get a glimpse of Keynes, who is emphatically the Man of the Moment,' said Mary Berenson. 'He told us a lot that he did not print about the personalities on whom the fate of the world depended during those awful months, when they were behaving in such a fatally stupid way.' Vanessa Bell was determined not to be impressed. 'Maynard is a huge success,' she reported to Roger Fry. 'At every meal there are nondescript foreigners and millionaires who hang on his lips.'[29]

The I Tatti house-party was invited to a sumptuous fête given by Charles Loeser, a Brooklyn-born department-store heir who had been Berenson's Harvard contemporary. Berenson and Loeser had feuded for a quarter of a century, and this great party was to mark their reconciliation. In Loeser's villa Torri di Gattaia, said Grant, 'one large room always seemed to lead to another even larger. The walls gleamed with beautiful things. Chattering people seemed to be everywhere. Great painted platters of cakes were handed round, and one's glass was constantly replenished with ice-cold marsala.' Loeser led Grant round introducing him to people who were startlingly deferential. It was only at the end of the party that Grant realized that Loeser had mistaken him for Keynes, and had been introducing him as *il gran' economista inglese* to eminent Italians, including the Governor of the Bank of Italy. Loeser owned ten or a dozen Cézannes, which he had bought for a few hundred francs apiece: while Grant dissimulated about economics, Keynes declaimed about painting to the collectors.[30]

An important Bloomsbury sub-section was the Memoir Club, which was formed in 1920 and disbanded in 1964. Its members (initially the luminaries of pre-1914 Bloomsbury) met to read aloud their reminiscences in acts of community remembrance which often, although not invariably, hallowed memories of Edwardian England: the club served to cherish souvenirs and recollections that became a cohesive part of what Leonard Woolf called 'communal psychology'. The Memoir Club met two or three times a year, dining together in a restaurant, and repairing to the Keynes house in Gordon Square, where one or two members would read aloud short memoirs devised to revive their common recollections. 'Lydia would usher us upstairs to the great room which Maynard had had constructed by throwing the drawing-rooms of Nos 46 and 47 into one,' recalled Bunny Garnett of the late 1930s. 'Maynard would lie, half-reclining on a couch, to rest his heart, with a reading-lamp beside him and his head in shadow, joining in sometimes with his own memories of the events or persons spoken of.'[31]

It was for the Memoir Club that Keynes wrote and read, in 1921, his reminiscences of the peace negotiations entitled 'Dr Melchior'. It awed Forster: 'A most wonderful paper. Privilege to listen to it.' But after sleeping the night at 46 Gordon Square, he commented: 'don't think these people are little; but they belittle all who come into their power unless the comer is strong, which I am not. Great as is my admiration for the Club, I shall resign.' Seventeen years later, in 1938, while convalescing after a life-threatening illness, Keynes read his memoir on his early beliefs – partly as a reproach to the gullible youngsters present who had been duped by Marxism. 'Maynard read a very packed profound & impressive paper so far as I could follow, about Cambridge youth; their philosophy; its consequences; Moore; what it lacked; what it gave,' Virginia Woolf noted. 'I was impressed by M. & felt a little flittery & stupid.' They ate ham sandwiches and hot cakes, and talked no politics.[32]

In 1929 Keynes was elected to the Cranium Club, which had been founded in 1924 by Francis Birrell and Garnett. Its members dined together on the first Thursday of every month in a private room in the Verdi restaurant in Wardour Street: dinner cost six and sixpence, and was paid individually; but wine was purchased from club funds. The entrance fee was two guineas. Seating at the table was chosen by lot (as it still is) on the model of the Apostles and the Keynes Club at King's. It is likely that Keynes had been blackballed in an early candidature (as Isaiah Berlin reputedly was, years later, by someone who considered him not bright enough). The Cranium's twenty-eight members in 1929 included Keynes's former lovers Birrell, Garnett, Grant, Sprott and Lytton Strachey; and fellow Apostles including Dickinson, Forster, Fry, Alec Penrose, Bertrand Russell, Saxon Sydney-Turner, Leonard Woolf and Russell's barrister friend Charles Sanger, who wrote a book on *Wuthering Heights*. Other members were familiar in Bloomsbury: Gerald Brenan, Raymond Mortimer, Eddy Sackville-West, Adrian Stephen and Arthur Waley. Oliver Strachey (Lytton's cryptographer brother) was a member with his sculptor son-in-law Stephen Tomlin (a former lover of Grant's) and the latter's barrister brother Garrow Tomlin. Most Cranium diners were inquisitive, knowledgeable, quick-witted, playful, even lightly flirtatious men. Their talk was expressive, thoughtful and cultivated. Although there might be earnest or emphatic exchanges, there was more banter than self-importance. There were no women members of this Bloomsbury adjunct until Keynes's nephew and godson Stephen Keynes proposed Frances Partridge in 1982: no one was so shameless as to blackball her.[33]*

---

* In the same year as his election to the Cranium, Keynes was elected a Fellow of the British Academy (having been rebuffed in 1920, as described at the close of chapter 3). His first impact was to prompt the election of Beatrice Webb as the first woman FBA in 1931 (outmanoeuvring the misogyny of his former Treasury chief, Lord Chalmers). Despite his official duties and deteriorating health, Keynes in 1940 accepted the chairmanship of the Economic Section of the British Academy, and devoted time and thought to its activities. In 1944–6 he strove unavailingly for the election of Joan Robinson as a second female FBA.

The Tuesday, the Other and the Cranium were all dining-clubs where like-minded men met to share ideas. Keynes was not an habitué of the Pall Mall or St James's Street clubs where members went to read newspapers, write letters, grumble, gossip, drink, tell tales, make bets and swap tips. He had no idle time for grazing in the pastures of clubland. He preferred to know whom he was likely to meet, and to feel sure that their views would be worth hearing. However, in 1942 he was elected a member of the Athenæum in Pall Mall, only a fortnight after being proposed, which was the Athenæum's equivalent of instantaneous election. The arrangement was convenient, for the Treasury, where Keynes then had an office, was a few minutes' stroll across St James's Park and up the Duke of York Steps. Many of its senior officials were Athenians, who used the club as a lunch-time canteen. Keynes's proposer was Sir Alan Barlow, a Treasury grandee and sometime chairman of the trustees of the National Gallery, who like Geoffrey Keynes had married into the Darwin family. Roy Harrod, Keynes's future biographer, seconded his nomination.

The Athenæum had not changed appreciably since it was pictured by Arthur Benson in 1904: 'The Ath is a rather terrible place, so much infirmity, such limping & coughing. The Abp of York, pale, iron-grey, stalking about in great dignity.' The club stood high on stilts of prestige, but low in comforts and spirits. A visitor, who was taken there in 1940 and needed a liqueur after his lunch to obliterate the taste of the food, was told there was only cooking-brandy available. 'At one time the Athenæum was a sort of Holy of Holies in club-land,' reflected the stinted guest. 'All the most respectable Bishops and Deans belonged to it, and famous scientists, judges and literary big-wigs considered their election as a sort of Order of Merit. Most of them had to wait a long time for the honour – no club in London can count so many white-haired and bald men among its members.' Keynes had often lunched there with such members as Ramsay MacDonald and Josiah Stamp. The cooking had never been good, and during the dour privations of wartime austerity, at the time of Keynes's election, it was sickening.[34]

The supreme coterie in Keynes's life was his college. He returned to King's in 1919. During the university terms of the inter-war years he journeyed by train to Cambridge on Thursday evenings, and remained at King's until Tuesday afternoons. His mid-weeks were spent at Gordon Square. In the vacations between the three university terms, Keynes stayed in London, or after 1926 at his house at Tilton in Sussex. His Cambridge schedule demanded a punishing round of meetings and socializing. In term-time, he attended the King's College Council, which met weekly on Saturdays from late morning onwards. 'Yesterday was a terrible day,' he told his wife on a Sunday in 1926. 'I had a College meeting (where I had to make speeches all the time) from 11 to 5.15. Very exhausting ... Then I was a fool in the evening. I played bridge in the Combination Room which was nice, but after the others had gone I stayed playing patience with myself with a bad head until half past one; so I am rather muzzy to-day.'[35]

In 1919, as second bursar of King's, Keynes took charge of college investments. He sat on the Estates Committee, and by the end of 1920 had induced the college to sell almost one-third of its land-holdings and to invest the proceeds in securities. From 1924 until his death he held the post of first bursar: by 1946 the initial funds, with no net addition, had multiplied in value twelve-fold under his stewardship. All this entailed a heavy burden of meetings beyond the College Council. As he complained on a bank-holiday Monday of 1924: 'This has been one of my dreadful wasted days, – I have spent more than eight hours in College and University Meetings and am much too tired to do anything sensible.'[36]

Sir Walter Durnford, who had been an Eton house master in Keynes's time until compelled to retire by gout, succeeded Monty

Rhodes James as Provost of King's in 1918, when James moved to the provostship of Eton. Durnford's death in 1926 marked the end of Etonian dominance in college history. The younger dons wished to elect Keynes as his successor, but the provostship went to a biblical scholar named Alan Brooke, who provided a stable interregnum, until the election of Jack Sheppard as Provost in 1933. One Council Meeting during Brooke's reign, in October 1931, showed the prim belief in self-denial, and the cavilling, parsimonious and ingrained puritanism of most Cambridge colleges. Council debated whether, given the country's financial crisis, King's should suspend the holding of Feasts, or at least stop serving wine at them. They vindicated their patriotism, said Keynes, by resolving 'to give Feasts but without ostentation substituting beer and cheap claret for champagne!'[37]

Sheppard became a monstrous poseur: clowning, petulant and callous to some Fellows; a self-travesty who gambolled, cut capers and showed off to undergraduates. Keynes found Sheppard 'a little dotty', but (as a former casual lover) forgave him much. When his proposal to create a fellowship for non-Kingsmen 'was defeated by the reactionaries' at the Council, he noted that Sheppard 'made a most painful speech – really making rather an exhibition of himself, quite losing control of his nerves'. As Provost, Sheppard was feeble, procrastinating and digressive when chairing Council. His maundering anecdotes in Council, which he treated as a congenial way to fill Saturdays, were so tedious that the frustration may have hurt Keynes's health. The mutual affection between Lydia Keynes and Sheppard survived her telling him that Geoffrey Keynes's son Stephen, who read history and then economics at King's immediately after the war, thought him 'a silly old man'.[38]

Keynes's progressive, outward-looking influence was far-reaching in a traditionally insular university. 'Cambridge is the one satisfactory English institution,' Francis Birrell said in 1932. Partly due to Keynes, it had in the 1920s 'really made an effort to keep up with the times.' Keynes's London commitments made him seem rather fast. 'He is not formidable & talks with ease & good temper about anything that I turn up,' Arthur Benson noted in 1924 after Keynes had dined at Magdalene. 'He is freely said to live with the famous Russian danseuse (Pavlovsky) but no one seems to care. He is much in the Bloomsbury set.'[39]

Keynes restricted himself to eight economics lectures, in the Michaelmas term, on his work in progress. There were none of the empty places and stolid apathy of other lecture-halls. 'It was as if we were listening to Charles Darwin or Isaac Newton,' recalled Michael Straight, who matriculated in 1934. Keynes also limited his tutorial supervision of undergraduates. Until the mid-1920s, his pupils were young men who were satisfied with obtaining second-class degrees before entering family businesses. In 1924–6 first-class minds began to come to him at King's.[40]

The Bells' son Julian, who went to read history at King's in 1927, found Cambridge rowdy – and he was a robust undergraduate who went beagling on most winter days. On one occasion a mob of hearties tried to raid his rooms. He had been mowing long grass earlier that day, and had left the whetstone of a scythe lying on a table. He hit the first man over his threshold on the shoulder with the whetstone, and broke his assailant's collar-bone. Thereafter, to meet any renewed attack, he kept Duncan Grant's knobkerrie by the door. Violence coexisted with leisurely fulfilment. 'The atmosphere of intellectual excitement was intoxicating,' recalled a man who won a scholarship in classics to King's in 1931. 'The dominant fashion was literary humanism fostered by close links with Bloomsbury, as represented by Maynard Keynes and George Rylands. For all its brilliance, King's was something of a lotus land; many of us had no ambitions to succeed in business or in public service; our main desire was to perpetuate the cultured intimacy we had just discovered. We were Epicureans.'[41]

The Apostles' Saturday-evening sessions were revived by Lucas and Sheppard: Richard Braithwaite, Alec Penrose, Sprott, Frank Ramsey and Rylands were among the young new Apostles of the 1920s who mattered in Keynes's life. Julian Bell felt that he 'had reached the pinnacles of Cambridge intellectualism' when he was elected to the Apostles in his second year as an undergraduate. The society remained more important in his life than any other institution. Politics were considered beneath discussion on the hearthrug in 1928: 'it was an intellectual climate of Bloomsbury *un peu passé*', with homage to the critical writings of I. A. Richards and a smattering of Freud.[42]

Keynes sat on King's Fellowship Committee, and was active in securing the election of Lucas as a Fellow in 1920, of Braithwaite and Ramsey in 1924, of Rylands in 1927 and of Richard Kahn in 1930. All but Kahn were Apostles. Whereas Sheppard pooh-poohed research and protected second-class minds, Keynes wanted superlative achievement. One criterion for recruitment was, in his words, 'how many Fellows will find a place in the *Dictionary of National Biography*'.[43]

Keynes abominated nail-biting. Aristotle, he emphasized, classed 'the biting of one's fingernails as bestiality along with buggering bulls and ripping open females with a view to devouring the foetus'. He inspected young men who were candidates for King's fellowships to check that their manicures were not bestial. On one occasion, at least, the fingernail inspection was to prove of historic importance. 'I had to lunch to-day the Fellowship candidate who seems much the cleverest on paper to inspect him and his fingernails,' he told his wife in 1935. 'He is *excellent* – there cannot be a shadow of doubt about it. Fingernails as long as yours (in proportion) – it is infallible. And he was very nice – Turing his name ...' On a Sunday evening a year later Keynes dined in hall at King's beside W. H. Auden, who was in Cambridge addressing undergraduate societies. 'He was most charming, intelligent, straightforward, youthful – a sort of senior undergraduate; altogether delightful, but but but – his finger nails are eaten to the bottoms with dirt and wet, one of the worst cases ever seen.' Such infantilism was disconcerting: 'all other impressions so favourable. But those horrid fingers cannot lie.'[44]

Christianity marred the beauties of King's chapel for Keynes. The memorial service for Provost Durnford 'touched me a little, but not much', he wrote in 1926. 'The choristers sang sweetly and the organ mumbled and the priests lifted up their mezzo-bassos, but somehow there was just a little pretending about it all, a sort of silly suggestion that the poor old provost now has wings.' His ambivalence about King's chapel extended to its music. Inviting a Hungarian Jewish exile to a service in 1939, Keynes promised, 'You would hear English Church music in its most exquisite form and in the grandest possible environment. To my thinking, though exquisite, it is lifeless and even moribund, and always falls on my emotions flatter than I expect.' Nevertheless, he continued, 'if you have never been to one of these highly respectable, quasi-aesthetic Victorian performances, where deathly moderation and pseudo-good taste have drowned all genuine emotions, you might find it an interesting experience.'[45]

A connoisseur should be a rentier. Patrons and collectors need investment income to support their benefactions and acquisitions. After resigning from the civil service in 1919, Keynes lost his salary of £1,200 a year and therefore sought new means to support his burgeoning interests. He joined the boards of the National Mutual Life Assurance Society in 1919, the Provincial Assurance Company in 1923 and the Independent Investment Company in 1924. He was associated in these businesses with his wartime Treasury colleague 'Foxy' Falk, empurpled and rasping in his bad moods, but 'boyish, pink and happy' after establishing himself in 1927 in 'an open and acknowledged ménage à trois' with Asquith's daughter Violet Bonham Carter and her husband. Keynes's ever-loyal friend Sidney Russell-Cooke, who was 'intensely enthusiastic' as a City director and 'never failed to inspire', was recruited to the board of National Mutual – doubtless at Keynes's instigation. The latter's speeches at annual general meetings of National Mutual, the board of which he chaired from 1921, were well reported: he retired from the board in 1938, on the pretext of ill-health, although his frustration at challenges to his investment strategy was the underlying reason.[46]

Keynes liked aggressive investment tactics. He and Falk believed in the 1920s that this entailed taking advantage of changes in the relative prices of long- and short-term fixed-interest securities and equities over the course of the credit cycle. They lost on the Stock Exchange between 1923 and 1929. After 1930, Keynes ceased to be an active dealer seeking short-term gains on predictions of changes in the credit cycle. Instead, he took long-term views, and concentrated on investing in a limited number of businesses which he felt were under-valued. During the 1920s he initially made substantial net gains in currencies and commodities; but lost heavily in commodity speculation at the end of the decade, when his net worth fell to under £8,000. In the early 1930s, however, his investment strategy recovered, and raised his net worth to over £500,000 in 1936. Slumps on Wall Street and in London meant that his investments depreciated during his illness of 1937–8. His net assets were worth £506,222 at the end of 1936, but only £181,244 by the end of 1938. His gross income fell from £18,801 in 1937–8 to £6,192 in 1938–9. However, his net assets doubled again by 1946.

Two (among many) of Keynes's statements about investment strategy can be quoted. 'It is from time to time the duty of a serious investor to accept the depreciation of his holdings with equanimity and without reproaching himself,' he told his National Mutual co-director Francis Curzon (a stockbroker at Panmure Gordon, and brother of the minister who had supported Treasury money being spent at the Degas studio auction in 1918).

> Any other policy is anti-social, destructive of confidence, and incompatible with the working of the economic system. An investor is aiming, or should be aiming primarily at long-period results, and should be judged solely by these ... The idea that we should all be selling out to the other fellow and should all be finding ourselves with nothing but cash at the bottom of the market is not merely fantastic, but destructive of the whole system.

Without perversity in his reading of markets, he upheld the Apostles' view that it is otiose to follow the beliefs that everyone else practises. 'My central principle of investment is to go contrary to general opinion, on the ground that, if everyone is agreed about its merits, the investment is inevitably too dear and therefore unattractive,' he told the banker Sir Jasper Ridley in 1944.[47]

Keynes, in his lecture 'Economic Possibilities for our Grandchildren' of 1928, imagined a time 'when the accumulation of wealth is no longer of high social importance'. Then, he hoped, 'we shall be able to rid ourselves of many of the pseudo-moral principles which have hag-ridden us for two hundred years, by which we have exalted some of the most distasteful of human qualities into the position of the highest virtues'. He predicted – uttering the hope of all Bloomsbury connoisseurs – an epoch when people infected by the money-bug would be recognized as self-degrading. 'The love of money as a possession – as distinguished from the love of money as a means to the enjoyments and realities of life – will be recognised for what it is, a somewhat disgusting morbidity, one of those semi-criminal, semi-pathological propensities which one hands over with a kind of shudder to the specialists in mental disease.' Distasteful social customs and unjust economic rewards and penalties, which society upheld because they promoted capital accumulation, would go. 'Of course there will still be many people with intense, unsatisfied purposiveness who will blindly pursue wealth … but the rest of us will no longer be under any obligation to applaud and encourage them.'[48]

John Buchan, Keynes's fellow member of the Other Club, was a socially climbing Scotsman who had laboured to make a comfortable fortune: he resented Keynes's attitude to money without noticing his respect for old institutions and families. Barralty, the cynical malefactor in Buchan's novel *The Island of Sheep*, who is based on Keynes, is mistrusted for his attitude to wealth: 'he professes to despise the whole money-spinning business. Says he is in it only to get cash for the things he cares about.' Barralty's money subsidizes 'a peevishly superior weekly journal, and he imports at his own expense all kinds of exponents of the *dernier cri*. His line is that he despises capitalism, as he despises all orthodoxies, but as long as the beastly thing lasts, he will try to make his bit out of it.' Keynes did not despise capitalism – he sacrificed his life trying to save it – but otherwise Buchan's summary is an accurate if unsympathetic summary of Keynes as an investor-connoisseur.[49]

Another side of Keynes's connoisseurship was expressed in his cherishing of English landscape. This began in 1924, when he leased from Lord Gage a farmhouse called Tilton, where he spent much of July and August with Lopokova. Tilton was a pleasant walk away from Charleston, just as poky and rudimentary as the Bell–Grant ménage, set amid lawns and orchards, and nestling beneath Firle Beacon. The billowing South Downs of Sussex were a soothing contrast to the Cambridge flatlands, with their scourging east winds and cold rain that fell like needles. Gage granted a twenty-one-year lease on the farmhouse to Keynes in 1926. The new tenant employed his fellow Old Etonian and Cranium member the architect George Kennedy to design a library annexe, an enlarged staircase, servant-quarters, bathrooms and other amenities. The house, though, was never commodious. Keynes bought the shooting-rights over Tilton wood in 1934. He took a new lease on the house and surrounding farmland, amounting to 3,000 acres, from Gage in 1935–6. He recruited an able farm manager, reared pigs and made Tilton prosper. Keynes never felt a need to own his own homes, but remained a leaseholder in Bloomsbury and Sussex. He improved the houses that he leased from the estates of the Duke of Bedford and Lord Gage without frets about his outlay. Although he urged house-building programmes as a means of providing employment and of improving national prosperity, it would have seemed to him irrational and even indecent for citizens to buy their homes as capital investments, and to make heavy borrowings in the hope of speculative profits out of their domestic settings. This was to mistake the value of house ownership, and to degrade the value of having a home.

The Sussex Downs provided the terrain that Vanessa Bell's elder son Julian celebrated in his poems about winter:

> Bare ploughland ridges sweeping from the down;
> Black hedges berryless; dead grass turned brown,
>   And brown-tipped rushes on each field,
>   And bare woods.

After Bell had been killed in the Spanish Civil War, to the fierce grief of his mother, Keynes ensured that her surviving son was protected from combat in 1939–45 by giving him a reserved occupation as a full-time farmworker at Tilton. Quentin Bell became the pig-man, and acquired a unique perspective as a Bloomsbury scion among the Tilton labourers. Although the younger men were proud of their employer's national eminence, his attempts to unite the hamlet in ceremonial feasts and bonfires drew a grudging response. The locals muttered that these events wasted money. Despite the respect accorded to Lord Gage for organizing festivities for his villagers at Firle, Keynes's expenditure seemed flashy. His problems as an incomer to a rural community were compounded by an eccentric Russian wife and a grey Rolls-Royce which smacked of the parvenu. There was incomprehension between Keynes and Tilton's estate-workers. 'He needed some reply to his fantastically brilliant conversation before he could be at ease with his interlocutors, or even before they could really exist for him,' Quentin Bell judged. 'When he talked about his labourers he described them as fantastic characters, as indeed they were, but they were for him *purely* fantastic, two-dimensional and not endowed with real passions. He found them comic but not sympathetic.' Keynes believed that squires should lead, meld and protect their communities. But to achieve these laudable aims, so Quentin Bell objected, 'he chose a role that is best played by the kind of stupid person who gets things right not by calculation but by instinct, and Maynard was wholly unfitted to play the part of a stupid person'.[50]

It was said, with justice, that Keynes knew little of England outside Cambridge and London; but he half understood the southern Sussex Downs. Tilton fulfilled him. He regretted the commodification of rural England and the loss of quiet privacy. As a schoolboy he had been influenced by his mentor, Luxmoore, who had sidled out at night to chop down an advertisement for Vinolia soap disfiguring a meadow at Eton, and pitched it into a pond where it floated with its legs in the air like a dead ox. Luxmoore later prosecuted, under regulations curbing the unbridled erection of advertising hoardings, a farmer who erected in a pretty meadow three eyesores advertising Heinz pickles. Morgan Forster had grown up in, and valued, as he wrote in *Maurice*, 'an England where it was still possible to get lost'. Maps, signposts, building-works and a busier tempo had robbed his country of its lonely places, Forster felt. Keynes had similar feelings of loss. From boyhood, he had travelled back and forth between Cambridge and London: the journeying boy, looking up from the pages of a book, will have seen the woods of Hertfordshire, and the leafy, rutted lanes to farms and fields; but the commuting man will have seen the scarring developments prefigured by Forster in his pre-war novel *Howards End*. Trains from King's Cross rattled through the station built in the 1920s for salubrious new Welwyn Garden City, past Welwyn, with Panshanger aerodrome to the east; traversed the valley of Tewin Water, and the cutting through the high chalk embankments at Hitchin; and ran parallel with the Hatfield bypass, on the A1 trunk road, which was built in 1927, with houses, roads, factories mushrooming everywhere except at the chalk downs near Royston. Trains from Liverpool Street chugged past the disfiguring developments of the Lee valley.

Similar encroachments near Tilton had been long foreseen. 'These Downs will last my time but I can see that their end is not distant,' Field Marshal Lord Wolseley, who lived nearby at Glynde, had told Henry James in 1902. 'Hideous towns & jerry-built villas now cover what was not many years ago … sheep-loved turf.' Day-trippers jeopardized Edwardian peace, said the Field Marshal: 'irredeemably vulgar citizens from London pour in here daily by train to rob this beautiful Downland of all its greatest charms'. Lord Gage, Keynes's landlord, was a doughty skirmisher determined to stop electricity pylons bestriding the Downs, stock-car racing destroying the peace, 'ribbon development, advertisement nuisances and bungalow atrocities'.[51]

Keynes welcomed the process begun by the Labour government in 1931 which resulted in a standing committee on National Parks and in the appointment in 1945 of his boyhood lover Arthur Hobhouse to chair a National Parks Committee. He did not live to see Hobhouse's recommendation in 1947 that twelve National

Parks should be created, the ensuing National Parks and Access to Countryside Act of 1949 and the accomplishment sixty years later of the South Downs becoming the twelfth and last of the National Parks recommended by Hobhouse. Keynes was grateful for the preservation schemes in the Labour government's Ancient Monuments Act of 1931, and for the controls in the Town and Country Planning Act of 1932. However, he deplored the tax on land values proposed in Philip Snowden's budget of 1931 for implementation after 1933. This levy was intended partly to raise revenue and partly to advance a pre-Edwardian radical agenda of breaking up big ancestral estates and dispersing land ownership.

Keynes feared that woodlands, playgrounds and agricultural land with building potential would be taxed. Certainly, owners of land beside roads and lanes would be put under pressure by the tax to sell land for building. Such sales would stimulate ribbon-developments along the roads, the sale of 'beauty-spots' coveted by jerry-builders and the pollution of the countryside with shoddy structures. Many unselfish people were preserving, for farming or as woodlands, sites which they might sell for building, simply from love of beauty, consideration of their neighbours and a traditional view that they held land in trust for posterity. 'These people are now to be penalised by taxation until the bungalow-builder and estate-breaker can have their way. If the state is going to use taxation as a means of forcing land into the market, it ought to decide what lands should in the public interest be built upon and what should not.' Keynes had too much respect for property to welcome its reduction to a speculative commodity. He was so shocked that the Liberals supported Labour's 'reactionary and … unworkable Land Tax', which he considered 'fifty years out of date', that he resigned as vice-president of the National League of Young Liberals.[52]

Keynes advocated the preservation of the English countryside for reasons of health, pleasure and natural beauty. It frustrated him that despite preponderant agreement on the urgency of preserving rural amenities, laissez-faire dogma, that 'perverted theory of the State', meant that 'when a stretch of cliff, a reach of the Thames, a slope of Down is scheduled for destruction, it does not occur to the Prime Minister that the obvious remedy is for the State to prohibit the outrage and pay just compensation' to the developers. Stanley Baldwin, a man of the shires, who published a homily *On England* in 1933, ought of all Prime Ministers to have realized the human importance of conserving natural beauty and wrest himself from 'the thrall of the sub-human denizens of the Treasury'. For Keynes, reaching decisions affecting the whole community on the basis of a narrow calculation of profit was 'the most dreadful heresy, perhaps, which has ever gained the ear of a civilised people'. In 1935 falls of masonry in Lincoln Cathedral threatened to collapse the Angel Choir and shatter the Great East Window: an emergency appeal raised private donations, but the government stinted any contribution. 'Since Lincoln Cathedral, crowning the height which has been for two thousand years one of the capital centres of England, can collapse to the ground before the Treasury will regard so uneconomic a purpose as deserving of public money, it is no matter for wonder that high authorities build no more hanging gardens of Babylon, no more Pyramids, Parthenons, Coliseums, Cathedrals, Palaces, no more Opera Houses, Theatres, Colonnades, Boulevards,' Keynes lamented on BBC radio. 'Our grandest exercise today in the arts of public construction are the arterial roads, which, however, creep into existence under a cloak of economic necessity and by the accident that a special tax earmarked for them brings in returns of unexpected size.' Keynes called for the appointment of a Commission of Public Places to prevent profiteering, eyesores and the wanton demolition of fine or historic buildings and to supplement the Royal Fine Art Commission's supervision of architecture.[53]

Keynes was a voracious reader. He had what he called 'one of the best of all gifts – the eye which can pick up the print effortlessly'. If one was to be a good reader, that is to read as easily as one breathed, practice was needed. 'I read the newspapers because they're mostly trash,' he said in 1936. 'Newspapers are good practice in learning how to skip; and, if he is not to lose his time, every serious reader must have this art.' Travelling by train from New York to Washington in 1943, Keynes awed his fellow passengers by the speed with which he devoured newspapers and periodicals as well as discussing modern art, the desolate American landscape and the absence of birds compared with English countryside.[54]

'As a general rule,' Keynes propounded as an undergraduate, 'I hate books that end badly; I always want the characters to be happy.' Thirty years later he deplored contemporary novels as 'heavy-going', with 'such misunderstood, mishandled, misshapen, such muddled handling of human hopes'. Self-indulgent regrets, defeatism, railing against fate, gloom about future prospects: all these were anathema to Keynes in literature as in life. The modern classic he recommended in 1936 was Forster's *A Room with a View*, which had been published nearly thirty years earlier. He was, however, grateful for the 'perfect relaxation' provided by those 'unpretending, workmanlike, ingenious, abundant, delightful heaven-sent entertainers', Agatha Christie, Edgar Wallace and P. G. Wodehouse. 'There is a great purity in these writers, a remarkable absence of falsity and fudge, so that they live and move, serene, Olympian and aloof, free from any pretended contact with the realities of life.' Keynes preferred memoirs as 'more agreeable and amusing, so much more touching, bringing so much more of the pattern of life, than ... the daydreams of a nervous wreck, which is the average modern novel'. He loved good theatre, settling into his seat at the first night of a production of Turgenev's *A Month in the*

Country with a blissful sigh and the words, 'Ah! this is the loveliest play in all the world.'[55]

Rather as Keynes was a grabby eater, with table-manners that offended Norton and other Bloomsbury groupers, so he could be impatient to reach the end of books. In the inter-war period publishers used to have a 'gathering' of eight or sixteen pages at the back of their volumes to publicize their other books-in-print. He excised these advertisements while reading a book, so that as he turned a page he could always see how far he must go before finishing.

A reader, said Keynes, should approach books 'with all his senses; he should know their touch and their smell. He should learn how to take them in his hands, rustle their pages and reach in a few seconds a first intuitive impression of what they contain. He should ... have touched many thousands, at least ten times as many as he reads. He should cast an eye over books as a shepherd over sheep, and judge them with the rapid, searching glance with which a cattle-dealer eyes cattle.' Keynes in 1927 reproached his fellow countrymen for their low expenditure in bookshops. 'How many people spend even £10 a year on books? How many spend 1 per cent of their incomes? To buy a book ought to be felt not as an extravagance, but as a good deed, a social duty which blesses him who does it.' He wished to muster 'a mighty army ... of Bookworms, pledged to spend £10 a year on books, and, in the higher ranks of the Brotherhood, to buy a book a week'. Keynes was a votary of good bookshops, whether their stock was new or second-hand. 'A bookshop is not like a railway booking-office which one approaches knowing what one wants. One should enter it vaguely, almost in a dream, and allow what is there freely to attract and influence the eye. To walk the rounds of the bookshops, dipping in as curiosity dictates, should be an afternoon's entertainment.'[56]

As an Eton boy he bought Aldines and Elzevirs (sixteenth-century editions prized by bibliophiles for their fine design and innovative typeface). As an undergraduate in 1903 he was a founder member of Cambridge's Baskerville Club, which published bibliographies intended for book-collectors, including in 1914 a bibliography of John Donne compiled by Geoffrey Keynes. Maynard Keynes had a Midas touch in his foraging. In his first term as an undergraduate at King's, he bought for a few shillings from a market stall a first edition of Isaac Newton's *Principia*, which turned out to have pencilled annotations by Edmond Halley. Until the 1930s he was a discriminating, erudite collector of good editions (not necessarily first editions) of the works of philosophers, economists, poets and dramatists. At the age of about fifty he determined to amass a library of the history of thought: Locke, Hume, Spinoza, Hobbes, Berkeley, Descartes, Leibnitz, Butler, Gibbon, Rousseau, Bentham, Bacon, Mandeville, Montesquieu, Kepler, Galileo, Hegel, Kant. He sat through the whole of the sale at Sotheby's in 1934 of Gibbon's Lausanne library. Lord Mersey, who liked Keynes as a fellow Liberal and bibliophile, received an amusing account from him, just before his final visit to the United States, describing how he had bought his Aristotle *editio princeps* from the Hermitage Library in Leningrad. 'The two Keynes brothers are experts at getting the best books from catalogues,' Mersey noted: 'the booksellers say, "Keen collectors telegraph, but the Keynes [sic] arrive in a taxicab."'[57]

Bibliophilia was an expression of Keynes's reverence for what he called 'the Higher Intelligentsia of England'. It represented a more essential part of him than buying pictures. 'M. adroit & supple & full of that queer imaginative ardour about history, humanity; able to explain flints & the age of man from some book he has read,' Virginia Woolf noted in 1934. 'He has a raging adventurous mind which I enjoy.' His pleasure in mental escapades and in connecting remote mentalities was inextirpable. In 1940 he urged Clive Bell's lover, Mary Hutchinson, to read the Dutch political economist Bernard Mandeville, whose *Fable of the Bees* had first been published in 1705. 'Here are two (not my best collector's copies!) for you to experiment on. He was a very odd and modern mind.'[58]

In 1939 Keynes started to collect the minor Elizabethans and Jacobeans. He judged that these writers were worth reading (it was his rule to read everything that he bought), realized that these editions were rarer than was thought, reckoned that many of them were cheap, partly because no one else was buying them, and knew that 'his was the last generation that would have an opportunity to buy them at any price'. Jacobean neuroses appealed to him in wartime. Sir William Davenant's *The Cruel Brother*, which he bought in 1944, had 'the most cruel and appalling plot that I had ever read. A pretty thrilling play, but ghastly.'[59]

A former Cambridge roller-skating rink sparked another side to Keynes's connoisseurship. Its site in St Andrew's Street was developed during the 1890s as the New Theatre. It was there, in vacations from Eton and as an undergraduate, that Keynes acquired his appreciation of drama. As a young Fellow of King's, staying in a cheap hotel in Birmingham with his actor boyfriend St George Nelson in 1913, he visited the city's Repertory Theatre, 'which is exactly what we ought to have at Cambridge', he said at the time. He continued to hanker for a Cambridge repertory theatre.[60]

In 1933, some years after the New Theatre's conversion into a cinema and following the destruction by fire of the university playhouse known as the ADC Theatre, Keynes proposed to build a new, efficient theatre on King's land a minute's walk from the college gates and twenty seconds from the small flat in St Edward's Passage that he shared with his wife. 'I was terribly exhausted at the College Meeting yesterday fighting through ... the first stage of the Theatre scheme,' he reported to her in 1934. 'I made eight speeches altogether, one lasting nearly half an hour and another three-quarters of an hour – so they must have got tired of me! But the scheme went through.' Inspired partly by his love for Lopokova, who was too old to continue ballet-dancing but had ambitions to interpret roles in Ibsen's repertoire, he persevered in countless conferences, site-meetings and fund-raising efforts. The project's total cost of £38,000 was mostly raised by loans, including £17,500 from Keynes. The arts must be self-supporting, he believed, and so the Cambridge Arts Theatre had by the time of his death repaid all these loans from its profits.[61]

The theatre opened in February 1936 with a cycle of Ibsen plays in which Lydia Keynes performed as Nora Helmer in *A Doll's House* and as Hilda Wangel in *The Master Builder*. In 1938 Keynes transferred control of the theatre to a charitable trust, so as to escape entertainment tax and to gain income tax relief on donations; but he remained chairman of the trustees. With the Cambridge Arts Theatre Keynes sought to entertain and edify both his university and his native town. It prepared him for his wartime responsibilities for national arts. He used Culture as his watchword even after the Nazis had sullied it with their use of *Kultur*.

Dadie Rylands, who helped to run the Cambridge Arts, felt vitalized, although occasionally exasperated, by Keynes's brio. 'The theatrical world is a baffling, enraging and exciting one, full of paradoxes and surprises and miscalculations and triumphs and disasters,' wrote Rylands. '[Keynes] was fascinated by statistics of bar-profits, and programme money, and matinée ices, and cups of coffee. Here was a change from Treasury finance and the balance-sheets of insurance companies and college audits. And when, in the early days, empty stalls or carping critics vexed or disappointed his fellow directors, he counselled patience and good humour.'[62]

Keynes became a part-time impresario who (for example) was involved in the first productions of the Auden–Isherwood plays *The Ascent of F6* and *On the Frontier*. 'The two authors have considerable talent, and I much looked forward to reading the ms.,' Keynes told a producer who had sent him the typescript of *The Ascent of F6*.

'But almost the greater part of it strikes me as both puerile and perfunctory, equally in theme, sentiment and diction. Since both the authors are as clever as monkeys, this return on their part to a sort of infantilism must be presumed to be deliberate.' The play resembled a charade composed by sparky pubescent boys and seemed inordinately long to him: 'by the time I got to the end I am afraid the whole thing seemed hopeless.' Lydia Keynes took the part of Anna Vrodny in *On the Frontier*: it included a love scene which made Louis MacNeice 'long for a sack to put one's head in'.[63]

The prestige of the Cambridge Arts Theatre was conceded by the philistines who imposed theatrical censorship from the Lord Chamberlain's Office. Before the war Jean Cocteau's play about the Oedipus myth, *The Infernal Machine*, had been refused a licence for performance because of its incestuous theme. But in 1943 Lord Clarendon, the Lord Chamberlain, relented after receiving advice from his official Henry Game, who was considered a liberal because he had wanted in 1939 to permit the performance of anti-Nazi plays so long as their subject-matter was 'ruritanianised' to reduce the offence to Hitler. Keynes's eminence impressed the censors, who were obsessed with immunizing the working classes from dangerous ideas, but judged that there was little danger of Cocteau exciting Cambridge men into incestuous lust. 'The production is now sponsored by the Cambridge Arts Theatre Trust, of which the trustees are … a galaxy of Economic, Municipal, Musical and Scholastic eminence,' Game advised Clarendon. 'The play will be performed before a cultured audience, and there is no fear of it later being performed before an un-cultured one: they would be bored to death and would never sit it out; the ordinary theatre-goer shuns the highbrow theatre like the plague-house.'[64]

Another mooted production was John Ford's *'Tis Pity She's a Whore* (1633). This had a title, Keynes hoped, likely to draw men serving in nearby RAF bases. Lord Clarendon licensed the play on condition that not a single word was omitted: his advisers intended to make it too long and verbose for plebeian audiences to endure. Keynes proposed mischievous publicity hinting at the salacity of an unexpurgated text: 'The Lord Chamberlain insists on our making no concession to modern squeamishness by the omission of a single expression ...'[65]

When the University of Cambridge's Public Orator presented Keynes (shortly before his death) with an honorary degree, he extolled him as a man who excelled in understanding the import-ance of Aristotle's dictum that the proper aim of business is to provide leisure. This strain of thinking was evident from 1928, when Keynes observed in a lecture that, for the first time in history, humankind faced the challenge of coping with permanent free-dom from economic worry: 'how to occupy the leisure, which science and compound interest will have won for him, to live wisely and agreeably and well'. There were no nations that could 'look forward to the age of leisure and of abundance without a dread. For we have been trained too long to strive and not to enjoy. It is a fearful problem for the ordinary person, with no special talents, to occupy himself, especially if he no longer has roots in the soil or in custom or in the beloved conventions of a traditional society.' Rich people of the 1920s, who were the advanced guard of the leisured classes, 'spying out the promised land for the rest of us and pitching their camp there', set depressing precedents. With 'independent income but no associations or duties or ties', said Keynes, 'they have most of them failed disastrously ... to solve the problem which has been set them.'[66]

This lecture bore the influence of Clive Bell's book, *Civilization*, published in 1928 and dedicated to Virginia Woolf. Bell defined civilization in the language of a Bloomsbury connoisseur: 'A taste for truth and beauty, tolerance, intellectual honesty, fastidiousness, a sense of humour, good manners, curiosity, a dislike of vulgarity, brutality, and over-emphasis, freedom from superstition and prudery, a fearless acceptance of the good things of life, a desire for complete self-expression and for a liberal education, a contempt for utilitarianism and philistinism, in two words – sweetness and light.' Bell argued that 'as a means to good and as a means to civility a leisured class is essential'. The Bloomsbury group was necessary because 'It is only when there come together enough civilized individuals to form a nucleus from which light can radiate, and sweetness ooze, that a civilization becomes possible. The disseminators of civilization are therefore highly civilized men and women forming groups sufficiently influential to affect larger groups, and ultimately whole communities.'[67]

In places Bell's book is precious and complacent, and carries the mistaken implication that sleeping with one's friends and agreeable supper-party talk are locomotives of civilization rather than minor by-products. Nevertheless, Bell's ideas had testamentary power for Keynes. They are indispensable in understanding the mainsprings of his later life. Given his precarious health after 1937, the effort that he made to promote Bloomsbury's faith in artistic civilization is an exemplary case of the Apostles putting their deliberated, heartfelt beliefs into action.

Keynes's ideas resembled those of Sir Kenneth Clark, the prodigious Director of the National Gallery, who had signalled his wish to democratize access to the arts by opening the gallery on Cup Final Day. During the war, Clark superintended the evacuation of the art collection from jeopardy under London bombardment to safety in Welsh caverns, organized morale-boosting lunch-time music recitals in the emptied gallery, and brought one masterpiece a month for display to Londoners who were avid for culture. England, Clark and Keynes both felt, was fighting for European arts and intellect against barbarism. They believed that the arts intensified people's appreciation of life. The two men's wartime collaboration began when Keynes became a trustee of the National Gallery in November 1941.

There were two counter-views of popularizing culture and disseminating civilization. Virginia Woolf pictured a London cinema queue in 1937: 'faces mobbed at the door of a picture palace; apathetic, passive faces; the faces of people drugged with cheap pleasures; who had not even the courage to be themselves, but must dress up, imitate, pretend'. She disbelieved that such people could be improved. The alternate view was put by a young poet. 'Habit makes me think,' Louis MacNeice wrote in 'Autumn Journal' (1939),

That freedom means the power to order, and that in order
    To preserve the values dear to the élite
The élite must remain a few. It is so hard to imagine
    A world where the many would have their chance without
A fall in the standard of intellectual living
    And nothing left that the highbrow cared about.
Which fears must be suppressed. There is no reason for thinking
    That, if you give a chance to people to think or live,
The arts of thought or life will suffer and become rougher
    And not return more than you could ever give.[68]

It almost seemed a response to MacNeice's optimistic urgings when an organization to promote and sustain cultural life in wartime, the Committee for the Encouragement of Music and the Arts (CEMA), was founded in January 1940 with £25,000 seed money from the Pilgrim Trust. It had been instigated by 'Buck' De La Warr, President of the Board of Education, which subsidized its activities with Treasury grants. Lord Macmillan, whose committee on industrial finance Keynes had animated in 1929–31, was its first chairman. In May 1940 Keynes proposed to CEMA that it should fund a provincial theatrical tour organized by the actor-manager Donald Wolfit, who had recently presented several plays at the Cambridge Arts Theatre. CEMA demurred, but agreed to give a financial guarantee against losses to Wolfit after Keynes had offered to pay one-quarter of the guarantee. This brought him forcibly to the attention of CEMA: in December 1941 (a month after becoming trustee of the National Gallery) he was offered the chairmanship, with his appointment to take effect from 1 April 1942. Kenneth Clark, CEMA's vice-chairman, deputized for him during his recurrent absences as an English financial envoy to the United States.

CEMA received a Treasury grant of £100,000 for its first year under Keynes's chairmanship, and a Parthian grant of £12,000 from the Pilgrim Trust. In an article entitled 'The Arts in Wartime', published by *The Times* in 1943, Keynes expressed relief that CEMA had 'an undefined independence, an anomalous constitution and no fixed rules, and is, therefore, able to do by misadventure or indiscretion what no-one in his official senses would do on purpose'. He believed in benefactors providing capital endowments, loans or bank guarantees against losses; but opposed subsidies to loss-making activities without hope of repayment. Perhaps only he could have accomplished – in wartime – CEMA's transition from a makeshift committee to a valiant new institution entitled the Arts Council of Great Britain and protected by a Royal Charter: still less, every year in wartime, cranked up its Treasury grant so that it reached £320,000 by the time of his death – with £500,000 promised for the coming year. This was a decisive moment in the history of English arts funding.[69]

Dadie Rylands insisted that the social and political criticism in Matthew Arnold's *Culture and Anarchy* of 1869 was as strong an influence on Keynes's outlook as any nineteenth-century economist. 'He shared Arnold's approval of Schiller's dictum that all art is dedicated to joy; he believed in sweetness and light, in spreading the best that has been thought and written in the world, as he believed that money was for spending.' His wartime work for national arts and intellect was commensurate with lifelong sentiments. 'Events are taking charge, and the near destiny of Europe is no longer in the hands of any man,' he had written in *Economic Consequences* in 1919. The continent was governed by unpredictable, subterranean, unstoppable forces. 'In one way only can we influence these hidden currents,' he had continued: 'by setting in motion those forces of instruction and imagination which change *opinion*. The assertion of truth, the unveiling of illusion, the dissipation of hate, the enlargement and instruction of men's hearts and minds, must be the means.' This was the ideal behind CEMA during the war and after.[70]

Music, drama and paintings were taken to air-raid shelters, hospitals, small halls, workshops and mining-villages. Keynes supported factory concerts and touring exhibitions, but he stopped CEMA from financing amateur choirs, and insisted on high quality rather than folksiness, sentimentality or cant. He wanted surpassing excellence, not amiable mediocrity. He fostered a project to rebuild the Crystal Palace site in south London to provide a sports stadium, swimming-pools, restaurant, concert hall or opera house, with facilities for outdoor spectacles and pyrotechnics. Philistine officials and meddling killjoys however dogged his path. Customs and Excise had an obtuse committee charged with assessing whether plays were amusements, and therefore liable to pay swingeing Entertainments Duty, or educational and therefore exempt from tax: Euripides and Ibsen were both suspected of being entertainers by tax-collectors whom Keynes called illiterates. He resented taxes being levied on entertainment as he did all examples of English puritanism. He fumed when, after CEMA had striven, at his instigation, to help repair and reopen the bombed Theatre Royal at Bristol, the city's Director of Education refused to let pupils attend performances of Shaw's *St Joan* because it was not on the examinations syllabus. The Scottish committee of CEMA exasperated him by its time-consuming claims for special treatment and thistly personnel. 'I would rather hand them over their share of the money, leaving them to stew in their own feeble juice,' he declared, 'than agree to a separatist precedent which would allow them to get the best of both worlds.'[71]

In 1944 a Conservative backbencher asked in a parliamentary question whether, given 'the poor quality and debasing effect of the pictorial art evinced at the exhibitions provided by CEMA', the Treasury grant of £100,000 could be cut, or CEMA restricted to music and drama. Contemporary artists had been included in only six of the twenty-five art shows sent on tour by CEMA, but several Royal Academicians, including Keynes's fellow member of the Other Club, Munnings, addressed a fulmination to *The Times*. These exhibitions were devised to promote 'the baleful influence of what is known as "modernistic" art', the RAs claimed. 'This is a subversive moment which, with its several "isms", has been for many years endeavouring to undermine the traditional glories of painting and sculpture.' The Academicians called on the government to halt 'public money being spent on the promulgation of objectionable painting'. Keynes retorted in *The Times* that Munnings's co-signatories 'do not explain whether it is their wish that no contemporary pictures should be circulated or only those of a particular school. The latter suggestion would be unworthy of the freedom and comradeship of art, besides being, in the light of the past history of taste, vain and childish'.[72]

'I do not believe it is yet realised what an important thing has happened,' Keynes said in a BBC broadcast on 8 July 1945 announcing the formation of the Arts Council of Great Britain as a permanent, peacetime successor to CEMA. 'It has happened in a very English, informal, unostentatious way – half-baked if you like.'

Public enjoyment would be the first aim. 'We have but little money to spill ... Our wartime experience has led us already to one clear discovery: the unsatisfied demand and the enormous public for serious and fine entertainment.' He doubted if this was merely a wartime phenomenon. 'I fancy that the BBC has played ... the predominant part in creating this public demand, by bringing to everybody in the country the possibility of learning these new games which only the few used to play, and by forming new tastes.' The Arts Council aimed to make theatres, concert halls and galleries into 'a living element in everyone's upbringing, and regular attendance at the theatre and concerts a part of organised education'. Keynes hoped that BBC regional programmes (resumed after the war) would revive localized interests in culture. He wanted as many differences between the provinces in their cultural avocations as there were in accents or landscape. 'Nothing can be more damaging than the excessive prestige of metropolitan standards and fashions. Let every part of Merry England be merry in its own way.' At a time when there were thirty million regular cinemagoers in Britain, he cried defiantly, 'Death to Hollywood!'[73]

There was one final related area of public service for Keynes. Covent Garden Theatre, owned by the Dukes of Bedford, had never prospered as an opera house. It was part of the property which passed, via Mallaby-Deeley the cut-price tailor, to Beecham the patent-medicine millionaire. The Beecham Estates & Pills Company, later renamed the Covent Garden Properties Company, contemplated the theatre's demolition during the inter-war period. At the last opera gala there, in the summer of 1939, before a five-year lease converted it into a Mecca dance hall, Winston Churchill strode about the foyer exclaiming, '*Götterdämmerung, Götterdämmerung*, we shall never see the like of this again.' But strenuous efforts by Keynes disproved Churchill's prophecy. In 1944, while at the Bretton Woods conference, which settled the new post-war global financial system, he accepted the chairman-ship of a committee to transform the building into the home of national opera and ballet companies. He undertook patient, subtle negotiations in Whitehall and with other interested parties: meet-ing the Earl of Lytton, chairman of the Sadler's Wells governors, in the House of Lords, where they had assembled to hear King George VI read his speech on the opening of the new parliamentary session, he buttonholed him for a few minutes, assuaged his doubts about financial and operational details, and after months of shilly-shallying thus secured the Sadler's Wells ballet company as the first resident company of dancers at Covent Garden.[74]

The cry of 'Death to Hollywood!' had echoes in the campaign for Covent Garden's revival. When raising Treasury money for the Royal Opera House, and in other planning, Keynes emphasized that the new institution would foster an English national style in opera and would employ English performers. This proviso excluded talented, experienced foreigners from the artistic direction, and had undoubted disadvantages; but it was well judged for the post-war temper. Twenty years later, Isaiah Berlin (who served intermit-tently on the Royal Opera House board from 1954 until 1987) wrote of the tendency of Labour governments since 1945 to insist that 'we can do as well as any foreigner – British singers, British players, British painters, British folk song, skiffle groups, arts and crafts, as against all this expensive, snobbish, highbrow nonsense.'[75]

Weeks before Keynes's death, in his last public appearance, on 20 February 1946, he attended the Royal Gala which celebrated the reopening of the Royal Opera House with its first post-war produc-tion, *The Sleeping Beauty*, with Margot Fonteyn in the title part. King George VI and Queen Elizabeth, the princesses Elizabeth and Margaret, and old Queen Mary graced a full house. 'Though it was a cheerful and enthusiastic audience, it was a drab one,' recorded the courtier Sir Alan Lascelles, who attended the royal family. The box which in Edwardian days had been rented by the Marchioness of Ripon, the patron who brought the Ballets Russes to London, was filled with cameras recording the gala for cinema newsreels. 'It was a gallant effort to open a new chapter,' Lascelles judged, 'largely due to the initiative of Keynes, who was there to welcome Their Majesties, but at the last moment got palpitations of the heart and had to remain in his box.' Keynes still took Sunday lunch at Harvey Road with his parents when he was in Cambridge. His father had stopped talking some years before, although he seemed to listen with comprehension. Describing the reopening of the Royal Opera House to his mother and to Stephen Keynes, who was a freshman at King's, he shed discreet tears as he told how the usherettes at the opera house had donated their clothes-rationing coupons to provide fabric for new lampshades for the bracket lights illuminating the auditorium in time for the Royal Gala.[76]

Discrimination was necessary in all culture that challenged, lifted and enlarged human possibilities, Keynes believed. 'This practice of regarding it as an act of impropriety to admit frankly and for the purposes of action that one man is better than another is sapping this country in every direction,' he wrote in 1946 after seven months of Labour government. Elite values should be privileged, specialist expertise should be respected, and failed ideas, botched compromises and second-rate people should never be encouraged. 'Honest plain speaking' was needed – not patronizing insincerity – about poor results, poor work, poor initiative, poor efforts: not ingratiating, face-saving half-truths. 'If we go down to perdition, it will', he warned, 'be in a foam of slop and soap.'[77]

CHAPTER SEVEN
ENVOY

'"No-one will ever want another war after this one,"' noted an anonymous article of 1916 attributed to Keynes: 'you can hear this said in any club or in any railway carriage, among any group of men who let their imagination touch, ever so momentarily, on the awful dull realities of the present conflict.' The sentiment against another war seemed universal. 'It is not enough to say that the Germans are not like ourselves, that a generation's systematic indoctrination at school, at the university, in the army, wherever bellicose mystics could get at them, of false ideas of the inevitability and glory of war, have made them much more warlike.' Common humanity meant that 'there is already, in all the belligerent countries, a deep-rooted hatred of war, before which even the Kaisers and Junkers will have to bow'. It was this optimistic view, certainly, that Keynes upheld until 1933. He recognized Germany's withdrawal from the Disarmament Conference at Geneva and from the League of Nations in that year as decisive blows against European peace. 'The hideous dilemma is presented – allowing them to call our bluff and re-arm as and when they choose with what results one can imagine, or the horror of a preventive war,' he commented. The next turning-point was, he judged, the Foreign Office's 'cowardly' response to the Italian invasion of Abyssinia, culminating in the Hoare–Laval Pact of December

1935, which he decried as 'the gravest and most disastrous error of policy'.[1]

Keynes liked to define an anti-semite as someone who disliked Jews *unreasonably*. In common with most of his nationality and generation, he had a thoughtless prejudice against what he found to be antipathetic manners and appearances, which was intensified by Bloomsbury's fastidiousness. The endemic anti-Jewish feeling of Edwardian England is chronicled in Anthony Julius's *Trials of the Diaspora* (2010), where various remarks by Keynes are quoted and contextualized. Although Edwardian Liberal parliamentary leaders had sought to minimize the impact of the Conservatives' Aliens Act of 1905, which targeted east European Jewish immigrants, Edwardian radicalism was permeated by anti-semitism derived, at least partly, from loathing of the influence of Johannesburg mining millionaires on the South African war. Keynes was tinged with this Edwardian radical tendency. His marriage to a Russian, in whom the bigotry of the Tsarist regime had been ingrained in girlhood, perpetuated this blight on his character. Their banter together included automatic jibes about the Jews: he considered Judaism as a subject for harsh, superior humour. 'I *smelt* it,' he told Lopokova in 1924 after hearing that the Gluckstein family, which owned Lyons Corner House, had bought the Café Royal where his Tuesday Club held its monthly dinners. Keynes had no hostile theory about the Jews, but enjoyed offering amateur psychology to explain mental traits that he generalized as Jewish. Jewish people whom he knew seldom met his preconceptions. 'The nicest, and the only talented person I saw in all Berlin,' he wrote after meeting Einstein in 1926, 'except perhaps old Fuerstenberg, the banker whom Lydia liked so much, and Kurt Singer, two foot by five, the mystical economist from Hamburg.' Carl Fürstenberg, Einstein and Singer were Jewish, he noted; 'my dear Melchior is a Jew too', and yet he felt that if he lived in Germany, 'I might turn anti-Semite.' He still remained enough of an Edwardian to regard immigrants from eastern Europe as schemers who outwitted less nimble-minded natives and polluted their environment: 'It is not agreeable to see a civilisation so under the ugly thumbs of its impure Jews who have all the money and the power and the brains,' he said of Weimar Germany.[2]

Keynes's callous flippancies disappeared with the advent of Hitler. Nazi racial hatreds revolted him from the first. 'To our generation Einstein has been made to become a double symbol – a symbol of the mind ... and a symbol of the brave and generous outcast,' he wrote in 1933 soon after the physicist had been forced into exile. 'It is not an accident that the Nazi lads vent a particular fury against him. He does truly stand for what they most dislike – intellectualist, individualist, super-nationalist, pacifist, inky, plump ... How should they know the glory of the free-ranging intellect and soft objective sympathy and smiling innocence of heart, to which power and money and violence, drink and blood and pomp, mean absolutely nothing?'[3]

The English loved peace more than they hated fascism, Keynes warned *New Statesman* readers in 1936, and no party would be elected that had peace secondary in its programme. The fact that 'the brigand powers', as he called Mussolini's Italy and Hitler's Germany, were readier to go to war than the English made their bluster more menacing. He advocated the amassing of armaments against the totalitarian bullies without making guarantees on their use. Liberals of his generation never forgot that in 1914 Asquith's government had been forced into declaring war on Germany by the treaty commitments by which it was tied. There had been no immediate German threat to the British Isles then; still less any need to rush the unready, ill-armed British Expeditionary Force, later known as the 'Old Contemptibles', into its costly shambles on mainland Europe. A deferred declaration of war, made when England was directly threatened, after its troops and armaments had been increased, and once Germany had begun to commit mistakes because its armies of occupation were overstretched, might have proved more effective.

Germany and Italy were spending a fortune on 'intensive propaganda to persuade the rest of the world that they are the enemies of the human race', Keynes noted in 1937, yet not even their Japanese allies thrilled to their crooning. 'They appear to be morbid, pathological, diseased. I gravely doubt their technical efficiency and expect that every sort of idiocy is going on behind the scenes.' Although it was 'humiliating to have to take so much lip' from Hitler and Mussolini, 'life and history are made up of short runs', and peace should be prolonged 'hour by hour, day by day, for as long as we can'. Implicitly recalling the errors of 1914, Keynes felt sure in 1937 that 'time and chance are with us', and urged that 'Britain should build up its naval strength and wait for the dictators *to make mistakes*'. Characteristically, too, he was depressed by the 'stale debating points, and personal jibes' of Labour speakers in the parliamentary debate following Anthony Eden's resignation as Foreign Secretary.[4]

The deterioration of European stability coincided with the collapse of Keynes's health. In 1937 he became dangerously ill with bacterial endocarditis, caused by septic tonsils disseminating bacteria which attacked his heart valves. From 18 June to 25 September he was treated at a costly sanatorium called Ruthin Castle in north Wales – 'a strange mixture of first-class medicine and first-class humbug', he decided. His poisoned tonsils were smeared with arsenic and iodine, but there was no outright cure for this condition until the invention of antibiotics. 'Maynard ... needs rest,' his wife wrote from Ruthin: 'his throat in view of his tonsils, drips, drips poison into his system and gives him long rises in temperature; as he is 53 they are reluctant to operate, but treat his throat with weed-killer'. The course of his illness was monitored not only by his friends but by the wider intelligentsia. 'Mr Keynes is unwell, in a nursing home,' Isaiah Berlin reported to Felix Frankfurter in August 1937. 'If people visit him he opens by saying he hasn't a minute to spare. The bed overflows with periodicals. Round him are rooms in which corpulent peers are trying to lose weight. The bulletins of their competitive activity are reported to Mr Keynes daily. He refers to them as the elephants.'[5]

After leaving Ruthin, Keynes spent most of the ensuing year convalescing at Tilton. His wife's cosseting delighted him, although he chafed at an invalid life. He spent half his day either in bed or on a couch. A writing-board helped him to work for two or three hours each morning. The talk of visitors over-excited him, and their departures left him demoralized. It was not only his wife's fierce, single-minded and devoted protection that prolonged his life and enabled him to resume work. In March 1939 he became the patient of János Plesch, a Hungarian Jewish exile, who combined medical work at the progressive Peckham Health Centre with a private practice in Mayfair. Plesch was ardent, charming, funny, unafraid of contradicting himself to patients, and never prone to aggrandize his expertise with Latin mumbo-jumbo. 'The Rabbi' and 'the Ogre' were the nicknames that Maynard and Lydia Keynes bestowed on him. Plesch issued orders: a saltless diet to reduce body fluids; an icebag to be put above Keynes's heart for three hours a day; less valetudinarian rest. He prescribed medicines too: opium pills; and – decisively – after finding that Keynes's throat was still swarming with streptococci, one of the newly discovered sulpha drugs, Prontosil. The injections of Prontosil made Keynes feel desperately ill, but cleaned his throat of the green streptococci, and revived his strength. Prontosil however had no effect on the bacteria lodged in his heart valves, which were bound to fore-shorten his life. Keynes certainly surmised that his life expectancy was poor.

Keynes's recuperation lifted his optimism about world events. In mid-August, for the first time in over two years, he was able to walk from Tilton to the top of Firle Beacon. Mogs Gage, whose husband owned the Firle estate and leased Tilton to Keynes, heart-ened her mother Ettie Desborough at about this time: 'We lunched with Keynes today, who says there will be no war. And that anyway the Germans will find it difficult to get along the single track roads in Poland, & that there are so *few* roads at all.' Keynes was always buoyant, never sinkable.[6]

After Germany's invasion of Poland forced England's declar-ation of war on 3 September 1939, Keynes seized on price policy and exchange control as urgent topics. He and other veteran economist-administrators who called themselves 'the Old Dogs' – William Beveridge, Hubert Henderson, Walter Layton and Arthur Salter – met regularly at 46 Gordon Square to concert their influence on the war effort. The Old Dogs were kept in touch by Robert Boothby with an all-party committee of MPs organized by a Liberal, Clement Davies. 'Keynes sometimes pursued a little too far the iridescent bubble of a new idea for its intrinsic beauty,' concluded Salter, who was Independent MP for Oxford University. 'You sometimes felt you had to class Keynes' doctrines by their year like a vintage wine ... his caustic, and sometimes cynical, wit was, in some sense, a form of self-protection against an excep-tionally sensitive temperament and the wounds of frustrated idealism.' Salter conjured up his friend in a series of exotic, mina-tory images. Keynes had 'feline grace, with something in his aura of a wizard's magnetism', he said. 'In argument a disputant felt, as with Socrates, the numbing influence of a basilisk's eye.' Alternately, with his long limbs and 'beady eyes', he resembled an 'intelligent and dangerous spider. But his voice was melodious, penetrating, persuasive, a perfect medium for his beguiling eloquence.'[7]

It became clear in November 1939 that Sir John Withers, the Conservative MP for Cambridge University, was dying. It had been Withers who, realizing that the college had shed its Old Etonian cohesion, had started the King's College Association and compiled a biographical register of its members. Keynes, the pre-eminent Kingsman, was asked by the chairman of the University Conservative Committee to stand as an unopposed Independent at the anticipated by-election. He was assured by Plesch that he was strong enough for parliamentary life; but (as before, when solicited as a candidate in the 1920s) he decided that the House of Commons was not his arena. Withers died in December, and at the ensuing by-election Keynes's brother-in-law A. V. Hill was elected Independent MP for the constituency. Hill saw his task as representing scientific expertise during a period of rapidly innovative technological warfare, and retired from parliament at the first post-war general election.

Another Cambridge episode diverted Keynes. Armistice Day, on 11 November each year, had become by the 1930s, for undergraduates ostensibly collecting donations for Poppy Day, an occasion for drunken ragging and intimidation. The mood on the streets around the colleges was, in Keynes's words, 'so hateful' that many Fellows remained in their precincts all day. Each year, as a culminating rite, the Poppy Day ringleaders, inflamed by alcohol, tried to break through the stage door of the Arts Theatre in order to raid its restaurant for booze. On 11 November 1939 the brawling was so nasty that the theatre manager was injured, and his wife insulted and frightened. Hearing the disturbance, outside his flat in St Edward's Passage, Keynes went to investigate, but, because of the wartime black-out, he found it hard to see what the mob was doing. Afterwards he strove to get undergraduate participation in future Poppy Days prohibited.[8]

On 14 and 15 November Keynes published in *The Times* his momentous articles 'Paying for the War'. He approached war finance not as an orthodox balancer of budgets, but with the aim of balancing total income with total demand. He recommended a large cut in general consumption in order to divert resources to the war effort: unless this was achieved by rationing and taxation there would be inflation. He therefore proposed that a graduated percentage of all incomes above a stipulated minimum should be paid to the government, partly as direct taxes, partly as compulsory savings. Some of this levy would be used to discharge income tax and surtax obligations. The rest would be credited to interest-bearing individual accounts in the Post Office Savings Bank, and would become repayable after the war in instalments. Keynes estimated that the levy would yield £400 million more than existing direct taxation. His proposed forced saving provoked abuse from Lord Beaverbrook's *Daily Express*. Keynes's recommendations were incomprehensible to Arthur Greenwood, deputy leader of the Labour party, who nevertheless accepted £100 in return for giving his name to a vituperative article written by a Beaverbrook dogsbody who likened Keynes's scheme to Hitlerism.

The great persuader was back on top form. Prompted by the publisher-politician Harold Macmillan, Keynes revised his November articles, and in February 1940 published *How to Pay for the War*. In it, he offered the sop of a post-war capital levy to appease his Labour critics (this levy presaging an annual wealth tax). He recommended measures to help poor households and publicized the notion of the 'iron ration' – a list of necessities at low, fixed prices affordable by people with low incomes. Most Labour leaders were sympathetic to these revised proposals, but Beaverbrook remained irreconcilable. As the controls of the war economy grew inexorable, Keynes, as a true Liberal, resisted social-ist regulation pursued by fiscal means. 'Even in war we cannot afford to dispense altogether with the economic incentive to effort – which a too exclusive financing by taxation would involve,' he warned in *How to Pay for the War*. 'We have already got danger-ously near to this in the case of the entrepreneurs and we must not make the same mistake with the working classes. There is a fatal family resemblance between bureaucracies in Moscow, Berlin and Whitehall; and we must be careful.'[9]

So far Keynes had dispensed advice and clarified opinions while striving not to meddle. But his status changed after Chamberlain was displaced as Prime Minister by Churchill in May 1940. A nondescript solicitor called Sir Kingsley Wood was installed as Chancellor of the Exchequer. Keynes was appointed in June by Wood to his Consultative Council, and in August he was allotted an office in the Treasury with access to official papers. His earliest discussions concerned the government's undertaking to bear the cost of wartime destruction, which was formalized in the War Damage Act of 1941. Soon he roamed over subjects that interested him, pushed them on the attention of ministers, and proffered advice about what should be done. By the autumn of 1940, fortified by his walks between Gordon Square and the Treasury, he often worked twelve hours a day. He spoke of the Treasury as having returned to his 'old home'.

'This has been very much a dons' war,' Isaiah Berlin wrote from the British Embassy in Washington in 1944. Arthur Salter, Gladstone Professor of Political Theory at Oxford, headed the British Shipping Mission in Washington; Oliver Franks, Professor of Moral Philosophy at Glasgow, ran the Ministry of Supply with the Oxford economist Robert Hall among his coadjutors; another Oxford economics don, John Maud, was at the Ministry of Food; Hubert Henderson and Dennis Robertson both became advisers at the Treasury; Richard Kahn was valued in the Board of Trade and Ministry of Production; Lionel Robbins headed the economic section at the Cabinet Office; and other academics commanded tactical positions. The methodical efficiency of the Oxbridge dons destroyed their 'reputation for starry-eyed incompetence once and for all', said Berlin. 'Nobody is so fiercely bureaucratic, or so stern with soldiers and regular civil servants, as the don disguised as temporary government official armed with an indestructible superiority complex.'[10]

Keynes's position was unique. As Sir Richard Hopkins of the Treasury explained, 'He was not a minister, but he was a friend of ministers. He was not a civil servant, but he was a friend of civil servants. He was also a critic of both, and, if need be, a castigator.' Keynes held conferences in his rooms that resembled seminar classes for colleagues, and was a forceful presence in meetings at the Treasury and with other departments. He illuminated discussions 'by the sudden flash of a forgotten fact', said Hopkins, listened as well as instructed, and thus affected decisions in many spheres: 'that influence was not the less weighty if it cannot be precisely weighed'.[11]

Another colleague described his voracity for paperwork: 'He sat in daily at the Treasury for long hours. He saw every important paper that the Treasury produced or that was wandering through the Treasury. Many he put away for reference, and out of any heap of papers in one of his locked drawers Keynes could unerringly pull out the one he wanted.' He had a knack of remembering what suited him, and sometimes invented facts that supported his arguments. Documents for him were tools for his intuition as well as part of his mental filing-system: 'He was increasingly impressed with the necessity of allowing the whole stream of official work to stream through his consciousness if he wanted to produce any economic plan whose structure would resist informed criticism.'

There was a sensual element to his use of official dossiers as there was to his collection of rare books. 'On the many journeys he made abroad he took care to receive and read regularly the most import-ant of the current papers reaching the Treasury. The feel and touch of things was to him a large part of the area of government.'[12]

At the Treasury, Keynes was a member of the Chancellor of the Exchequer's budget committee. Wood's first budget of July 1940 increased the standard rate of taxation from seven shillings and sixpence in the pound to eight shillings and sixpence, which, when combined with a top surtax rate of nine shillings and sixpence in the pound, gave a top marginal tax rate of 90 per cent (eighteen shillings in the pound). This was heavier taxation than Keynes thought necessary, but proved insufficient to curb inflation in the government's short-term debt. A new fiscal instrument, purchase tax, was levied on luxury articles. To satisfy the Labour members of Churchill's all-party wartime coalition, excess profits tax, which had been fixed at 60 per cent in September 1939, was hiked to 100 per cent, despite warnings from Treasury officials that such a puni-tive rate removed the incentive for businesses to economize on resources or take risks with new investment.

At first, as protection from aerial bombardment, Keynes slept at night in a bunk bed in the basement at 46 Gordon Square. The Blitz of London began on 7 September 1940. Eleven days later, on 18 September, while he and his niece, with his chauffeur, cook and housemaid, were eating a duck from Fortnum & Mason, a land-mine exploded outside. The shuttered windows saved them from flying glass, but the front door was blown from its hinges. Keynes was luckier than Josiah Stamp, who, some months later, was killed alongside his wife and son when a bomb fell on the air-raid shelter in his garden. Keynes shifted his base to Tilton, which he left by motor-car at eight every morning for the Treasury, and to which he returned by about 8.30 each evening. Because of strict petrol rationing, there were few private vehicles on the roads, from which signposts had been stripped in case of a German parachute invasion. The buildings that he passed were battened down, and the lush landscape of Sussex and Surrey had been turned to war production. As to his bombed London district, it was pictured by Graham Greene: 'the untidy gaps between the Bloomsbury houses – a flat fireplace halfway up a wall, like the painted fireplace in a cheap doll's house, and lots of mirrors and green wall-papers, and from round a corner of the sunny afternoon the sound of glass being swept up, like the lazy noise of the sea on a shingled beach'.[13]

While Wood's 1941 war budget was being formulated, Keynes convinced the Treasury to use national income accounting to estimate the additional revenue that must be raised if there was to be no inflation, and to discard the traditional practice of confining the budget to a balance of government revenue and expenditure. Two younger economists, James Meade and Richard Stone, both destined for high influence, prepared estimates of national income intended to make budget calculations more intelligible. The duo huddled in a cubby-hole with a single desk. Stone crouched by a corner of the desk with a quill pen and hand calculator, while Meade cranked the calculator's handle. By these quaint means they produced, with encouragement from Keynes, the first double-entry social accounts for any country, which were utilized in framing the 'Keynesian' budget of April 1941 and were published with it. Although Keynes, using national income analysis, estimated that upwards of £300 million could be raised in additional taxation, Wood opted to aim at £250 million after Churchill criticized the tax proposals as onerous.

Keynes hailed this budget, with its accompanying paperwork, as 'a revolution in public finance'. It sought, for the first time, to restrain inflation by raising taxation to make civilian expenditure equal to the goods and services available. The standard rate of income tax was raised to ten shillings in the pound, bringing a top marginal rate of nineteen shillings and sixpence. The number of people liable to pay income tax was increased, because income and personal allowances were reduced. This amounted to forced saving through taxation, as propounded by Keynes in his November 1939 articles in *The Times*. In order to make this extension of direct taxation more palatable, Keynes's idea of post-war credits was adopted. The thinking was that post-war credits could be repaid to prevent a post-war slump, such as had occurred in 1920–1; but inflationary pressure after 1945 created a very different situation from that envisaged by Keynes.[14]

Britain was financially crippled by the war against the Nazis, yet hoped to remain a world power, whereas most Americans wanted to dismantle the British Empire. In this conflicting situation Roosevelt, in December 1940, unveiled the Lend-Lease programme, whereby American goods were to be supplied to Britain without cash payment. For this consideration, Britain was to be stripped of its dollar assets and to relinquish export markets. After stout resistance in the US Congress, the Lend-Lease Act was passed in March 1941. In the ensuing fire-sale, Courtauld's American subsidiary, the Viscose Corporation, the most profitable English holding in north America, was sold to an American banking consortium for $54 million – about half what it was worth. Roosevelt's Treasury Secretary, Henry Morgenthau, had a secondary war aim, after defeating Nazi Germany, of impoverishing British imperialism and of reducing the reach of the City of London in post-war finance. Morgenthau's tactics drove Keynes to complain in March that US officials were hustling England as if it was the humblest, most feckless Balkan nation.

'How the English hate being rescued by the Americans,' reflected Charles Ritchie of the Canadian High Commission in London in April.

They know they must swallow it, but God how it sticks in their throats. The Americans are thoroughly justified in their suspicions of the English, and the English I think are justified in their belief that they are superior to the Americans. They have still the steadiness, stoicism and self-discipline that make for a ruling race, but what will these qualities avail them if the tide of history and economics has turned against them? How will the volatile, generous, imaginative, spoiled and impatient Americans manage ... the after-war world?

This was a question that would come to dominate the last years of Keynes's working life. The history of his wartime dealings with Washington officials combines stupendous Anglo-American cooperation with shocking Anglo-American miscomprehension and annoyance. The two powers had incompatible global aims; there was never any doubt which nation would prevail; and English envy of American supremacy, coupled with dismay at the British Empire's irreversible decline, led to trenchant complaints. Depiction of the strains in the Atlantic alliance cannot be shirked, even if the tensions of the 1940s still have the power to arouse resentment.[15]

It was decided to send Keynes to Washington as an envoy charged with improving Anglo-American handling of Lend-Lease. On 2 May, flanked by his wife whose vigilance protected his health, he left Poole harbour by flying-boat for Estoril in Portugal. Two other distinguished men were waiting in Estoril for the next leg of the flying-boat's trip to America. Both were travelling to New York, like Keynes, to put England's case to American friends and to the American public. One was A. L. Goodhart, scion of a rich New York family, who, when he had gone to Cambridge as an undergraduate in 1912, had opted to read law rather than economics after being advised against having Keynes as his tutor: Goodhart was currently Professor of Jurisprudence at Oxford. The other traveller was also a jurist, Lord Greene, the Master of the Rolls and quondam Fellow of All Souls. The trio went in the evening to Estoril casino where Keynes and Greene, following a carefully planned system, lost steadily while Goodhart, a novice, recouped their depleted finances. As they left the casino, Keynes explained that 'a player's success depended more on intuition than intelligence'. Casino-owners had little to fear, Keynes knew, from gamblers who felt they were indulging in a logical activity, subject to deductive reason and capable of systematization, but should beware of those who played without long-term principles. From Estoril an American Clipper flew this party westward, with stopovers in the Azores and Bermuda, and despite engine-trouble which forced the machine to turn back.[16]

Keynes's dealings in Washington were bumpy, especially with Morgenthau, a sullen man who suspected that the purpose of the Englishman's mission was to wreck the Viscose deal. Although Keynes met officials, he never visited Congress, and knew few legislators. He was exasperated by the American reliance on telephones, by interminable discussions without documentation, and by the dependence on lawyers. He trusted intuitions, and objected to lawyers because they codified human experience, treated intuitive thinking as hazardous, were paid to find pitfalls, inhibited their clients, propagated dehumanizing legalese and busied themselves making good sense illegal. On 28 July he lost his temper when the Americans sought a binding declaration from the British government of non-discrimination in post-war trade and equal tariff treatment of all countries. This became Article VII of the Lend-Lease agreement, which was devised by the American to hasten the dismantling of the British Empire by prohibiting imperial tariff preference and thus unravelling imperial economic unity. In England the business community warned that the renunciation of post-war trade barriers and exchange regulations, as required by Article VII, would expose their post-war domestic market to a flood of cheap imports. The substance of Article VII was nevertheless soon agreed between Churchill and Roosevelt.

Decision-taking in London government departments followed a strict procedure based on the circulating file: officials wrote policy papers, prepared summaries and recommended decisions in a file that rose through the ministry in strict hierarchical order, with each official suggesting revisions, minuting their concurrence or disagreement with proposals, until the file finally reached the political head of the department who signed it off. Keynes, who had a preternatural mastery of documentation, liked this methodical, hierarchical, paper-bound system, which seemed to eliminate random intrusions from policy-making. After returning to England in August, Keynes vented his frustrations with Washington procedures. As the diplomat Oliver Harvey noted, 'he gave most amusing description of chaotic conditions of work of U.S. Government departments – each department letting down the other – no coordination and no overriding authority – no records or written descriptions are kept of anything – all oral and all that can be repudiated'. This three-month sojourn in the USA set the pattern for his later visits. In Robert Skidelsky's summary, the relentless round of fencing discussions with American officials, 'the crippling workload imposed by overambitious schedules, the small size of the British delegations, the fact that he doubled the roles of expert and plenipotentiary, his constant need to refer back to London – all tended to leave him exhausted, baffled, angry and frustrated'. Keynes's consequent impatience, condescension and sarcasm were as maddening to American negotiators as were their informalities with paperwork to him.[17]

Keynes became a director of the Bank of England in September 1941 (filling the vacancy created by the bomb that destroyed Josiah

Stamp's air-raid shelter). This appointment confirmed his transition from outspoken and unwelcome outsider to reputable and trusted insider to whom there was no longer any reflex of resistance. 'A Director as such has, as you know, no more knowledge of or influence over policy than the man in the moon,' he wrote to Falk, 'so you might argue that I am putting on a muzzle for nothing. But for the war I am muzzled anyhow by having returned to the old home [the Treasury]. And anything one can do in the near future can only be from the inside.' He found the balance of sympathies and policies in Whitehall was shifting towards his own.[18]

Keynes and his wife spent most weekends in Cambridge, returning on crowded trains on Friday evening, so that he could attend College Council on Saturdays and transact bursarial business. It was counter-intuitive of them to live in the Sussex countryside on weekdays, and to spend a long weekend in town. In war conditions it was also a test of fortitude. Keynes proved hardier than Sir John Clapham, the King's economic historian, who was depleted by the delays, discomforts and black-out of his wartime commuting from Cambridge to the Bank of England, where he was official historian, and to the British Academy, where he was president. Clapham died of heart failure, in mid-sentence, in a train compartment carrying him south for another day of meetings in London.

During the war year Keynes was too tired and overworked to make new friends. With his London dining-clubs suspended, he valued more than ever the good talk and familiar companions at King's high table: even with rationed food. He and his wife also attended concerts, plays and talks in the evenings. 'Maynard Keynes didn't approve of Morgan Foster's lecture on Virginia Woolf, which he said was in baby language,' Edward Marsh reported from Cambridge in 1942 a year after Woolf had drowned herself. That weekend there was a concert of madrigals sung on a floating platform moored under the bridge at King's, the river lined with canoes and punts, crowds sitting on the banks, in a joyful interlude from wartime hardships. To the delight of his mother, Keynes succeeded Lord Eltisley as High Steward of the Borough of Cambridge in 1943: he was twenty-ninth holder of the sinecure, which had been instituted in 1529. His predecessors included Francis Bacon, Oliver Cromwell, Clarendon, Macaulay and various ceremonially imposing dukes. His successor, after his death, was G. M. Trevelyan.[19]

'I am getting too elderly to have any fresh ideas well in advance of the times,' Keynes complained in 1942 aged fifty-nine. 'I have run as fast as I could and am now out of breath. If practical forces catch one up, what can one do about it?' Nevertheless, during dinner at King's, he continued to send out whizzing sparks like a Catherine wheel. On a typical occasion he advocated the segmentation of Germany into the kingdoms, principalities and grand duchies which had existed before unification, proposed the creation of an enlarged Habsburg state comprising Austria, Slovakia and Serbia, and predicted that the German population would be evicted from east Prussia, control of which would be transferred to Poland: 'then Russia could have the Baltic Republics, which anyhow couldn't be denied to her'. He ended with the words, 'So it will be our role to save Europe from Germany, Russia and America, which will take us all our time.' Given all that followed in Washington, it is notable that he thought England's post-war task was to save Europeans from US hegemony as well as Nazi conquest or Soviet occupation.[20]

In June 1942 Keynes was gazetted with a barony: Lord Keynes was the title he took, with Tilton as his territorial designation. He was the forerunner of numerous economist peers, including Beveridge (1946), Layton (1947), Robbins (1959), Kahn (1965), Balogh (1968), Kaldor (1974), Jackson (Barbara Ward; 1976), Bauer

(1983), Peston (1987), Desai (1991), Eatwell (1992) and Layard (2000). The enlistment of economic experts in the parliamentary management of the state, which he had presaged in his criticisms of inexpert political bungling in *The Economic Consequences of the Peace*, began with him. 'I dare to speak for the much-abused so-called experts,' he told his fellow peers in a parliamentary debate. 'I even venture sometimes to prefer them, without intending any disrespect, to politicians. The common love of truth, bred of a scientific habit of mind, is the closest of bonds.' Once (at Cambridge in 1924) Keynes had declaimed at election hustings against the hereditary prerogatives of the House of Lords; but by 1942 he had hopes of the Upper Chamber becoming a Senate of wise men (women were excluded from sitting in the House of Lords until 1958).[21]

As an Eton boy Keynes had a passionate phase of interest in medievalism and genealogy. Now he diverted himself in discordant correspondence with Sir Gerald Wollaston, Garter King of Arms, about the design of the supporting figures on either side of his heraldic shield. Keynes wished to commemorate the two institutions that most mattered to him by taking scholars of Eton and King's as his supporters. However, Wollaston vetoed the Eton scholar from sporting a top-hat, as Keynes had requested, and tried to stop the King's scholar from wearing a mortar-board. Keynes was dissatisfied by the sketches made by the College of Arms' heraldic artist: he complained that the Eton scholar resembled 'a tawny Scot' and had too lined a face for his age. 'The King's undergraduate is dreadfully old and worried-looking, and appears, though rather ambiguously, to wear a fluffy moustache.' Keynes arranged for Quentin Bell, who was working as his pig-man at Tilton, to redraw the heraldic design, with more boyish-faced supporters. In the event, the Eton scholar was permitted by Wollaston to hold a book in his hand and the King's scholar to wear a cap and gown. Keynes took as his motto, *Me Tutore Tutus Eris*, meaning 'Under my tutelage you will be safe': the phrase is derived from 'me duce tutus eris' in Ovid's *Ars Amatoria*, with the literal meaning 'with me as a leader you will be safe'. If all this seems recondite midway through the century of the common man, it is notable that the peak year in English heraldic history for the registering or granting of coats-of-arms was 1945 – the year of the Labour general election landslide. There are backlashes even in heraldry.[22]

'Here I am back again in the Treasury like a recurring decimal – but with one great difference,' Keynes replied to a Labour front-bencher's congratulations on his peerage. 'In 1918 most people's only idea was to get back to pre-1914. *No-one* today feels like that about 1939. This will make an enormous difference when we get down to it.' Forces were mustering in many institutions to promote Keynesian policies – not least in the Church of England. Keynes invited William Temple, who was enthroned as Archbishop of Canterbury in 1942, to address the Tuesday Club on Christian notions of post-war capitalism. He had first met Temple nearly forty years earlier when they spoke against each other at a university debating contest in which Keynes represented Cambridge and Temple spoke for Oxford. Although Keynes objected to signing portentous, ineffectual, round-robin letters, he had made an exception for one organized in 1934 by Temple beseeching Hitler to stop the brutality of the concentration camps (Hitler refused to receive it, but his special adviser on foreign relations, Joachim von Ribbentrop, sent a formal acknowledgement). Thereafter Keynes maintained contacts with Temple, who was Archbishop of York before his promotion to Canterbury.[23]

'Economics, more properly called political economy, is a side of ethics,' Keynes wrote to Temple from the Treasury in 1941. 'Marshall used always to insist that it was through ethics he arrived at political economy, and I would claim myself in this, as in other respects, to be a pupil of his.' He was then helping Temple to write *Christianity and the Social Order*, which sold 139,000 copies after its publication by Penguin in 1942. It is a lucid, rousing tract written with the doughty optimism and practical compassion of Keynesian enlightenment. Keynes made numerous suggestions, read the galley-proofs and convinced Temple to add an appendix which is indispensable reading for those interested in his influence. Overall, the Archbishop urged that there should be a five-day working week and guaranteed minimum standards in housing, education, employment and holiday-allowances. Although both he and Keynes foreshortened their lives by choosing to overwork, they recognized that civilized and free lives preclude excessive working-hours and oppressive conditions of work, and allow respite from the tensions of work. Rested minds and valued recreations were priorities for Keynesian capitalism. Guarantees of free speech and free assembly were part of Temple's programme – as were regional devolution and worker-nominated directors on boards of companies. He called for the nationalization not only of the Bank of England but of the joint-stock banks. He wanted public ownership of land development sites; security of tenure for tenants; restrictions on borrowings secured on property.[24]

Christianity and the Social Order, although forgotten by secularized historians, is one of the foundation piers of the welfare state and perhaps the most-read Keynesian tract of all. After the Beveridge scheme for post-war social security and unemployment benefits proposals was published in a government white paper, Temple observed that this was the first time that the spirit of Christian ethics had been embodied in an act of parliament. Violet Bonham Carter lunched with Keynes shortly after publication of *Christianity and the Social Order*: 'very well and excellent company', she found him. If Churchill perished, the only man with the authority to succeed him, said Keynes, was Archbishop Temple, with his support of state planning and of Beveridge's proposals.[25]

The Treasury was wary about post-war levels of unemployment, and therefore about the level of national income. Consequently its senior men resisted Beveridge's project as unaffordable. Keynes felt more sanguine than them about employment prospects, was robust in his support of Beveridge's scheme, and helped to make the costing estimates for the welfare system more acceptable to his department. The Treasury remained so uneasy, however, that its officials besought Keynes not to use his maiden speech in the House of Lords in May 1943 to welcome the Beveridge proposals as good value. He complied, like the loyal Treasury man that he had become, and instead spoke about his proposed International Clearing Union. This maiden speech proved an expository triumph as well as inspiriting. 'I sat wrapt in admiration at the lucidity, the clarity and indeed the gems of economic wisdom,' Lord Melchett of ICI said afterwards: Keynes had been, since 1919, 'a beacon of light in an extremely dark world'.[26]

'The optimistic view', Keynes wrote to a Treasury colleague in June 1943, 'which I am charged with maintaining is by no means intended as a prophecy of what is certain to happen.' His set of ideas to maintain employment was hypothetical; but he maintained that only his hypothesis gave a chance of survival to capitalist initiative. If it transpired that 'free enterprise is incapable of dealing with the problem of structural unemployment', then solutions based on competition and profit would be jettisoned in favour of socialist controls. However, he still believed 'that something like free enterprise can be made to work. I think we ought to have a good try at it.' Although Keynes had little part in drafting the momentous government policy document on unemployment issued in 1944, with its opening declaration accepting government responsibility for maintaining 'a high and stable level of employment after the war', it was as Keynesian as *Christianity and the Social Order*. Both documents showed how Keynes's notions had turned from heresy to the ruling authority in ten years.[27]

From the autumn of 1941, Keynes worked at creating a post-war global capitalist economy that avoided the instabilities, fluctuations, excesses and failures of the pre-war system. He envisaged a post-war international monetary system, which would supersede the gold standard and impose a system of permanent regulations to manage the divergent needs, conflicts and weaknesses of the world's national economies. With Treasury colleagues, he devised a scheme to enable money that was earned by selling goods in one country to be spent on purchasing the products of any other country. All else in the proposals was ancillary to that object. The Keynes scheme, as it became generally known, was first published in April 1943. It proposed that an International Clearing Union would issue a universal currency valid for trade transactions across the world to an amount totalling an equivalent in gold of US $26 billion. Creditor nations (pre-eminently the USA, which was the only nation in the world that was neither impoverished nor deep in deficit) would allocate funds, and debtor nations would reduce or settle their debts. The expansion of world trade would be financed by deploying the surpluses of creditor nations to enable debtor nations to meet their needs. It was a characteristically Keynesian scheme, with expansion providing a keynote.

The Keynes scheme was published simultaneously with American counter-proposals, which were designated the White plan – named after its progenitor Harry Dexter White. White's alternative was a Stabilization Fund capitalized at $5 billion to issue loans accompanied by a world bank to finance post-war reconstruction capitalized at $10 billion. His mechanisms were designed to benefit American power. The war, as he saw, gave an unrepeatable chance to install the US dollar as the global currency: so much so that he pressed for the dollar to be the sole money used by the liberation forces, Allied as well as American, when they occupied Europe, and recommended the over-valuation of European currencies so that liberated citizens preferred to use the dollar. White's plan fitted the US Treasury aim of reorienting the world's financial centre from the City of London.

Harry Dexter White – the son of Jewish Lithuanians – had worked for years in his family's hardware store before wartime military service widened his aspirations. He was teaching economics at a minor liberal arts college in Appleton, Wisconsin when he was recruited to Washington in 1934. Probably in the following year he began working for Soviet Russian agents – providing documents and advice – although his economic thinking was more Keynesian than Marxist. He never shed the manners of the hardware store: he resembled a shop assistant who was so determined not to be servile that he browbeat customers on the other side of the counter. Lionel Robbins reported that, at a monetary meeting held in 1943 in a Washington room with noisy air-conditioning, White 'shouted all day like a man directing the movements of a ship without a rudder in a hurricane'.[28]

The artificial currency for the multilateral clearing system was called 'Bancor' in the Keynes proposals and 'Unitas' in the White scheme. 'Bancor? Unitas? Both of them in my opinion are rotten bad names, but we racked our brains without success to find a better,' Keynes told the House of Lords. 'What would your Lordships say to dolphin? A dolphin swims, like trade, from shore to shore. But the handsome beast, I am afraid, also goes up and down, fluctuates, and that is not at all what we require.' Another possibility mooted by Keynes was bezant, the gold unit of Byzantium and the world's previous international currency. Even in the greatest world affairs, he seemed to say, people must be allowed verbal frivolity. He also stressed that interim versions of the new arrangements must be published and debated. 'The economic structure of the post-war world cannot be built in secret,' he said in the Lords. Democracy's hallmark was 'the consciousness of consent'.[29]

In September 1943 Keynes and his wife traversed the Atlantic on the *Queen Mary* to discuss the monetary rules of the reconstructed post-war global economy. His first speech, on 21 September, at a plenary session in Washington, appealed for a unified approach both to reducing unemployment and to improving standards of living. 'I have never heard him better – more brilliant, more persuasive, wittier or more truly moving,' commented James Meade. Keynes's priority was to agree a plan which Congress might accept: he expected the negotiations to end by adopting White's scheme with subordinate English modifications. Nevertheless, the different Anglo-American traditions of managing meetings, accentuated by jarring personalities, led to daily clashes. 'What absolute Bedlam these discussions are!' Meade exclaimed after a fortnight. 'Keynes and White sit next each other, each flanked by a long row of his own supporters. Without any agenda or any prepared idea of what is going to be discussed they go for each other in a strident duet of discord which after a crescendo of abuse on either side leads up to a chaotic adjournment.'[30]

Keynes's summary of White strove to be fair. 'He is over-bearing, a bad colleague, always trying to bounce you, with harsh rasping voice, aesthetically oppressive in mind and manner; he has not the faintest conception how to behave or observe the rules of civilised intercourse,' he reported in October 1943. 'At the same time, I have a very great respect and even liking for him. In many ways he is the best man here. A very able and devoted public servant, carrying an immense burden of responsibility and initiative.' Keynes concluded that the best way to influence White was 'to respect his purpose, arouse his intellectual interest ... and to tell him off very frankly and firmly when he has gone off the rails of relevant argument'. But White and other Americans often experienced this approach as disdainful or snubbing. It was for this reason that White called Keynes to his face 'Your Highness', and sneered to English officials that their leader pissed perfume. The university backgrounds of leading English negotiators inclined them to behave to their American counterparts like examiners giving marks on term papers or writing job-references for their students. Their patronizing, donnish approach, unconscious though it may have been, was typified by Lionel Robbins in 1943 assessing the US Assistant Secretary of State Dean Acheson, who had attended both Yale and Harvard Law School, as 'amiable, able, but decidedly not alpha'. Americans, too, had their prejudices: a consultant at the State Department warned Robbins (son of a Middlesex smallholder) that London sent to Washington 'too many Englishmen with the wrong sort of accent. Why didn't we send more people from the North and from Scotland – they went down so much better.'[31]

It was common to both London and Washington that the post-war international monetary system must stabilize exchange rates, promote international financial cooperation, prohibit currency devaluations intended to weaken other economies, halt arbitrary changes in the value of currencies and discourage destabilizing short-term speculation. A managed global financial system would replace the unregulated, destructive disarray of pre-war years. The rules about currency values would be enforced by a body that came to be known as the International Monetary Fund. The complementary body to finance post-war reconstruction came to be called the World Bank. The notion of an artificial currency – be it bancor, dolphin or bezant – was discarded. Ultimately, despite their committee-room antics and outcries, White and Keynes agreed a Joint Statement of intentions in which American wishes prevailed. It was to the credit of these two incompatible men that, during a global war, they persuaded two imperial powers, whose long-term interests were irreconcilable, to reform global capitalism along lines that were not only interventionist and cooperative, but idealistic about human fulfilment. They wanted governments to guarantee economic security and material comforts to their citizens. They sought fixed but adjustable exchange rates, which would enable governments to pursue domestic aims (such as welfare programmes) without impairing their international competitiveness.

Violet Bonham Carter recorded an 'amusing lunch with Keynes and Lydia' in January 1944. During a rationed, makeshift meal at a restaurant in Charlotte Street, Antoine's, which was popular with the literary intelligentsia, he praised the US Ambassador in London, John Winant, and similar Ivy Leaguers with their distinct-ive mid-Atlantic twang known as Park Avenue lockjaw, but regret-ted that 'they have ceased to represent or control the country'. America's new rulers aroused in him patrician unease. Their mobility unsettled him, and their lack of historical background diminished their authority in government, he felt. 'With no roots anywhere and no power to stay in one house even for as long as 3 months,' so he told Bonham Carter, 'America has *no* future in the long run.' This remark may seem absurd seventy years later, but it shows how some English leaders expected that American suprem-acy could not endure because, although this new super-power was the richest in history, it lacked the heritage and rooted traditions for world leadership. It had long been a refrain of Keynes's that instability jeopardized the capitalist system more grievously than inequitable distribution of wealth or resources. Restiveness seemed destabilizing to him. By 1944 his parents had lived in the same house in Harvey Road for sixty years. This tenure was a matter of pride to every Keynes, who felt confident in their parts and imbued with authority by such continuities, and doubted the staying-power of callow families who moved every few years.[32]

The first quarter of 1944, following Keynes's return to England, was dominated by his defence of the commitments made in the Joint Statement. There was resistance by the Bank of England, which felt threatened by the notion of a World Bank, and fear at the Treasury about expense and limitations in their prerogatives. There were attacks in Cabinet, led by the irresponsible trouble-maker Beaverbrook, and from motley parliamentarians spurred by dislike of all things American. On 23 May Keynes gave a robust defence of the Joint Agreement, and indeed of the constructive generosity of the United States, in the House of Lords. He warned against 'little Englandism', which pretended that 'this small coun-try' could survive by 'a system of bilateral and barter agreements', or by 'keeping to itself in a harsh and unfriendly world'. It seemed to him that 'those who talk this way' were 'pretty near frenzy' in their nationalism. Moreover, the Anglo-American proposals for international monetary cooperation would adjust the instabilities that 'before the war did more than any other single factor to destroy the world's economic balance and to prepare a seed-bed for foul growths'. The commitments undertaken would be liberating and enriching – not constricting.

Sometimes alone, in popular articles in the press, in pamphlets, in dozens of letters to *The Times*, in textbooks, in enormous and obscure treatises, I have spent my strength to persuade my coun-trymen and the world at large to change their traditional doctrines and, by taking better thought, to remove the curse of unemploy-ment. Was it not I, when many of to-day's iconoclasts were still worshippers of the Calf, who wrote that 'Gold is a barbarous relic'? Am I so faithless, so forgetful, so senile that, at the very moment of triumph of these ideas when, with gathering momentum, Govern-

ments, parliaments, banks, the press, the public, and even economists, have at last accepted these new doctrines, I go off to help
forge new chains to hold us fast in the old dungeons? I trust, my
Lords, that you will not believe it.[33]

As the sequel to the Joint Statement, Roosevelt invited non-Axis
states to the United Nations Monetary and Financial Conference,
which was convened for 1 July 1944 with the task of agreeing the
forms of the proposed new global institutions. Keynes had long
suffered during American summers. 'One sweats all day and the
dirt sticks to one's face,' he had complained after a visit in 1934.
'The nights are as hot as the days. Nobody sleeps. Everyone is kept
on the go all day long.' He insisted that the conference must be held
somewhere cooler than the federal capital. The Mount Washington
Hotel in the White Mountains of New Hampshire was accordingly
selected as the location of the conference. The hotel had its own
electricity plant, post-office, golf-course, church, beauty-parlour,
barber-shop, bowling-alley and cinema, but had been closed for
two years. There was pandemonium in readying it before finance
ministers, economic experts and journalist hordes converged by
train at an adjacent village called Bretton Woods.[34]

First there were preliminary sessions in Atlantic City, where
Keynes dominated the Anglo-American meeting about the World
Bank on 24 June. 'Keynes was in his most lucid and persuasive
mood; and the effect was irresistible,' Robbins recorded. 'Keynes
must be one of the most remarkable men who ever lived – the
quick logic, the birdlike swoop of intuition, the vivid fancy, the
wide vision, above all the incomparable sense of the fitness of
words.' Only Churchill surpassed him, Robbins reckoned; but
Keynes achieved his effects without the Prime Minister's grandilo-
quence. 'He uses the classical style of our life and language, it is
true, but it is shot through with something which is not traditional,

a unique unearthly quality of which one can only say that it is pure genius.'[35]

At Bretton Woods there were speeches of mind-numbing orotundity, hours of deadly boredom, parades of egomania, interminable but necessary procedural rigmaroles, bargaining, schisms, mediation, sub-committees, informal parleys, crashing disorganization, incidents of comic absurdity, grumpiness, tale-telling and much else. None of this signified as much as the tenacity, dedication, subtlety and patience of the leading delegations. Keynes's part in the conference is detailed in the Royal Economic Society's edition of his works. His activities are narrated by Skidelsky particularly, but also by Moggridge, in their biographies. Specialist studies by Richard Gardner, Benn Steil, Ed Conway and others provide further analysis. Countless memoirs and histories illumine its side-lines and personalities. Here only a summary is needed.

At Bretton Woods, Keynes faced his greatest test yet. There had not been so lively, supple and technically masterful a negotiator since the days of Talleyrand. Yet he faced manifold obstacles. The American press and many Congressmen feared that the United States would be duped into subsidizing a pauperized world by a delegation that was more astute than their own experts. They decried the bailing out of bankrupt Britain, with American money, or the financing of improved social services, under the guise of stabilizing currencies. Many of the Bretton Woods delegates did not speak or understand the conference language of English, and were uncomprehending of global monetary and banking techniques in any argot. Keynes described the insupportable workload to Wood's successor as Chancellor of Exchequer, his fellow Tuesday Clubber Sir John Anderson. 'It is as though, in the course of three or four weeks, one had to accomplish the preliminary work of many interdepartmental and Cabinet committees, the job of the

Parliamentary draftsmen, and the passage through several Houses of Parliament of two intricate measures of major dimensions.' Discussions involved 'up to 200 persons in rooms with bad acoustics, shouting through microphones, many of those present, often including the Chairman, with an imperfect knowledge of English.' All this had to be borne by a man with cardiac disease. Keynes had one evening of prostration in Atlantic City, two in the first week at Bretton Woods, then three more attacks. His health teetered on a precipice.[36]

White chaired Commission I on the International Monetary Fund, and Keynes chaired Commission II on the International Bank. Keynes had so eager a mind, and such command of the subject, that he hurtled through the agenda ahead of everyone else, and aroused resentment from the plodders and those relying on translators. Yet his speech at the closing banquet on 22 July, after agreement had been reached on the International Monetary Fund and World Bank, had delegates standing in tribute and applauding like thunder. One passage praised those present for performing combined 'tasks appropriate to the economist, to the financier, to the politician, to the journalist, to the propagandist, to the lawyer, to the statesman – even, I think, to the prophet and to the soothsayer'. It was perhaps after flying back in August that Keynes said, 'When I come home, I don't come home to England, I come home to *Europe*.'[37]

After only a month in Whitehall and Tilton, a new round of negotiations for Stage II of Lend-Lease required Keynes and his wife to return to America on the *Île de France* liner in September. They remained there for two and a half months, until 6 December. Keynes sought $3 billion on the military side, and got $2.8 billion, which seemed an excellent outcome. His negotiating team did not, however, get near their target of $3 billion for non-military items. The English wished to resume exporting on 1 January 1945, but the

Americans insisted that export freedom could not be contemplated before victory over Germany. Nor could Keynes wrest from the Americans the desired guarantee that Lend-Lease would continue for a year after the end of the war. Frank Lee, a member of the Treasury delegation in Washington, praised his 'matchless chief' in December 1944: 'occasionally he over-played his hand and occasionally wore himself out struggling for points which were not worth winning. But in general he was an inspiration to us all ... His industry was prodigious, his resilience and continual optimism were a constant wonder to those of us more inclined to pessimism, while I doubt whether he has ever written or spoken with more lucidity and charm.' Lee was sure that the London delegation could never have reached $3 billion without 'Maynard's inspired leadership'.[38]

Hitler killed himself on 30 April 1945, and the German capitulation was signed in Berlin on 8 May. Vanessa and Clive Bell, with Duncan Grant, attended the two-stage Victory festivities at Tilton, as she recounted. First there was a dinner party. 'Chicken, champagne and very good red wine so it was most enjoyable,' she wrote with quivers of anti-royalist resentment. 'I was a bit shocked to find that afterwards we were expected to listen to the King's speech [on the radio]. All the retainers were led in and everything was so solemn that after the first moments of hysteria induced by His Majesty's stutter I nearly went to sleep.' To her relief the solemnities were broken by 'wild shrieks from Lydia' when a puppy dashed into the room, and cannoned about before settling on Vanessa Bell and nipping her exuberantly. 'Maynard,' she continued, 'because he's a lord, has become completely feudal and does all the right things. We had to drink His Majesty's health.' Then, with the blackout curtains lifted, the party opened windows and saw bonfires, distant fireworks and even, they fancied, the lights of London. On the following night the Bells and Grant returned to Tilton, where the farmworkers were assembled with bevies of small boys. Beer and cheese were handed round. Lydia Keynes danced and recited, there was a sing-song, in which Quentin Bell struck a hit with an American trade union recruitment anthem. A straw figure of Hitler with a lurid papier-mâché head was then put on trial, with Keynes presiding as judge, Quentin Bell prosecuting and Grant as defending counsel jabbering in broken English and grimacing like a fiend. Finally Hitler's effigy was carried in a torchlight procession to the top of the hill behind the house where it was burnt on a bonfire.[39]

Keynes spent the weekend of 18–21 May at King's, where a conference of Canadian diplomats and financial experts met to discuss the post-war transition. One evening, after dinner, they strolled over the bridge across the Cam, past the punts and swans, and into the Fellows' Garden on the other side of Queen's Road. The gardens were heavy with blossom, and the variegated colours, textures and shapes of the trees and shrubs looked breathtaking. The Canadians congratulated Keynes on the artistry of the place. 'Yes, it is beautiful,' Keynes replied, 'and we want to keep it, you know. That's why you're here!' King's, for him, remained the acme of English civilization.[40]

On 26 July Clement Attlee's newly elected Labour government replaced Churchill's caretaker national government. As a member of the House of Lords Keynes had no vote in the general election: he donated £25 to the Liberal party's fighting-fund, and spoke of their candidates as 'Funnies'. Few of the incoming Labour ministers understood the country's predicament as the world's greatest debtor nation, which was committed to full employment and prodigal in its overseas expenditure. They trusted instead to the rectitude of their crusade for social justice vanquishing heathen ill-wishers. In a memorandum of 13 August, Keynes advised the Cabinet that Britain was overspending its income by £2,100 million a year – of which £1,100 million was supplied by Lend-Lease. 'The more or less sudden drying up of these sources of assistance shortly after the end of the Japanese war will put us in an almost desperate plight,' he predicted. 'The gay and successful fashion in which we undertake liabilities all over the world and slop money out to the importunate represents an over-playing of our hand, the possibility of which will come to an end quite suddenly and in the near future unless we obtain a new source of assistance.' He advised the government to anticipate national bankruptcy, enforce an austerity programme and defer its social and economic reforms. US economic support would have to be sought as a gift, even at the risk of the Americans imposing conditions detrimental to British trade. 'Beyond question we are entering into the age of abundance. All the more reason not to mess things up and endanger the prizes of victory.'[41]

On 20 August, following the use of atomic weapons to force Japan's surrender, Washington declared the immediate severance of Lend-Lease: no further goods would be supplied; those already ordered must be paid for. The abruptness of this cancellation, without prior consultation, added insult to the fell blow. At an emergency meeting in the Cabinet Room on 23 August Keynes sounded so optimistic that Ernest Bevin, the Foreign Secretary, fancied that he could hear the money jingling in Keynes's pocket. The moral case for the United States making an outright gift to Britain in recompense for its wartime sacrifices, and the practical advantages for the United States in treating Britain munificently as a means of hastening the return of world prosperity, seemed to Keynes unassailable. It was decided that he and the British Ambassador to the USA, who was on furlough in England, should hurry to Washington to meet the crisis. 'Keynes and Halifax are off to the USA,' noted a Conservative backbencher, '2 Etonians to the rescue of the Labour Party!' Keynes, despite his resilience in the Cabinet Room, recognized that he faced his trickiest negotiations with limited chances of success. On 27 August he and his wife left Southampton on a Canadian troopship accompanied by one official each from the Board of Trade, Foreign Office and Treasury.[42]

The Foreign Office man was Bevin's principal economic adviser, Edmund Hall-Patch: one of those idiosyncratic talents who were then cherished in the English civil service. Hall-Patch's father had been majordomo at the British legation in Brussels before becoming verger of Brompton Oratory. While playing in the band in a Paris cabaret in 1919 Hall-Patch was spotted by a Treasury official who thought his linguistic gifts were wasted as a musician and got him a job with the Supreme Allied Economic Council. He was financial adviser to the government of Siam during the 1920s, and learnt to speak Thai. He went in 1932 to America, where he supported himself as saxophonist in a speakeasy; then became a riding-instructor in London. He visited Romania in 1934 as part of a League of Nations commission; was next recruited to the Treasury, and became its financial commissioner responsible for China, Japan and the Far East. Like Keynes he was charming and pleasure-loving. It was said of him, as it might be of Keynes, that it was 'surprising that with his sceptical and traditional cast of mind, Hall-Patch often seemed a pioneer and even a rebel involved in great changes'. Unlike Keynes he was a mordant pessimist, whose dire forebodings became a laughing-matter. 'Send for 'All-Patch: 'e'll make yer flesh creep,' Bevin used to say. Hall-Patch urged that Britain's future lay with Europe: not in the bogus notions of a special relationship with the USA or economic autarky with the Commonwealth. 'He was a very private person and cultivated an air of myth,' wrote an ambassador named Lord Henniker. 'He tended to appear and disappear like a magician ... His dress – slightly theatrical and antique, with stocks and stick-pins – an inscrutable air behind thick spectacles, and a tendency to break suddenly into French, all added to the enigma.'[43]

In August 1945 the American literary intellectual Malcolm Cowley contemplated his country's future after the atomic bombing of Japan. 'In the short run we're living in the great imperial republic of the twentieth century, we'll be rich, we'll all have three automobiles, we'll have to have them, by law, whether or not we want to sleep with Mae West we'll have to sleep with her, we'll eat too much and then take expensive cures to be slenderized.' More unsettling to Cowley, though, than capitalist nirvana was the perilous insularity underlying the sudden ending of Lend-Lease: 'we had god damn better well have sympathy and imagination, for now we're on the top of the heap and all the envy of an envious world is going to be directed at us – and the world will whoop when the first atom bomb falls on New York'. Generally, though, the Truman administration's termination of Lend-Lease was popular, Isaiah Berlin reported from Washington in September. 'Although regrets have been widely expressed over the abrupt handling of the affair, there has also been, especially in the Middle West, fiery indignation at what is viewed as our ingratitude in criticizing this move. The idea that America is used as a Santa Claus by an ungrateful and largely undeserving world still flourishes luxuriantly here.'[44]

Keynes's double triumphs of 1944 – at Bretton Woods and in the second stage of Lend-Lease negotiations – buoyed him too high when he approached the difficulties of 1945. Morgenthau had resigned, White's influence was receding, and when he reached America in September he faced William Clayton, Assistant Secretary of State for Economic Affairs, and Fred Vinson, Morgenthau's replacement as Secretary of the Treasury. Clayton, who had left school at thirteen and became the world's biggest cotton trader (shifting his base from Oklahoma City to Texas), was judged by the Washington Embassy to be efficient, lucid and congenial. Vinson, a crony of the new President Truman, had been born in the county gaol at Louisa, Kentucky, where his father was warden, and worked as a professional baseball player before setting up as a lawyer and getting elected to Congress. The Embassy in Washington regarded him as slow-thinking but sensible, liberal-minded and well disposed towards the English. Partly to disguise his awkwardness with new ideas, he was prone to cracker-barrel speechifying.

Lord Halifax and Lord Keynes went to Washington hoping to persuade the US to accept a moral obligation to rescue their nation with a grant-in-aid, or at worst an interest-free loan, as a reward for defending world freedom. On 25 September Clayton and Vinson met them, without State Department cognizance, to clarify that neither Washington officials nor the American public would entertain claims for special treatment based on past sacrifices. Still less were they attracted by the argument that American generosity would enable England to join Washington in shaping world commerce and currency on sound lines. 'This led to some rather tense exchanges,' reported Hall-Patch, who warned London that 'Congress & the outside world are blanketed in an impenetrable fog ... of downright hostility.' At another meeting between Clayton and Vinson on one side, with Keynes and Halifax on the other, Keynes erupted in exasperation: 'why do you persecute us like this?' Halifax was more nonchalant about these exasperations: 'a man who tried to flick off everything that might be a nuisance', Isaiah Berlin called him.[45]

Attlee's inexperienced government blundered in its approach. Although Washington had insisted that an Anglo-American trade agreement must precede any request to Congress for financial aid to Britain, ministers did not include trade negotiators in the delegation sent to the USA. After Keynes's expositions in September of his country's predicament, the financial talks stalled until the expert commercial negotiators arrived at the end of the month. There was later another delay of a fortnight while the negotiators awaited further instructions from the Cabinet in London. During each hiatus feelings in Congress and in the American press grew more anti-English. A swift visit to Washington by Attlee was no help to the financial negotiators.

Keynes never ceased to be an Apostle whose beliefs governed his actions. Virginia Woolf had categorized him as 'a moralist', and his political sense was overborne by his sense of morality in 1945. He believed that his country was a virtuous global power, which had fought a just war against the evil of the totalitarian brigands. The injustice seemed inordinate to Keynes, as to his compatriots, that the nation which had battled and ultimately vanquished the Nazis should in consequence be so ruined in its finances as to be emasculated as a world power. Few in Whitehall or Westminster could face the truth that the victors were bust: in some quarters it seemed treasonable to think it. It must be stressed that in 1945–6 Keynes was not craving imperial greatness. He was a Liberal who cherished freedom, believed that competition was invigorating, opposed collectivism and regarded state controls as tantamount to communism. He dreaded the British Isles succumbing to a fortress mentality, retreating within a shrunken and insignificant sterling bloc, cowering behind closed borders, closed minds and customs barriers except with nations that had conceded bilateral trade agreements.[46]

'The "smoked-filled room" technique with no witnesses and no record is a form of negotiation which is only possible if you are supremely confident that the people with whom you are dealing are powerful enough to put through what they agree with you,' Hall-Patch warned in November. He had been shaken by Marriner Eccles, chairman of the Federal Reserve Bank, insisting on 'safeguards' against American money being 'used to raise your standard of living or to meet military expenditure'. It seemed 'fantastic' to Hall-Patch in 1945 that his country would ever submit control of its standard of living or defence budget to foreign lenders. Yet the stipulation by Eccles, whose policy outlook had been described by a New York banker as 'curried Keynes', seems reasonable. Hall-Patch's touchiness at Eccles's proviso was a measure of how ill adapted to post-war realities were the tired, fraught negotiators from London.[47]

Throughout the 1920s and 1930s Keynes had decried the inefficiencies in capitalism that occurred when data was ill coordinated and decisions were taken without full information. Output fell and unemployment rose because of administrative obfuscation, as he insisted on many occasions. The negotiating procedure in Washington, with its dependence on imprecise and disorganized data, therefore infuriated him as inimical to efficiency. 'Life here for the past three weeks or longer has been absolute hell,' he reported to a Treasury official on 21 November.

> Everything that we think we have settled with the Top Committee is then transmitted by them inaccurately to experts and lawyers, who have not been present at the discussion. The latter work without consultation with us and produce to their own top lads something which bears not the slightest resemblance to what we have agreed. Then it is adopted by the American Top Committee and hurled at us in what looks very like an ultimatum. We then in a series of exasperated meetings have to throw out as much as possible.

This frustrating cycle of confusion happened 'time after time after time'.[48]

Keynes, in addition to leading negotiations with the Americans, had to negotiate on a second front with Attlee's Cabinet and

Treasury officials in London. He persevered, often with a splash of gaiety that rallied his delegation colleagues; but his exasperation, irritability and jibes often nettled the Americans, and his troubles with London were almost worse. These difficulties arose despite the fact that no one apart from him had the expertise or subtlety to negotiate such intricate technicalities or the self-reliance to face such momentous global issues without flinching. 'His nature was protean,' said a Canadian financial adviser who saw much of Keynes during 1945. 'He could be magisterial, analytic, scornful, withering, contemptuous, insinuating, persuasive.'[49]

In September, with ministerial authority, Keynes had agreed to the American demand for full sterling convertibility by the end of 1946. In November Hugh Dalton, Labour's Chancellor of the Exchequer, and Attlee's Cabinet had a belated realization of what this meant, and foresaw a crisis a year hence with a headlong exodus of funds from London. Dalton sought to rescind this undertaking on sterling convertibility, but the Americans had no reason to budge. Relations between Dalton and Keynes belied accusations that people wearing the same school tie stick together in class complicity. They had been within a few years of one another at both Eton and King's. They had been interviewed together by the Berlin sexologist Magnus Hirschfeld about the gay scene in Edwardian Cambridge. They also exemplified the informed disdain with which ambitious people who have been educated together often view each other. Dalton did not find Keynes as impressive as the world did, or as authoritative as Keynes thought himself. Keynes reciprocated: he remembered Dalton as a vehement under-graduate supporter of Imperial Preference until converted to socialism, while drunk, by Rupert Brooke, on whom he had sexual designs.

During November, Keynes reached the verge of collapse and resignation. Bank of England and Treasury officials felt that they were wrestling with his views as much as with the Americans. Finally, the Cabinet Secretary, Sir Edward Bridges, went to Washington to conclude the Anglo-American negotiations. Bridges vindicated Keynes's position by recommending Attlee's Cabinet to accept similar terms to those previously reached. At this critical juncture the Cabinet still baulked at the commitment to sterling convertibility, but the Americans would do no more than agree to defer conversion until 1947. If the American terms had been refused, Attlee's government would have been unsustainable. Intolerable austerity, amounting to starvation, would have ensued. Without American rescue-money, it would have been impossible for Labour to nationalize the iron and steel industries, coal-mining, electricity and transport – a socialist experiment that was to fail because of recurrent political meddling, the elimination of individual incentives and initiative, underinvestment, market insensitivity and weakened management. The social security system inaugurated by Beveridge's proposals, which Keynes prized, would have been long deferred if the American terms had been refused. The nationalization and attempted standardization of the abundant existing welfare services – the self-funding and self-governing hospitals, the local-authority clinics, independent charities, local poor relief boards, private insurance schemes, friendly societies and state insurance benefits – which in 1946–8 created the National Health Service would not have been viable. Participation by the Attlee government in the Bretton Woods agreement would have collapsed. This would have renewed the instabilities of pre-war international finance: as Keynes always emphasized, the great vulnerability of the capitalist system is not its inequities or injustices but its instability.

The loan agreement was signed on 6 December. The US granted the UK a line of credit of $3,750,000,000 (equivalent to £1,100,000,000, or to $56 billion in 2014 values) at interest of 2 per cent. Britain was to begin the interest payments in 1951, with provision for fifty annual repayment instalments, which could be deferred in any financial year if British finances were parlous. The American debt was finally liquidated by the transfer of $83.25 million in 2006 when Tony Blair was Prime Minister and George W. Bush was President. In addition, $650 million (about six-sevenths of the outstanding Lend-Lease account) was cancelled by the Americans: Keynes thought this concession was handsome, and felt dismay at the ingratitude with which it was received by his compatriots.

Keynes could never decide whether he might have obtained better terms if Roosevelt had still been alive. 'If he had been in full health and at the height of his political power, the answer would probably be Yes,' he told Kingsley Martin. 'Suppose Winston had survived [in power] too, undoubtedly there would have been brisk messages from one to the other, and very probably Roosevelt would have used his authority to get us better terms.' But he fancied that Congress would have rejected any such terms, and that those which had now been obtained were the utmost that was politically practicable. If the negotiations had collapsed without a loan agreement, he doubted if 'the Labour Government could have lasted a year', and suspected that this foreknowledge might have motivated 'some of those who seemed so complacent at the idea of things breaking down' – for example in the Bank of England (which was facing nationalization by the Labour government). 'It would have been a real disaster if, for the second time, a Labour Government should be destroyed by an external financial situation, for which they scarcely could be regarded as primarily responsible.' He equally doubted 'if the poor, silly Cabinet caught a glimpse of that … probability … even out of the corner of their eyes'. He was driven by the knowledge that 'a permanent splitting up of the world into separate economic blocs, of which ours would be far the weakest, founded on sand and almost certain to collapse within a brief period, would have been a major disaster'.[50]

On 11 December Keynes and his colleagues embarked on the liner *Queen Elizabeth* heading for Southampton. Most of the others were so exhausted by their recent labours that they spent their days as well as nights asleep. Keynes liked to relax on Atlantic voyages by absorbing himself in such nineteenth-century masterpieces as Walter Scott's *The Heart of Midlothian*, Charles Reade's *The Cloister and the Hearth* and Sir George Trevelyan's *The Life and Letters of Lord Macaulay*. But on the *Queen Elizabeth* he had little respite from the toxins of fatigue. The news from England was dismaying. Government speeches recommending the agreement were lukewarm. Ministers were failing to rebut misrepresentations, and indeed sometimes misunderstood the terms. None urged the advantages for the world in Anglo-American cooperation. It was exasperating when Robert Boothby in the House of Commons dubbed the loan agreement reached by Keynes and Bridges 'an economic Munich' – a capitulation by weakling appeasers of an overweening power – and added that the British Empire had been sold for a packet of cigarettes. 'This is the greatest economic defeat we have ever had,' declared Boothby. 'Lord Keynes is a siren beckoning us to our doom from the murky bogs of Bretton Woods.'[51]

'In the press at large, all the tadpoles and tapers who had sucked up to Keynes in the past were now accusing him of betraying our interests,' recalled Robbins, who was travelling with him. He lay in his cabin receiving, with mounting scorn and anger, wires from the liner's radio operators summarizing the newspaper and parliamentary misrepresentations of his efforts and the loan settlement. Sometimes, although all exercise now overtaxed his heart, he crept along to the radio room to collect the latest mortifying calumnies. Then, lying down again in his state-room, he prepared for the political fight that awaited him in England. He sharpened the phrases, and polished the arguments, with which he intended to vanquish his detractors.[52]

Keynes reached Southampton on 17 December, the opening day of the House of Lords debate on the loan and the Bretton Woods agreements. After visiting Gordon Square, he attended five hours of the debate, which opened with a weak presentation of the government's case by an elderly member of Attlee's Cabinet, Lord Pethick-Lawrence. After the destruction of the House of Commons by German bombs in 1941, MPs had occupied the House of Lords debating chamber, and the peers shifted to improvised accommodation in the royal robing-room. There, on 18 December, Keynes gave his masterly speech. 'The smaller chamber', recalled Lord Hailsham, who was present, 'was admirably suited to hear Lord Keynes's quiet but beautifully modulated voice.' Lord Addison thought it 'a brilliant, penetrating discourse, to which it was a joy to listen, and which I am sure will be a perpetual inspiration to read'. Lord Samuel agreed that this was Keynes's greatest oration. 'Although he looked so ill after his return from his labours in America, he spoke with much energy. That speech was a model of cogent argument, illuminated by brilliance and by wit, and it had a profound effect at a critical moment.' This debate in the royal robing-room was the last time that Bertrand Russell saw Keynes. Many peers were dubious about the Anglo-American agreement when Keynes rose to speak, recalled Russell, 'but when he had finished there remained hardly any doubters except Lord Beaverbrook and two cousins of mine with a passion for being in the minority. Having only just landed from the Atlantic, the effort he made must have been terrific.'[53]

In this superlative parliamentary performance, Keynes made clear, as no one had dared do before, that the free world had entered a period of American hegemony, and that his own country was broke. 'The Americans – and are they wrong? – find a post-mortem on relative services and sacrifices amongst the leading allies extremely distasteful.' They found it 'more practical and more realistic – to use two favourite American expressions – to think in terms of the future and to work out what credits, of what amount and upon what terms, will do most service in reconstructing the post-war world'. The United States was a business nation, where money-making seemed a moral duty: 'the American Administration and the American people' accordingly directed their efforts 'towards influencing the future and not towards pensioning the past'. Keynes spoke of his own feelings and position. 'I shall never so long as I live cease to regret that this is not an interest-free loan. The charging of interest is out of tune with the underlying realities. It is based on a false analogy.' Nevertheless, he told the Lords, 'a point comes when in a matter of this kind one has to take No for an answer ... it is not for a foreigner to weigh up the cross-currents, political forces and general sentiments which determine what is possible and what is impossible in the complex and highly charged atmosphere of that great democracy'. Throughout his time in Washington, 'there was not a single Administration measure of the first importance that Congress did not either reject, remodel, or put on one side'. He asked: 'Is it not putting our claim and legitimate expectations a little too high to regard these proposals, on top of Lend-Lease, as anything but an act of unprecedented liberality? Has any country ever treated another country like this, in time of peace, for the purpose of rebuilding the other's strength and restoring its competitive position?'[54]

Many peers spoke against the agreement or regretted American conduct. Lord Portsmouth, from whom Keynes had bought his cache of Isaac Newton manuscripts, regretted 'the mournful masochism of those who have supported the bill'. It showed the swift changes overcoming England that a High Tory agriculturalist now used, by reflex, the jargon of sexual psychology in the House of Lords. Portsmouth and the Duke of Bedford spoke for rural England, and there was telling resistance from businessmen. Lord Piercy, a former personal assistant to Attlee and head of the wartime Petroleum Mission in Washington who had been ennobled weeks earlier, expressed the widespread belief 'that this loan should have been a gift'. The motor-car and aero-engine manufacturer Lord Kenilworth complained about American ruthlessness, as represented by the price paid for Courtauld's Viscose subsidiary. 'We fought at Dunkirk,' said Lord Woolton, formerly managing director of a department store and now chairman of the Conservative party, 'but to-day we are surrendering what I conceive to be our just rights. We are surrendering them to the power of the dollar, because those responsible for the affairs of this country do not dare to retreat on the economic fastnesses of the Empire.' If Britain was the largest debtor nation in history, the USA 'had become rich beyond her dreams'. He supported Keynes's call 'for rightful restitution of the dollars we paid in advance of what became a common cause'.[55]

Above all the newspaper magnate Lord Beaverbrook, who had the touchy parvenu's dislike of the upper chamber, where there was no automatic deference to self-made millionaires, launched a vehement attack on the American loan. He denied that the country was in such financial straits that it needed foreign loans for assistance, and produced a string of figures about sterling balances and import values to justify his assertion. Keynes interrupted Beaverbrook's talk of millions with a deadly interjection: 'in a long and rugged life spent in the statistical jungle, I have never heard statistics so phoney' (the official parliamentary record, Hansard, euphemistically printed the last word as 'funny'). Beaverbrook retorted that Keynes 'has been derelict in duty', and was culpable for the British Empire 'being needlessly and wantonly and wickedly thrown away'.

There were many abstentions in the Lords division, but ninety votes for the agreement, and only eight votes against.[56]

After resting at Tilton, Keynes resumed Treasury work, albeit with mistrust of his ministers and antipathy between him and Dalton. Years before he had explained his Liberalism in terms which still held for him in 1946. 'The political problem of mankind is to combine three things: economic efficiency, social justice, and individual liberty. The first needs criticism, precaution and technical knowledge; the second, an unselfish and enthusiastic spirit, which loves the ordinary man; the third, tolerance, breadth, appreciation of the excellencies of variety and independence, which prefers, above everything, to give unhindered opportunity to the exceptional and the aspiring.' In theory, at least, socialists loved their fellow men, although their internecine strife suggested difficulties in practice; but 'the great party of the proletariat', as Keynes called Labour, had little interest, he judged, in fostering individual rather than collective aspirations, opportunities, excellence. The political prospects did not please.[57]

'The time has come', Keynes confided to Halifax on New Year's Day of 1946, 'for me to slip out of the Treasury, if not suddenly, at least steadily.' He was not attuned to the Labour administration: 'I shall not last long in this galère ... so I had better go ... quietly and friendly.' He deprecated the proposed spending on overseas and military commitments of £700 million for 1946 against £925 million from the Loan. He warned of a forced retreat in these engagements unless there was a swift, voluntary, planned modification. The number of forces outside Europe should be halved, and the burden of feeding hungry Germans should be lifted. His criticisms of the London government and of public opinion were no less severe than his strictures on the Washington administration and on popular sentiments in the USA. 'The mixed chauvinism and universal benevolence of the F.O. and other departments, and the weakness of the Chancellor in these matters, are slopping away on everybody and everything in the world except the poor Englishman the fruits of our American loan,' he warned on 29 January. The irresponsible level of expenditure was not premeditated. 'No-one knows what is happening ... The Ministers, I am told, are reluctant to read their official papers and reach half the ramshackle decisions, particularly on overseas affairs, in the absence of anyone who really knows what it is all about.' Outside government, too, 'England is sticky with self-pity and not prepared to accept peacefully and wisely the fact that her position and her resources are *not* what they once were.'[58]

In March Keynes attended the inaugural meetings of the board of governors of the International Monetary Fund and of the World Bank at Wilmington Island, Savannah. He made believe that something pleasant must happen in Savannah's balmy air and bright colours, which offered an antidote to damp, cold London with its weary, drab, sickly, tetchy inhabitants. The location, structure and personnel of the IMF and World Bank were to be settled at Savannah. Keynes wanted to divert the Americans from their decision to locate both institutions in Washington, where they would seem mere appendages of the US government, rather than in New York; but the Americans had organized an assorted bloc of voters who gave large majorities to all of their wishes.

The Americans wished to appoint full-time executive directors, supported by a battery of expert technical staff, to the International Monetary Fund. The proposed salaries exceeded, in Keynes's view, their burden of work and responsibilities. He urged that the directors should be part-timers, holding posts with their national banks or governments, backed by about thirty full-time staff (as opposed to 300 as contemplated by the Americans). Part of the difference was that Keynes still hankered for his model of an International Credit Union, acting as an international lender of last resort, with a bias towards expansion, whereas the Americans wanted an interventionist body which coordinated monetary policies globally, and implemented ambitious financial schemes. Keynes understood that his resistance to the American proposals on remuneration and staffing was doomed to fail. 'They plainly intend to force their own conceptions on the rest of us,' he told Richard Kahn on 13 March. 'The result is the institutions look like becoming American concerns, run by gigantic American staffs, with the rest of us very much on the side-lines.' The only negative vote recorded at Savannah was by Keynes's delegation against the salary provisions. He was resoundingly outvoted by the American bloc in all his last efforts to curb US hegemony.[59]

There was anguish from the old Empire in recession at the new imperium in the making. The mismatch between American and English officialdom had far deeper causes than Keynes's superiority complex. The Washington Embassy's important despatch to the Foreign Office, which was sent as a final assessment of the Savannah conference, showed either painful confusion in English diplomatic readings of the Americans or the gaping incompatibilities in the Washington administration's approach. Written in the accents of traditional diplomacy, and signed by Halifax, the despatch reported that the proceedings at Savannah 'confirmed the prevalent American tendency to view international problems in emotional terms (the turgid sentimentality of the opening and closing speeches was oppressive to the point of suffocation)'. Then Halifax's despatch either contradicted itself or identified a contradictory characteristic of the Washington administration: having asserted that Americans were too emotive, it accused them of simultaneously pretending to scientific infallibility. The Savannah conference, continued the Washington Embassy, 'also showed how prone are the American officials of the State Department and the Treasury to view the financial problems of the world from the vacuum of a statistical laboratory in Washington, and how wedded they are to the idea that the solution of these problems can be found by a collection of highly qualified economists and statisticians "following trends" from Washington'. The conflicts, disappointments and even odium between old statecraft and new were to continue in both London and Washington for decades.[60]

The negotiations over Lend-Lease, American post-war rescue loans and global financial institutions showed repeatedly that London's trust in a special Anglo-American relationship, on a fair and equal footing, was naive. The United States was intent on world leadership, and saw its London allies as useful but not needing much respect. There were parallel experiences with the Anglo-American nuclear partnership, which was agreed in 1943, but from which English scientists were excluded by the US authorities for the first crucial year (during which the Americans overtook their allies in expertise). The English were finally ejected, unceremoniously, from American collaboration by the McMahon Act of 1946, which prohibited the sharing of technological information with foreign allies.

Keynes knew that his strenuous efforts were killing him. Although exhausted beyond measure, his indomitable will-power and his wife's loving protection kept him alive. On 19 March, on a long, buffeting train carrying him to Washington, he collapsed after walking through swaying carriages on his way to the restaurant car; and collapsed again, giddy and swirling, on his first attempt to return to his compartment. During a turbulent Atlantic crossing he caught a stomach bug in an insalubrious cabin, which had previously been used for the transport of the brides of American soldiers and their babies.

Keynes returned to England as a champion. He had done more than any other single person to create the world institutions whereby currency, external investment, reconstruction, international trade would be managed. He stood at the summit of his prestige. No intellectual had stamped so indelible a mark upon his age; no economist had left such footprints on policy. He was peerless in developing technical theory, explaining it to doubters and applying it to practical business. He had, too, done more than anyone to secure state funding for the arts at a time when private patronage was at its nadir. In doing so, he had upheld civilized values in a decade of lowest barbarism. He helped to provide cultural abundance and discrimination for the coming years of penny-pinching austerity and gimcrack populism. He had also given voice to those who wished to protect English landscape and urban environments from money-grabbing speculators and brutish developers: in the twenty years after his death, many rural amenities were preserved, although many towns and cities were despoiled.

Fame turned Keynes into an epithet. He lived long enough to see the emergence of a school of economists known as Keynesian, and to joke in his intimate circle that Maynard Keynes was not a Keynesian. Already the adjective 'Keynesian' was being applied to describe policies that had been implemented in European industrialized democracies and by the Roosevelt administration without any debt in ideas to him or to his *General Theory*. Although Keynes is nowadays identified with deficit finance, as a wartime Treasury official he opposed his government going into debt in order to maintain individual levels of consumption: 'the ordinary Budget should be balanced at all times', in his own words. 'If serious unemployment does develop, deficit financing is absolutely certain to happen, and I should like to keep free to object hereafter to the more objectionable forms of it,' he warned Treasury colleagues in 1943. Deficit finance seemed to him a 'rather desperate expedient'. He deplored profligacy. He proposed the use of counter-cyclical demand management policies during periods of economic depression and higher unemployment, but affirmed that in ordinary times the budget should always be balanced. Despite recommending public-works programmes to stimulate aggregate demand, he remained a good enough Liberal to oppose ever-increasing government deficits.[61]

In the years after his death some economists invoked Keynes's name as a Good Fairy blessing their own ideas, while others claimed to know what he would recommend to solve the quandaries of later times. This was often spurious stuff. If he had lived into the late twentieth century (his father died in 1949 aged ninety-seven, his mother in 1958 just before her own ninety-seventh birthday, his sister Margaret in 1974 aged eighty-nine, his brother Geoffrey at ninety-five in 1982), his ideas would have developed and transmuted: he was, after all, both brilliant and brave in having second thoughts. He did not believe in mental standstills. He knew that most of his ideas had only a transitive value. The recognition that previous systems of thought, including one's own, have miscarried or are inadequate was the mainspring of his intellectual vigour. Under the influence of Keynes's revisions, the thinking of his peers, the policies of governments, the expectations of consumers, the economic situations of industrialized economies and the scope of possible improvisations towards prosperity would all have developed in ways that can only be guessed at hazard. Keynes's underlying principles of life are more distinct. In 1938 he endorsed a remark of the eighteenth-century Anglican clergyman and moral philosopher William Paley: 'although we speak of communities as of sentient beings; although we ascribe to them happiness and misery, desires, interests, and passions; nothing really exists or feels but *individuals*'. This belief in the primacy of individual effort, self-respect and fulfilment was the ineradicable core of his economic thinking.[62]

During a fortnight in London, after his return from Savannah,

Keynes felt exigent and perplexing business pressing hard on him. Towards the end he attended a performance of John Gielgud's production, with Cecil Beaton's decor, of Oscar Wilde's *Lady Windermere's Fan*: a valiant flourish of flamboyance in the dismal London scene; and an apt play for Keynes, who was so intellectually debonair. One line of Wilde's, though, proclaiming 'the astounding stupidity of optimism', is the antithesis of all that Keynes believed and personified. For him pessimism and anxiety were degradations, like everything that constricted human choices and hopes. Optimism was generous and therefore intelligent, because it enriched, expanded and enhanced life.

After enjoying Wilde's play, Keynes went to Tilton. There, for a week, he toiled on official papers, drafted a post-budget memorandum, inspected his farm, read in the garden, welcomed his mother on a holiday visit, planned to write about his long-dead lover Lytton Strachey for the Memoir Club, and inveighed against Labour's decision to include long-distance road-hauliers alongside the railway companies in the nationalization of transport. Then, on the morning of Easter Sunday 21 April, in the downstairs boot-room by the front door where he slept at night so as to avoid the strain of mounting the stairs, as Lopokova brought him a cup of tea in bed, he had a final heart attack. He died within three minutes before his wife's eyes – held in the arms of his mother who had hurried to the room at the sound of her cries.[63]

Keynes was a sunny man who never iced over. Napoleon's last words in *The Dynasts* provide his immediate epitaph:

> Great men are meteors that consume themselves
> To light the earth. This is my burnt-out hour.

Selflessness killed Keynes. In 1944–5 he had the choice of conserving his life, or of sacrificing himself by overwork. With altruism in his heart he chose to dissipate the last remnants of his strength in public service. For the national good he signed, as it were, his own death warrant. He took a heroic course.

Acknowledgements

All readers will recognize the heavy debt that my book owes to the scholarship and solicitude that Donald Moggridge has devoted to the writings and activities of John Maynard Keynes. The infallibility of Moggridge's editorial work on the thirty volumes of Keynes's papers, and the dedicated, attentive scruples of his Keynes biography, are all the more attractive for being unostentatious. His volumes are indispensable aids. The virtuosity of Robert Skidelsky's work, and the urbane intelligence of his approach, have been no less important to my work.

My own book is neither milk-and-water Moggridge nor gin-and-bitters Skidelsky. It owes some of its flavour to the writings of Richard Overy, Graham Robb, Richard Roberts, Brendan Simms and Robert Tombs. Stephen Keynes made time to see me and to talk freely when he was beset by other responsibilities. I have profited, too, from suggestions, information and corrections from Michael Bloch, Kevin Bucknell, Sir Charles Chadwyck-Healey, Anne Chisholm, Patric Dickinson (Clarenceux King of Arms), Henry Hardy, Simon Malloch, Philip Mansel, Tom Perrin, James Stourton and Donald Winch. Roger Louis twice invited me to speak at the British Studies seminar in the University of Texas at Austin, and thus enabled me to quarry material in the Harry Ransom Center from which parts of this book have been hewn. Various ideas and sentiments in *Universal Man* derive from the discussions of a reading-group that I attend: I thank Edward Behrens, Susie Boyt, Henrietta Bredin, Jonathan Keates, Alan

Moses, Nicola Normanby, Miranda Seymour and Giles Waterfield for all their thoughtful nudges and zestful provocations, which I have recycled.

It is not just a dutiful rigmarole to add that Martin Redfern, my editor at HarperCollins, annotated the penultimate text of this book with candour, sympathy and shrewdness that I had no right to expect. Every reader should be grateful for his improving influence. A publisher at Penguin said some years ago that the book-production dream-team was Peter James as copy-editor with Christopher Phipps as indexer. I feel privileged to have had them both work with unflurried level efficiency on *Universal Man*. I would add Stephen Guise of HarperCollins as the third member of my dream-team: in superintending this book's design and production he has been immaculate.

I thank the archivists of the Berenson Library, I Tatti, Florence; the British Library; Cambridge University Library; Harry Ransom Center at the University of Texas at Austin; Hertfordshire Record Office; the House of Lords Record Office; King's College, Cambridge; Magdalene College, Cambridge; the School of Oriental & African Studies, University of London; and Sheffield University Library. The amenities of the London Library were helpful in the research of this book.

Unpublished writings of J. M. Keynes are © The Provost and Scholars of King's College, Cambridge 2015. Extracts from the *Collected Writings of John Maynard Keynes*, edited by Donald Moggridge *et al.* (1971–89) are © The Royal Economic Society, published by Cambridge University Press. Extracts from letters written by Isaiah Berlin © the Trustees of the Isaiah Berlin Literary Trust 2015 are quoted by permission of the Trustees. For their consent to my use of copyright material I thank the Society of Authors, as agents of the Strachey Trust; Lord Williams of Oystermouth and the Fellows of Magdalene College, Cambridge, where Arthur Benson's diaries are held; and Faber & Faber and the estate of Louis MacNeice for extracts from 'Autumn Journal'.

Susannah Burn, the daughter of Polly Hill and granddaughter of Margaret Keynes and A. V. Hill, has permitted the use of family photographs deposited in the archive at King's, and together with her husband Alastair Burn has given the friendliest help with illustrations. Patricia McGuire, the archivist at King's, has been painstaking in providing us with images. Geoffrey Keynes's grandson Professor Simon Keynes, of Trinity College, Cambridge, has also been generous with his time and advice.

The patient support and smiling tolerance of Christopher Phipps and Jenny Davenport, despite my neglect of many simple decencies and responsibilities during work on the seven lives of Maynard Keynes, makes my all-surpassing debt to them.

> So now, in the end, if this the least be good,
> If any deed be done, if any fire
> Burn in the imperfect page, the praise be thine.

Notes

Abbreviations

BL: British Library
CUL: Cambridge University Library
CW: *Collected Writings of John Maynard Keynes*, ed. Donald Moggridge *et al.*, 30 vols (London: Macmillan/Cambridge: Cambridge University Press, for the Royal Economic Society, 1971–89)
HLRO: House of Lords Record Office
HRC: Harry Ransom Center, University of Texas at Austin
JMK: John Maynard Keynes
JNK: John Neville Keynes
King's: Archives of King's College, Cambridge
NA: National Archives, Kew
Skidelsky: Robert Skidelsky, *John Maynard Keynes*, 3 vols (London: Macmillan, 1983–2000)
SOAS: School of Oriental & African Studies
VWD: *The Diary of Virginia Woolf*, ed. Anne Olivier Bell, 5 vols (London: Hogarth Press, 1977–84)

One: Altruist

1. CW, XX, p. 84.
2. A. C. Pigou, 'John Maynard Keynes, 1883–1946', *Cambridge Review*, 18 May 1946, vol. 67, p. 381.
3. Isaiah Berlin, *Enlightening: Letters 1946–1960* (London: Chatto & Windus, 2009), pp. 62, 208; Lord Beaverbrook, House of Commons debates, 18 December 1945, vol. 138, col. 866.
4. CW, XX, p. 469.
5. Leonard Woolf, 'The Listener's Book Chronicle', *Listener*, 25 January 1951, p. 151.

6. Magdalene College Old Library, 146/1, diary of Arthur Benson, 30 May 1914; CW, XXI, p. 244; Sir Austin Robinson, 'John Maynard Keynes, 1883–1946', *Economic Journal*, 57 (March 1947), p. 67.

7. CW, II, pp. 11–13.

8. D. H. Robertson, 'Review of J. M. Keynes', *Economic Journal*, 30 (March 1920), p. 84.

9. CW, IX, pp. 268–9.

10. John Buchan, *The Island of Sheep* (London: Hodder & Stoughton, 1936), pp. 104–6.

11. Kingsley Martin, 'J. M. Keynes', *New Statesman*, 3 February 1951, p. 133.

12. Clive Bell, *Old Friends* (London: Chatto & Windus, 1956), pp. 52, 61.

Two: Boy Prodigy

1. CW, X, p. 73.

2. 'Horticultural Show at Kensington', *The Times*, 12 September 1861, p. 10.

3. 'Death of Mr John Keynes', *Salisbury & Winchester Journal*, 23 February 1878, p. 8.

4. Virginia Woolf, *The Years* (London: Hogarth Press, 1937), p. 210; CW, II, p. 6.

5. *Letters of H. E. Luxmoore* (Cambridge: Cambridge University Press, 1929), p. 106.

6. Magdalene College Old Library, 46/55, diary of Arthur Benson, 2 February 1904.

7. CW, X, p. 213.

8. King's, PP/20/1, remarks by JMK at his father's ninetieth birthday, August 1942.

9. CUL, Add 7837, diary of JNK, 29 January 1888.

10. CUL, Add 7864, diary of JNK, 20 April & 12 July 1914.

11. CUL, Add 7833, diary of JNK, 5 & 6 June 1883.

12. *Ibid.*, 8 & 27 July, 11 August 1883.

13. CUL, Add 7836, diary of JNK, 5 June, 30 August, 10 September, 9 & 23 December 1887.

14. *Ibid.*, 8 October 1887.

15. *Ibid.*, 29 April & 19 May 1888; Florence Ada Keynes, *Gathering up the Threads* (Cambridge: Heffer, 1950), p. 64.

16. CUL, Add 7837, diary of JNK, 2 December 1888 & 2 September 1894.

17. CUL, Add 7844, diary of JNK, 8 October 1894.

18. C. D. Broad, 'William Ernest Johnson, 1858–1931', *Proceedings of the British Academy*, 17 (1931), p. 513; J. T. Sheppard, 'John Maynard Keynes, 1883–1946', *Cambridge Review*, 18 May 1946, vol. 67, p. 380.

19. CUL, Add 7847, diary of JNK, 12 January 1897, 14, 15, 17, 19 & 25 April 1897, 28 June 1897.

20. *Ibid.*, 5 July 1897.

21. *Ibid.*, 24 July 1897.

22. *Ibid.*, 18 September 1897.

23. Esmé Wingfield-Stratford, *Before the Lamps Went Out* (London: Hodder & Stoughton, 1945), pp. 130–1; Rudyard Kipling, 'The Islanders' (1902).

24. Wingfield-Stratford, *Lamps*, p. 128; Lord Vansittart, *The Mist Procession* (London: Hutchinson, 1958), p. 23.

25. Percy Lubbock, *Shades of Eton* (London: Jonathan Cape, 1929), pp. 13–14; HRC, Ives papers III/IV, diary of George Ives, 25 February 1906; Luxmoore, *Letters*, p. 186; 'A Nation under Orders', *The Times*, 24 May 1915, p. 3; Vansittart, *Mist Procession*, pp. 23–4.

26. King's, PP/45/321/290, holograph note on Keynes at Eton by Bernard Swithinbank, March 1948.

27. Wingfield-Stratford, *Lamps*, pp. 124–5, 129–32, 133–4.

28. 'Mr. S. G. Lubbock, the Best of Eton', *The Times*, 31 January 1958, p. 13; CUL, Add 7848, diary of JNK, 12 June 1898.

29. 'Mr. H. E. Luxmoore, A Great Etonian', *The Times*, 12 November 1926, p. 19; Lubbock, *Shades of Eton*, pp. 168, 171; CUL, Add 7850, diary of JNK, 26 December 1900.

30. CUL, Add 7848, diary of JNK, 29 June, 8, 9 & 23 July 1898.

31. Phyllis Deane, *The Life and Times of J. Neville Keynes: A Beacon in the Tempest* (Cheltenham: Edward Elgar, 2001), p. 178.

32. CUL, Add 7851, diary of JNK, 4 April 1901; Luxmoore, *Letters*, p. 123.

33. Keynes, *Gathering Up the Threads*, p. 73; CUL, Add 7852, diary of JNK, 10 February 1902.

34. Bertrand Russell, 'The Study of Mathematics', *New Quarterly*, 1 (1907–8), pp. 33–4.

35. CW, X, pp. 353, 355, 356.

36. Luxmoore, *Letters*, p. 110; Sir Denis Proctor, ed., *The Autobiography of G. Lowes Dickinson* (London: Duckworth, 1973), p. 65.

37. Polly Hill and Richard Keynes, eds, *Lydia and Maynard: Letters between Lydia Lopokova and John Maynard Keynes* (London: André Deutsch, 1989), p. 256; 'West and East Camb', *Cambridge Independent News*, 9 December 1910, p. 4.

38. CW, X, p. 438.

39. G. H. Hardy, *A Mathematician's Apology* (Cambridge: Cambridge University Press, 1940), p. 23.

40. William C. Lubenow, *The Cambridge Apostles 1820–1914* (Cambridge: Cambridge University Press, 1998), p. 33.

41. Magdalene College Old Library, 76/55, diary of Arthur Benson, 5 December 1905; Hardy, *Apology*, p. 7.

42. VWD, I, p. 135; Goldsworthy Lowes Dickinson, *J. McT. E. McTaggart* (Cambridge: Cambridge University Press, 1931), p. 58.

43. BL, Add 57930A, JMK to Duncan Grant, 14 August 1908; Keith Hale, ed., *Friends and Apostles: The Correspondence of Rupert Brooke and James Strachey 1905–1914* (London: Yale University Press, 1998), pp. 74–5.

44. Dickinson, *McTaggart*, p. 49; Virginia Woolf, *The Voyage Out* (London: Duckworth, 1915), p. 242.

45. Magdalene College Old Library, 46/55 & 71/52, diary of Arthur Benson, 2 February 1904 & 3 July 1905.

46. Norman Mackenzie, ed., *The Letters of Sidney and Beatrice Webb*, 3 vols (Cambridge: Cambridge University Press, 1978), II, p. 372.

47. CW, X, p. 435.

48. CW, X, pp. 447–8.

49. CW, XX, pp. 436–7.

50. King's, UA/22/6–8, JMK, 'Modern Civilisation', paper read to the Apostles, 28 October 1905; King's, UA/31/1 & 7, paper on 'Paradise' (1908?).

Three: Official

1. King's, PP/45/331/1, G. M. Trevelyan to JMK, nd [June 1906?].

2. BL, Add ms 48680, diary of Sir Edward Walter Hamilton, 3 September 1902.

3. Barbara Strachey and Jayne Samuels, eds, *Mary Berenson: A Self-Portrait from her Letters & Diaries* (London: Victor Gollancz, 1983), p. 135.

4. Virginia Woolf, *Jacob's Room* (London: Hogarth Press, 1922), p. 282; King's, PP/45/316/3/22, JMK to Lytton Strachey, 7 March 1907.
5. King's, PP/45/316/3/120, JMK to Lytton Strachey, 13 September 1907.
6. CUL, Add 7858, diary of JNK, 1 March 1908; Strachey and Samuels, *Mary Berenson*, p. 147.
7. Magdalene College Old Library, 120/2 & 141/50, diary of Arthur Benson, 12 March 1911 & 16 November 1913.
8. CW, X, p. 41.
9. Sir Ernest Cable, 'The Hoarded Wealth of India', *The Times*, 17 August 1908, p. 7.
10. In the section that follows I depend upon a steady and stylish guide in Richard Roberts, *Saving the City: The Great Financial Crisis of 1914* (Oxford: Oxford University Press, 2013).
11. CW, XI, pp. 254–5.
12. CW, XI, p. 248.
13. Skidelsky, I, p. 289; Bertrand Russell, 'Portraits from Memory', *Listener*, 17 July 1952, p. 97.
14. CW, XVI, pp. 7–15.
15. CW, XVI, pp. 16–19, 32–9.
16. CW, XVI, p. 31; David Lloyd George, *War Memoirs*, 6 vols (London: Ivor Nicholson & Watson, 1933–6), I, pp. 111–12; CW, XI, pp. 238, 266–8.
17. CW, XVI, pp. 297–300.
18. CW, X, p. 440.
19. CUL, Add 7865, diary of JNK, 6, 14 & 17 January 1915; HRC, Morrell papers 11/5, JMK to Lady Ottoline Morrell, 13 January 1915; CW, XVI, pp. 46–8; VWD, I, p. 24.
20. Sir Otto Niemeyer and Sir Richard Hopkins, 'Public Servant', *Proceedings of the British Academy*, 32 (1946), p. 401; Sheffield University Library, Hewins papers 58/133, Sir Vincent Caillard to William Hewins, 26 September 1915.
21. CUL, Add 7865, diary of JNK, 18 September & 3 October 1915; HRC, Morrell papers 2/3, Clive Bell to Lady Ottoline Morrell, 26 September 1915; CW, XVI, p. 213; Niemeyer and Hopkins, 'Public Servant', p. 402.
22. CW, XVI, p. 198.
23. CW, XVI, p. 201.
24. CW, XVI, p. 211.

25. CW, X, pp. 33–5.
26. CW, XVI, p. 221; Laird M. Easton, ed., *Journey to the Abyss: The Diaries of Count Harry Kessler 1880–1918* (New York: Random House, 2013), pp. 771–2.
27. CW, X, pp. 340, 448; Clive Bell, *Old Friends* (London: Chatto & Windus, 1956), pp. 46–7.
28. 'The Great Rally', *The Times*, 4 October 1915, p. 5a; 'Bulgaria and the War', *ibid.*, p. 9a.
29. Viscount Sandhurst, *From Day to Day 1914–15* (London: Edward Arnold, 1928), pp. 287, 296.
30. HRC, Morrell papers 11/5, JMK to Lady Ottoline Morrell, 4 January 1916.
31. CUL, Add 7866, diary of JNK, 6 & 14 January 1916; VWD, I, p. 25.
32. BL, Add 57931, JMK to Duncan Grant, 14 January 1917 (while staying with McKenna at Munstead).
33. David Garnett, ed., *Carrington* (London: Jonathan Cape, 1970), pp. 56–7; David Garnett, *The Flowers of the Forest* (London: Chatto & Windus, 1955), pp. 144–5; Quentin Bell, 'Recollections and Reflections on Maynard Keynes', in Derek Crabtree and A. P. Thirlwall, eds, *Keynes and the Bloomsbury Group* (London: Macmillan, 1980), p. 72.
34. E. M. Forster, *Goldsworthy Lowes Dickinson* (London: Edward Arnold, 1934), p. 107.
35. CW, XVI, p. 264; Strachey and Samuels, *Mary Berenson*, p. 217; D. E. Moggridge, *Maynard Keynes: An Economist's Biography* (London: Routledge, 1992), p. 277; BL, Add 57931, JMK to Duncan Grant, 17 October 1917.
36. King's, PP/45/168/9/55, JMK to Florence Keynes, 24 December 1917; CW, XVI, p. 287.
37. King's, EC/7/2/2, JMK note of 1919.
38. CW, XXVIII, p. 163; R. B. McCallum, *Public Opinion and the Last Peace* (London: Oxford University Press, 1944), pp. 7, 39, 42, 70.
39. CW, X, p. 390.
40. *Ibid.*
41. King's, UA/36/11 & 13, JMK's presidential address to the Apostles, 21 June 1921.
42. CW, X, p. 393.
43. CW, X, p. 395.

44. CW, X, pp. 404–5.

45. CW, X, pp. 413–15.

46. CW, X, pp. 423–4.

47. Moggridge, *Maynard Keynes*, pp. 298–9.

48. John Vincent, ed., *The Crawford Papers* (Manchester: Manchester University Press, 1984), p. 401.

49. 'The starving children of Austria', *Manchester Guardian*, 8 May 1919, p. 5.

50. Lord Vansittart, *The Mist Procession* (London: Hutchinson, 1958), p. 218; CW, II, pp. 2–3; Sir Roy Harrod, *The Life of John Maynard Keynes* (London: Macmillan, 1951), p. 239.

51. CW, II, p. 143.

52. Leo Amery, *My Political Life*, 3 vols (London: Hutchinson, 1953–5), II, p. 111.

53. BL, Add 57931, JMK to Duncan Grant, 14 May 1919.

54. CW, XVI, p. 464; Sir Andrew MacFadyean, 'Lord Bradbury', *The Times*, 11 May 1950, p. 8; BL, Add 57931, JMK to Duncan Grant, 1 June 1919.

55. HRC, Morrell papers 11/5, JMK to Lady Ottoline Morrell, 8 August 1919; CW, XVII, pp. 7–8.

56. Vansittart, *Mist Procession*, p. 224.

57. CW, II, pp. 18–19.

58. CW, II, pp. 27–8.

59. CW, II, pp. 19–20.

60. CW, II, pp. 2, 21–2.

61. CW, II, p. 142.

62. CW, II, pp. 184–5; Richard Davenport-Hines, 'Vickers and Schneider', in Alice Teichova, Maurice Lévy-Leboyer and Helga Nussbaum, eds, *Historical Studies in International Corporate Business* (Cambridge: Cambridge University Press, 1989), pp. 123–34.

63. CW, II, p. 185.

64. Robert Self, ed., *The Austen Chamberlain Diary Letters* (Cambridge: Royal Historical Society, 1995), p. 122; Robert Self, ed., *The Neville Chamberlain Letter Diaries* (Aldershot: Ashgate, 2000), p. 358.

65. Vincent, *Crawford Papers*, pp. 404–5; NA FO 371/4591, A1157/1157/45, despatch 279 of R. C. Lindsay, 24 February 1920, with undated minute by Lord Hardinge of Penshurst; Trevor Wilson, ed., *The Political Diaries of C. P. Scott 1911–1928* (London: Collins, 1970), p. 380; P. J. Grigg, *Prejudice and Judgment* (London: Jonathan Cape, 1948), p. 104.

66. SOAS, PP Ms 14/4, diary of Sir Charles Addis, 23 December 1919; 'A Critic of the Peace', *The Times*, 5 January 1920, p. 17.

67. Mark Pottle, ed., *Champion Redoubtable: The Diaries and Letters of Violet Bonham Carter 1914–1945* (London: Weidenfeld & Nicolson, 1998), pp. 107–8; Hertfordshire Record Office, DERV C407/40, Violet Bonham Carter to Lady Desborough, 28 December 1919; cf. Julia Davis and Dolores Fleming, eds, *The Ambassadorial Diary of John W. Davis* (Morgantown: West Virginia University Press, 1993), p. 215; Sir George Arthur, *Further Letters from a Man of No Importance 1914–1929* (London: Geoffrey Bles, 1932), p. 77.

68. Lord Perry, House of Lords debates, 23 May 1944, vol. 131, col. 860; Lord Melchett, House of Lords debates, 15 April 1943, vol. 127, col. 241; Valerie Eliot, ed., *The Letters of T. S. Eliot*, I (London: Faber & Faber, 1988), p. 353; CW, II, p. 76.

69. Robert Boothby, 'A decade which struck down greatness', *Listener*, 15 February 1951, p. 253.

70. Vansittart, *Mist Procession*, pp. 223–5.

71. Robert Tombs, *The English and their History* (London: Allen Lane, 2014), p. 650.

72. Rupert Hart-Davis, ed., *Siegfried Sassoon Diaries 1923–1925* (London: Faber & Faber, 1985), p. 42; Donald Winch, 'Keynes and the British Academy', *Historical Journal*, 57 (2014), pp. 757, 759; CW, XVII, pp. 165–6; Roy Harrod, *The Prof* (London: Macmillan, 1959), p. 49.

Four: Public Man

1. 'Mock Trial of Economists', *The Times*, 14 July 1933, p. 11; King's, PP/45/316/1/173, JMK to Lytton Strachey, 15 November 1905.

2. King's, PP/45/316/2/177, JMK to Lytton Strachey, 2 April 1906; Kingsley Martin, 'John Maynard Keynes', *New Statesman*, 27 April 1946, p. 295.

3. VWD, I, p. 288; Martin, 'John Maynard Keynes', p. 295.

4. CW, IX, pp. 297, 299.

5. SOAS, Addis papers 14/407, JMK to Sir Charles Addis, 25 July 1924; CW, IX, p. 304; David Kynaston, *City of London*, 4 vols (London: Chatto & Windus, 1994–2001), III, p. 123.

6. CW, XX, p. 561; CW, X, p. 234.

7. Donald Moggridge, ed., *Keynes on the Wireless* (Basingstoke: Palgrave Macmillan, 2010), p. 168.

8. CW, XVIII, pp. 33–4; CW, XIX, p. 642.

9. CW, IX, pp. 267–8; CW, XIX, p. 641.

10. BL, Add 57930B, JMK to Duncan Grant, 3 October 1911; cf. J. H. Morgan, 'The Eighty Club Visit to Ireland', *Manchester Guardian*, 6 October 1911, p. 7, and 'Eighty Club's Tour, Limerick Visited under Difficulties', *Manchester Guardian*, 27 September 1911, p. 8.

11. Sir Frederick Leith-Ross, *Money Talks* (London: Hutchinson, 1968), p. 148.

12. Sir Colin Coote, *The Other Club* (London: Sidgwick & Jackson, 1971); Sir Newman Flower, ed., *The Journals of Arnold Bennett*, 3 vols (London: Cassell, 1932–3), III, p. 218; James Hepburn, ed., *Letters of Arnold Bennett*, 4 vols (London and Oxford: Oxford University Press, 1966–86), IV, p. 601.

13. CW, X, pp. 173–4.

14. CW, X, pp. 364, 373–4; Sir Edward Marsh and Christopher Hassall, *Ambrosia and Small Beer* (London: Longmans, 1964), p. 243; Sarah Dry, *The Newton Papers* (Oxford: Oxford University Press, 2014).

15. Lord Kahn, 'On Re-Reading Keynes', *Proceedings of the British Academy*, 60 (1974), p. 368; CW, IV, p. 65 (Keynes's italics).

16. CW, IX, p. 306.

17. VWD, V, p. 129; CW, X, p. 446.

18. CW, XXI, pp. 241–2.

19. Lowes Dickinson, *McTaggart*, p. 57; CW, II, pp. 11–12.

20. Sir Ernest Cable, 'The Hoarded Wealth of India', *The Times*, 17 August 1908, p. 7.

21. VWD, II, p. 268.

22. King's, PP/45/190.3/28, JMK to Lydia Keynes, 15 November 1925.

23. CW, XIX, pp. 220, 222; HLRO, Viscount Davidson papers, DAV/160, Wilfrid Ashley to Philip Lloyd-Greame, 8 August 1923.

24. CW, XIX, pp. 228–9, 230–1.

25. F. L. Lucas, 'Criticism', *Life and Letters*, 3 (1929), p. 434.

26. G. M. Young, *Stanley Baldwin* (London: Hart-Davis, 1952), p. 46; Robert Blake, *The Unknown Prime Minister* (London: Eyre & Spottiswoode, 1955), pp. 492–5; J. Mordaunt Crook, 'G. M. Young', in S. J. D. Green and Peregrine Horden, eds, *All Souls and the Wider World* (Oxford: Oxford University Press, 2011), p. 310.

27. SOAS, Addis papers 14/397, JMK to Sir Charles Addis, 26 October 1921.

28. SOAS, Addis papers 14/407, JMK to Sir Charles Addis, 25 July 1924.

29. P. J. Grigg, *Prejudice and Judgment* (London: Jonathan Cape, 1948), pp. 182–3.

30. CW, XX, p. 323.

31. CW, XIX, p. 473; CW, IX, p. 258.

32. HRC, Morrell papers 11/5, JMK to Lady Ottoline Morrell, 2 May 1928; CW, XVIII, pp. 34–5, 38; Julian Bell, *Essays, Poems and Letters* (London: Hogarth Press, 1938), pp. 21, 67.

33. VWD, I, p. 194; CW, VII, p. 374.

34. Mark DeWolfe Howe, ed., *Holmes–Laski Letters*, 2 vols (Oxford: Oxford University Press, 1953), I, p. 400.

35. CW, XXVIII, p. 107; CW, II, p. 166; Harrod, *Keynes*, p. 239.

36. CW, XVII, pp. 370, 372–3

37. CW, XIX, p. 765; Peter Clarke, *The Keynesian Revolution in the Making 1924–36* (Oxford: Clarendon Press, 1988), pp. 49, 74.

38. 'Mr Keynes on Labour Predicament', *Manchester Guardian*, 4 December 1923, p. 13.

39. 'Vote – and Vote Right', *Blackpool Times*, 4 December 1923, p. 7; 'Great Liberal Rally', *Blackpool Times*, 7 December 1923, p. 5; 'The Campaign', *Barrow Guardian*, 1 December 1923, p. 2; 'Remarkable Enthusiasm at Final Meeting', *Barrow News*, 8 December 1921, p. 21; J. D. Scott, *Vickers* (London: Weidenfeld & Nicolson, 1962), pp. 144–5; 'London Solicitor Found Shot', *Manchester Guardian*, 1 May 1929, p. 11; 'Inquest on Shot Solicitor', *The Times*, 4 May 1929, p. 4.

40. Polly Hill and Richard Keynes, eds, *Lydia and Maynard: Letters between Lydia Lopokova and John Maynard Keynes* (London: André Deutsch, 1989), pp. 135–6.

41. *Ibid.*, pp. 234, 242; Magdalene College Old Library, 177/20, diary of Arthur Benson, 25 October 1924.

42. 'Liberals' Big Rally', *Cambridge Daily News*, 27 October 1924, p. 6.

43. King's, PP/45/190/3/100, JMK to Margot Oxford, 30 May 1926.

44. King's, PP/45/190/4/22, JMK to Lydia Keynes, 25 February 1928; CW, XIX, p. 735; Keith Middlemas, ed., *Thomas Jones: Whitehall Diary*, 3 vols (London: Oxford University Press, 1969–71), II, p. 130.

45. CW, IX, p. 122.

46. CW, IX, pp. 123, 125.

47. 'Sunday Cinemas', *Sydney Morning Herald*, 22 April 1931, p. 11; Sir Harold Nicolson, *Diaries and Letters 1930–1939* (London: Collins, 1966), p. 72; House of Commons debates, 20 April 1931, vol. 251, cols 633–766.

48. N. J. Crowson, *Fleet Street, Press Barons and Politics: The Journals of Collin Brooks, 1932–1940* (London: Royal Historical Society, 1998), p. 241; CW, XVIII, pp. 399, 400, 402, 403; Clive Bell, *On British Freedom* (London: Chatto & Windus, 1923), p. 35.

49. David Lloyd George, *War Memoirs*, 6 vols (London: Ivor Nicholson & Watson, 1933–6), II, p. 684.

50. Eric Homberger, William Janeway and Simon Schama, eds, *The Cambridge Mind* (London: Jonathan Cape, 1970), pp. 48, 50.

51. CW, XX, pp. 243–5, 249, 256, 262–3.

52. Clarke, *Keynesian Revolution*, p. 192.

53. Lord Macmillan, *A Man of Law's Tale* (London: Macmillan, 1952), pp. 196–7; information from Lord Crowther's son-in-law Colin Luke, 6 August 2013.

54. Sir Charles Chadwyck-Healey, *Cecil Lubbock* (Bassingbourne: Penchant Press, 2008), pp. 46–52; Grigg, *Prejudice and Judgment*, pp. 253–4.

55. Leith-Ross, *Money Talks*, p. 129.

56. Grigg, *Prejudice and Judgment*, p. 257.

57. Valerie Eliot and John Haffenden, eds, *The Letters of T. S. Eliot*, IV (London: Faber & Faber, 2013), p. 262.

58. Lionel Robbins, *Autobiography of an Economist* (London: Macmillan, 1971), pp. 151, 154.

59. CW, XX, pp. 378–80.

60. CW, XXI, pp. 233–4, 236, 237, 239.

61. CW, XVIII, pp. 185–6; VWD, IV, pp. 272–3; CW, XVIII, p. 155.

62. CW, XX, pp. 490, 505.

63. CW, XX, p. 569; Nicolson, *Diaries*, p. 87.

64. VWD, IV, pp. 107–8.

65. Sir Arthur Salter, 'Support for the Keynes Plan', *Manchester Guardian*, 21 March 1933, p. 9.

66. Robert Self, ed., *The Austen Chamberlain Diary Letters* (Cambridge: Royal Historical Society, 1995), p. 434.

67. Moggridge, *Keynes on the Wireless*, p. 112.

68. E. H. Carr, *International Relations between the World Wars, 1919–1939* (London: Macmillan, 1939), p. 150.
69. Kahn, 'Re-Reading Keynes', pp. 364, 368; Sir Austin Robinson, 'John Maynard Keynes: Economist, Author, Statesman', *Proceedings of the British Academy*, 57 (1971), pp. 201–3.
70. CW, VI, p. 132.
71. Sir Austin Robinson, 'John Maynard Keynes, 1883–1946', *Economic Journal*, 57 (March 1947), p. 40; Joan Robinson, 'What Has Become of the Keynesian Revolution?', in Milo Keynes, ed., *Essays on John Maynard Keynes* (Cambridge: Cambridge University Press, 1975), p. 125.
72. Robinson, 'John Maynard Keynes, 1883–1946', pp. 44–5.
73. Kahn, 'Re-reading Keynes', p. 369; CW, VII, p. 247; Clarke, *Keynesian Revolution*, p. 305.
74. CW, IX, p. 332; Leo Amery, *My Political Life*, 3 vols (London: Hutchinson, 1953–5), I, p. 252.
75. CW, XIX, p. 733.
76. CW, XIX, p. 542.

Five: Lover

1. King's, PP/45/149/9, JMK to Arthur Hobhouse, 27 April 1905; PP/45/316/155, JMK to Lytton Strachey, 11 March 1906; Lady Cynthia Asquith, *Diaries 1914–1918* (London: Hutchinson, 1968), p. 391; VWD, II, pp. 69, 266.
2. Robert Gathorne-Hardy, ed., *Ottoline at Garsington* (London: Faber & Faber, 1974), p. 50; Sir Harold Nicolson, 'Maynard Keynes', *Observer*, 28 January 1951, p. 7; BL, Add 57930A, JMK to Duncan Grant, 31 January 1909; Regina Marler, ed., *Selected Letters of Vanessa Bell* (London: Bloomsbury, 1993), p. 163.
3. BL, Add 57930B, JMK to Duncan Grant, 6 December 1910; CW, X, p. 42; Hertfordshire Record Office, DERV C/1882/1, Edwin Montagu to Ettie Desborough, 8 April 1917. Montagu's repressed sexuality is to be evaluated in a forthcoming book entitled *Closet Queens* by Michael Bloch, to whom I am grateful for his suggestive talk.
4. SOAS, PP Ms 14/4, diary of Sir Charles Addis, 23 February 1921; Polly Hill and Richard Keynes, eds, *Lydia and Maynard: Letters between*

Lydia Lopokova and John Maynard Keynes (London: André Deutsch, 1989), p. 318; CW, X, pp. 382–3.

5. CW, XX, pp. 158–9; VWD, V, p. 346.
6. Hill and Keynes, *Lydia and Maynard*, p. 118; Sir Austin Robinson, 'John Maynard Keynes, 1883–1946', *Economic Journal*, 57 (March 1947), p. 49; BL, Add 57931, JMK to Duncan Grant, 14 January 1917; CW, X, p. 415; Niall Ferguson, *High Financier: The Lives and Time of Siegmund Warburg* (London: Allen Lane, 2010), p. 39.
7. King's, PP/45/321/164, JMK to Bernard Swithinbank, 7 June 1906; BL, Add 57930B, JMK to Duncan Grant, 24 January 1910.
8. King's, PP/45/109/1, Morgan Forster to JMK, 8 December 1914.
9. King's, PP/45/316/2/197, JMK to Lytton Strachey, 19 April 1906.
10. Private information and personal knowledge.
11. BL, Add 57930A, JMK to Duncan Grant, 26 December 1908.
12. *Ibid.*, JMK to Duncan Grant, 26 July 1908 & Add 57930B, JMK to Duncan Grant, 11 October 1910.
13. BL Add 57931, JMK to Duncan Grant, 23 January & 12 February 1913.
14. Willa Cather, *Stories, Poems and Other Writings* (New York: Library of America, 1992), pp. 877–8.
15. CUL, Add 7844, diary of JNK, 21 October 1894.
16. Jesse Bering, *Perv* (London: Doubleday, 2013), p. 78; Francis B. Smith, *The People's Health 1830–1910* (London: Croom Helm, 1979), pp. 298–9; 'Sheffield Medico-Chirurgical Society', *Lancet*, 20 June 1891, p. 1384; 'The Barbarity of Circumcision as a Remedy for Congenital Abnormality', *Lancet*, 20 June 1891, p. 1387.
17. Lord Hailsham, *A Sparrow's Flight* (London: Collins, 1990), p. 17.
18. Richard Davenport-Hines, *Auden* (London: Heinemann, 1995), pp. 31–2; King's, PP/45/316/2/70, JMK to Lytton Strachey, 1 February 1906.
19. Sir Lawrence Jones, *A Victorian Boyhood* (London: Macmillan, 1955), pp. 152–3.
20. CUL, Add 7849, diary of JNK, 2 April 1899; J. A. Gere, *Bensoniana and Cornishiana* (Settrington: Stone Trough Books, 1999), p. 55.
21. Percy Lubbock, *Shades of Eton* (London: Jonathan Cape, 1929), pp. 168, 171; King's, PP/45/321/190, holograph note by Bernard Swithinbank for Roy Harrod, March 1948.
22. King's, PP/20A/2, list of sexual partners 1901–15.

23. King's, PP/45/316/2/143–4 & 155, JMK to Lytton Strachey, 5 & 11 March 1906; BL, Add 57930B, JMK to Duncan Grant, 28 July 1909 & 21 August 1910.

24. Magdalene College Old Library, 45/64, diary of Arthur Benson, 24 January 1904.

25. Michael Holroyd, *Lytton Strachey*, 2 vols (London: Heinemann, 1967–8), I, p. 200; BL, Add 57930a, JMK to Duncan Grant, 10 May 1909.

26. Magdalene College Old Library, Cambridge, 52/65, diary of Arthur Benson, 24 May 1904.

27. King's, PP/45/53/19, Oscar Browning to JMK, 17 August 1918; *Dictionary of National Biography 1922–1930* (Oxford: Oxford University Press, 1937), p. 127.

28. King's, PP/45/109/14, JMK to E. M. Forster, 30 August 1933; William C. Lubenow, *The Cambridge Apostles 1820–1914* (Cambridge: Cambridge University Press, 1998), p. 70. Dickinson had smudgy backward-sloping handwriting, used cheap, flimsy note-paper and was an inept typist who made messy, annoying corrections to his mistyped missives.

29. Keith Hale, ed., *Friends and Apostles: The Correspondence of Rupert Brooke and James Strachey 1905–1914* (London: Yale University Press, 1998), p. 157.

30. King's, PP/45/283/3, Harry Norton to JMK, nd; King's, UA/22/7, JMK, 'Modern Civilisation', paper read to the Apostles, 28 October 1905.

31. Holroyd, *Lytton Strachey*, I, pp. 218–19; BL, Add 60706, Lytton Strachey to James Strachey, 1 August 1907.

32. Michael Holroyd, ed., *Lytton Strachey by Himself* (London: Heinemann, 1971), p. 172.

33. Hale, *Friends and Apostles*, p. 251; Sir Geoffrey Keynes, ed., *The Poetical Works of Rupert Brooke* (London: Faber & Faber, 1970), p. 31.

34. King's, UA/36/3, JMK presidential address to the Apostles, 21 June 1921; Angus McLaren, *Impotence: A Cultural History* (Chicago: University of Chicago Press, 2007), p. 190.

35. BL, Add 57930A, JMK to Duncan Grant, 28 July 1908.

36. King's, PP/45/316/2/113, JMK to Lytton Strachey, 15 February 1906; CW, XI, pp. 559–60.

37. King's, PP/20A/1, 2, 3 & 4; HRC, Morrell papers 11/5, JMK to Lady Ottoline Morrell, 5 July 1915.

38. King's, PP/20A/3–4; David Felix, *Keynes* (London: Greenwood Press, 1999), p. 108; Graham Robb, *Strangers* (London: Picador, 2003), p. 172.

39. BL, Add 57930B, JMK to Duncan Grant, 7 September 1911.

40. HRC, Ives papers III/V, diary of George Ives, 15 & 16 February 1906, 5 March 1906, 15 August 1907, 6 April 1909; Paul Sieveking, ed., *Man Bites Man: The Scrapbook of an Edwardian Eccentric* (London: Jay Landesman, 1980).

41. 'Scotland from the Firth to the Grampians', *Manchester Guardian*, 3 January 1906, p. 9; 'David Erskine', *The Times*, 1 June 1922, p. 13.

42. 'Army Officer's Suicide', *The Times*, 20 May 1911, p. 4.

43. David Garnett, *The Flowers of the Forest* (London: Chatto & Windus, 1955), pp. 29–30.

44. BL, Add 60707, Lytton Strachey to James Strachey, 15 & 23 July 1908; Hale, *Friends and Apostles*, p. 55.

45. BL, Add 57930A, JMK to Duncan Grant, 28 July & 9 August 1908; D. E. Moggridge, *Maynard Keynes: An Economist's Biography* (London: Routledge, 1992), p. 170; Skidelsky, I, p. 196.

46. BL, Add 57930B, JMK to Duncan Grant, 24 December 1910.

47. Hale, *Friends and Apostles*, pp. 159–61.

48. BL, Add 57931, JMK to Duncan Grant, 11 & 14 September 1913.

49. 'Mr Francis Birrell, Conversationalist and Writer', *The Times*, 4 January 1935, p. 14; 'Mr Francis Birrell, Conversationalist, Critic and Bookseller', *Manchester Guardian*, 5 January 1935, p. 9.

50. George Zytaruk and James Boulton, eds, *The Letters of D. H. Lawrence*, II (Cambridge: Cambridge University Press, 1981), pp. 320–1.

51. Hale, *Friends and Apostles*, p. 36; 'Dr Hargreaves and Mr Farnell', *City of London School Magazine*, July 1938, pp. 76–7; 'Obituary', *City of London School Magazine*, December 1952, p. 94.

52. Hale, *Friends and Apostles*, p. 55; BL, Add 57930B, JMK to Duncan Grant, 24 January & 4 February 1910; Robb, *Strangers*, pp. 276–7.

53. King's, PP/45/301/1, Mary Berenson to JMK, nd [February–March 1906]; Barbara Strachey and Jayne Samuels, eds, *Mary Berenson: A Self-Portrait from her Letters & Diaries* (London: Victor Gollancz, 1983), pp. 128–9.

54. King's, PP/45/149/28, JMK to Arthur Hobhouse, 31 March 1906; Richard M. Dunn, *Geoffrey Scott and the Berenson Circle* (Lampeter: Edwin Mellen Press, 1998), pp. 30–2.

55. Strachey and Samuels, *Mary Berenson*, p. 134.

56. Kings, PP/45/285/12, Geoffrey Scott to JMK, nd [late March or early April 1907]; Dunn, *Geoffrey Scott*, pp. 47–8.

57. King's, PP/45/316/3/46–7 & 51, JMK to Lytton Strachey, 10 & 12 April 1907.

58. King's, PP/45/316/3/164, JMK to Lytton Strachey, 6 November 1907; Marler, *Selected Letters of Vanessa Bell*, p. 163; Gathorne-Hardy, *Ottoline at Garsington*, p. 50.

59. VWD, III, p. 244; Richard Davenport-Hines and Adam Sisman, eds, *One Hundred Letters from Hugh Trevor-Roper* (Oxford: Oxford University Press, 2014), pp. 295–6.

60. Arthur Pound and Samuel Taylor Moore, eds, *They Told Barron: Conversations and Revelations of an American Pepys in Wall Street* (London: Harper, 1930), pp. 188–9; HRC, Hutchinson papers 19/6, Lytton Strachey to Mary Hutchinson, 15 May 1919; Lord Vansittart, *The Mist Procession* (London: Hutchinson, 1958), p. 223.

61. 'Charge against Barrister', *The Times*, 15 March 1934, p. 4; 'Constable and a Barrister', *Manchester Guardian*, 28 March 1934, p. 3; 'Accused Barrister Vindicated', *The Times*, 28 March 1934, p. 9.

62. Hale, *Friends and Apostles*, p. 286; CW, X, p. 336.

63. In this section I depend upon Judith Mackrell, *Bloomsbury Ballerina* (London: Weidenfeld & Nicolson, 2008).

64. Sir Osbert Sitwell, *Laughter in the Next Room* (London: Macmillan, 1949), p. 14; King's, CHA/1/341/3/2, JMK to Vanessa Bell, 22 December 1921.

65. King's, PP/45/74/9, Sidney Russell-Cooke to JMK, 13 December 1921; King's, Sheppard papers, JTS/2/12, JMK to Jack Sheppard, 6 July 1930; 'Stockbroker found shot', *The Times*, 4 July 1930, p. 18, & 5 July 1930, p. 11; Philip Williams, ed., *The Diary of Hugh Gaitskell 1945–1956* (London: Jonathan Cape, 1983), p. 427; HRC, Snow papers 166/8, C. P. Snow to J. H. Plumb, 18 April 1961. On Campbell Stuart, see also King's, PP/45/39/6, Violet Bonham Carter to JMK, 30 July 1919; BL, Add 62985, diary of Lord Riddell, 14 January 1920; I Tatti archives, Frank Giles to Bernard Berenson, 16 May 1954.

66. King's, PP/45/316, JMK to Lytton Strachey, 17 May 1920; Magdalene College Old Library, 173/48, diary of Arthur Benson, 22 February 1924.

67. Hill and Keynes, *Lydia and Maynard*, p. 38; Mackrell, *Bloomsbury Ballerina*, pp. 201–2; Frances Partridge, *Ups and Downs* (London: Weidenfeld & Nicolson, 2001), p. 86.
68. VWD, III, pp. 18, 181.
69. Milo Keynes, 'Maynard and Lydia Keynes', in Milo Keynes, ed., *Essays on John Maynard Keynes* (Cambridge: Cambridge University Press, 1975), p. 7.
70. King's, PP/45/190/3/177, JMK to Lydia Keynes, 21 February 1927.
71. HRC, Hutchinson papers 17/7, Lydia Lopokova to Mary Hutchinson, postmarked 19 July 1923.
72. King's, PP/45/316/3/126, JMK to Lytton Strachey, [13 September 1907]; BL, Add ms 58695, JMK to Marie Stopes, 30 January 1924; BL, Add ms 58596, Marie Stopes to JMK, 16 January 1925, with Keynes's marginal response, 19 January 1925; BL, Add ms 58721, JMK to Marie Stopes, 26 March 1939.
73. Norman Mackenzie, ed., *The Letters of Sidney and Beatrice Webb*, 3 vols (Cambridge: Cambridge University Press, 1978), III, p. 790; Norman and Jeanne Mackenzie, eds., *The Diary of Beatrice Webb*, 4 vols (London: Virago, 1982–5), IV, p. 357; CW, IX, pp. 302–3.
74. King's, PP/45/316/3/126, JMK to Lytton Strachey, 13 September 1907; King's, PP/45/128/17, J. B. S. Haldane to JMK, nd; John Haffenden, ed., *Selected Letters of William Empson* (Oxford: Oxford University Press, 2006), pp. 8, 12–13.
75. CW, XVIII, pp. 78, 116–17; 'Personal', *New Statesman*, 23 July 1938, p. 165; 30 July 1938, p. 197; 13 August 1938, p. 265.
76. King's, PP/45/316/3/87, JMK to Lytton Strachey, 13 July 1907; C. R. Fay, 'The Undergraduate', in Milo Keynes, ed., *Essays on John Maynard Keynes*, p. 36.
77. Bertrand Russell, 'Portraits from Memory', *Listener*, 17 July 1952, p. 97; Kenneth Clark, *The Other Half* (London: John Murray, 1977), p. 27.
78. Malcolm MacDonald, *People and Places* (London: Collins, 1969), pp. 176–9.

Six: Connoisseur

1. Richard Shone, 'A General Account of the Bloomsbury Group', in Derek Crabtree and A. P. Thirlwall, eds, *Keynes and the Bloomsbury Group* (London: Macmillan, 1980), p. 25.

2. HRC, Morrell papers 2/3, Clive Bell to Lady Ottoline Morrell, undated [?April 1915].

3. Sir Osbert Sitwell, *Laughter in the Next Room* (London: Macmillan, 1949), p. 17; J. A. Gere, *Bensoniana and Cornishiana* (Settrington: Stone Trough Books, 1999), p. 17.

4. Clive Bell, *On British Freedom* (London: Chatto & Windus, 1923), p. 60; David Garnett, *The Flowers of the Forest* (London: Chatto & Windus, 1955), pp. 23–4.

5. Raymond Mortimer, 'London Letter', *Dial*, 84 (February 1928), p. 239; George Zytaruk and James Boulton, eds, *The Letters of D. H. Lawrence*, II (Cambridge: Cambridge University Press, 1981), p. 319.

6. A. C. Pigou, 'John Maynard Keynes, Baron Keynes of Tilton', *Proceedings of the British Academy*, 32 (1946), p. 398; Virginia Woolf, *The Years* (London: Hogarth Press, 1937), p. 442; Clive Bell, *Civilization* (London: Chatto & Windus, 1928), p. 220.

7. Bell, *Civilization*, p. 176; Bell, *British Freedom*, p. 85; Duncan Grant, 'I Tatti: A Question of Labels', *Charleston Magazine*, 10 (1994), p. 6; Julian Bell, *Essays, Poems and Letters* (London: Hogarth Press, 1938), p. 156.

8. HRC, Morrell papers 31/13, Lytton Strachey to Lady Ottoline Morrell, 12 July 1912; Norman and Jeanne Mackenzie, eds., *The Diary of Beatrice Webb*, 4 vols (London: Virago, 1982–5), IV, pp. 93–4.

9. CW, XXIV, p. 628.

10. VWD, V, p. 77; Woolf, *The Years*, pp. 232, 358.

11. CW, X, p. 444.

12. Trevor Wilson, ed., *The Political Diaries of C. P. Scott 1911–1928* (London: Collins, 1970), p. 380; F. L. Lucas, 'Criticism', *Life and Letters*, 3 (1929), pp. 434–5.

13. Leonard Woolf, *Barbarians at the Gate* (London: Victor Gollancz, 1939), pp. 11–13, 16, 18, 31.

14. F. L. Lucas, *Journal under the Terror, 1938* (London: Cassell, 1939), p. 15.

15. King's, PP/45/149/21, JMK to Arthur Hobhouse, 3 September 1905.

16. CW, XXII, p. 155.

17. Raymond Mortimer, 'London Letter', *Dial*, 84 (1928) p. 240.
18. BL, Add 57931, JMK to Duncan Grant, 5 October 1912.
19. CW, IX, p. 139; CW, XVIII, p. 348.
20. David Garnett, *The Flowers of the Forest* (London: Chatto & Windus, 1955), p. 146.
21. James Stourton and Charles Sebag-Montefiore, *The British as Art Collectors* (London: Scala, 2012), p. 281.
22. Bell, *Old Friends*, p. 60.
23. 'A Wayfarer', *Nation*, 13 December 1919, p. 381.
24. Lady Cynthia Asquith, *Diaries 1915–1918* (London: Hutchinson, 1968), p. 226; CW, X, p. 39; private information, 27 June 2011.
25. Robert Gathorne-Hardy, ed., *Ottoline at Garsington* (London: Faber & Faber, 1974), p. 50.
26. Viscount D'Abernon, *An Ambassador of Peace*, 3 vols (London: Hodder & Stoughton, 1929–30), III, p. 212; Richard Davenport-Hines, *Ettie: The Intimate Life of Lady Desborough* (London: Weidenfeld & Nicolson, 2008), pp. 294–5.
27. Bell, *Civilization*, p. 244.
28. HRC, Morrell papers 11/5, JMK to Lady Ottoline Morrell, 29 March 1918; Garnett, *Flowers of the Forest*, pp. 148–50.
29. Barbara Strachey and Jayne Samuels, eds, *Mary Berenson: A Self-Portrait from her Letters & Diaries* (London: Victor Gollancz, 1983), p. 233; Regina Marler, ed., *Selected Letters of Vanessa Bell* (London: Bloomsbury, 1993), pp. 240–2.
30. Grant, 'I Tatti: A Question of Labels', p. 11; King's, PP/45/190/3/177, JMK to Lydia Keynes, 21 February 1927.
31. CW, X, p. 387. I follow in this account S. P. Rosenbaum, *The Bloomsbury Group Memoir Club* (Basingstoke: Palgrave Macmillan, 2014).
32. Philip Gardner, ed., *The Journals and Diaries of E. M. Forster*, 3 vols (London: Pickering & Chatto, 2011), II, pp. 62–3; VWD, V, pp. 168–9.
33. King's, PP45/116/44, David Garnett to JMK, 26 April 1929. Other non-Bloomsbury groupers in 1929 were the scientific pundit, encyclopaedist and esoteric philosopher Gerald Heard, the architect George Kennedy (whom Keynes employed at King's and Tilton), the sculptor Frank Dobson, Dobson's friend the novelist Leo Myers, the sociologist Tom Marshall, Charles (Harris Curtis) Prentice

(1892–1949), a discriminating publisher at Chatto & Windus, and Ralph Wright, who worked in the bookshop run by Birrell and Garnett.

34. Magdalene College Old Library, Cambridge, 61/17, diary of Arthur Benson, 27 October 1904; Percy Colson, *White's 1693–1950* (London: Heinemann, 1951), p. 121.

35. King's, PP/45/190/3/75, JMK to Lydia Keynes, 7 March 1926.

36. Polly Hill and Richard Keynes, eds, *Lydia and Maynard: Letters between Lydia Lopokova and John Maynard Keynes* (London: André Deutsch, 1989), p. 217; cf. King's, PP/45/190/1/138, JMK to Lydia Lopokova, 12 May 1924: 'To-day has been a regular dreary Monday for work – I sat in meetings from 11 to 5.15, and then had pupils.'

37. King's, PP/45/190/5/44, JMK to Lydia Keynes, 11 October 1931.

38. King's, PP/45/190/1/191, JMK to Lydia Lopokova, 12 June 1924; King's, PP/45/190/4/66, JMK to Lydia Keynes, 3 June 1928.

39. Francis Birrell, *Letter from a Black Sheep* (London: Hogarth Press, 1932), p. 16; Magdalene College Old Library, 174/40, diary of Arthur Benson, 11 May 1924.

40. Michael Straight, *After Long Silence* (London: Collins, 1983), p. 57.

41. 'George Christopher Stead', *Biographical Memoirs of Fellows of the British Academy*, IX (Oxford University Press, 2010), p. 302.

42. Bell, *Essays, Poems and Letters*, pp. 6, 20–1.

43. Noël Annan, *The Dons* (London: HarperCollins, 1999), p. 116.

44. King's, PP/45/316/2/56, JMK to Lytton Strachey, 24 January 1906; King's, PP/45/190/7/33 & 159, JMK to Lydia Keynes, 11 March 1935 & 15 November 1936.

45. King's, PP/45/190/3/80, JMK to Lydia Keynes, 25 April 1926; King's, PP/45/255/32, JMK to János Plesch, 28 May 1939.

46. King's, PP/45/190/3/213, JMK to Lydia Keynes, 5 June 1927; 'Mr S. R. Cooke', *The Times*, 5 July 1930, p. 19.

47. CW, XII, pp. 38–9, 111.

48. CW, IX, p. 329.

49. John Buchan, *The Island of Sheep* (London: Hodder & Stoughton, 1936), pp. 105–6.

50. CW, X, p. 359; Quentin Bell, 'Recollections and Reflections on Maynard Keynes', in Crabtree and Thirlwall, *Keynes and the Bloomsbury Group*, pp. 84–5.

51. Philip Horne, ed., *Henry James: A Life in Letters* (London: Allen Lane, 1999), p. 374; Lord Gage, 'Bungalows and Town Planning', *The Times*, 2 September 1936, p. 8.

52. CW, XX, pp. 525–6, 527–8.

53. CW, XXVIII, pp. 342–4; Earl of Yarborough, 'The Cathedral at Lincoln', *The Times*, 28 November 1935, p. 10.

54. Donald Moggridge, ed., *Keynes on the Wireless* (Basingstoke: Palgrave Macmillan), pp. 164–5.

55. King's, PP/45/321/22, JMK to Bernard Swithinbank, 7 September 1902; Moggridge, *Keynes on the Wireless*, pp. 165–8; Mary Glasgow, 'The Concept of the Arts Council', in Milo Keynes, ed., *Essays on John Maynard Keynes* (Cambridge: Cambridge University Press, 1975), pp. 264–5.

56. Moggridge, *Keynes on the Wireless*, pp. 172–3; CW, XIX, p. 670.

57. Viscount Mersey, *Journal and Memories* (London: John Murray, 1952), p. 54.

58. VWD, IV, pp. 236–7; HRC, Hutchinson papers 17/6, JMK to Mary Hutchinson, 20 March 1940.

59. A. N. L. Munby, 'The Book Collector', in Milo Keynes, *Essays on John Maynard Keynes*, pp. 294, 296; Sir Edward Marsh and Christopher Hassall, *Ambrosia and Small Beer* (London: Longmans, 1964), p. 280.

60. BL, Add 57931, JMK to Duncan Grant, 11 September 1913.

61. King's, PP/45/190/6/118, JMK to Lydia Keynes, 18 February 1934.

62. Dadie Rylands, 'The Arts', *Proceedings of the British Academy*, 32 (1946), p. 401.

63. Peter Parker, *Isherwood* (London: Picador, 2004), p. 334; Alan Heuser, ed., *Selected Literary Criticism of Louis MacNeice* (Oxford: Oxford University Press, 1987), p. 101.

64. Steve Nicholson, *The Censorship of British Drama 1900–1968*, 4 vols (Exeter: University of Exeter Press, 2003–14), II, pp. 19, 241.

65. D. E. Moggridge, *Maynard Keynes: An Economist's Biography* (London: Routledge, 1992), p. 697.

66. CW, IX, p. 328.

67. Bell, *Civilization*, pp. 163–4, 166, 208.

68. Woolf, *The Years*, p. 419; Louis MacNeice, 'Autumn Journal' (1939), canto 3 in E. R. Dodds, ed., *The Collected Poems of Louis MacNeice* (London: Faber & Faber, 1966), pp. 105–6.

69. CW, XXVIII, p. 360.
70. Rylands, 'The Arts', pp. 398–9; CW, II, p. 188.
71. Glasgow, 'The Concept of the Arts Council', p. 268.
72. Captain Alan Graham, House of Commons debates, 15 February 1944, vol. 397, cols 27–8; D. Y. Cameron *et al.*, 'C. E. M. A. and Modern Art', *The Times*, 11 March 1944, p. 5; JMK, 'Pictures for the Public', *The Times*, 14 March 1944, p. 5.
73. CW, XVIII, pp. 368, 369, 371.
74. Duff Hart-Davis, ed., *King's Counsellor: The Diaries of Sir Alan Lascelles* (London: Weidenfeld & Nicolson, 2006), p. 388.
75. Isaiah Berlin, *Building: Letters 1960–1975* (London: Chatto & Windus, 2013), p. 210.
76. Hart-Davis, *King's Counsellor*, pp. 388–9; information from Stephen Keynes, 29 May 2014.
77. King's, Sheppard papers 6/13, JMK to Sheppard, 15 February 1946.

Seven: Envoy

1. CW, XXVIII, pp. 20–1, 55, 64; CW, XVI, pp. 181–2; cf. Daniel Waley, *British Public Opinion and the Abyssinian War 1935–6* (London: Maurice Temple Smith, 1975).
2. Anthony Julius, *Trials of the Diaspora* (Oxford: Oxford University Press, 2010), pp. 268–84, 397–8; King's, PP/45/1901/1/101, JMK to Lydia Lopokova, 14 March 1924; CW, X, pp. 383–4.
3. CW, XVIII, pp. 21–2.
4. CW, XVIII, pp. 48, 55, 62, 63, 64, 96, 120.
5. Susan Howson and Donald Moggridge, eds, *The Wartime Diaries of Lionel Robbins and James Meade, 1943–45* (Basingstoke: Macmillan, 1990), p. 93; HRC, Hutchinson papers 17/7, Lydia Keynes to Mary Hutchinson, 4 July 1937; Isaiah Berlin, *Flourishing: Letters 1928–1946* (London: Chatto & Windus, 2004), pp. 251–2.
6. Hertfordshire Record Office, Desborough papers D/ERV C899/493, Lady Gage to Lady Desborough, nd [August 1939].
7. Sir Arthur Salter, 'Maynard Keynes', *Spectator*, 26 April 1946, p. 421.
8. King's, PP/80/7/164.
9. CW, XXII, p. 46.
10. Berlin, *Flourishing*, p. 502.

11. Sir Otto Niemeyer and Sir Richard Hopkins, 'Public Servant', *Proceedings of the British Academy*, 32 (1946), p. 404.

12. Sir Austin Robinson, 'John Maynard Keynes, 1883–1946', *Economic Journal*, 57 (March 1947), pp. 52–3.

13. Graham Greene, *The Ministry of Fear* (London: Heinemann, 1943), p. 1.

14. CW, XXII, p. 354.

15. Charles Ritchie, *The Siren Years: Undiplomatic Diaries 1937–1945* (London: Macmillan, 1974), p. 100.

16. A. L. Goodhart, 'Lord Keynes', *The Times*, 28 March 1972, p. 15.

17. John Harvey, ed., *The War Diaries of Oliver Harvey* (London: Collins, 1978), p. 32; Skidelsky, III, p. 158.

18. BL, Add ms 57923, JMK to Oswald Falk, 25 September 1941.

19. Sir Edward Marsh and Christopher Hassall, *Ambrosia and Small Beer* (London: Longmans, 1964), p. 215.

20. BL, Add ms 57923, JMK to Oswald Falk, 23 June 1942; Marsh and Hassall, *Ambrosia*, p. 241.

21. JMK, House of Lords debates, 23 May 1944, vol. 131, col. 848.

22. King's, PP/9/62, JMK to Sir Gerald Wollaston, 12 August 1943; Grant 107/253 at College of Arms, 16 May 1944. *Arms*: Azure a Bend wavy cottized wavy between two Fleurs de Lys Argent. *Crest*: on a wreath of the colours, a Talbot passant Sable gorged with a Collar Flory counter Flory with line reflexed over the back and attached to a Fleur de Lys Or. *Supporters*: on the dexter side a Scholar of King's College Cambridge in his Cap and Gown, and on the sinister side a Scholar of Eton College in his Gown holding in his exterior a closed Book all proper. *Motto*: Me Tutore Tutus Eris.

23. Moggridge, *Maynard Keynes*, p. 695.

24. F. A. Ironmonger, *William Temple* (Oxford: Oxford University Press, 1948), p. 438.

25. Mark Pottle, ed., *Champion Redoubtable: The Diaries and Letters of Violet Bonham Carter 1914–1945* (London: Weidenfeld & Nicolson, 1998), pp. 241, 244, 246.

26. Lord Melchett, House of Lords debates, 18 May 1943, vol. 127, col. 542.

27. CW, XXVII, p. 354.

28. Howson and Moggridge, *Robbins and Meade*, p. 71.

29. JMK, House of Lords debates, 18 May 1943, vol. 127, cols 528–9.

30. Howson and Moggridge, *Robbins and Meade*, pp. 110, 127.

31. CW, XXV, p. 356; Howson and Moggridge, *Robbins and Meade*, pp. 13, 76.

32. Pottle, *Champion Redoubtable*, p. 291.

33. JMK, House of Lords debates, 23 May 1944, vol. 131, cols 840, 842, 844.

34. VWD, IV, p. 235.

35. Howson and Moggridge, *Robbins and Meade*, pp. 158–9.

36. CW, XXVI, pp. 106–7.

37. CW, XXVI, p. 101; Mary Glasgow, 'Discussion', in Derek Crabtree and A. P. Thirlwall, eds, *Keynes and the Bloomsbury Group* (London: Macmillan, 1980), p. 108.

38. CW, XXIV, p. 188.

39. Regina Marler, ed., *Selected Letters of Vanessa Bell* (London: Bloomsbury, 1993), pp. 496–7.

40. Douglas Lepan, *Bright Glass of Memory* (Toronto: McGraw-Hill Ryerson, 1979), pp. 95–6.

41. *Documents on British Policy Overseas*, series 1, vol. 3 (London: Her Majesty's Stationery Office, 1986), pp. 29, 37.

42. Stuart Ball, ed., *Parliament and Politics in the Age of Churchill and Attlee: The Headlam Diaries 1935–1951* (Cambridge: Royal Historical Society, 1999), p. 477.

43. Lord Henniker, 'Sir Edmund Leo Hall-Patch', *Dictionary of National Biography 1971–1980* (Oxford: Oxford University Press, 1986), pp. 375–6.

44. Hans Bak, ed., *The Long Voyage: Selected Letters of Malcolm Cowley, 1915–1987* (Cambridge, Mass.: Harvard University Press, 2014), pp. 358–9; H. G. Nicholas, ed., *Washington Despatches, 1941–1945* (London: Weidenfeld & Nicolson, 1981), p. 616.

45. *Documents on British Policy Overseas*, series 1, vol. 3, p. 156; Isaiah Berlin, *Building: Letters 1960–1975* (London: Chatto & Windus, 2013), p. 310.

46. VWD, V, pp. 255–6.

47. *Documents on British Policy Overseas*, series 1, vol. 3, pp. 320–1.

48. CW, XXIV, p. 591.

49. LePan, *Bright Glass*, p. 91.

50. CW, XVIII, pp. 217–18, 220–1.

51. 'An Onerous Burden: Mr Boothby's Criticism of Agreement', *The Times*, 13 December 1945, p. 6; 'Mr Dalton's Blunt Question', *Manchester Guardian*, 13 December 1945, p. 3.

52. Lionel Robbins, *Autobiography of an Economist* (London: Macmillan, 1971), p. 210.
53. Lord Hailsham, *A Sparrow's Flight* (London: Collins, 1990), p. 273; Lord Addison, House of Lords debates, 30 April 1946, vol. 140, col. 913; Lord Samuel, House of Lords debates, 30 April 1946, vol. 140, col. 916; Bertrand Russell, 'Portraits from Memory', *Listener*, 17 July 1952, p. 97.
54. JMK, House of Lords debates, 18 December 1945, vol. 138, cols 781–2, 784, 785, 787.
55. Earl of Portsmouth, Lords Piercy and Kenilworth, House of Lords debates, 18 December 1945, vol. 138, cols 854, 803 and 770.
56. Lord Beaverbrook, House of Lords debates, 18 December 1945, vol. 138, cols 861–2, 869. The eight negative votes came from the Duke of Bedford, Lord Portsmouth, the blimpish backwoodsman Lord Redesdale, Beaverbrook and his fellow Canadian peer Bennett, the playboy Lord Stanley of Alderley and two Scottish aviators, Lords Balfour of Inchrye and Sempill.
57. CW, IX, p. 311.
58. CW, XXIV, p. 628; CW, XXVII, pp. 463–4.
59. CW, XXVI, p. 217.
60. *Documents on British Policy Overseas*, series 1, vol. 4 (London: Her Majesty's Stationery Office, 1987), p. 193.
61. CW, XXVII, pp. 225, 353–4.
62. CW, X, p. 449.
63. Information from Stephen Keynes, 29 May 2014.

Index

Index

Index

Index

Index

Index